OpenOffice.org 2,
Firefox and Thunderbird
for Windows

Greg Perry
M. T. Cozzola
Jennifer Fulton

SAMS
**Teach
Yourself**

Sams Publishing, 800 East 96th Street, Indianapolis, Indiana 46240 USA

Sams Teach Yourself OpenOffice.org 2, Firefox, and Thunderbird All in One

International Standard Book Number: 0-672-32808-9

Library of Congress Catalog Card Number: 2005901786

Printed in the United States of America

First Printing: July 2005

08   07   06   05   4   3   2

Trademarks

All terms mentioned in this book that are known to be trademarks or service marks have been appropriately capitalized. Sams Publishing cannot attest to the accuracy of this information. Use of a term in this book should not be regarded as affecting the validity of any trademark or service mark.

Warning and Disclaimer

Every effort has been made to make this book as complete and as accurate as possible, but no warranty or fitness is implied. The information provided is on an "as is" basis. The author and the publisher shall have neither liability nor responsibility to any person or entity with respect to any loss or damages arising from the information contained in this book or from the use of the CD or programs accompanying it.

Bulk Sales

Sams Publishing offers excellent discounts on this book when ordered in quantity for bulk purchases or special sales. For more information, please contact

U.S. Corporate and Government Sales

1-800-382-3419

corpsales@pearsontechgroup.com

For sales outside of the U.S., please contact

International Sales

international@pearsoned.com

Acquisitions Editor
Betsy Brown

Development Editors
Jonathan Steever
Alice Martina Smith

Managing Editor
Charlotte Clapp

Project Editor
Elizabeth Finney

Indexer
Lisa Wilson

Proofreader
Suzanne Thomas

Technical Editors
Jason Perkins
Dallas Releford

Publishing Coordinator
Vanessa Evans

Multimedia Developer
Dan Scherf

Designer
Gary Adair

Page Layout
Bronkella Publishing

Contents at a Glance

Continued on next page

611 42757

Contents at a Glance

Continued from previous page

About the Author

Greg Perry is a speaker and a writer on both the programming and application sides of computing. He is known for his skills at bringing advanced computer topics to the novice's level. Perry has been a programmer and a trainer since the early 1980s. He received his first degree in computer science and a master's degree in corporate finance. Perry has sold more than 2 million computer books worldwide, including such titles as *Digital Video with Windows XP in a Snap, Sams Teach Yourself Windows XP in 24 Hours, Sams Teach Yourself Visual Basic 6 in 21 Days*, as well as the phenomenal bestseller *Sams Teach Yourself Office 2003 in 24 Hours*. He also writes about rental property management and social and political issues, creates and manages websites, loves to travel, and enjoys home life with his lovely wife Jayne and their two fluffy dogs Casper and Zucchi.

M.T. Cozzola has been writing, developing, and editing computer books for 10 years. She lives in Chicago, and has no comment regarding the Chicago Cubs.

Jennifer Fulton, iVillage's former "Computer Coach," is a computer consultant and trainer with more than 20 years of experience. Jennifer is also the best-selling author of more than 100 computer books written for both the education and retail markets, including *Digital Photography with Photoshop Album in a Snap, Paint Shop Pro 8 in a Snap*, and *Photoshop Elements 3 in a Snap*.

Dedications

Joseph Farah, a man I've admired for a long time, became my long-distance friend two years ago. I'll be forever grateful that our paths crossed. Joseph, a book dedication is the least I can do to express my gratitude for all you do for America.
—Greg Perry

To my Aunt Betty, who succumbed to lung cancer last year after a hard-fought battle. Aunt Betty never met a person she didn't like, and along with her endearing Scottie dogs, she filled my life with love and laughs. I miss her.
—Jennifer Fulton

Acknowledgments

I want to send special thanks to Betsy Brown for putting up with me on this project. She was the driving force behind the work, and I cannot express how glad I am that she wanted me to do this project.

Jason Perkins had to wade through all the problems I put into this book's first draft. Any problems that might be left are all mine. In addition, the other staff and editors on this project, namely Jon Steever, George Nedeff, and Bart Reed, made this book better than it otherwise could be.

Finally, I want to express massive thanks to readers who keep coming back to my titles. Teaching you how to do something is nothing but a pleasure for me.

—Greg Perry

Thanks go first to Betsy Brown and Alice Martina Smith—a dream team of editorial excellence. Thanks also to Greg himself—for writing such a wonderful book to begin with. I also want to thank Dave Belden for his support and insight, and *you*, the reader, for joining the OpenOffice.org community. Spread the word!

—M.T. Cozzola

What can I say? Betsy and Alice will always have my eternal gratitude—on every book I've ever worked on with them, they have put their hearts and souls into the project, with excellent results as you can now see. Thanks also to Greg for providing the backbone for this book, and to the OpenOffice.org community for jointly creating such a wonderful product to write about.

—Jennifer Fulton

We Want to Hear from You!

As the reader of this book, *you* are our most important critic and commentator. We value your opinion and want to know what we're doing right, what we could do better, what areas you'd like to see us publish in, and any other words of wisdom you're willing to pass our way.

You can email or write me directly to let me know what you did or didn't like about this book—as well as what we can do to make our books stronger.

Please note that I cannot help you with technical problems related to the topic of this book, and that due to the high volume of mail I receive, I might not be able to reply to every message.

When you write, please be sure to include this book's title and author as well as your name and phone or email address. I will carefully review your comments and share them with the author and editors who worked on the book.

Email: consumer@samspublishing.com

Mail: Mark Taber
         Associate Publisher
         Sams Publishing
         800 East 96th Street
         Indianapolis, IN 46240 USA

Reader Services

For more information about this book or others from Sams Publishing, visit our Web site at www.samspublishing.com. Type the ISBN (excluding hyphens) or the title of the book in the Search box to find the book you're looking for.

PART I

Writing Words with Writer

IN THIS PART:

✔ Start Here

Set your sights high because OpenOffice.org helps you work more efficiently and more effectively. OpenOffice.org offers an integrated set of tools that includes a word processor, a spreadsheet, a presentation program, a drawing program, and a database program. OpenOffice.org is a pleasure to use, and its price is stunning.

Did I mention that OpenOffice.org's price is stunning?

OpenOffice.org costs you nothing. It's free. Absolutely free. No strings attached. Free as in no money down and no payments afterwards. Free as in, if you bought 25 copies it wouldn't cost you any more than if you bought one.

▶ NOTE
Wal-Mart became the nation's leading retailer based on price competition. But even Wal-Mart cannot compete with OpenOffice.org!

When you hear OpenOffice.org's price, you'll probably say to yourself, "It must be worth what they charge for it." For most things, you'd be correct. You'd be wrong here. OpenOffice.org is jam-packed full of features that make even the most loyal Microsoft Office fan cringe when he or she pays hundreds of dollars every year or two for yet another Office upgrade.

What OpenOffice.org Is and What OpenOffice.org Does

OpenOffice.org is a set of integrated programs maintained by the OpenOffice.org team that you download from the OpenOffice.org website. Talk about name branding!

Originally, a German company named *StarDivision* created *StarOffice* in the mid-1980s. Sun Microsystems purchased StarOffice in 1999 and added features, lowered the price (to *free*), and changed the name to OpenOffice.org. OpenOffice.org works on the Windows, Linux, Macintosh, FreeBSD, and Solaris operating systems too. Current versions of OpenOffice.org share most features and an almost identical interface with Sun Microsystem's StarOffice package, a suite offered for sale as another alternative to Microsoft Office.

▶ **NOTE**

This book assumes you use a Windows operating system environment, although OpenOffice.org works uniformly on any supported operating system. So even if you work on a Solaris or Macintosh computer, you'll feel right at home here as you learn OpenOffice.org along with Windows readers.

OpenOffice.org offers integrated software tools that are powerful yet easy to learn and use. Offices large and small can use OpenOffice.org–based applications for many of their day-to-day computer needs, as can families and home-based businesses that want simple but robust writing and analysis tools for their computers.

With each new revision, OpenOffice.org takes you to the next step with an improved user interface and more solid features that help you become more productive in the way you use the OpenOffice.org products. The OpenOffice.org website is loaded with information, technical support, white papers, forums, press information, upcoming events, and manuals that give you support and background information about OpenOffice.org.

With OpenOffice.org's help, you'll get your work done better and more quickly. OpenOffice.org automates many computing chores and provides tools that work in unison and share data between them.

▶ **NOTE**

OpenOffice.org is often abbreviated *OOo*.

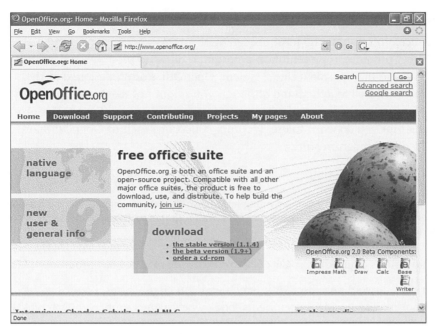

The OpenOffice.org website dedicates itself to helping you use OpenOffice.org better.

There can be no hiding the fact that OpenOffice.org is a direct competitor to Microsoft Office. On a price/performance comparison, OpenOffice.org mangles Microsoft Office, even though Microsoft Office is more powerful than OpenOffice.org, at rare times more stable (depending on which Microsoft Office updates you've applied recently and how stable they are), and is better refined in certain tasks. For example, cropping an image isn't quite as simple as the same task in Office. Yet, those fine-tuned advances in Microsoft Office come at a price, and the price is steep compared to the free OpenOffice.org system.

Lots of politics exist between those in the OpenOffice.org camp and those in the Microsoft Office camp. Throughout this book, I'll do my best to display my encouragement and strong support for OpenOffice.org, its concepts, and its power. At the same time, I don't want to enter the political debate between those on the OpenOffice.org side and those on the Microsoft Office side. I see no reason why both cannot coexist, especially given the ease with which OpenOffice.org works with Microsoft Office files.

▶ NOTE

One of OpenOffice.org's primary strengths (in addition to its free price tag) is its strong support for Microsoft Office files. OpenOffice.org opens, converts, and lets you edit virtually any document that you or someone else created in Word, PowerPoint, Access, or Excel. When you move to OpenOffice.org, you don't lose work created elsewhere.

What's in OpenOffice.org?

OpenOffice.org contains the most needed applications—a word processor, a spreadsheet program, a presentation program, a drawing program, a database program—and more inside a single system. OpenOffice.org is designed so that its programs work well together, and although you might not need every program in OpenOffice.org, you can easily share information between any OpenOffice.org programs that you do want to use. Program collections such as OpenOffice.org are often called program *suites*.

▶ **KEY TERM**

Suite—An application that contains multiple programs, each of which performing a separate function. These programs generally work well together, with each one easily reading the other programs' data.

The following is a quick overview of the primary OpenOffice.org programs:

- **Writer**—A word processor with which you can create notes, memos, letters, school papers, business documents, books, newsletters, and even web pages.

- **Calc**—An electronic spreadsheet program with which you can create graphs and worksheets for financial and other numeric data. After you enter your financial data, you can analyze it for forecasts, generate numerous what-if scenarios, and publish worksheets on the Web.

- **Impress**—A presentation graphics program with which you can create presentations for seminars, schools, churches, web pages, and business meetings. Not only can Impress create the presentation overheads, but it can also create the speaker's presentation notes and print compacted audience handouts.

- **Draw**—A powerful drawing program that you use to create drawings, utilize predesigned shapes, develop logos, and even design web page graphics.

- **Base**—A database management system you use to store large amounts of data such as an inventory, mailing lists, even movie and CD collections. Not only does Base store the data, it lets you analyze it, create forms, and generate reports, all quickly and easily.

▶ **NOTE**

Base is new to OpenOffice.org 2.0.

In addition to these five major programs, OpenOffice.org includes several other features, such as an HTML editor for web page design and editing as well as a mathematical formula editor that you use to create complex math equations (see **30 Use Mathematical Formulas in Documents**).

All the OpenOffice.org programs share common features and common menu choices. The next two figures show an Impress editing session and a Draw editing session. Even though the Impress screen shows a slide from a presentation and the Draw screen shows a flier being created, the surrounding interface elements are extremely similar. The menus, toolbars, and status bar buttons are almost identical for both programs. When you learn one OpenOffice.org program, you are well on your way to knowing quite a bit about all the other OpenOffice.org programs, too.

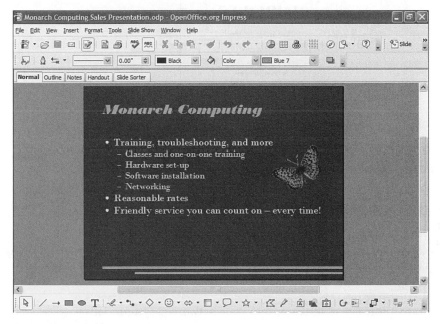

When you design and edit presentations with Impress, you'll recognize the interface because OpenOffice.org programs share a similar interface.

▶ NOTE

Unlike other application suites, OpenOffice.org was designed as one single software package, right from the start.

In addition to working with familiar interfaces in the OpenOffice.org products, you can insert data that you create in one program into another program within the OpenOffice.org suite. If you create a financial table with Calc, for instance, you can put the table in a Writer document that you send to your board of directors and embed the table in an Impress presentation to stockholders. Once you learn how to use any program in the OpenOffice.org suite, you will be far more comfortable using all the others because of the common interface.

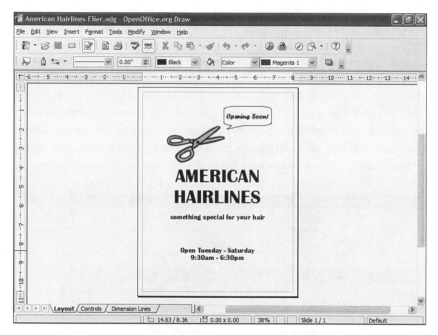

Draw's menu, toolbars, and status bar elements are virtually identical to those of other OpenOffice.org programs, especially those of Impress.

OpenOffice.org Is Versatile

The OpenOffice.org products are general purpose, meaning that you can customize applications to suit your needs. You can use Calc as your household budgeting program, for example, and also as your company's interactive balance-sheet system.

You can integrate OpenOffice.org into your networked system. This way, OpenOffice.org provides useful features whether you are networked to an intranet, to the Internet, or to both. You can share OpenOffice.org information with others across the network. OpenOffice.org fits well within the online world by integrating Internet access throughout the OpenOffice.org suite.

Introducing Writer

When you need to write any text-based document, look no further than Writer. Writer is a word processor that supports many features, including the following:

- Automatic corrections for common mistakes as you type using special automatic-correcting tools that watch the way you work and adapt to your needs

- Templates and styles that make quick work of your document's formatting

- Advanced page layout and formatting capabilities

- Numbering, bulleting, bordering, and shading tools

- Integrated grammar and spelling tools to help ensure your document's accuracy

- Newsletter-style multiple columns, headers, footers, and endnotes in your publications

- Graphical tools that enable you to emphasize headers, draw lines and shapes around your text, and work with imported art files in your documents

The next figure shows a Writer editing session. Even though Writer is a word processor, you can see from the figure that it supports advanced formatting, layout, and graphics capabilities so that you can produce professional documents, covers, and title pages using Writer.

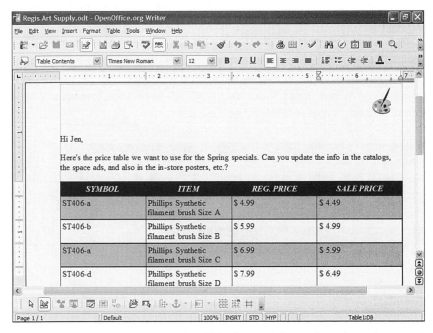

Writer easily handles text, graphics, and advanced formatting of any document you wish to create.

Introducing Calc

Calc's primary goal is to help you organize and manage financial information such as income statements, balance sheets, and forecasts. Calc is an electronic spreadsheet program that supports many features, including the following:

- Automatic cell formatting

- Automatic worksheet computations that enable you to generate a worksheet that automatically recalculates when you make a change to a portion of the worksheet

- Built-in functions, such as financial formulas, that automate common tasks

- Automatic row and column completion of value ranges with automatic completion of ranges of data

- Formatting tools that let you turn worksheets into professionally produced reports

- Powerful data sorting, searching, filtering, and analyzing tools that enable you to turn data into an organized collection of meaningful information

- Powerful charts and graphs that can analyze your numbers and turn them into simple trends

The following figure shows a Calc editing session. The user is entering income statement information. If you have worked with other worksheet programs, you might be surprised at how fancy Calc can get. Calc's automatic formatting capabilities make creating advanced worksheets easy.

Calc helps you create, edit, and format numeric worksheets.

Introducing Impress

Have you ever given a presentation and longed for a better approach to messy overhead slides? Have you seen the pros wow their audiences with eye-catching, professional computerized presentations? With Impress, there is simply no reason why you shouldn't be wowing your audiences as well. Professional presentations are now within your reach.

Impress supports many features, including the following:

- The use of the Wizard feature to generate presentations automatically
- Sample design templates that provide you with a fill-in-the-blank presentation
- A screen display that imitates how a slide projector displays slides
- Complete color and font control of your presentation slides
- A collection of art files, icons, and sounds that you can embed to make your presentations more attention-getting
- Numerous transitions and fades between presentation slides to keep your audience's attention
- The capability to save presentations as web pages that you can then present on the Internet

The next figure shows an Impress editing session. The user is getting ready for a presentation and has only a few minutes to prepare six color slides for the meeting. With Impress, a few minutes is more than enough time!

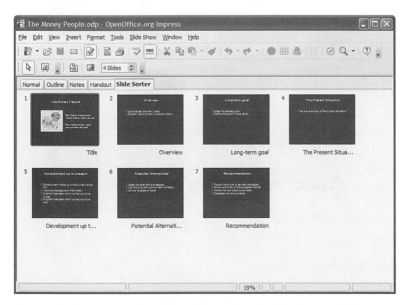

Impress helps you create, edit, and format professional presentations.

Introducing Draw

With Draw, you can generate drawings and graphics. Draw supports all popular graphics formats, both for importing images and for the drawings you want to save. You can create freeform drawings and you can use Draw's predesigned shapes to create more modern artwork, such as a commercial artist may require.

Here are just a few features that Draw supports:

- The use of predefined geometric shapes to include in your drawings

- The ability to create and use built-in three-dimensional shapes to add depth to your images

- The ability to adjust the perceived light source on the objects you draw to add realism

- The ability to convert two-dimensional text and graphics to three dimensions

- The ability to logically connect objects so that when you move or resize one, other objects adjust accordingly

The next figure shows a Draw editing session. The drawing contains both text and graphics. Draw's ability to combine both text and graphics makes it great for businesses that need to design brochures, ads, fliers, and logos.

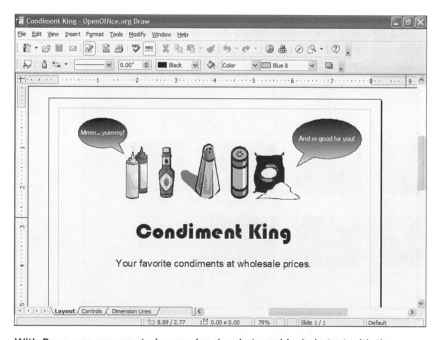

With Draw, you can create impressive drawings and include text with them.

Introducing the Base Database

Base puts the power of information right at your fingertips. Whether you're a soccer dad who wants to create a contact sheet for the team or a store manager with a warehouse full of products, Base can keep you on track. Base is a database management program that supports many features, including the following:

- The ability to create, modify, search, and sort large amounts of data in table format

- The ability to index your database tables to speed up data access

- The ability to perform simple or complex queries

- The ability to generate meaningful reports from your data

- The ability to create forms that you or others can complete to gather data

- A choice of views to suit all levels of database users—wizards for beginnings, design views for more experienced users, and SQL for advanced folks

- The choice of using your own database or Base's own built-in HSQL database engine

The next figure shows a Base database session. As you can see, the application can manage a lot of data and offers tools for sorting, grouping, and presenting the data in meaningful ways. Base also makes it easy to connect to existing databases. It offers native support for many popular databases including Microsoft Access, MySQL, and LDAP-compliant address books.

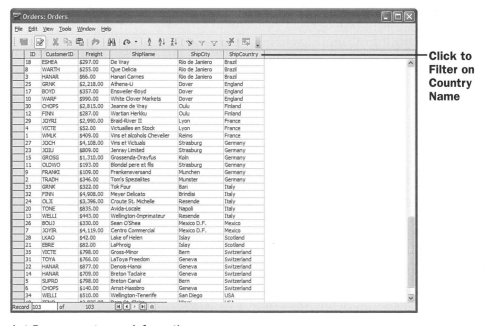

Let Base manage your information.

Installing OpenOffice.org

For most users, installing OpenOffice.org takes little more than an Internet connection and some time (and more than some time if you don't have a high-speed broadband connection such as DSL or a cable modem). Basically, one needs only to go to the OpenOffice.org website, download OpenOffice.org, and install it onto a computer. Users will be creating Impress presentations and Draw drawings soon after that.

To download OpenOffice.org, you only need to surf to the OpenOffice.org website. One of the first and most prominent links on the page is the **Download** link. To download OpenOffice.org, you click this **Download** link, choose your preferred language, operating system, and download site, and the download begins.

▶ **TIP**

As the owner of this book, you don't need to download OpenOffice.org because it's included with this book's CD-ROM!

Once the download completes, the user needs only click the **Open** button on the **Download complete** dialog box, and OpenOffice.org begins its installation. Even though you don't have to download OpenOffice.org, you'll need to remember where you read these instructions so when an updated version is released, you'll know where to get it. You download and install new versions the same way as you would download and install the very first installation.

▶ **NOTE**

The installation routine may request that you restart your computer after the installation finishes to set up all the files properly.

To uninstall OpenOffice.org (why would you want to?), select **Add/Remove Programs** from the Windows **Control Panel** dialog box. Locate the entry for OpenOffice.org and click **Remove**.

Starting OpenOffice.org

Generally, you'll start one of the OpenOffice.org applications by clicking your Windows **Start** toolbar button and doing one of the following:

▶ **NOTE**

You can edit Microsoft Office data files without converting them to OpenOffice.org format because OpenOffice.org can read and write Office files.

▶ **TIP**

A quick way to start OpenOffice.org is to use the **QuickStarter** icon on the taskbar. Right-click this icon; from the context menu, choose any OpenOffice.org program to launch it, use a template, or load an existing document. The **QuickStarter** icon is available only if the **Load OpenOffice.org during system startup** option is enabled. To enable this option, select the **Memory** category in the **OpenOffice.org** options list in the **Options** dialog box of any OpenOffice.org program.

- Select the **OpenOffice.org** menu from your Windows **Programs** menu and select from the list of OpenOffice.org programs. If, for example, you select **OpenOffice.org Draw**, Draw will start and offer you a blank drawing area where you can begin a new drawing or load an existing drawing into the editing area.

You can start any OpenOffice.org program from your Windows Programs menu.

- From any Windows Explorer–like window that displays a file listing, select any OpenOffice.org file and the appropriate OpenOffice.org program automatically launches with that file loaded. If, for example, you select a Writer document, Writer automatically opens and loads that document so you can edit the contents. If you select a Calc spreadsheet, Calc starts and loads that spreadsheet file. Of course, you can also select a Microsoft Office Word, Excel, or PowerPoint file and Writer, Calc, or Impress, respectively, will open that file. You then can save the file into a converted OpenOffice.org format if you wish.

▶ **NOTE**

As **133** **Use Both OpenOffice.org and Microsoft Office** demonstrates, you can assign Microsoft Office data filename extensions to OpenOffice.org files so that when you click on a DOC file inside a Windows Explorer window, Writer and not Word will automatically open the file.

- From any OpenOffice.org program, you can start any other OpenOffice.org program by selecting **File**, **Open** and selecting a file. If, for example, you are writing a letter inside Writer and remember that you have to update a spreadsheet, you don't need to start Calc. Instead, from Writer's **File**, **Open** menu, select the spreadsheet to open. Calc will open and load that spreadsheet for you. Writer remains open with your document loaded for when you're ready to return to it.

Options for All

All of the OpenOffice.org programs provide their own set of options so that you can customize the program to suit the way you work. For example, if you are using Draw on an older computer, your drawing has to update when you add or change a shape on your screen. If you have one or more three-dimensional objects in the drawing, the screen update can be very slow. Therefore, Draw offers an option whereby you can display an image icon and frame, instead of the image itself, everywhere the image appears in your drawing. Once you've positioned all your images onto the drawing area, you can turn the graphic display back on to review the drawing.

▶ **NOTE**

The images always print even if you've chosen to suppress their display on the screen.

Throughout this book's tasks, you'll find descriptions of each OpenOffice.org program's options that you can modify. For example, **106** **Set Draw Options** explains all the Draw options and why you may want to change some of them.

From any individual OpenOffice.org program, you can program specific options, as well as global options. These global options determine how all the OpenOffice.org programs behave and appear as you use OpenOffice.org. Because these general options are generic across all the OpenOffice.org programs, this would be a good time to review them. Doing so not only makes sense because these options are global in scope and the tasks in the chapters that follow are specific to individual OpenOffice.org programs, but also reading about the general OpenOffice.org options will give you an early feel of what OpenOffice.org is all about.

Table 1.1 describes the 6 general OpenOffice.org option categories from which you can select. From any OpenOffice.org program, you only need to select **Tools**, **Options** from the menu and click the plus sign to expand the **OpenOffice.org** entry to see the numerous global option categories.

TABLE 1.1   OpenOffice.org Option Categories

OpenOffice.org Option Category	Explanation
OpenOffice.org	Describes general settings for all OpenOffice.org programs, such as your user information, path settings, and accessibility settings.

TABLE 1.1 Continued

OpenOffice.org Option Category	Explanation
Load/Save	Describes how you want to load and save documents. For example, you can request that a backup copy of the previous version of any document is saved every time you save a file.
Language Settings	Defines the default language used by the OpenOffice.org programs as well as how you want writing aids to work, such as correcting the misuse of upper- and lowercase characters.
OpenOffice.org Base	Describes general settings for external data sources you use in OpenOffice.org documents and tables.
Charts	Describes basic chart color settings for charts you insert in documents.
Internet	Describes how you want OpenOffice.org to interact with the Internet, such as which search engines you want OpenOffice.org to use.

The following figure shows the options available in Writer. As you can see, there are global options as well as Writer-specific ones.

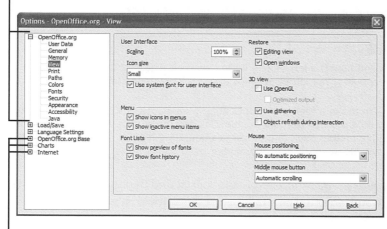

Review the OpenOffice.org option categories.

OpenOffice.org Toolbars

OpenOffice.org contains several toolbars, many of which are similar across all the OpenOffice.org programs. Some toolbars change depending on the program you're using at the time, and some toolbars are exclusive to a particular program. The **Presentation** toolbar, for example, appears only in Impress, whereas the **Standard** toolbar appears in all programs.

▶ **TIP**

Select from the **View**, **Toolbars** menu option to display and hide specific toolbars.

You can position toolbars wherever you like. You can *dock* a toolbar—that is, position it along an edge of the document window—or lock it so that it cannot be moved (by selecting **Lock Toolbar Position** from the toolbar menu), or let it **float**. To move a toolbar, drag the handle located at the left end of the toolbar.

▶ **KEY TERM**

Dock—To align a toolbar along the top or side of the document window, drag its handle to the desired location or double-click its title bar.

In addition to opening toolbars using the **View**, **Toolbars** menu option, you can also display certain toolbars by ***long-clicking*** or clicking a button arrow. Long-clicking is available for some selections and allows you to open a palette and then drag it into the document window as a ***floating toolbar***.

▶ **KEY TERMS**

Long-click—Click and hold the left mouse button, without dragging the mouse, until a toolbar or option appears. The left click takes about a half second to trigger its option.

Floating toolbar—To make a toolbar into a floating toolbar, drag its handle into the document window, or hold the **Ctrl** key and double-click any blank spot within the toolbar. To return the floating toolbar back to its fixed position, drag it by its handle or hold **Ctrl** and double-click any blank spot within the toolbar once again.

The following figure shows examples of both locked and floating toolbars, as well as a palette. The **Standard** toolbar and the **Presentation** toolbar are docked along the top of the document window. The **Gluepoints** toolbar floats in the document window. Last but not least, the **Connector** palette is open. You can drag the handle at the top of the palette into the document window if you want the palette to become a floating toolbar.

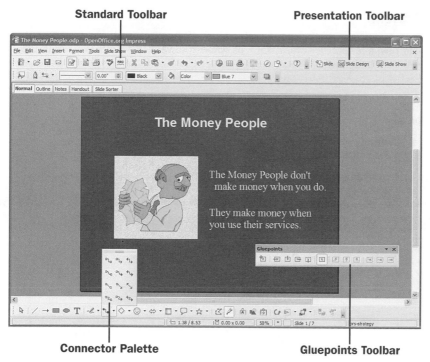

Standard Toolbar · Presentation Toolbar · Connector Palette · Gluepoints Toolbar

Toolbars in OpenOffice.org change depending on the program you're using.

Getting Help

Any time you need help, press **F1** to produce a *context-sensitive help* screen.

► KEY TERM

Context-sensitive help—An automated system that looks at what you're currently doing and provides assistance for that particular menu, button, or command.

OpenOffice.org is surprisingly accurate at displaying the help you need when you need it. For example, suppose you're selecting from the **Tools** menu and you want to know what the **AutoCorrect** command does. Simply select **Tools** and move your mouse to the **AutoCorrect** option. Without clicking to trigger that option, press **F1** with the option still highlighted, and OpenOffice.org opens a help window that provides help on the **AutoCorrect** feature. Throughout most of OpenOffice.org's help screens, you'll find many *hyperlinks* that take you to other areas within the help system for more detailed assistance on topics related to the **AutoCorrect** menu option.

► KEY TERM

Hyperlinks—Text that's usually underlined in help screens (and web pages, too) that you can click to navigate to other areas, such as when you want to learn more about the topic mentioned in the help text.

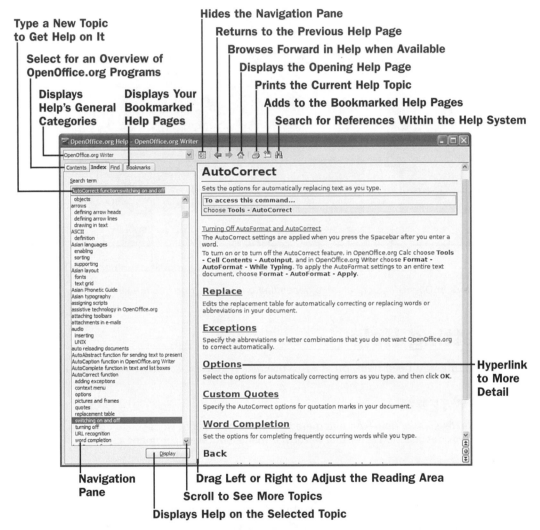

OpenOffice.org's help screens provide context-sensitive help for whatever topic you request.

In addition to the traditional help screens, OpenOffice.org provides three more kinds of help tools, described next. You can display or hide any of these help elements from the **Help** menu of any OpenOffice.org program:

- **Help Agent**—Displays a small window in the lower-right corner of your OpenOffice.org program when a task you're currently performing might be better done another way or when additional information about what you're doing may be of some assistance to you. If you click the Help Agent's window, the extra help appears in a window that you can read for more details.

▶ NOTE

The Help Agent works a lot like Microsoft Office's animated *Clippit* assistant but is far less obtrusive and annoying!

- **Tips**—Also called *ToolTips* in Windows terminology, these are names that pop up in hovering description boxes over toolbar buttons and other areas of your screen that tell you the name or purpose for a particular object.

- **Extended Tips**—Display a description of almost any item on the screen (except for menus) when you hover your mouse over these objects. To activate this feature, select **What's This** from the **Help** menu.

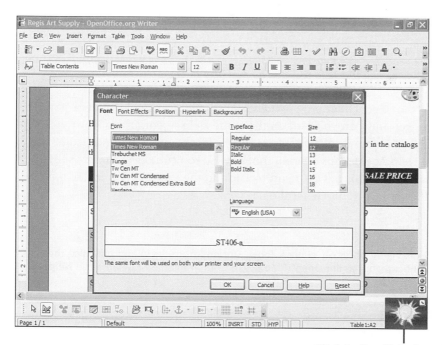

Click to See Help Agent's Advice

The Help Agent offers advice as you use OpenOffice.org programs.

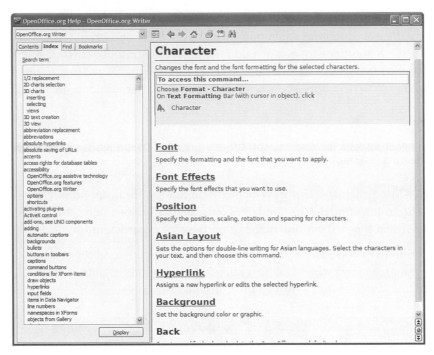

Help Agent produces this help screen when you click the Help Agent window while format-ting a text selection; this help provides an overview of character formatting.

The help that OpenOffice.org provides is always customizable on your part. For example, not only can you turn off the entire Help Agent, if you leave the Help Agent on but ignore its offered advice three times in a row in a particular situa-tion, the Help Agent stops offering that advice. You can always reset the Help Agent and restart this advice again by clicking the **Reset** button inside the OpenOffice.org **Option's General** dialog box.

▶ **TIP**

To turn Help Agent on or off, choose **Tools, Options** from the menu bar, click the **General** subcategory under **OpenOffice.org**, and then enable or disable the **Help Agent** check box.

2

Learning Writer's Basics

IN THIS CHAPTER:

Writer is a full-featured word processor that you can use to produce notes, reports, newsletters, brochures, and just about anything that requires text and perhaps graphics as well. If you want to do something in Writer, Writer probably offers a way to do it.

In spite of all its bells and whistles, Writer's primary goal is to get text into a document. Hardly any word processor does that as easily as Writer (or as cheaply!). This chapter gets you started if you are new to Writer. You'll master the basic text-entering and document-navigation skills.

▶ **NOTE**

Start Writer by selecting **OpenOffice.org** from the **OpenOffice.org** program group on the **Start** menu, or by selecting **File, New, Text Document** from the menu bar in any OpenOffice.org program window.

---

1   Set Writer Options

→ **SEE ALSO**

2 Create a New Document
4 Type Text into a Document
5 Edit Text

1

Not everybody works the same way, so not every Writer user wants to use Writer the same way. By setting some of Writer's many options, you will make Writer conform to the way you like to do things. For example, you may want Writer to hide its horizontal scrollbar so you get more space on your screen for text. If so, Writer has an option to display or hide the horizontal scrollbar.

As a matter of fact, Writer has an option for just about anything! Table 2.1 describes Writer's options. You'll learn a lot about what Writer can do just by looking through the options available to you.

TABLE 2.1   Writer's Text Document Options

Writer Option Category	Explanation
General	Describes general Writer settings such as the default unit of measurements and the width of tab stops (see **11** **About Paragraph Breaks and Tabs**).
View	Describes how Writer appears on the screen and which Writer special elements, such as graphics and rulers, appear by default.
Formatting Aids	Describes how Writer displays formatting elements such as line breaks, spaces, and hidden text.

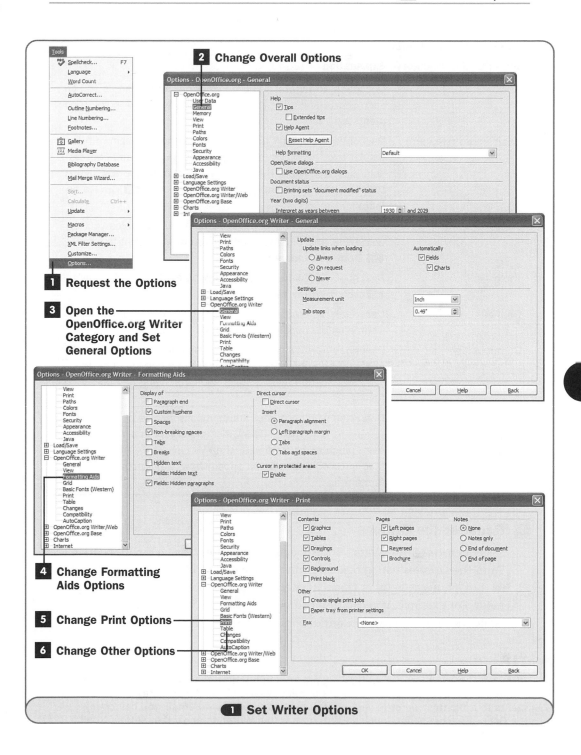

2 **Change Overall Options**

1 **Request the Options**

3 **Open the OpenOffice.org Writer Category and Set General Options**

4 **Change Formatting Aids Options**

5 **Change Print Options**

6 **Change Other Options**

1 **Set Writer Options**

TABLE 2.1   Continued

Writer Option Category	Explanation
Grid	Describes how Writer's grid appears on the screen so you can align charts and other graphic elements with text in your documents.
Basic Fonts (Western)	Describes the default fonts you want Writer to begin with for regular text, headings (see **33 About Headers and Footers**), lists (see **19 Add a Bulleted List**), captions (see **27 Insert Graphics in a Document**), and the index (see **22 Create an Index**).
Print	Describes how Writer prints documents and enables you to determine which installed printer you want to print to (see **9 Print a Document**).
Table	Describes how Writer formats tables and data within cells (see **23 About Writer Tables**).
Changes	Describes how Writer displays revisions made in documents when multiple people perform group editing.
Compatibility	Describes how Writer handles certain aspects of document formatting when importing a Microsoft Word document so that you can fine-tune options such as line spacing and object positioning.
AutoCaptioning	Describes whether Writer automatically inserts a caption when you insert any type of OpenOffice.org object in a Writer document (such as *Illustration 1* when you insert a picture you created in Draw) and lets you specify how the caption should be formatted.

1 Request the Options

Select **Options** from Writer's **Tools** menu. The **Options** dialog box appears. From the **Options** dialog box, you can change any of Writer's options as well as the options from other OpenOffice.org programs that affect a Writer document. For example, you can also change Base settings that affect how a Writer document accesses external data sources.

▶ TIP

Often you'll work in one OpenOffice.org program and realize that you need to change an overall option. For example, if you want to print several kinds of OpenOffice.org documents to a file (instead of to your printer) to send to others via email, you can change the OpenOffice.org option labeled **Print**, from within Writer, to apply that setting to all OpenOffice.org programs.

2 Change Overall Options

Select any option in the **OpenOffice.org** category to modify OpenOffice.org-wide settings such as pathnames. For example, if you don't like the pathname you see when you open or save a file, click the **Paths** option and change it to a different default file path.

If you're new to OpenOffice.org, consider leaving all the OpenOffice.org options "as is" until you familiarize yourself with how the OpenOffice.org programs work.

3 Open the OpenOffice.org Writer Category and Set General Options

Click the plus sign next to the **Text Document** option to display the 10 Writer-specific options listed in the table at the beginning of this task.

Click the **General** options category; the dialog box changes to show options you can select to make changes to the general Writer options. The **Update** section enables you to determine when Writer updates, or refreshes, linked data in a document such as an external worksheet that you link to your current document to use as a table. The **Settings** section enables you to determine how you want Writer to measure items. For example, you can click to open the **Measurement unit** drop-down list to change the default measurement from inches to centimeters if you work in, or travel to, a country that uses the metric system.

4 Change Formatting Aids Options

Click the **Formatting Aids** options category under the **OpenOffice.org Writer** category; the dialog box changes to show options that modify the display of various Writer formatting characters such as spaces and line breaks.

Enable the check box for any formatting options you want to see in documents onscreen. For example, if you want to see the space format character (a horizontally centered dot in place of a space) every time you press the spacebar in a document, enable the **Spaces** check box.

▶ TIP

Some users prefer to see all formatting characters, such as the space format character and the end-of-paragraph mark (¶). Such characters can make some editing chores easier. For example, you'll know you pressed the spacebar seven times if you see seven space formatting characters, whereas it's far more difficult to know how many spaces appear if there are no characters to "mark." You can also turn these features on or off by clicking the Nonprinting Characters button on the Standard toolbar.

▶ **NOTE**

The more formatting characters you display, the more cluttered your screen will look; when you print the document that's onscreen, none of the formatting characters will be printed; the formatting characters are there to help you edit your document.

5 Change Print Options

Click to select the **Print** category under the **OpenOffice.org Writer** option category. View or set any print-related options you want to adjust. For example, if you want to print a draft of your current document's text, you could uncheck the **Graphics** and **Drawings** options so these elements don't print until you select them again.

6 Change Other Options

Continue viewing and changing the remaining options in the **OpenOffice.org Writer** options category by first selecting the category and then looking at the individual options. You might find, for example, that you want to eliminate the scrollbars to give yourself more screen real estate to see the document. You could uncheck the scrollbar options on the **View** page of the **OpenOffice.org Writer** options set.

When you're done specifying Writer options, click the **OK** button to close the **Options** dialog box.

2

---

2   **Create a New Document**

✔ **BEFORE YOU BEGIN**	→ **SEE ALSO**
1 Set Writer Options	**4** Type Text into a Document
	9 Print a Document
	18 Use a Template

Writer gives you two ways to create new documents: You can create a new document from a completely blank document (if you choose this approach, you must decide what text to place in the document and where you want that information to go) or you can use a **Wizard** to open a blank, preformatted document. If you use the Wizard approach to document creation, you can choose from several Wizard options that preformat your new document according to selections you make:

1 Request a New Document   **2** Compose Your Document

3 Request a New Document Using a Wizard

4 Specify Letter Options

5 Select Additional Options

6 Create the Letter

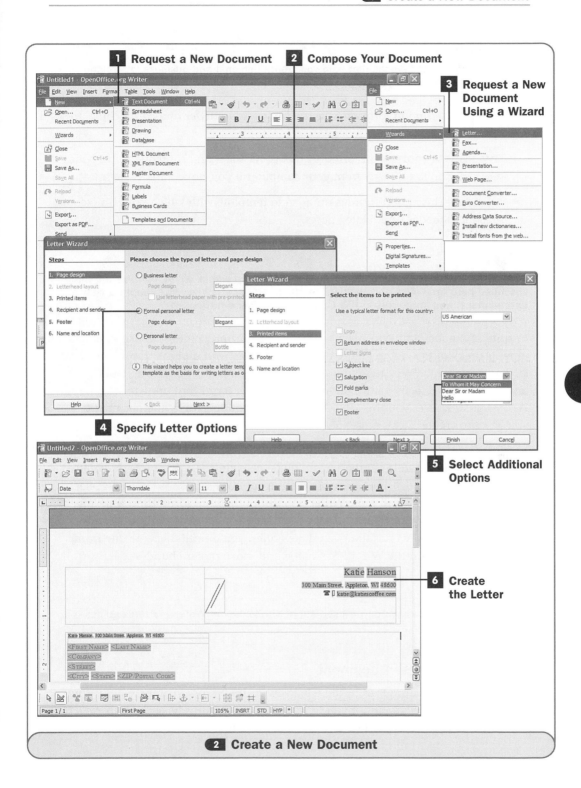

▶ **KEY TERM**

Wizard—Preformatted guides that help you create personal and business letters and forms more easily than if you began with a blank page.

- **Letter**—This option formats a business or personal letter and can include an optional logo in various styles.

- **Fax**—This Wizard option formats a fax cover sheet and subsequent fax pages that you can fax directly from your computer if you have a fax modem.

- **Agenda**—This option formats an agenda template with which you can create meeting agendas and related notes.

▶ **NOTE**

Several Wizard guides appear when you view them from within Writer, but only the three described here are Writer documents. The others are for Calc (see **40** **Create a New Spreadsheet**) and Impress (see **81** **Create a New Presentation**).

In spite of the fact that Wizards provide a great starting point for the special documents you want to create, many times you'll begin with a blank document (that is, you'll bypass the Wizard's guides). Starting with a blank document, without any preformatted logos, return addresses, and other items that appear with the Wizard guides, gives you the most flexibility in creating exactly the document you want to create.

Nevertheless, the Wizard guides are difficult to beat when you want to create special documents that fall into the Wizard guide categories. For example, it would probably take too much time to create a fax form from scratch, so you can select the Wizard **Fax** guide and have Writer do most of the hard formatting work for you. Of course, if you or your company requires a special fax form that differs dramatically from the ones the Wizard generates, you'll need to create one from scratch or begin with the Wizard Fax guide and make major changes to it.

▶ **NOTE**

If you've used Microsoft Word, you'll see strong similarities in Writer's Wizards guides and Word's wizards.

1 **Request a New Document**

Select **Text Document** from the **File**, **New** menu option. Writer creates a completely blank document for you to work with. Alternatively, click the **New** toolbar button to open a new blank Writer document quickly.

2 Compose Your Document

Create your document using the blank work area Writer gives you. Start typing as you would in any word-processing document. Press **Enter** to end a block of text (be it a paragraph, an item you want to be part of a list of similar items, or a signature block). You can save your work (choose **File**, **Save**) and print your document (see **9** **Print a Document**) at any time.

3 Request a new Document Using a Wizard

To create a document using a Wizard, choose **File**, **Wizards**. From the submenu that opens, you can select from a number of Wizards; choose the one that suits the kind of document you want to create. For example, if you want to create a fax, choose **Fax** from the **File**, **Wizards** submenu. A dialog box showing options for that particular kind of document appears.

A list of numbered steps on the left side of the dialog box shows where you are in the Wizard process. As you move through each step, you can select options to fine-tune your document. You can click the **Next** button to proceed or the **Back** button if you change your mind and want to return to a previous step, or you can click any number in the list to jump directly to that step in the Wizard. You can click the **Finish** button at any time to create the document using the current settings.

In this example, I'll use a Wizard to create a Formal Personal letter. Consequently, I'll select **Letter** from the **File**, **Wizards** submenu. The **Letter Wizard** dialog box opens.

▶ **NOTE**

The Wizard actually creates a template you use to create your document. See **18** **Use a Template** to learn more about Writer's templates.

4 Specify Letter Options

Specify the kind of letter you want to write by selecting **Business letter**, **Formal personal letter**, or **Personal letter**. From the drop-down list next to the selected letter type, choose a page design for your letter. If you are creating a **Business letter** or a **Formal personal letter**, you can choose from three page designs: **Elegant**, **Modern**, or **Office**. If you are creating a **Business letter** and have preprinted letterhead, you can enable the **Use letterhead paper with preprinted elements** check box and specify where the printed elements are located on the page. These options help you customize the Wizard to your company letterhead. If you are creating a **Personal letter**, you have a choice of four page designs: **Bottle**, **Mail**, **Marine**, and **Red Line**.

2

▶ **TIP**

You can see a preview of your document as it takes shape behind the dialog box.

5 Select Additional Options

Depending on the type of letter you've chosen, the steps in the Wizard dialog box change to provide appropriate choices for that type of letter. In my example, I am creating a **Formal personal letter**, so the next step is selecting which items I want to print. You can specify a letter format appropriate to your country (helpful when conducting international correspondence), and select from a list of individual items such as a **Subject line**, **Salutation**, and so on. Disable the check box for any item you don't want included in the letter.

▶ **TIP**

The preview area behind the dialog box updates as you select Wizard options so that you can see what your document layout looks like so far.

6 Create the Letter

When you have selected the options appropriate to the type of letter you want to create, you have the choice to continue setting more options by clicking the **Next** button or you can click **Finish** to create the letter with the options you've set so far. Many times you'll end a Wizard early by clicking **Finish** before you've looked at all the options. This is because Writer puts the most critical options and the ones most subject to change at the beginning of the Wizard.

For now, click the **Finish** button to create your letter. By doing this, you bypass options such as specifying sender and recipient information. The **Letter** Wizard dialog box closes, and a document is created that's preformatted according to the options you've selected.

In the preformatted letter that the Wizard creates, you'll find notes telling you where to place certain parts of your document, such as opening text, a logo (if you chose to include one), the fax page count (if you had selected the Fax Wizard), and other hints that help you complete the document you requested through the Wizard.

▶ **NOTE**

Your screen might differ slightly from the one shown here depending on the options you selected as you went though the Wizard process. If you entered user information when you installed OpenOffice.org, the Wizard uses this information to personalize the document.

3   Open an Existing Document

✔ BEFORE YOU BEGIN	→ SEE ALSO
1 Set Writer Options	**9** Print a Document
2 Create a New Document	

Opening an existing document to edit with Writer is simple. You tell Writer you want to open a document file and then locate the file, and Writer loads the document in the editing area.

One important Writer feature is its capability to open documents you create in other word processing programs. Most notably, Writer opens Microsoft Word documents with ease. Although Writer might not fully support 100% of Microsoft Word's advanced features, Writer does a super job of loading Word documents into Writer's workspace so that you can edit the documents using Writer's interface.

1   Request a Document

Select **Open** from Writer's **File** menu to display the **Open** dialog box.

Beginning with OpenOffice.org 2.0, Writer uses the document extension .odt (OpenDocument Text) for its documents. You can still open .sxw documents created in earlier versions of Writer. Microsoft Word uses the .doc file extension, and all three types of documents (.odt, .swx, and .doc files) display when you want to locate files to open in Writer.

▶ NOTE

OpenOffice.org 2.0 uses the new OASIS (Organization for the Advancement of Structured Information Standards) standard XML (eXtensible Markup Language) file format as its default file format. This new file format is also used in StarOffice, KOffice, and a growing number of products that support the new standard.

2   Navigate to the Document's Location

The document you want to open might not appear at the default location shown in the **Open** dialog box, so navigate to the folder in which the document you're looking for resides using the **Look in** drop-down list.

▶ TIP

You can open documents from your computer's disk or from elsewhere in the file system. If you want to open a document located on the Web, preface the filename with **http://** or **ftp://** to open document files from those sources.

3

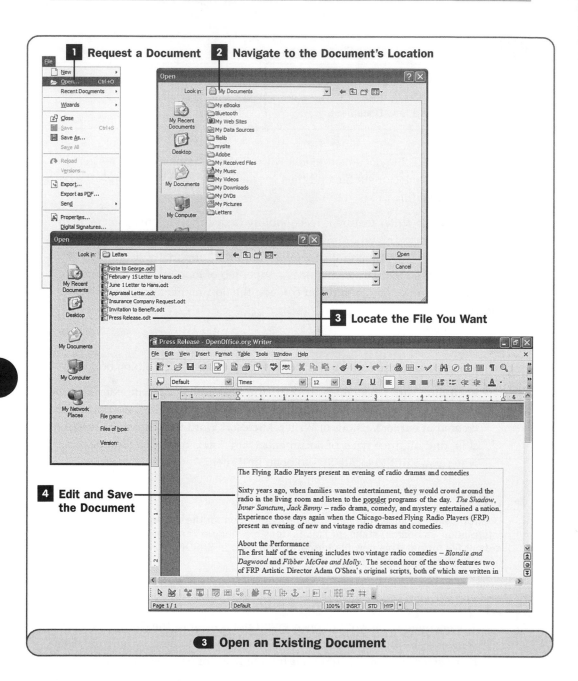

3 Locate the File You Want

3 Locate the File You Want

When you locate the folder that holds the document file, select the file you want to open. Then click the **Open** button to open the selected file in Writer's editing workspace.

▶ **TIP**

Feel free to open more than one file by holding the **Ctrl** key while clicking multiple file-names. Writer opens each document you select in its own window. Use the **Window** menu to select an open document to edit.

4 **Edit and Save the Document**

After the file opens in the Writer workspace, you can edit the file. Navigate to where you wish to make edits (see **5** **Edit Text**) or move to the end of the document and add to it (see **4** **Type Text into a Document**).

Once you've made all the changes you wish to make, select **File**, **Save** to save your document. Your recent changes will be saved in the document file for your next editing session.

4 **Type Text into a Document**

✔ **BEFORE YOU BEGIN**	→ **SEE ALSO**
2 Create a New Document	**5** Edit Text
3 Open an Existing Document	**9** Print a Document

4

If you've ever used any word processor before, even a simple one such as WordPad found in Windows, you'll have no trouble editing text in Writer. Writer's editing area remains fairly clear of clutter so you can concentrate on your work.

Writer has tools to help you make the most of your editing sessions. For example, you may want to see more of your document at one time, perhaps to help keep your current paragraph in context with the one before and after it. The **Full Screen** view removes all menus and toolbars from your editing area to give the maximum amount of space to your editing. Writer's various toolbars are there to provide one-click access to tools. For example, Writer's common *Standard toolbar* is one of the handiest of all the available toolbars because it puts the common editing tasks just to the left of your editing area, where you can quickly access them. To select an item from the Standard toolbar, you'll simply click one of the buttons.

This task walks you through a short editing session, just to give you a feel for the kinds of movements and tools available to you. Many of the editing skills you acquire in one OpenOffice.org program, such as Writer, will apply to the other OpenOffice.org programs as well. For example, all OpenOffice.org programs offer the capability to display or hide any toolbar. The Standard toolbar changes slightly depending on which program you use, but most of its functions are similar across the OpenOffice.org programs.

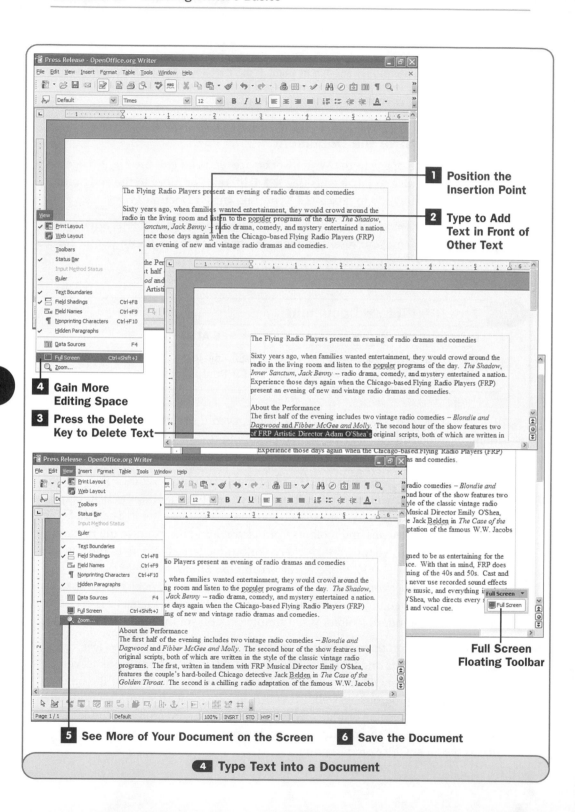

1 Position the
Insertion Point

2 Type to Add
Text in Front of
Other Text

4

4 Gain More
Editing Space

3 Press the Delete
Key to Delete Text

**Full Screen
Floating Toolbar**

5 See More of Your Document on the Screen   **6** Save the Document

4 Type Text into a Document

1 **Position the Insertion Point**

Press the arrow keys to see the text cursor move around your screen. The text cursor is called the *insertion point* and moves as you press any arrow key. You can also click your mouse within the document to place the insertion point where you next want to type.

▶ **KEY TERM**

Insertion point—A vertical text cursor that shows where the next character you type will appear.

Text that you type appears at the insertion point. If you make a mistake, press **Backspace** and Writer moves the insertion point backwards, erasing as you press **Backspace**. When you get to the right edge of a paragraph, Writer automatically wraps your paragraph onto the next line. Do not press **Enter** unless you want to end a paragraph and begin a new one. Writer may or may not insert a blank line between paragraphs, depending on how you set up your page (see **14** **Set Up Page Formatting**).

If you press **Shift**|**Enter** instead of **Enter**, Writer ends the current line and begins at the start of the line below without actually creating a new paragraph. You can easily see where paragraphs begin and end by displaying nonprinting characters (see **5** **Edit Text**). If you press **Ctrl+spacebar** instead of the normal **spacebar**, Writer inserts a *nonbreaking space* and will not end a line on that space but, if necessary, will move both the word before and after the nonbreaking space to the next line in a word wrap. If you press **Ctrl+Enter**, Writer begins a new page in the document, even if you had not yet filled up the previous page.

▶ **KEY TERM**

Nonbreaking space—A space that appears between words when you print the document but does not break at the end of a line. When you want to keep two words together without the end of a line causing them to separate, use a nonbreaking space so that Writer will wrap them both to the next line.

For more information about paragraph breaks and using tabs, see **11** **About Paragraph Breaks and Tabs**.

2 **Type to Add Text in Front of Other Text**

When you place the insertion point before existing text on a line, Writer normally inserts the text you type in front of the existing text and moves the existing text over to the right. This is called *insert mode* and is normal behavior for most editors and word processors. If your typing replaces text on the screen, you're in *overtype mode* instead of insert mode.

4

▶ KEY TERMS

Insert mode—The state of Writer where new text you type is inserted before existing text. It is indicated by the **INSRT** message on the status bar.

Overtype mode—The state of Writer where new text replaces existing text as you type. It is indicated by the **OVER** message on the status bar.

Press the **Insert** key to switch between overtype and insert modes. If you have a lot of text to replace, you'll find that it's easier to do so in overtype mode because you'll have less text to delete.

3 Press the Delete Key to Delete Text

Select text and press the **Delete** key to delete characters where the insertion point appears. Every time you press **Delete**, Writer removes one character (including a space, number, or even a blank line if that's where the insertion point is positioned).

4 Gain More Editing Space

Select **Full Screen** from the **View** menu to temporarily hide your toolbars, menu, and the status bar. You will be able to see more of your document at one time. Notice that even when all the other toolbars are hidden in **Full Screen** mode, the floating **Full Screen** toolbar appears in the editing area.

▶ TIP

Often you'll start typing a word, such as *following*, but before you type the fifth letter, Writer finishes the word for you with its word completion feature. You can press **Enter** to accept the proposed word, or just keep typing to finish the word yourself. Also, if you type a word incorrectly, such as *windoes*, Writer very well might correct it using its automatic spelling checker. You can turn off this AutoComplete feature from the **Tools, AutoCorrect** dialog box.

Click the floating **Full Screen** toolbar's **Full-Screen On/Off** button to return to the normal editing workspace with full menus, toolbars, and the status bar.

5 See More of Your Document on the Screen

Select the **Zoom** option from the **View** menu to adjust how much of your document appears on the screen at any one time. In the **Zoom** dialog box that opens, select from the given list of percentages or click **Variable** and enter another percentage. The default zoom percentage is **100%**, which means that what you see on the screen is the same size as what appears when you print your document. If you change to a higher percentage, such as **200%**, you'll zoom more into your document, making the characters look larger on the screen. If you change to a lower percentage, such as **75%**, you'll zoom away from your document, seeing more of the page, although you won't see as much up-close detail.

Click **OK** to close the dialog box and see the result of your screen adjustment.

6 Save the Document

After you have edited the text in the document—and periodically while you are editing—you should save your changes to the hard disk. To save the document, choose **File**, **Save** or click the Save icon on the **Standard** toolbar (the third icon from the left). Writer saves the current version of the file, overwriting the previous version of the file.

▶ **TIP**

If you're not sure that you want the current version of the file to overwrite the existing version when you save, choose **File**, **Save As** instead. Writer asks you for a new filename for the current version of the document, saves it under that name, and doesn't touch the original version.

---

5 | **Edit Text**   **5**

✔ BEFORE YOU BEGIN	→ SEE ALSO
2 Create a New Document	**9** Print a Document
3 Open an Existing Document	

Writer makes it easy to edit your documents. Whether you want to edit a letter, add to your novel, or edit a report once more before sending it to clients, Writer provides quick and simple tools that help you get the job done right.

If your document is long, you can navigate to the place you want to edit using the keyboard (see **6** **Move Around a Document**). If you know of a key word or phrase that is close to the text you want to edit, you can search for that key word or phrase to move there quickly (see **7** **Find and Replace Text**). Writer's formatting and spell-checking tools will help you ensure accuracy while making your documents look good too. You'll find help with formatting starting in **12** **Apply Character Formatting**, and you'll learn how to check your document's spelling using Writer's built-in word dictionary in **8** **Check a Document's Spelling**.

▶ **TIP**

Always select **File**, **Save** to save your document after making changes to it. If you attempt to exit Writer before you save your changes, Writer kindly reminds you to save the file.

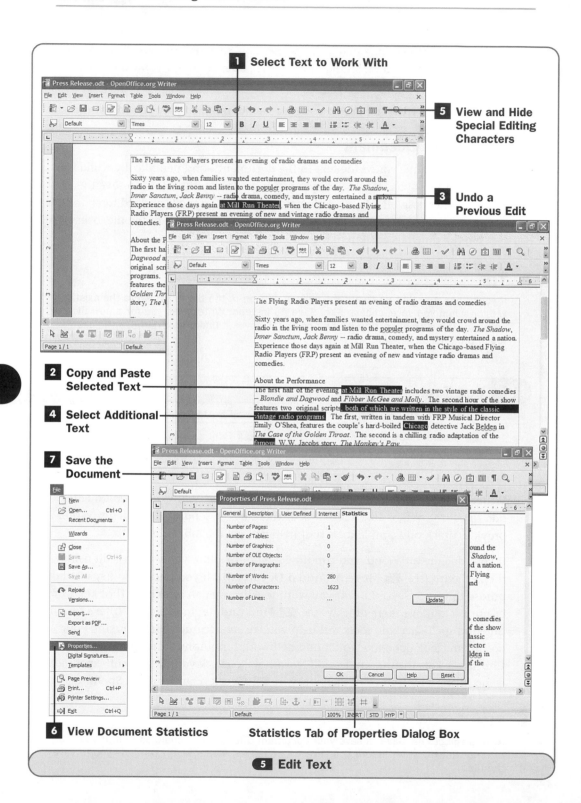

1 Select Text to Work With

5 View and Hide Special Editing Characters

3 Undo a Previous Edit

2 Copy and Paste Selected Text

4 Select Additional Text

7 Save the Document

6 View Document Statistics

Statistics Tab of Properties Dialog Box

5 Edit Text

▪ Select Text to Work With

Select text using standard Windows selection tools (such as holding the **Shift** key as you press arrow keys) to select more than one character at a time. You might want to select a large block of text for deletion or to apply a special format to that selected text (see **12** **Apply Character Formatting**). The selected text appears in "reverse video," meaning that it is white text on a black background.

▶ **TIP**

Press **Ctrl+A** to select the entire document. You can also make multiple selections by first making one selection and then holding the **Ctrl** key while selecting additional text.

▪ Copy and Paste Selected Text

After you've selected text, you can press **Ctrl+C** to copy the selection to your Windows Clipboard. The original text remains unchanged in the document. After you've copied the selection to the Clipboard, move your insertion point to another place in your document (the text you originally selected is deselected) and press **Ctrl+V** to paste a copy of the text in the new location.

You can keep pressing **Ctrl+V** to paste the text as many times as you wish in your document. The normal Windows keyboard shortcuts work in Writer, so if you instead want to move the originally selected text to a new location, press **Ctrl+X** (for cut) instead of **Ctrl+C** (for copy) to delete the text from its original location; then reposition the insertion point and press **Ctrl+V** to paste the text in its new location.

Writer's **Edit** menu contains the typical **Cut**, **Copy**, and **Paste** options in case you don't want to use the keyboard shortcuts. In addition, the **Standard** toolbar provides **Copy**, **Cut**, and **Paste** buttons for you to use.

▶ **TIPS**

To quickly move a paragraph up or down by one line, you can click anywhere in the paragraph and then press the **Up Arrow** or **Down Arrow** key.

You can press **Shift+Delete** to cut a selection; press **Shift+Insert** to place the cut selection into its new location.

▶ **NOTE**

You can paste selected text into another OpenOffice.org program or another Windows program that accepts text. The Windows Clipboard is handy for copying and moving data between programs.

3 Undo a Previous Edit

Writer's **Undo** feature undoes your previous edit—whatever that may have been. To invoke it, press **Ctrl+Z**, choose **Edit**, **Undo**, or click the **Undo** button on the **Standard** toolbar. So if you accidentally erased a large block of text, press **Ctrl+Z** and Writer puts the text right back. You can undo just about any edit you make in Writer other than a style change.

▶ **TIP**

You can redo an Undo! Press **Ctrl+Y**, select **Edit**, **Redo**, or click the **Redo** button in the **Standard** toolbar to reverse the previous Undo operation you performed.

4 Select Additional Text

Writer doesn't limit you to one selection at a time. You can select multiple blocks of text within your document at the same time. After you've selected the first block, hold the **Ctrl** key and select another block of text. You may keep doing this as often as needed to select all the text you need to select.

By selecting multiple items, you'll be able to work with them all as a group. For example, you may be writing about great works of literature and you realize you did not italicize each title. Instead of selecting the titles and italicizing them individually, you can select all the titles and apply italics to them in one step (see **12** **Apply Character Formatting**).

5 View and Hide Special Editing Characters

Click the **Nonprinting Characters** button in the **Main** toolbar (or press **Ctrl+F10**) to turn on nonprinting characters, which show you where paragraph divisions, blank spaces, and other editing elements occur. These nonprinting characters don't print (unless you change the printing option to show them, as mentioned in **1** **Set Writer Options**) but can appear on the screen so that you'll know exactly what you're editing.

Click the **Nonprinting Characters** button on the **Main** toolbar button (or press **Ctrl+F10**) again to turn off the display of nonprinting characters.

▶ **TIP**

If you want to count the words in a particular passage of text rather than in the whole document, use the **Word Count** feature. First, select the text you want to count—it can be a sentence, a paragraph, or any text selection within a document. Then choose **Tools**, **Word Count** and view the results in the **Word Count** dialog box.

6 **View Document Statistics**

As you type text into your document, you can maintain an accurate word count, along with other document statistics, by selecting the **Properties** option from the **File** menu.

Click the **Statistics** tab to view the **Statistics** page in the **Properties** dialog box. Here you see counts of various objects in your document, such as the number of paragraphs, words, characters, and lines. If you're writing for a magazine, for example, word count is an important statistic to track; if you're trying to fit all the text on a single page, you might want to keep track of the number of lines.

When you've viewed the statistics for your current document, click **OK** to close the **Properties** dialog box and return to the editing area.

▶ **NOTE**

Click the **Statistic** page's **Update** button to force Writer to perform an update of the statistics before you fully rely on the numbers.

7 **Save the Document**

After you have edited the text in the document—and periodically while you are editing—you should save your changes to the hard disk. To save the document, choose **File**, **Save** or click the **Save** icon in the **Standard** toolbar (the third icon from the left). Writer saves the current version of the file, overwriting the previous version of the file.

▶ **TIP**

If you're not sure that you want the current version of the file to overwrite the existing version when you save, choose **File, Save As** instead. Writer asks you for a new filename for the current version of the document, saves it under that name, and doesn't touch the original version.

6 **Move Around a Document**

✔ **BEFORE YOU BEGIN**

2 Create a New Document
3 Open an Existing Document

→ **SEE ALSO**

7 Find and Replace Text
5 Edit Text

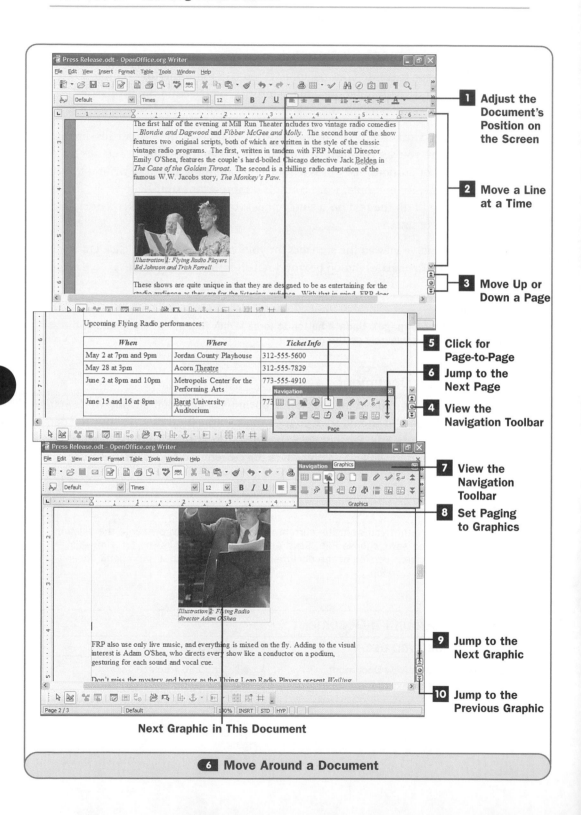

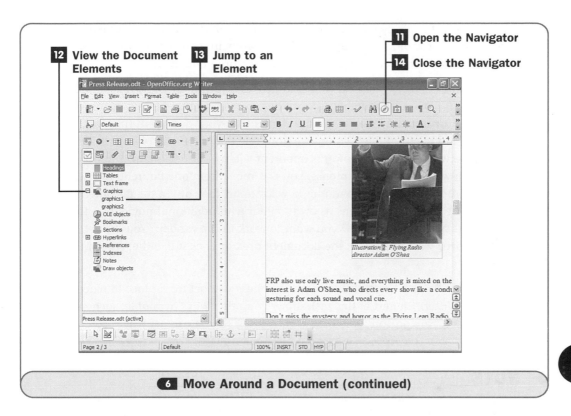

12 View the Document Elements

13 Jump to an Element

11 Open the Navigator

14 Close the Navigator

6 Move Around a Document (continued)

6

The faster you can move around a document, the faster you'll get your work done. If most documents consumed less than a screen of real estate, the ability to move around the document wouldn't be needed. Most documents, however, require far more than a single screen of room. Being able to navigate from place to place becomes second nature quickly because it's a skill needed before you can edit seriously.

Writer and the other OpenOffice.org programs help you move from place to place with onscreen elements, a Navigator window, and a bevy of keyboard shortcuts. In this task, you'll get a chance to use onscreen elements such as the scrollbars, the **Navigation** toolbar, and a more sophisticated set of navigation tools called the **Navigator**.

The **Navigation** toolbar lets you move from one element to another (such as from one graphic to another, or one heading to another) with a click of the mouse. You can specify whether that element is graphics, charts, or whatever and then use the toolbar's navigation buttons to jump from one to another. By treating your document as a set of objects rather than as one cohesive whole, the **Navigation** toolbar lets you navigate quickly through a very long document. This feature is invaluable when you're working with a multi-page document. Suppose that you want to quickly check that all the graphics in a 100-page document look good. Instead of scrolling through the whole document, you can use the **Navigation** toolbar to quickly jump from one picture to the next.

The **Navigator** is more powerful cousin to the **Navigation** toolbar. It's a window that contains icons and a toolbar for working more efficiently in long documents. The **Navigator** displays icons for all the elements in your document (pictures, headings, and so on) and lets you move from one to another simply by clicking icons in the window. Its true power is apparent when your document is many pages long; with a click of the mouse, you can move from one figure to the next or one heading to the next, no matter how far apart they are in the document. The **Navigator** window contains its own toolbar with additional navigation tools that let you specify exactly how you want to work in the window. You can let the **Navigator** window float in the document area or dock it to either side of the window.

Table 2.2 lists several keystroke shortcuts that help you get from place to place quickly in Writer. The rest of this task shows you other ways available, such as the scrollbars, **Navigation** toolbar, and Navigator, so you can get where you want to go.

6

▶ **NOTE**

Writer supports a wealth of additional keyboard shortcuts. Table 2.2 lists only the ones found to be among the most popular or useful for moving around a document.

TABLE 2.2   Keyboard Navigation Shortcuts

Keyboard Shortcut	Description
Ctrl+left arrow	Moves the text cursor to the beginning of the word
Ctrl+Shift+left arrow	Moves the text cursor to the left, word by word and extends the selection left
Ctrl+right arrow	Moves the text cursor to the end of the word
Ctrl+Shift+right arrow	Moves the text cursor to the right, word by word and extends the selection right
Up arrow	Moves the text cursor up one line at a time
Down arrow	Moves the text cursor down one line at a time
Home	Goes to the beginning of the current line
End	Goes to the end of the current line
Ctrl+Home	Moves the text cursor to the beginning of the document
Ctrl+End	Moves the text cursor to the end of the document
PageUp	Moves up one screen at a time
PageDown	Moves down one screen at a time

TABLE 2.2   Continued

Keyboard Shortcut	Description
Ctrl+Delete	Deletes text to the end of the current word
Ctrl+Backspace	Deletes text to the beginning of the current word
Ctrl+Shift+Delete	Deletes text to the end of the current sentence
Ctrl+Shift+Backspace	Deletes text to the beginning of the current sentence

1 Adjust the Document's Position on the Screen

When editing your document, drag either the vertical or the horizontal scroll-bar to position a different part of your document on the screen.

▶ **NOTE**

Dragging the vertical scrollbar up and down the screen is much faster than paging through a very long document.

2 Move a Line at a Time

Click any scrollbar arrow to move one line up or down. You can hold down your mouse button to scroll rapidly up or down the screen.

6

3 Move Up or Down a Page

Click the Writer's **Previous Page** or **Next Page** button on the scrollbar to move up or down one page at a time. You can hold down your mouse button to scroll rapidly up or down the screen one page at a time.

▶ **NOTE**

The **Previous Page** and **Next Page** scrollbar buttons may take on another function (such as paging to the next graphic or header or footer) if you've used the **Navigation** toolbar this session.

4 View the Navigation Toolbar

Click the **Navigation** button on the vertical scrollbar to display the **Navigation** floating toolbar. With the Navigation toolbar, you can page through your document and move between different elements easily.

5 Click for Page-to-Page

Click the **Navigation** toolbar's **Page** button to set the vertical scrolling to move from page to page. If you've never used the **Navigation** toolbar before, the **Page** button will already be selected.

6 Jump to the Next Page

Click the vertical scrollbar's **Next Page** button to jump to the next page in the document.

At this point you may be wondering what good the **Navigation** toolbar did. After all, you clicked the **Next Page** button in the scrollbar in step 3 without having to display the **Navigation** toolbar first. That's because when you first use Writer, the **Navigation** toolbar mode is set to the **Page** button. The **Navigation** toolbar does not have to remain set to **Page**, however, as the next two steps show.

7 View the Navigation Toolbar

Click the scrollbar's **Navigation** button once again to display the **Navigation** toolbar once again.

8 Set Paging to Graphics

Click the **Navigation** toolbar's **Graphics** button to set the paging to graphics instead of a page of text.

6

▶ **TIP**

Remember, if you can't see your scrollbars and you want to, or if you can see them and you'd rather hide them, you can decide which scrollbar (either one, both, or neither) you want to see from the OpenOffice.org Writer Options **View** page (see **1** **Set Writer Options**).

9 Jump to the Next Graphic

Click the **Next Graphic** button that now appears on your vertical scrollbar to jump to the next graphic image in your document. Notice the floating ToolTip that describes the scrollbar has changed from **Next Page** to **Next Graphic**. That's because you just selected a graphic image when you used the **Navigation** toolbar in the previous step. As long as your document has a graphic image somewhere below your current position, Writer jumps to that image. If no graphic image appears in the document, Writer remains where it is.

10 Jump to the Previous Graphic

Click the **Previous Graphic** button to move back to the previous graphic image you viewed (assuming your document has multiple graphic images).

⑪ Open the Navigator

Click the Navigator button on the Standard toolbar, or press **F5**, to open the **Navigator** window. The **Navigator** window differs from the Navigation floating toolbar, although their similar names never cease to confuse users. The **Navigation** toolbar is more directly linked to your vertical scrollbar, as the previous steps showed. The **Navigator** window provides a high-level look at your document's various elements (or possible elements, such as a header that you may not have yet added).

▶ TIP

If the **Navigator** takes up too much room docked to a border of the document window, you can drag it into the document window where it will float as a smaller, scrollable window.

⑫ View the Document Elements

View the Navigator options to see various Writer-related elements that can appear in your document. If your document has multiple elements, such as the two graphic images found by Navigator here, Navigator displays a check mark next to the item on the list. Click the check mark to see a list of the items.

⑬ Jump to an Element

In this example, you can double-click either entry, **graphics1** or **graphics2**, in the Navigator to see either graphic image. Writer scrolls directly to that item in the document window.

⑭ Close the Navigator

When you're finished using the Navigator to look for something, press **F5** or click the **Navigator** button on the Standard toolbar.

---

7 **Find and Replace Text**

✔ **BEFORE YOU BEGIN**

- ③ Open an Existing Document
- ⑤ Edit Text
- ⑥ Move Around a Document

→ **SEE ALSO**

- ⑫ Apply Character Formatting

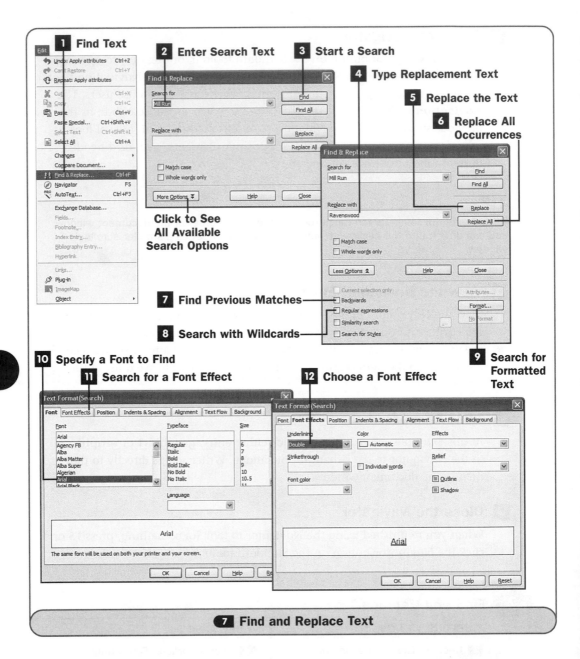

7 Find and Replace Text

Long documents make quickly locating what you need important. Perhaps you need to make changes to some text in a table or perhaps a caption is wrong on a figure. Writer provides text-locating tools that will be familiar to you if you've done similar text-locating tasks in the past.

Of course, along with finding text, you'll need to replace the text you find sometimes. For example, you may have written a press release about a show at the Mill Run Theater and learned that the venue for the show has changed to the Ravenswood Theater. With Writer's Find and Replace tools, you can make quick work of changing all the Mill Run references to Ravenswood throughout the document. Whether the document is one page or 100 pages, you'll be able to find and replace text such as this just as quickly and easily.

▶ **NOTE**

The **Navigator** and the **Navigation** toolbar are great for locating generic elements within your document, but use the **Find and Replace** tools, shown in this task, to locate specific text and editing marks within your document.

1 Find Text

Select the **Find & Replace** option from the **Edit** menu to display the **Find & Replace** dialog box. You can also click the **Find & Replace** toolbar button or press **Ctrl+F** to display the **Find & Replace** dialog box. Click the **More Options** button to display all the Search options available in this dialog box.

2 Enter Search Text

Type the text you want to find in the **Search for** text box.

▶ **TIP**

If you've searched for the same text before, you can click the down arrow to open the **Search for** drop-down list box and select the text to search for it once again.

3 Start a Search

Click the **Find** button. Writer searches from the current text cursor's position in the document to the end of the file. If Writer finds the text, it highlights the text. You may be able to see the highlighted text, but if not you can move or close the **Find & Replace** dialog box to see the highlighted text. (If you had clicked the **Find All** button instead of **Find**, Writer would have highlighted all occurrences of any matching text in the document.)

4 Type Replacement Text

If you want Writer to replace found text with new text, type the new text into the **Replace with** text box.

7

5 Replace the Text

If the **Search for** text is found, Writer replaces that text with the text you entered in the **Replace with** text box.

6 Replace All Occurrences

Instead of **Replace** (or after you do a replacement), if you click the **Replace All** button, Writer replaces all the matches with your replacement text throughout the document. Such a change is more global and possibly riskier because you may replace text you didn't really want replaced. By clicking **Find** before each replace operation, you can be sure that the proper text is being replaced; however, such a single-occurrence find and replacement takes a lot of time in a long document.

7 Find Previous Matches

Click to select the **Backwards** option before doing a find or replacement if you want to find or replace from the current text cursor's position back to the start of the document.

8 Search with Wildcards

Click to select the **Regular expressions** option if you want to perform a ***wildcard search*** using OpenOffice.org's ***regular expressions***. Table 2.3 describes some of the more common regular expressions you may use in the **Search for** text box and gives an example of each.

▶ KEY TERMS

Wildcard search—Allows you to use wildcard characters, such as *, to replace characters in a search.

Regular expressions—The name given to OpenOffice.org's extensive wildcard character support; OpenOffice.org supports far more wildcard characters than most Windows programs.

TABLE 2.3   Regular Expressions That Form Advanced Wildcard Searches

Regular Expression Character	How Used
.	Represents one and only one character in a search. Therefore, h.s matches *his* and *has* but not *hands* (similar to the question mark wildcard character in other programs).
^	Requests that a match be made only if the search term appears at the beginning of a paragraph. Therefore, ^The matches all occurrences of *The* that begin paragraphs, but it does not match any other *The* in the document.

TABLE 2.3   Continued

Regular Expression Character	How Used
$	Requests that a match be made only if the search term appears at the end of a paragraph. Therefore, success$ matches all occurrences of *success* that fall at the end of paragraphs, but it does not match any other *success* in the document.
*	Represents zero, one, or more characters. Therefore, i*n matches *in*, *i123n*, and *ion*.
\>	Represents a search term located at the end of a word. Therefore, \>door matches *outdoor* and *indoor* but not *doorknob*.
\<	Represents a search term located at the beginning of a word. Therefore, \<door matches *doorknob* but not *outdoor* and *indoor*.
^$	Locates empty paragraphs.

9 Search for Formatted Text

If you want to search only for certain text values that are formatted in a particular way, such as all italicized instances of Mill Run but not boldfaced instances of Mill Run, you can do so by clicking the **Format** button to display the **Text Format (Search)** dialog box.

10 Specify a Font to Find

Select the font name, typeface, and size that the text must match before being considered found.

11 Search for a Font Effect

If you want to further refine your search to a specific font color or effect, click the **Font Effects** tab to display a page with those attributes you can look for.

12 Choose a Font Effect

Select the font effect you want to find. If the matching text also matches the font effects you select (as well as any font name and size you may have selected in step 10), Writer considers the match to be successful and highlights the found text.

▶ **NOTE**

Click the tabs on the other pages within the **Text Format (Search)** dialog box to see the other refinements you can make when searching and replacing text. You can even specify the background color that must appear behind any matching text before the text is to be considered a match.

When you finish finding and replacing all the text for this search session, click the **Find & Replace** dialog box's **Close** button to close the dialog box and return to the document's work area.

---

8   **Check a Document's Spelling**

✔ BEFORE YOU BEGIN	→ SEE ALSO
2 Create a New Document	**9** Print a Document
3 Open an Existing Document	

Writer can check your spelling in two ways:

- All at once after you've composed or opened a document

- As you type by highlighting your words with a red, wavy line beneath the misspelled ones

▶ NOTE

Don't rely solely on Writer's spelling check capabilities. Writer's spelling checker does not replace the need for proofreading on your part. As a good example, consider that Writer will find absolutely no misspelled words in the following sentence: *Wee went two the fare too search the bares.*

If Writer flags a word as misspelled but the word is spelled correctly, you can tell Writer to add that word to its spelling dictionary or to ignore the word for the rest of the editing session. Writer might flag some proper nouns and technical terms as misspelled that are not.

▶ TIP

In addition to spellchecking, Writer can also offer synonyms from its online thesaurus. Don't type *confused* when *obfuscated* will baffle more people!

1 Request a Spelling Check

Choose **Tools, Spellcheck** from the menu bar to check the spelling of your current document. Writer begins checking the spelling of your document, starting at the current location of the insertion point and continuing to the end of the document. If the insertion point was not at the beginning of the document, Writer prompts you to continue the spelling check from the beginning of the document before it completes the check to make sure that nothing was missed. If Writer finds a misspelled word, Writer displays the **Spellcheck** dialog box, which shows the misspelled word and the sentence in which that word occurs. Writer also suggests alternate spellings if they are available.

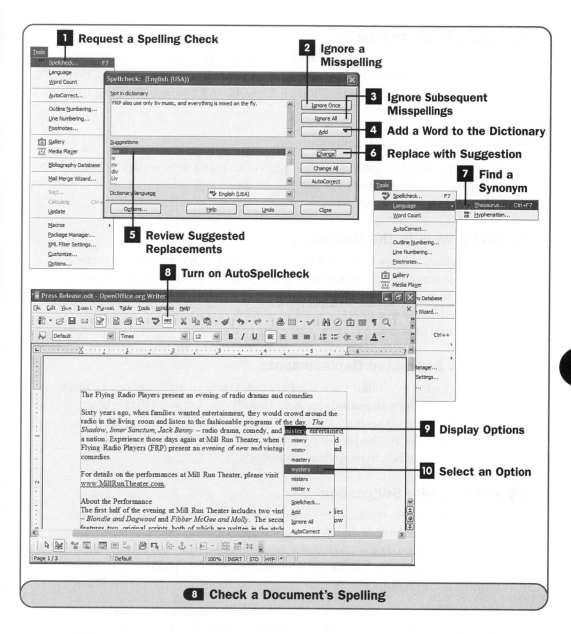

1 Request a Spelling Check

2 Ignore a Misspelling

3 Ignore Subsequent Misspellings

4 Add a Word to the Dictionary

6 Replace with Suggestion

7 Find a Synonym

5 Review Suggested Replacements

8 Turn on AutoSpellcheck

9 Display Options

10 Select an Option

8

8 Check a Document's Spelling

▶ **TIP**

If you cannot see the highlighted misspelled word and you want to view it in the context of your document, you may have to drag the **Spellcheck** dialog box up or down to see the highlighted word that Writer considers to be misspelled.

2 Ignore a Misspelling

If Writer finds a word that is not really misspelled (perhaps it's an abbreviation that you don't want to add to the Writer's spelling dictionary), click the **Ignore Once** button. Writer will ignore the word and continue checking the rest of your document.

3 Ignore Subsequent Misspellings

If you often type the abbreviation or other word found to be misspelled but really isn't, click the **Ignore All** button and Writer will ignore that word in all subsequent spelling check sessions.

4 Add a Word to the Dictionary

If Writer finds a properly spelled word that it thinks isn't, such as a strange last name, you can add that word to Writer's spelling dictionary by clicking the **Add** button. Not only will Writer not flag the word as misspelled in the future, but Writer will offer the word as a possible correction for subsequent words found to be misspelled that are close to that one.

5 Review Suggested Replacements

If Writer finds a word that truly is misspelled, Writer tries to offer one or more suggestions in the **Suggestions** list box. Usually, the top word that is highlighted is the correct spelling for the misspelled word, but you may have to scroll down to locate the proper correction, depending on how many close matches Writer finds in its spelling dictionary.

6 Replace with Suggestion

If the top highlighted word is the word to replace the misspelled word with, click the **Change** button and Writer will replace the misspelled word with the selected correction. If the correction is not the top word in the **Suggestions** list box but appears farther down the list, click the correct replacement word and then click the **Change** button to make the replacement.

Click **OK** to close the **Thesaurus** dialog box. When you're done checking the spelling, click the **Close** button to close the **Spellcheck** dialog box.

▶ TIPS

If Writer does not suggest a correct spelling for the current misspelled word, you can correct the spelling yourself by clicking the text in the **Not in Dictionary** box and making edits there.

If you want Writer to replace all instances of the misspelled word with the suggested word, click the **Change All** button instead of the **Change** button.

7 Find a Synonym

If you want to see synonyms of any word, select that word and then choose **Tools, Language, Thesaurus** from the menu bar to display the **Thesaurus** dialog box. Review the suggested synonyms for the each meaning of the word (if multiple meanings are listed). If you find a better word than the one you selected, click that word in the **Synonym** list in the **Thesaurus** dialog box.

▶ **TIP**

The **Thesaurus** dialog box is also available via the **Tools, Thesaurus** menu or the **Ctrl+F7** keyboard shortcut.

8 Turn on AutoSpellcheck

To turn on the automatic spelling checker so that Writer checks your spelling as you type words into your document, select the **AutoSpellcheck** button on the Standard toolbar. The highlighted button indicates that Writer turned on the automatic spelling checker.

▶ **NOTE**

You can turn off Writer's automatic spelling checker by clicking the **AutoSpellcheck** button on the Standard toolbar. The button will no longer appear highlighted, indicating that Writer has turned off the automatic spelling check feature.

9 Display Options

As you type, misspelled words appear with a red wavy line beneath them. Right-click over the misspelled word to see several options (including suggested replacement words) from which you can choose.

One of the options, **Spellcheck**, opens the **Spellcheck** dialog box, so just because you've turned on AutoSpellcheck doesn't mean you can't work within that dialog box as you did in step 1. You may also elect to add the word that Writer thinks is misspelled to the dictionary so future spelling checks of that word won't be flagged as incorrect. If you select the **Ignore All** option, Writer will not flag the word as incorrect for the rest of this session, but subsequent editing sessions will still view the word as incorrect because you didn't add it to the dictionary.

The **AutoCorrect** option tells Writer that if this word ever appears in the future, instead of marking it as misspelled, automatically correct the word with one of the options you suggest. If you find yourself mistyping the same word frequently, such as typing *mispell* for *misspell*, you could request that Writer automatically change *mispell* to **misspell** if and when you make that

8

mistake in the future. Writer corrects that misspelling as you type, and often you'll not notice the correction took place, but you will have a more accurate document. For more information on Writer's AutoCorrect feature, see **32** **Use AutoCorrect to Improve Your Typing**.

10 Select an Option

From the right-click menu, select the option you want to choose to handle the misspelled word. Although the **Spellcheck** dialog box offers more suggestions than this right-click menu, the right-click menu often brings up as many options as you will routinely need to ensure spelling accuracy when you type.

---

9 Print a Document

✔ BEFORE YOU BEGIN

2 Create a New Document
3 Open an Existing Document
4 Type Text into a Document

→ SEE ALSO

10 About the Rulers
14 Set Up Page Formatting

9

Once you're done creating your document, you'll want to print it to paper. Writer supports the standard printing options that most Windows programs support. If your document has color charts and you have a color printer, the charts will print just fine. Otherwise, the charts will print in shades of black and gray (and still look fine!).

Be sure to save your document before you print it. Actually, it's a good idea to select **File**, **Save** to save your document throughout the editing of that document. If your printer jams or the Windows print queue messes up during the printing process (rare but it can happen), you could lose changes you made to the document before you print it.

If you select **File**, **Export as PDF**, Writer saves your document in the common PDF format, which you can send to any computer with *Adobe Acrobat Reader* and that user will be able to view or print your document with all the formatting preserved, even if his or her word processing program doesn't support the OASIS standard file format (see **36** **Save a Document as a PDF File**).

▶ KEY TERM

Adobe Acrobat Reader—A free program, available from www.Adobe.com, that reads and prints PDF document files. All formatting of the document can be preserved, displayed, and printed by Adobe Acrobat Reader even if the user's computer is not Windows based. The full-featured Adobe Acrobat program lets you create, edit, and work with PDF files, but you must pay for the privelege.

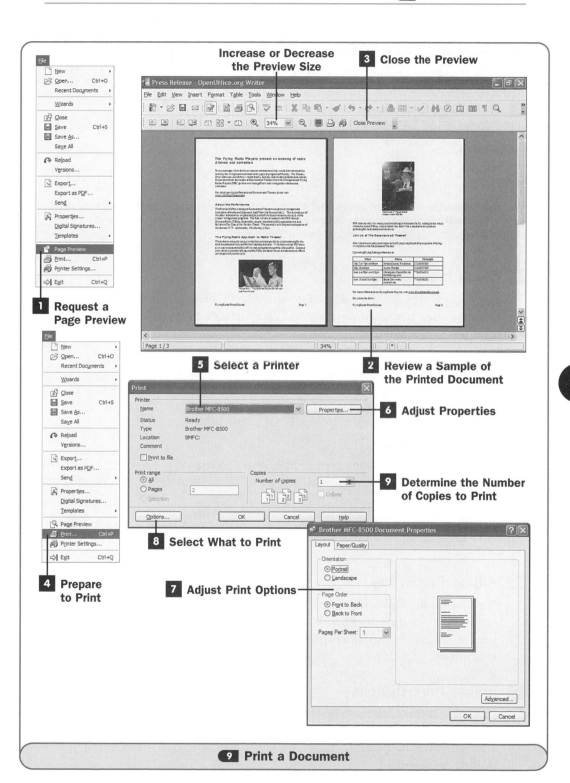

Increase or Decrease the Preview Size

3 Close the Preview

1 Request a Page Preview

5 Select a Printer

2 Review a Sample of the Printed Document

6 Adjust Properties

9 Determine the Number of Copies to Print

8 Select What to Print

4 Prepare to Print

7 Adjust Print Options

1 Request a Page Preview

Select the **Page Preview** option from the **File** menu.

2 Review a Sample of the Printed Document

Look over the preview of the document to see if it appears to be properly formatted.

▶ **TIP**

You can adjust the number of pages that Page Preview shows at one time by clicking to select the **Multiple Pages** toolbar button and designating the number of rows and columns of sample pages you want to view at one time.

3 Close the Preview

Once you've previewed what your document will look like printed, click the **Close Preview** button. If you need to make further edits to your document, do so now.

4 Prepare to Print

Once you're satisfied that the document is ready to print, select the **Print** option from the **File** menu. The **Print** dialog box appears.

5 Select a Printer

Select the printer you want to print to from the **Name** drop-down list.

▶ **TIP**

If you have a fax modem, you can select your fax from the **Name** list to send your document to a fax recipient.

6 Adjust Properties

If you want to adjust any printer settings, click the **Properties** button. The dialog box that appears when you click **Properties** varies from printer to printer. Close the printer's **Properties** dialog box once you've made any needed changes.

7 Adjust Print Options

Click the **Options** button to display the **Printer Options** dialog box. From the **Printer Options** dialog box, you can adjust several print settings, such as whether you want graphics, tables, and drawings printed or omitted from the printed document.

▶ **NOTE**

Although it's called *Printer Options*, the **Printer Options** dialog box is not printer specific but rather controls the way your document appears when printed. If, for instance, you want to print for a binder, you could click to select the **Left pages** and **Right pages** options to leave an extra middle margin on every other printed page.

Click the **OK** button to close the **Printer Options** dialog box.

8 Select What to Print

Click to select either **All** or **Pages** to designate that you want to print the entire document or only a portion of it. If you click **Pages**, type the page number or a range of page numbers (such as **2-5** or **1-10, 15-25**) that you want to print.

9 Determine the Number of Copies to Print

Click the arrow box next to the **Number of Copies** option to determine how many copies you want to print.

Once you've determined how many pages and copies to print, click the **OK** button to print your document and close the **Print** dialog box.

9

3

Making Your Words Look Good

IN THIS CHAPTER:

Writer adds flair to your documents. Not only can Writer make your words read more accurately with its automatic correction tools, but Writer makes your writing look better too. Writer supports character, paragraph, and even complete document formatting.

When you begin learning Writer, don't worry about the formatting. Just type your text before formatting it so that you get your thoughts in the document while they are still fresh. After you type your document, you can format its text. Many writers follow this write-then-format plan throughout their entire careers.

10	**About the Rulers**

✔ **BEFORE YOU BEGIN**	→ **SEE ALSO**
1 Set Writer Options	**11** About Paragraph Breaks and Tabs
4 Type Text into a Document	**13** Apply Paragraph Formatting
	14 Set Up Page Formatting

10

Writer has two rulers: the *horizontal ruler* and the *vertical ruler*. Both of these rulers are onscreen guides that display measurement values so you'll know where on the page your text will appear. For example, if your measurements are set to inches (see **1** Set Writer Options), the 2 on your horizontal ruler means that all text beneath that ruler's 2 is exactly 2 inches from the left margin.

▶ KEY TERMS

Horizontal ruler—A guide you can display across the top of your document that shows the horizontal position of text and graphics on the page.

Vertical ruler—A guide you can display down the left side of your document that shows the vertical position of text and graphics on the page.

By default, Writer displays the horizontal and vertical rulers. If you do not see the rulers, choose **View, Ruler** from the menu bar to display them.

The ruler measurements are relative to the left and right margins. For example, in this figure, the ruler's left edge is the left edge of the page, but the ruler's white area shows where the left and right margins appear.

▶ TIP

Right-click either ruler to change the measurement to a different setting, such as from inches to centimeters.

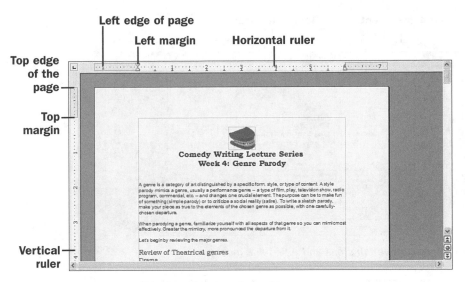

Left edge of page

Left margin   Horizontal ruler

Top edge
of the
page

Top
margin

Vertical
ruler

Rulers show the positioning of text and graphics.

In addition to showing margins and the page width, the horizontal ruler also shows this additional information:

- *Tab stop* (see **11** About Paragraph Breaks and Tabs)
- Paragraph *indent* (see **13** Apply Paragraph Formatting)
- Border (see **13** Apply Paragraph Formatting)
- Columns (see **15** Create a Multicolumn Newsletter)

▶ KEY TERMS

Tab stop—Controls the horizontal placement of text on a line.

Indent—The space between the left and right page margins and the current paragraph.

If you format different paragraphs in your document differently from one another, the ruler will change to reflect those differences. In other words, if the first paragraph has three tab stops and a first-line indent, when you click anywhere within that paragraph, the ruler changes to show those tab stops and the first-line indent, as shown in the following figure.

If a subsequent paragraph has a different set of indents, tab stops, and margins, the ruler will show those differences if you click within that paragraph, as shown in the next figure.

10

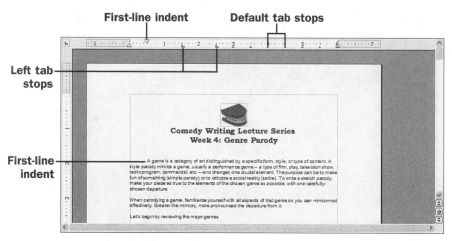

First-line indent **Default tab stops**

Left tab stops

First-line indent

A ruler showing three tab stops and a first-line indent.

Left-margin indent

A ruler showing default tab stops and a left-margin indent.

10

The horizontal ruler is so tied to paragraph formatting that if you double-click the ruler, the **Paragraph** formatting dialog box appears. **13 Apply Paragraph Formatting** explains how to use the **Paragraph** dialog box.

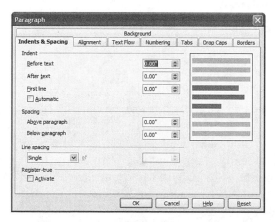

The Paragraph dialog box appears when you double-click the ruler.

Obviously, it's important that you keep in mind that the current horizontal ruler showing at any one time is only reflecting the current paragraph's tab and margin settings. A ruler can reflect each paragraph differently.

▶ **NOTE**

Don't confuse the ruler's half-inch default tab stops with the centered tab stop. Both look the same, but the centered tab stop will be larger, when present, than the default tab stops. See **11** **About Paragraph Breaks and Tabs** for more information on centered tabs.

The ruler does more than update to reflect the current paragraph's settings. You can use the ruler to change tab, indent, and margin settings without using dialog boxes. Unless pinpoint precision is required, the ruler is actually the best place to make these changes.

For example, click anywhere on the ruler and a tab stop will appear at that location. You can drag that tab stop left or right to adjust its position. You can drag any tab stop left or right, even those you applied using the **Paragraph** formatting dialog box. To change the type of tab you place, first click the tab character box at the left of the ruler to change the next tab you place on the ruler.

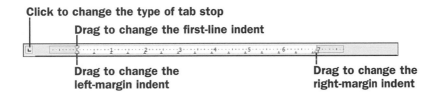

Click to change the type of tab stop

Drag to change the first-line indent

Drag to change the left-margin indent

Drag to change the right-margin indent

10

Click the tab character box to change the kind of tab you want to place on the ruler.

If you want to increase a paragraph's *left-margin indent*, click in that paragraph to display its horizontal ruler. Then, drag the ruler's left-margin indent character to its new location. After you drag the ruler's left-margin indent character, the paragraph's actual left-margin indent changes to reflect the new setting. To change the *first-line indent*, drag the ruler's first-line indent character to a new location. To change the *right-margin indent*, drag the ruler's right-margin indent character to a new location.

▶ **KEY TERMS**

Left-margin indent—An indention of the left edge of all lines in a paragraph, usually more so than in surrounding paragraphs, to set off the paragraph, as might be done for a quotation.

First-line indent—A right indent of the first line in a paragraph where subsequent lines in the same paragraph align closer to the left margin.

Right-margin indent—An indention of the right edge of all lines in a paragraph, usually more so than in surrounding paragraphs, to bring in the paragraph's right edge, as might be done for a quotation.

Although the horizontal ruler is constantly linked to individual paragraphs, the page's overall left and right margins also appear on the horizontal ruler. The margins are set off of the gray areas on either end of the ruler. You can change the left or right margin by dragging the ruler's edge of either margin (the position between the gray and the white of the ruler's typing area) left or right.

▶ **NOTE**

Be careful that you leave enough room for your printer's required margin. For example, many laser printers will not print less than one-half inch to the edge of the paper, no matter how wide you attempt to make your margins.

You won't use the vertical ruler as much as the horizontal ruler, but it can be handy for showing the top and bottom margins on a page as well as the general position on a page where certain elements appear. For example, you can tell from the vertical ruler exactly how many inches down on a page a graphic image will appear when printed.

One of the most common uses of the vertical ruler is to show the top and bottom margin used by the document and drag these margins to a different location.

▶ **TIP**

Select **Edit**, **Undo** (or **Ctrl+Z**) to undo changes you make to the horizontal or vertical ruler.

11

11	**About Paragraph Breaks and Tabs**

✔ **BEFORE YOU BEGIN**	→ **SEE ALSO**
1 Set Writer Options	**13** Apply Paragraph Formatting
10 About the Rulers	

Understanding exactly how Writer treats paragraphs is the first step in understanding Writer's formatting capabilities. Knowing exactly where a paragraph begins and ends is not always obvious. For example, in the next figure, it appears that the document has three paragraphs.

If you glance at the screen or print the document, three paragraphs certainly appear to be there. As far as your readers are concerned, the document does contain three paragraphs. Nevertheless, as far as Writer is concerned, this particular document contains only a single paragraph! Clicking the **Nonprinting characters** button on this particular document shows nonprinting characters that reveal this document contains only a single paragraph, as the following figure shows.

▶ **NOTE**

The nonprinting characters enable you to see the hidden elements that Writer uses to determine where certain formatting should begin and end (see **4** **Type Text into a Document**).

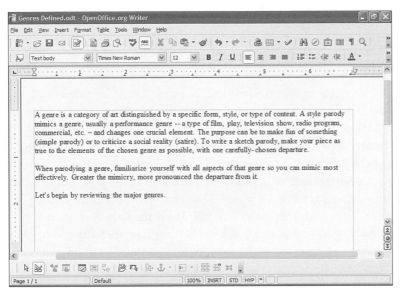

Seeing isn't always believing—how many paragraphs are in this document?

Nonprinting characters button

11

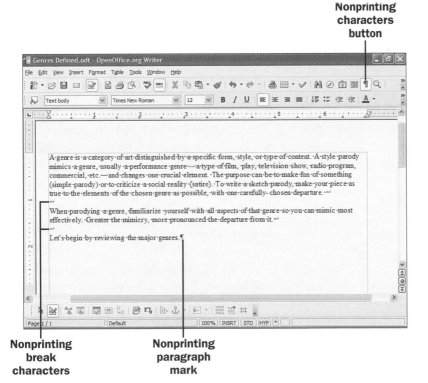

Nonprinting break characters

Nonprinting paragraph mark

Only one paragraph mark appears, meaning that Writer views the entire document as one long paragraph.

You can press **Shift+Enter** to start a new line without starting a new paragraph. The newline nonprinting character will appear when you turn on nonprinting characters. Without the nonprinting characters appearing, it looks as though the document will have multiple paragraphs.

You won't want to create an entire document this way. There are times, though, when you want to do this so that Writer formats all the lines uniformly as though they were different paragraphs. In other words, if you are typing a section of text that is more than one paragraph, and you want to format that section differently from the rest of the document, one way to do so is to keep the text all one paragraph. You'll press **Shift+Enter** to give the lines the look of multiple paragraphs, but Writer will see them as being only one. Then, any paragraph formatting you apply to the text—either from the ruler (see **10 About the Rulers**) or from the **Paragraph** formatting dialog box (see **13 Apply Paragraph Formatting**)—applies to all the text in that section. You won't have to format more than one paragraph individually.

▶ **TIP**

Another advantage of keeping a section as one long paragraph is if you make a paragraph adjustment to the text later, your change applies to all the text and you won't have to apply the change multiple times over multiple paragraphs.

This multiparagraph trick using **Shift+Enter** is wonderful to remember for the times when you have a couple or more paragraphs that you may need to adjust formatting for later. If, however, you have several paragraphs to format differently from surrounding text, or even a page or more of text, you may be better off creating a new *section* for that text. You can then easily change the formatting of all the paragraphs in that section without affecting the surrounding text. **14 Set Up Page Formatting** discusses sections in more detail.

▶ **KEY TERM**

Section—A block of document text that contains its own formatting, including possible headers and footers, that will differ from surrounding text.

Tab stops are critical in most documents. Tab stops enable you to align values consistently across multiple lines. Also, when you use a tabstop, you don't have to press the **spacebar** many times to jump to the right spot on a line. Tab stops enable you to start paragraphs with an indented first line. Writer supports four types of tab stops, as detailed in Table 3.1.

TABLE 3.1   Writer's Four Types of Tab Stops

Tab Stop	Description
Left tab	After you press **Tab**, the insertion point jumps to that tab stop and the text you then type appears to the right of the tab stop's position. A left tab is the tab most people are familiar with and use.
Right tab	After you press **Tab**, the insertion point jumps to that tab stop and the text you then type appears to the left of the tab stop's position. In other words, as you type, the text moves left toward the left margin, against the tab stop. A right tab stop is useful for page or chapter numbers in a list because it ensures that the right edge of the numbers will align together.
Decimal tab	After you press **Tab**, the insertion point jumps to that tab stop and the numeric values you then type will position themselves so that the decimal points all align on multiple lines.
Centered tab	After you press **Tab**, the insertion point jumps to that tab stop and the text you then type adjusts to remain centered around the tab stop.

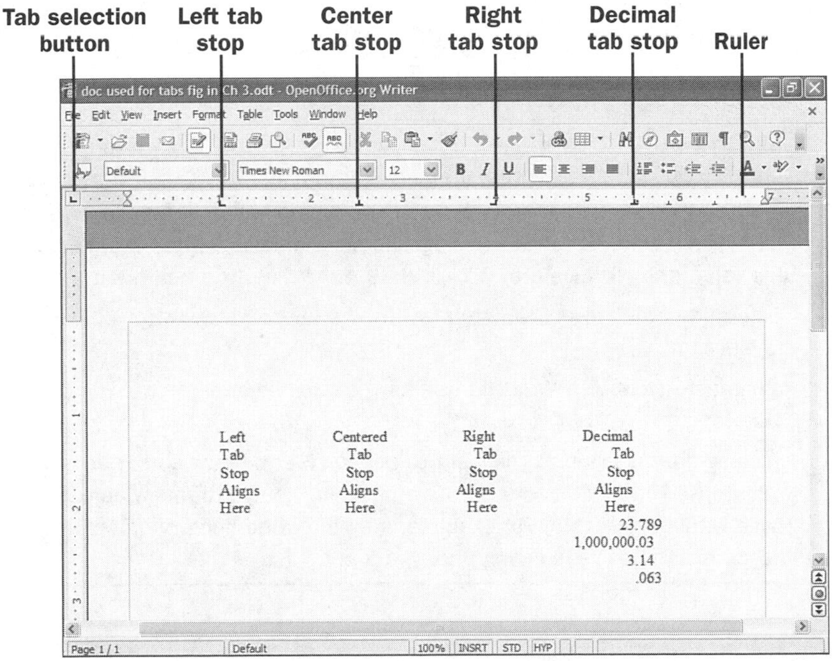

Use the ruler to set and change tab stops.

To set a tab stop, use either the ruler or the **Tabs** page in the **Paragraph** dialog box. You can click the **Tab** selection button on the ruler to select which tab stop you want to place. Every time you click the **Tab** selection button, the symbol changes to a different kind of tab stop. When you then click anywhere on the ruler, that kind of tab appears on the ruler where you click.

To use the **Tabs** page, double-click the ruler or select **Format**, **Paragraph** to display the **Paragraph** dialog box. Click the **Tabs** tab to display the **Tabs** page.

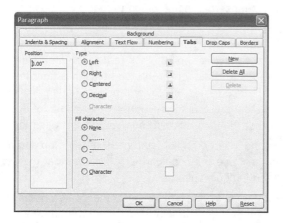

The Tabs page enables you to set tabs for the current paragraph.

Table 3.2 describes each of the options in the **Tabs** page.

TABLE 3.2 The Tabs Page Options

Option	Description
Position	Enables you to enter individual measurement values, such as **0.25"**, to represent one-fourth of an inch. After you type a value, click **New** to add that value to the list of tab settings. To clear an existing tab stop, select the value and click **Delete**. Click **Delete All** to clear the entire tab list.
Type	Determines the type of tab stop (such as a left tab stop) that you want to place.
Character	A character you want Writer to use as the decimal separator for decimal tab stops.
Fill Character	Leading characters that you want to appear, if any, between values and tab stops. The fill character forms a path for the eye to follow across the page within a tab stop. For example, a fill of dotted lines often connects goods to their corresponding prices in a price list.

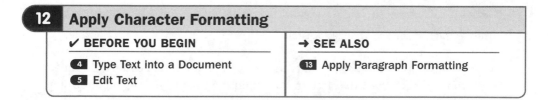

12 **Apply Character Formatting**

✔ **BEFORE YOU BEGIN**

  4 Type Text into a Document

  5 Edit Text

→ **SEE ALSO**

  13 Apply Paragraph Formatting

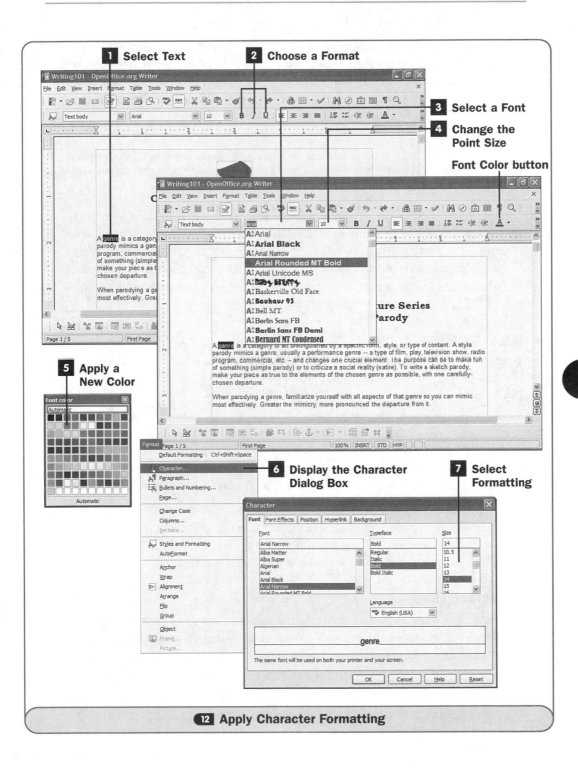

1 Select Text

2 Choose a Format

3 Select a Font

4 Change the Point Size

Font Color button

5 Apply a New Color

6 Display the Character Dialog Box

7 Select Formatting

12 Apply Character Formatting

When you want to make a point, you can format your text to modify the way it looks. Common character formatting styles are underline, boldface, and italicized text. Writer offers several additional character formats you can apply to your document's text.

▶ NOTE

Although they're called *character* formats, you can easily apply them to multiple characters, paragraphs, and even complete documents as easily as to single characters. Writer applies character formats to any text you select.

One of the most common character formats you can apply is to change the **typeface** (loosely called a **font** in general discussions) in your document. The typeface determines the way your characters look, whether artsy or elegant. Fonts have names, such as **Courier** and **Times New Roman**. The size of a font is measured in **points**. As a standard rule of thumb, a 10- or 12-point size is standard and readable for most word-processed documents.

▶ KEY TERMS

Typeface—A character design that determines the size and style of how your characters look.

Font—Loosely used as another name for typeface.

Point—Approximately 1/72nd of an inch.

As you type and move the insertion point, Writer displays the current font name and size on the Formatting toolbar, and indicates whether the current character is boldfaced, italicized, or underlined. Writer also enables you to change the color of your text.

When using character formatting, express but don't impress. Too much formatting, such as italicizing and underlining the same selection, makes your document look busy and distracts the reader from your message.

1 Select Text

When you want to format characters, select the characters first. You can select a single character, an entire word, a sentence, a paragraph, or multiple paragraphs. Whatever text you select before applying a format is the text that will take on the character formatting you apply.

You can also apply a character format to text before you type it. Instead of selecting text first, pick a character format and then type the text. The text you type will have those character format attributes.

12

▪2 Choose a Format

Click the **Bold**, **Italic**, or **Underline** button on the **Formatting** toolbar to apply that format. You can click two or all three to combine the character styles.

▶ TIP

Ctrl+B, **Ctrl+I**, and **Ctrl+U** are all shortcut keys to apply boldface, italics, and underlining.

▪3 Select a Font

To change the font of selected text (or text that you're about to type), click the drop-down arrow to the right of the **Font Name** box and select a new font. Each font name appears in its own font, so you'll know what your text will look like before you apply the format. After you select a new font, your selected text will change to that font.

▪4 Change the Point Size

To choose a new point size for the selected text, click the drop down arrow to the right of the **Point Size** list. When you click to select a size, your selected font will change to that size.

▪5 Apply a New Color

To change the color of selected text (or text you're about to type), click the **Font Color** button's list arrow on the **Formatting** toolbar. A **Font Color** *palette* appears. Click a color on the palette to change your selected text to that color.

▶ KEY TERM

Palette—A collection of colors from which you can choose.

▪6 Display the Character Dialog Box

Instead of using the **Formatting** toolbar to apply character formats, you can set such formats in the **Character** dialog box. Display the **Character** dialog box by selecting **Format**, **Character** from the menu bar.

7 Select Formatting

The **Character** dialog box's **Font** page enables you to select common character formats such as the font name, bold, italics, and the size. The **Font Effects** page offers more options, including underlining, color selection, and special effects such as a shadow and blinking text. The **Position** page enables you to select a subscript or superscript version of your font as well as rotate your text so it travels up and down the page instead of across it.

▶ **TIP**

Text rotated 90 degrees in the **Character** dialog box's **Position** page works well in some letterheads, for titles, or as a sidebar that travels down the length of your page.

The **Hyperlink** page enables you to add a link to a Web page or a filename to your text. Web pages often use such hyperlinks. The **Background** page enables you to set a background color for your text.

13 Apply Paragraph Formatting

✔ BEFORE YOU BEGIN	→ SEE ALSO
12 Apply Character Formatting	14 Set Up Page Formatting

You can change the format of entire paragraphs of text, such as the line spacing, justification, and indention of text. You can apply that format to selected paragraphs or to all the paragraphs in your document.

▶ **TIP**

You can set up a paragraph format before typing a paragraph, and Writer applies the format to the newly typed paragraph.

One of the most common ways to format a paragraph is to **align** it. Writer supports these justification options:

▶ **KEY TERM**

Alignment—Determine the paragraph text's position in relation to the right and left margins.

- **Left**—Aligns (makes even) text with the left margin. Personal and business letters are often left-justified.

- **Center**—Centers text between the left and right margins. Titles and letterheads are often centered atop a document.

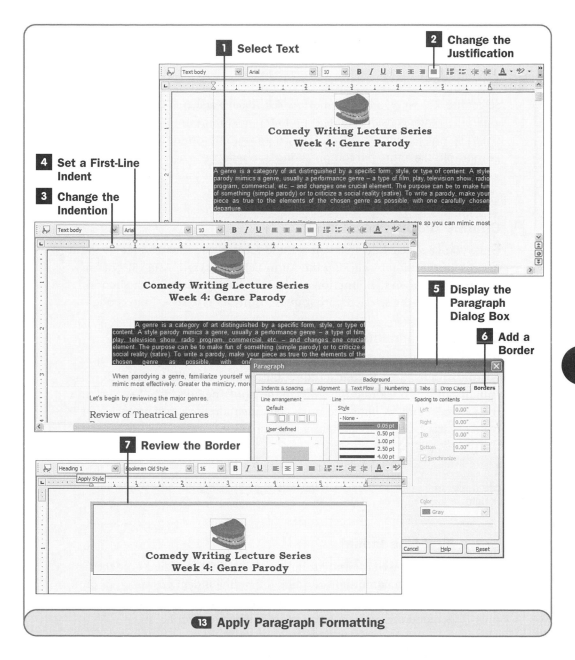

1 Select Text

2 Change the Justification

4 Set a First-Line Indent

3 Change the Indention

5 Display the Paragraph Dialog Box

6 Add a Border

7 Review the Border

13 Apply Paragraph Formatting

- **Right**—Aligns text with the right margin, and the left margin's text is not kept straight.

- **Justified**—Aligns text with both the left and right margins. Newspaper and magazine columns are usually justified; the text aligns with the left and right margins evenly.

Writer provides many additional ways to format your paragraphs, such as the capability to put a border around them and indent the first lines.

1 Select Text

Select the text you want to format. As **11 About Paragraph Breaks and Tabs** explains, Writer considers all text up to the next nonprinting paragraph symbol to be one paragraph. If you apply a paragraph format to any part of a paragraph, the entire paragraph changes to reflect the new format. You can format multiple paragraphs at once by selecting multiple paragraphs before changing the format.

2 Change the Justification

Once you've selected the text you want to format, you may change the paragraph's justification by clicking the **Align Left**, **Centered**, **Align Right**, or **Justified** button on the **Function** toolbar. As soon as you click the button, Writer changes the selected paragraph's justification to reflect the change.

3 Change the Indention

13

If you want to indent the entire selected paragraph to the right, click the **Formatting** toolbar's **Increase Indent** button. For each click of the **Increase Indent** button, the paragraph shifts to the right one-half inch. You can click the **Decrease Indent** button to move the indention back half an inch. (Of course, **Ctrl+Z** undoes indentions you make also.)

▶ TIP

You can make more precise paragraph indentions by dragging the ruler's **Indent** button left or right.

4 Set a First-Line Indent

Drag the ruler's **First-Line Indent** button to the right to indent only the first line of the selected paragraphs. Adding a first-line indent ensures your paragraphs have their initial lines indented to the right without you having to press **Tab** manually each time you begin a new paragraph.

5 Display the Paragraph Dialog Box

All the paragraph-formatting commands are available from the **Paragraph** dialog box. Select **Format**, **Paragraph** to display the **Paragraph** dialog box.

The **Paragraph** dialog box's **Indents & Spacing** page enables you to set precise indents as well as specify a default number of blank lines to appear between your paragraphs. The **Alignment** page enables you to set the precise alignment of your paragraphs.

The **Text Flow** page enables you to set automatic hyphenation so that Writer can insert hyphens as needed to make long words wrap better at the end of a line. The **Numbering** page enables you to number paragraphs as you might do for legal pleadings. The **Tabs** page enables you to set tab stops (see **11** **About Paragraph Breaks and Tabs**).

The **Drop Caps** page lets you specify a *drop cap* letter format to start your paragraphs with. The **Borders** page enables you to create borders around paragraphs, color them, and add drop shadows.

▶ KEY TERM

Drop cap—A large starting letter or word, sometimes twice the size of the other letters in the same paragraph, that provides a visual starting point for paragraphs of text.

6 Add a Border

Click the **Borders** tab to display the **Borders** page. Click one of the line arrangements to determine whether you want to enclose all four sides of the paragraph with a border or only two opposing sides. The line style list determines how thick the border will appear. You can also adjust how far from the margins and text the border will appear by adjusting the **Left**, **Right**, **Top**, and **Bottom** settings. Special border effects, such as a shadowed effect, are also available here.

Your entire document can appear with a border around it, too. **14** **Set Up Page Formatting** explains how to create such a border.

▶ TIP

As you change values throughout the **Paragraph** dialog box, many of the box's pages display a thumbnail image that changes to show you what effect your new paragraph format will have on the selected paragraphs.

7 Review the Border

Once you've set up a bordered paragraph, click **OK** to close the **Paragraph** dialog box and review the bordered paragraph to ensure you've got the right effect. Remember to reserve your use of borders, shadowing, and other special effects for those times when you want to emphasize a title or a statement. Don't overdo the use of special formats. Your document can look too busy with too many formats, making it difficult to read.

13

14 Set Up Page Formatting

✔ BEFORE YOU BEGIN	→ SEE ALSO
5 Edit Text	**15** Create a Multicolumn Newsletter
12 Apply Character Formatting	
13 Apply Paragraph Formatting	

You will often need to make format changes to your entire document. Perhaps you want to change the printed margins on the page. You may want to add a background color or even put a border around the document.

The **Page Style** dialog box contains all of Writer's options that enable you to modify your document's format. Any changes you make to the current page applies to all pages in your document.

▶ TIP

If your document contains multiple sections, page formatting changes apply only to the current section unless you first select your entire document, with **Ctrl+A**, before modifying the page format.

If you want to start a new section, as you might do if you wanted to format several pages within a document differently from surrounding pages, select **Insert**, **Section** and click **Insert** to make Writer begin a new section. Any page formatting that you apply to the section stays in that section.

1 Open the Page Style Dialog Box

Select **Page** from the **Format** menu to open the **Page Style** dialog box.

The **Page Style** dialog box contains several categories you can use to modify the pages in your document. Click each tab across the top of the dialog box to select different options. The **Organizer** page determines the default style currently used and enables you to select a different style. See **16** **About Styles and Templates** for help with understanding and using styles. The **Page** tab enables you to format your paper statistics, such as selecting a page length as well as margin settings. The **Background** page enables you to place a background color on the page.

▶ TIP

As with character formats, don't overuse background colors. You should use a colored stationery in your printer for best effect if you want to print on a colored background.

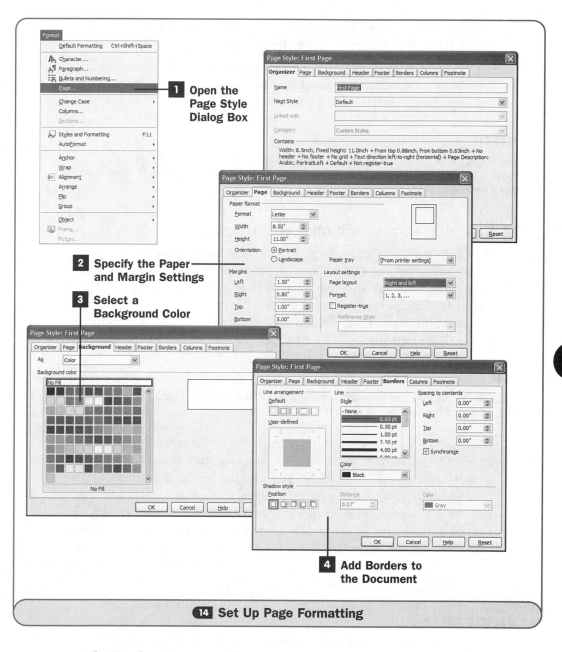

1 Open the Page Style Dialog Box

2 Specify the Paper and Margin Settings

3 Select a Background Color

4 Add Borders to the Document

14 Set Up Page Formatting

The **Header**, **Footer**, and **Footnote** pages provide you the ability to place a header, footer, and footnotes on the pages of your documents. For example, you might want to place a company logo on the page header of your first page, and you'd do so inside a header. **33** **About Headers and Footers** explains how to use headers and footers. **35** **Add a Footnote or Endnote** explains how to add footnotes and endnotes to your document. The **Borders** page lets you apply a border to your page.

Use the **Columns** page to turn your document into a multicolumned document, as you might do for a newsletter. **15 Create a Multicolumn Newsletter** explains how to work with multiple columns.

▶ **NOTE**

You cannot undo many of the changes you make from the **Page Style** dialog box. If you apply a change and want to undo it, you'll have to display the **Page Style** dialog box again and change the incorrect setting.

2 Specify the Paper and Margin Settings

Click the **Page** tab to show the page options. When you change the type of paper you use in your printer, such as going from letter size to legal, you'll need to select the proper option, such as **Legal**, from the **Format** list. If you use a nonstandard paper size, one that is not letter, legal, or one of the other options in the **Format** list, you can click to adjust the **Width** and **Height** settings to the unique settings of your paper.

14

▶ **TIP**

The **Format** list contains common envelope sizes for when you want to print addresses and return addresses from your printer.

You also may want to change the orientation of your printed page from *Portrait* to *Landscape*. In addition, you can give your margins more or less room by adjusting the **Left**, **Right**, **Top**, and **Bottom** measurements. If you have multiple paper trays in your printer, such as an envelope feeder, you may want to select a different tray from the **Paper tray** option. Finally, the **Layout settings** area enables you to control how the pages print in relation to one another; for example, if you plan to bind your output into a booklet, you may want the left and right margins to be mirrored to leave more room in the middle for the binding or hole punching.

▶ **KEY TERMS**

Portrait—Displays and prints with the page oriented vertically, as you might do for a letter.

Landscape—Displays and prints with the page oriented horizontally, as you might do for a wide report.

3 Select a Background Color

Click the **Background** tab to add a background color to your page. Although you may want to use colored paper for extensive coloring, you might want to lightly highlight a report page that appears inside your document with a highlighted background color.

4 Add Borders to the Document

Click the **Borders** tab to display the border options. As with paragraph borders (see **13 Apply Paragraph Formatting**), you can specify which edges you want to use as a border (the sides, top and bottom, or all four sides) and the line thickness of the border (from the **Line Style** list). If you want to add an additional effect to your border, you can adjust the position and add a drop-shadow.

---

15 Create a Multicolumn Newsletter

✔ **BEFORE YOU BEGIN**	→ **SEE ALSO**
10 About the Rulers	**16** About Styles and Templates
13 Apply Paragraph Formatting	

15

When you want to create newspaper-style columns—such as those that appear in newsletters and brochures—configure Writer to format your text with multiple columns. You can assign multiple columns to the entire document or to specific sections. By applying multiple columns to certain sections, you'll be able to span a headline across the top of two or three columns of text.

▶ **TIP**

Generally, you should type your document's text before breaking the document into multiple columns.

1 Type the Document

Create your initial document without worrying about column placement. Type your headline and other text using Writer's default styles and formats.

▶ **TIP**

If you routinely write a newsletter or other multicolumned document, you may want to create a template that contains your headline and column layout and then apply that template to create each issue. For more, see **16 About Styles and Templates**.

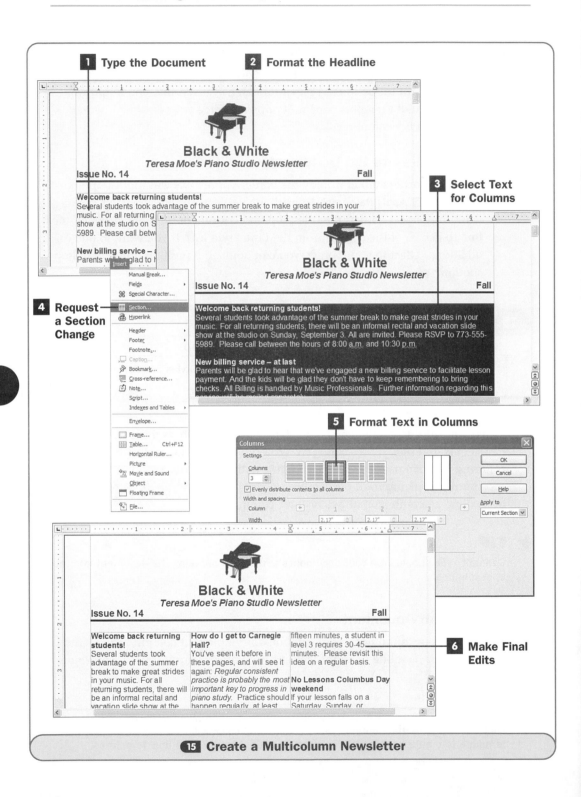

15 Create a Multicolumn Newsletter

2 Format the Headline

Change your headline's format to match the style you want your newsletter to take on. Not all multicolumn documents have headlines across the top of the columns, but many do.

3 Select Text for Columns

Select all the text that will be converted to multiple columns. This generally begins immediately following your headline.

▶ **TIP**

Turn on nonprinting characters to ensure that you don't select any part of the headline. Start selecting following the headline's nonprinting paragraph character.

4 Request a Section Change

Select **Insert**, **Section** from the menu bar. This menu option is slightly misleading. You are actually converting the selected text to a new document section because you selected the text before selecting the **Section** option.

5 Format Text in Columns

Click **Columns** on the **Format** menu to open the **Columns** dialog box. Because you converted this text to a new document section, the headline will not be affected. You can select the number of columns you want by clicking to change the number in the **Columns** list. Generally, it's quicker to click the thumbnail image that displays the number of columns you want to convert to. The options beneath the **Settings** section enable you to precisely adjust each column's width and the space between them. Generally, Writer's default width and spacing values work well.

Feel free to select a separating line by selecting from the **Line** drop-down menu. Each option provides a different line width that will appear between your columns. You can also specify, from the **Height** option, if you want the line to run the entire column length (**100%**) or less and where you want to position it (**Top, Centered,** or **Bottom**).

6 Make Final Edits

Once your document appears in columns, you'll almost certainly need to make some final adjustments. For example, with three or more columns, the text becomes lumpy with too many spaces between the words if you've justified the columns. Newspapers often use full justification, but they suffer from

15

this extra spacing at times. Most of the time, columns that you left-justify look the best with three or more columns. Also, subheadings that you format-ted before converting to multiple columns may be too large in their columns, so you can decrease the font size of such subheadings (see **12 Apply Character Formatting**).

---

16 **About Styles and Templates**

✔ BEFORE YOU BEGIN	→ SEE ALSO
5 Edit Text	**17** Use a Style
	18 Use a Template

You can begin with a *template* to create a document that has a prearranged look. You can apply a *style* you've created previously to text within any docu-ment. By reusing templates and styles, you reduce the amount of work you have to do to create a document.

16

▶ **KEY TERMS**

Template—A predefined document with styles and other formatting, such as columns and tables, that forms a model for new documents.

Style—A set of character and paragraph formats you can apply to text to change that text's format details.

Suppose you find yourself typing a weekly report for your company and you often quote your corporate office's weekly sales records. If you format the sales record portion of your report differently from the rest of your report, perhaps putting it into a table with a heading and a lightly colored background with boldfaced numbers and titles, you can create a style for that section of text. In the future, when it's time to type that information, instead of formatting the corporate sales records, you only need to select the corporate sales records and apply your prede-fined style to that selection. By defining the style one time, you won't ever need to go through the motions of formatting the text again; instead, you just apply the style, and Writer formats the text according to the style.

Templates take styles further. Actually, a template is to an entire document what a style is to selected text. When creating a document that's to look like another that you often create, such as a fax letter that requires special formatting, you can elect to use a fax template you've already created with the **To:**, **From:**, and **Cover Page Note** fields already placed where they belong and you only need to fill in the details.

▶ **NOTE**

In reality, you always use a template when you create new Writer documents. Writer uses a default template named **Default** unless you specify another template. The font and margin settings offered when you create a new document come from this default template.

Keep in mind that a template is a model for a document. A style is often a model for smaller blocks of text, usually paragraphs. A template may contain several styles. If you want to use a style that's available to your current document or template, you can easily select that style and apply it to existing paragraphs or text you're about to type.

The **Styles and Formatting** window, available from the **Format** menu or by pressing **F11**, lists every style available in the current document. Each style has a name. If you create a new document using **File**, **New**, the styles in this window will display the default template's styles. If you create a new document using a predefined template, the styles listed come from the styles defined in that template.

—Styles

*The **Styles and Formatting** window displays the current styles available to you.*

You can also see the styles available to you in a different way. You can also display a catalog of styles that shows the styles in a format you may prefer over the **Styles and Formatting** window. Press **Ctrl+F11** to see the **Style Catalog** dialog box. You can select paragraph styles, character styles, and other kinds of styles currently available to you.

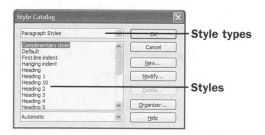
—Style types

—Styles

*The **Style Catalog** lists styles by paragraph style types, among other types.*

When you want to use a template, you'll select **File**, **New**, **Templates and Documents** to choose the template you want to work from.

▶ **TIP**

When you learn about styles and templates in Writer, you also learn about them in the other OpenOffice.org products, because they all use styles and templates in the same way.

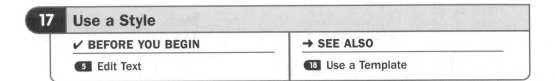

17 **Use a Style**

✔ **BEFORE YOU BEGIN**	→ **SEE ALSO**
5 Edit Text	**18** Use a Template

Using a style is simple. You can apply a style to selected text to format that text with the style's character and paragraph formatting. Writer comes with several styles, and you can add your own.

Suppose that you routinely write résumés for other people. You might develop three separate sets of character and paragraph formats that work well, respectively, for the title of a résumé and an applicant's personal information and work history. Instead of defining each of these formats every time you create a résumé, you can format a paragraph with each style and store the styles under their own names (such as **Résumé Title**, **Résumé Personal**, and **Résumé Work**). The next time you write a résumé, you need only to select a style, such as Résumé Title, before typing the title. When you then type the title, the title looks the way you want it to look without your having to designate any character or paragraph format.

One of the easiest ways to apply a style is to keep the **Styles and Formatting** window open at all times by pressing **F11** (or by selecting **Styles and Formatting** from the Format menu). If you don't have the screen room to keep the **Styles and Formatting** window showing, you can display it when you want to apply a style and then click its **Close** button to hide the **Styles and Formatting** window once again.

▶ **TIP**

The **Styles and Formatting** window provides existing styles, and you can define your own from text you select before displaying the window.

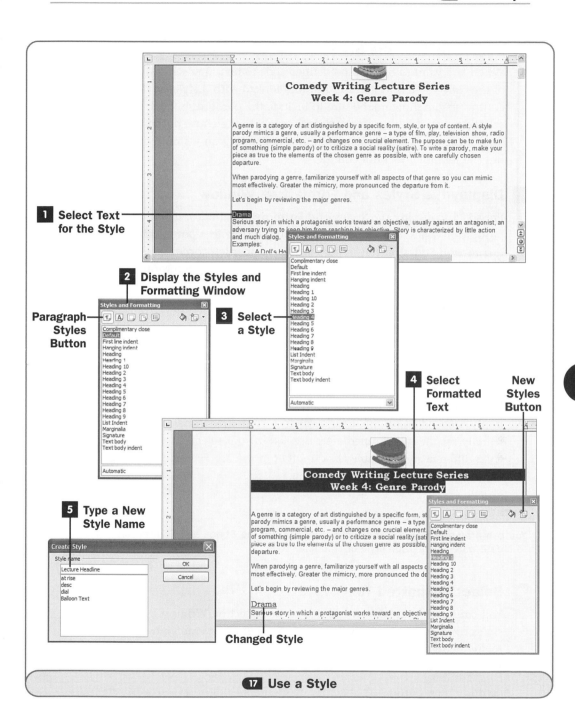

1 Select Text for the Style

2 Display the Styles and Formatting Window

Paragraph Styles Button

3 Select a Style

4 Select Formatted Text

New Styles Button

5 Type a New Style Name

Changed Style

■ Select Text for the Style

When you want to apply a predefined style to text, first select the text. Most of the time you'll select a paragraph to format with a style, so if nonprinting characters are showing, be sure to include the paragraph mark when you select the text if you want the style to apply to the entire paragraph. The format of the text will completely change depending on which style you apply, but the text itself will not change.

② Display the Styles and Formatting Window

Press **F11** to display the **Styles and Formatting** window. If you don't see paragraph styles (assuming you're adding a style to a paragraph), click the **Paragraph Styles** button in the window's upper-left corner. The style names will then appear that you can apply to your selected paragraph text.

▶ NOTE

The **Styles and Formatting** window provides styles for characters, frames, pages, and numbered lists in addition to paragraph styles.

17

③ Select a Style

In the **Styles and Formatting** window, double-click the style that you want to apply. Depending on the arrangement of your screen and windows, you can usually see the style immediately applied to your selected text. If you want to try a different style, double-click another in the list. Feel free to keep the **Styles and Formatting** window open.

▶ TIP

You can drag and drop a text selection directly into the **Styles and Formatting** window to create a new paragraph style or character style.

④ Select Formatted Text

You can easily add your own styles to the collection Writer provides. You add styles by example. In other words, you format text to match a style you want to create and then tell Writer to create a new style based on that formatted text.

To add a new paragraph style, for example, format and then select an entire paragraph (including its paragraph symbol if nonprinting characters are showing). Press **F11** to display the **Styles and Formatting** window if it's not currently showing.

5 Type a New Style Name

Click the **New Styles** button (the first button from the right at the top of the **Styles and Formatting** window) and then click **New Style from Selection** in the submenu that opens. Writer displays the **Create Style** dialog box.

Type a name for the style (one that does not already exist in the **Styles and Formatting** window—unless you want to replace one). When you click **OK**, Writer creates the new style based on your selected text. The next time you select text and then select your new style, Writer applies the new style's formatting to the text.

The other two options in the **New Style from Selection** submenu will become more useful to you as you work more with styles. If you previously created a style but want to make changes to it, modify the formatting of the text, and then follow this step and click the **Update Style** option in the submenu; the style is updated based on the current text selection. If you want to use styles from another document, click the **Load Style** option in the submenu and use the resulting dialog box to import styles from another document.

18 Use a Template   **18**

✔ BEFORE YOU BEGIN	→ SEE ALSO
2 Create a New Document	**34** Use AutoCorrect to Improve Your Typing
16 About Styles and Templates	

Templates contain formatting for complete documents. All the OpenOffice.org programs support templates. If you create a new document without specifying a template, Writer uses the **Default** template style to create the empty document and to set up initial font, margin, and other formatting-related details.

The *Templates and Documents dialog box* lists all the templates available to you. You often work with templates, selecting and adding them, from the **Templates and Documents** dialog box.

▶ KEY TERM

Templates and Documents dialog box—An organizer of templates and styles that enables you to use and organize your templates.

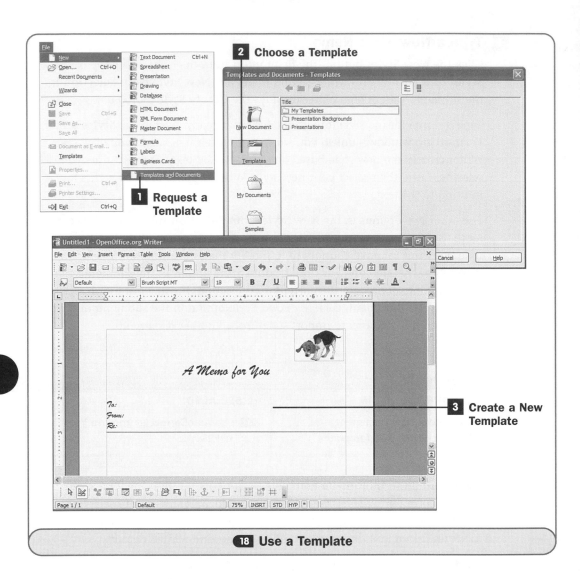

18 Use a Template

1 Request a Template

Select **File, New, Templates and Documents** to open the **Templates and Documents** dialog box. Click the **Templates** icon to see folders of templates such as **My Templates** and **Presentations** (for Impress, see **86 Use an Impress Template**).

2 Choose a Template

Decide which template you want to work with. If you've recently installed Writer or have not added new templates, you may see only two templates:

Presentation Backgrounds and **Presentations**. These are for Impress; OpenOffice.org does not include any Writer templates beyond the blank default document template.

▶ **NOTE**

Writer organizes templates in folders. The name of the folder tells you the kind of templates that are inside. The **Default** folder may contain multiple templates, but a blank default template is used when you select **File**, **New** to create a new document.

▶ **TIP**

Click the **Preview** button atop the **Templates and Documents** dialog box to see a graphic thumbnail image of a blank document created with the selected template.

3 Create a New Template

Feel free to create your own templates! For example, you might write many memos, so you can create a memo template. Create the model for the template, including the title, recipient, and subject areas, but don't add memo-specific text. Keep the text general. Feel free to include instructions to the user of this template, such as [Type Body of Memo Here].

You can create a document using a Wizard (see **2 Create a New Document**), personalize it with your information and formatting, and then save it as a template. *Voila*—your own custom template, compliments of OpenOffice.org!

When you select **File**, **Templates**, **Save**, Writer opens the **Templates** dialog box, where you can assign a name and category folder for your template (such as **Default**). The next time you create a new document from a template, your new template will appear in the list.

18

4

Adding Lists, Tables, and Graphics

IN THIS CHAPTER:

Writer lets you add flair to your documents, such as bulleted lists and numbered lists, tables, charts, and graphics. With today's graphical technology, documents are far from text only, and you can easily add formatted graphic elements to get your point across to your audience.

So many of Writer's features, such as bulleted and numbered lists, work automatically. You just begin typing the list and Writer takes care of all the formatting and keeps track of the proper indention for you. When you want to return to regular text once again, Writer can easily return to regular paragraph mode.

► **NOTE**

Writer recognizes most lists in documents that you import from other word processors. For example, if you open a Microsoft Word document with a numbered list, Writer recognizes the list and retains its formatting.

19 **Add a Bulleted List**

✔ BEFORE YOU BEGIN	→ SEE ALSO
13 Apply Paragraph Formatting	**20** Add a Numbered List

19

OpenOffice.org Writer supports 10 levels of bulleted lists. Therefore, as you might do in an outline, you can indent portions of a bulleted list to create sublists.

Writer makes bulleted lists easy to produce. You only need to type an asterisk or a hyphen before your list's first item, and when you press **Enter** at the end of the line, Writer recognizes the start of the list, converts the asterisk or hyphen to a bullet character, and automatically indents the next line and adds its bullet so you can quickly continue the list.

► **TIP**

Writer supports several bullet styles, such as check marks and arrows.

1 **Type the First Item**

When you begin a bulleted list, start on a new line. Type an asterisk (*) or a hyphen (–) followed by a space and then type the first line of your list.

► **NOTE**

If you type a hyphen instead of an asterisk, Writer uses a hyphenated bullet instead of a rounded bullet.

Writer will recognize that you've begun a bulleted list when you press **Enter**.

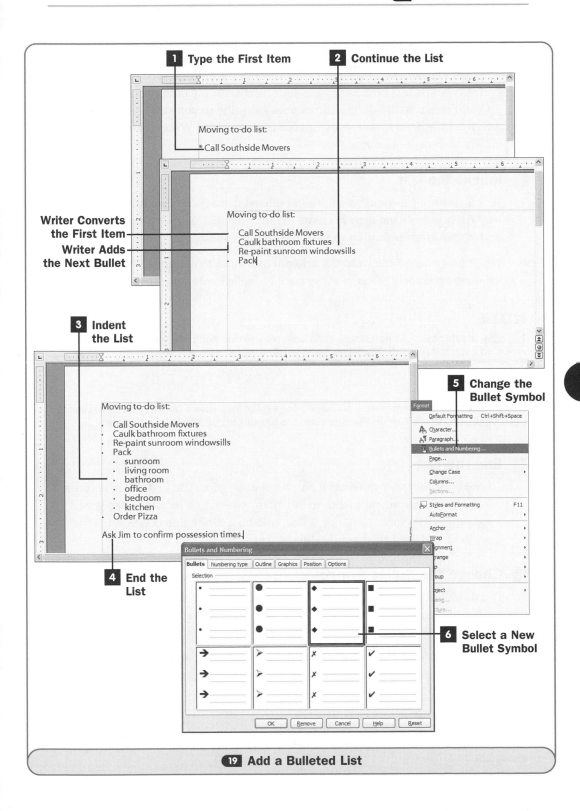

1 Type the First Item

2 Continue the List

Moving to-do list:

* Call Southside Movers

Writer Converts the First Item

Writer Adds the Next Bullet

Moving to-do list:

Call Southside Movers
Caulk bathroom fixtures
Re-paint sunroom windowsills
Pack

3 Indent the List

Moving to-do list:

· Call Southside Movers
· Caulk bathroom fixtures
· Re-paint sunroom windowsills
· Pack
    · sunroom
    · living room
    · bathroom
    · office
    · bedroom
    · kitchen
· Order Pizza

Ask Jim to confirm possession times.

4 End the List

5 Change the Bullet Symbol

Format

Default Formatting   Ctrl+Shift+Space
Character...
Paragraph...
Bullets and Numbering...
Page...

Change Case
Columns...
Sections...

Styles and Formatting   F11
AutoFormat

Anchor
Wrap
Alignment
Arrange
Group
Object
Name...
Picture...

6 Select a New Bullet Symbol

Bullets and Numbering

Bullets | Numbering type | Outline | Graphics | Position | Options

Selection

OK   Remove   Cancel   Help   Reset

19

2 Continue the List

You won't have to continue typing the asterisk once Writer recognizes that you're typing a list. Writer converts your asterisk to the bullet item on the first line and puts a bullet at the start of your next line so you can continue typing. You only need to worry about your list items, and Writer takes care of the bullets and the indention.

3 Indent the List

When you want to create a sublist of bulleted items, press **Tab** after the bullet. Writer indents the item to create the indented list. Keep typing the list, and Writer keeps indenting the list, creating the sublist.

When you want to return to the original indention to continue your primary list items, press **Shift+Tab** to move back to the left column.

▶ NOTE

Typically, a sublist should have more than one item. Writer supports up to 10 levels of indented lists, but three or four levels deep is often as far as you'll need to go.

19

▶ TIP

If you want to change a bulleted list back into regular text, select the list and then click the **Bullets On/Off** button on the **Standard** toolbar to turn off the list formatting.

4 End the List

To end your list, after the final item press **Enter** twice. The first **Enter** keypress tells Writer that you don't want to indent anymore. The second **Enter** keypress moves the cursor to the next line, adding a blank line between the list's final item and your next regular line of text.

5 Change the Bullet Symbol

You don't have to settle for the default bullet symbol that Writer uses. Highlight your bulleted list if you want to change the bullet symbol used in the list.

Select **Bullets and Numbering** from the **Format** menu to show the **Bullets and Numbering** dialog box. Click the **Bullets** tab to show the **Bullets** page.

▶ TIP

If you only want to change some of a list's bulleted symbols, such as the indented sublists, select only those portions of the list before opening the **Bullets and Numbering** dialog box.

6 Select a New Bullet Symbol

Click any of the bullet formats to select a new bullet symbol. When you click **OK**, Writer converts your bulleted list so that the symbol you selected appears in your document.

20 Add a Numbered List

✔ BEFORE YOU BEGIN	→ SEE ALSO
13 Apply Paragraph Formatting **19** Add a Bulleted List	**21** Create a Table of Contents

OpenOffice.org supports the use of numbered lists, indented lists with numbered items, in much the same way it supports bulleted lists (see **19** **Add a Bulleted List**). Writer handles not only the formatting of your numbered list but also the renumbering if needed. Therefore, if you add items anywhere within or after a numbered list, Writer updates the numbers to reflect the new items. If you delete an item from a numbered list, Writer renumbers the remaining items to reflect the change.

As with bullets, OpenOffice.org Writer supports 10 levels of numbered lists. Therefore, as you might do in an outline, you can indent portions of a numbered list to create sublists.

To start a numbered list, you only need to type 1., i., or I. to signal to Writer that you're typing the first item in a numbered list.

▶ **TIP**

You can use a closing parenthesis after the number instead of a period when typing the first item in a numbered list. Therefore, you can type 1) or i) or I) to start a numbered list.

After you type the first line in the numbered list and press **Enter**, Writer recognizes the start of the numbered list, continues the numbering using the same format you used in the first item, and automatically indents the next line and adds its number so you can quickly continue the list.

▶ **TIP**

Writer supports several numbering styles, including letters; a "numbered list" might begin with **A)**, **B)**, **C)**.

20

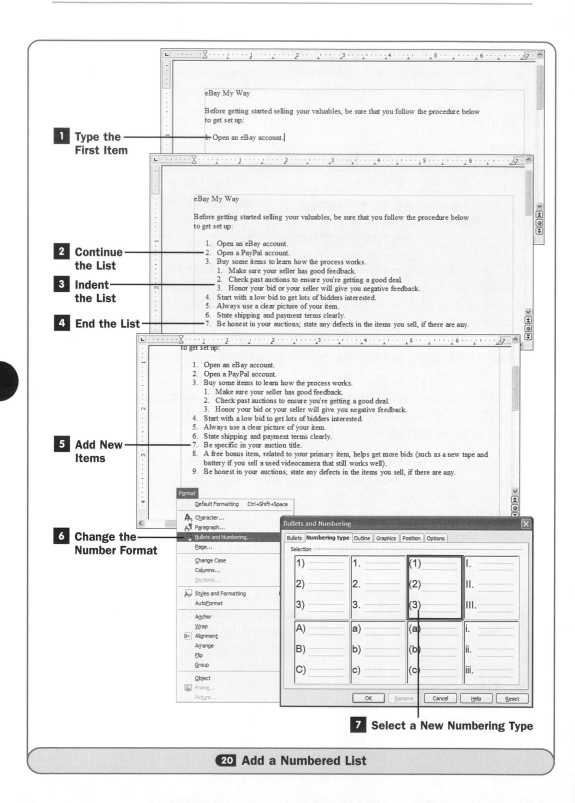

1 Type the First Item

2 Continue the List

3 Indent the List

4 End the List

20

5 Add New Items

6 Change the Number Format

7 Select a New Numbering Type

20 Add a Numbered List

1 Type the First Item

When you want to begin a numbered list, start on a new line. Type a number followed by a period or closing parenthesis, such as 1. or 1), followed by a space and then the first line of your list.

Writer recognizes that you've begun a numbered list when you press **Enter**.

2 Continue the List

You won't have to continue typing the number once Writer recognizes that you're creating a numbered list. Writer puts the second number at the start of the next line so you can continue typing. You only need to worry about your list items, and Writer takes care of the numbers and the indention.

▶ TIP

You can add bullets or numbering to your tables by clicking the **Numbering On/Off** or **Bullets On/Off** button on the **Formatting** toolbar. See **24** **Create a Table**.

3 Indent the List

When you want to create a sublist of numbered items, press **Tab** after the number. Writer indents the item and starts the numbering once again from 1. Keep typing the list, and Writer keeps indenting and creating the sublist.

When you want to return to the original indention to continue your primary list items, press **Shift+Tab** to move back to the left column and continue the numbering of the original list.

▶ NOTE

Typically, a sublist should have more than one item. Writer supports up to ten levels of numbered lists, but three or four levels deep is often as far as you'll need to go.

4 End the List

To end your list, after the final item press **Enter** twice. The first **Enter** keypress tells Writer that you don't want to indent anymore. The second **Enter** keypress moves the cursor to the next line, adding a blank line between the list's final item and your next regular line of text.

5 Add New Items

The true power of Writer's numbered lists is Writer's ability to renumber the entire list when you add or remove list items. To insert new items, put your text cursor at the end of any item and press **Enter**. Writer inserts a new line with the next number and renumbers all subsequent items accordingly. You may keep inserting new items, and Writer handles all the renumbering for you.

If you delete a line, Writer renumbers the list to reflect the change.

6 Change the Number Format

You don't have to settle for the default number format that Writer initially uses. Highlight your numbered list if you want to change the kind of number used in the list.

Select **Bullets and Numbering** from the **Format** menu to show the **Bullets and Numbering** dialog box. Click the **Numbering type** tab.

▶ **TIP**

If you only want to change some of a list's number style, such as an indented sublist, select only that portion of the list before opening the **Bullets and Numbering** dialog box.

7 Select a New Numbering Type

Click any of the number formats to select a new numbering type. When you click **OK**, Writer converts your numbered list so that the new number format appears in your document.

21 Create a Table of Contents

✔ BEFORE YOU BEGIN	→ SEE ALSO
5 Edit Text	**22** Create an Index
17 Use a Style	

When you write for others, a *table of contents* provides easy access for your readers. They can quickly go to whatever subject, or chapter, they want to go to. Making a table of contents used to be tedious, but Writer makes it easy. If you make changes to your document, such as adding new chapters, you can easily regenerate the table of contents to keep it fresh.

▶ **KEY TERM**

Table of contents—A table in the front of many books that lists the page number on which a book's chapters and other elements appear.

1 Find Text for the Table

2 Request the Heading 1 Style

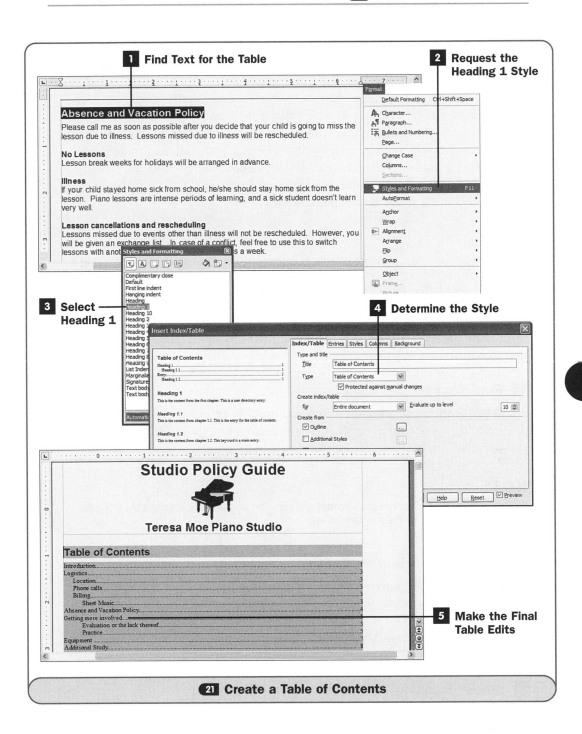

3 Select Heading 1

4 Determine the Style

5 Make the Final Table Edits

21 Create a Table of Contents

Generally, paragraphs to which you apply the **Heading 1** style will end up in your table of contents. With 10 heading styles, **Heading 1** through **Heading 10**, you have plenty of title, heading, and subheading styles with which to format your text. If any or all of these styles do not format paragraphs exactly the way you want them to, you can modify the styles. The important thing to note is that if you do use the **Heading 1** style, whether or not you've modified the style, Writer considers each of those paragraphs to be part of the table of contents. All the contents should appear in the currently open document; otherwise, Writer won't be able to locate the entries. The only exception would be for a Master Document (see **130 About Master Documents**).

▶ **NOTE**

Writer doesn't continually update a table of contents even when you use the **Heading 1** style. When you're ready for a table of contents, you'll request the **Insert Index/Table** dialog box, and at that point Writer generates the table.

You may request that Writer use paragraph styles other than the **Heading 1** style by clicking the **Additional Styles** option in the **Insert Index/Table** dialog box and selecting more styles by clicking the ... button.

1 Find Text for the Table

Select one or more paragraphs that you want to include in your table of contents. If you're writing a book, generally such a paragraph will consist of the introduction, chapter titles, and appendixes (if any).

▶ **NOTE**

If you formatted your introduction, chapter titles, and appendixes with the **Heading 1** style, you don't need to reapply the style.

2 Request the Heading 1 Style

If you've selected paragraphs to apply the **Heading 1** style to, select **Styles and Formatting** from the **Format** menu to display the **Styles and Formatting** window. You'll see a list of styles from which you can choose. (Click the **Paragraph Styles** button from the drop-down box if it's not already selected.)

3 Select Heading 1

Select **Heading 1** from the style list and click **OK**. Continue applying the **Heading 1** style to all paragraphs in your document that you want to include in the table of contents. As you apply the **Heading 1** style, the format of those paragraphs typically changes to become boldface.

▶ **TIP**

Add chapter numbers in front of chapter titles so the chapter numbers automatically appear in the table of contents.

4 Determine the Style

Once you've applied the **Heading 1** style to all the paragraphs you want to include in your table of contents, you can generate the table of contents. Move the text cursor to the beginning of your document (assuming you want the table of contents to appear there).

Select **Insert, Indexes and Tables** to display the **Insert Index/Table** dialog box. You can change various aspects of your table of contents, such as the title. As you change various options, the preview image of your table will update to the left of the dialog box. Deselect the option labeled **Protected against manual changes** if you want the ability to modify the actual table of contents after Writer generates it.

Once you're ready to generate the table of contents, click **OK**. Writer generates the table from your selected styles.

5 Make the Final Table Edits

You now must make final edits to the table of contents. You can format the table, put page breaks around it (using **Control+Enter**), and add spacing between the lines if you wish. If you find that Writer doesn't let you change the table, you didn't uncheck **Protected against manual changes** when you generated the table in the **Insert Index/Table** dialog box. You can regenerate the table with the option unchecked and then make any edits you wish.

22 Create an Index

✔ BEFORE YOU BEGIN	→ SEE ALSO
13 Apply Paragraph Formatting	**24** Create a Table
21 Create a Table of Contents	

The longer your document, the more your audience will appreciate an ***index***. As you write your document, or after you've written the document, you can mark any word in the document that you want to include in the index, and Writer can then generate the index showing the proper page numbers. If you make changes to the document, you can regenerate the index to keep it fresh.

22

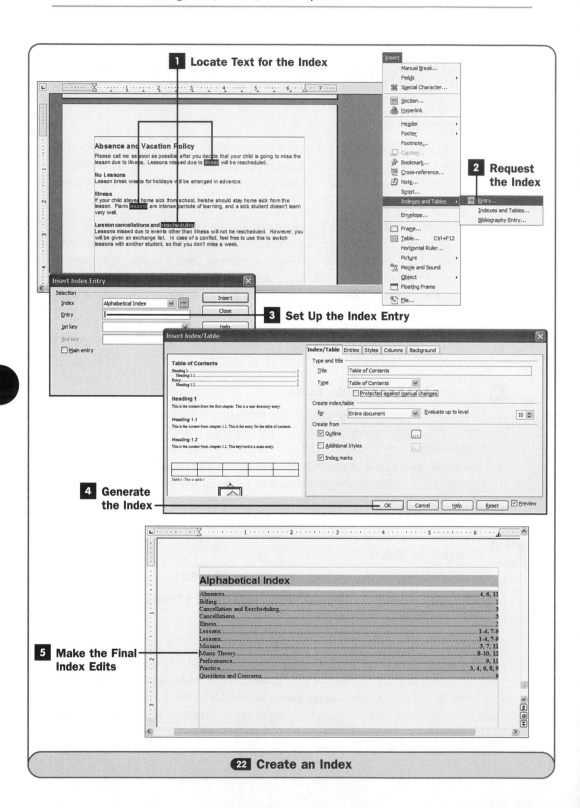

22 Create an Index

▶ KEY TERM

Index—A table that appears in the back of some books that lists the page numbers of certain key words, people, and terms in the book.

You might wonder why you have to do all the work of marking every index entry. Writer is smart, but it's not *that* smart! Writer could never know which words you want to include in the index, so it's up to you to mark each of them. Unlike the days of old, however, once you mark which words go in the index, your job is over because Writer will search out the page numbers and generate the index.

▶ NOTE

A Writer document can support multiple indexes. When you define index entries, you can determine to which of multiple indexes the entries are to go. Most documents have only a single index, however.

1 Locate Text for the Index

Highlight a word or words and phrases that are to appear in your index. By using **Ctrl**, you can select many index entries at once or you can select them one at a time and then add each to the index individually.

Whatever you choose, make sure you've selected any word or phrase you want in the index before continuing.

▶ NOTE

You don't have to select every index entry and add them all at once. You can add them individually. You can add some now, make additional edits, and add others later.

2 Request the Index

With the text selected, choose **Insert, Indexes and Tables, Entry** from the menu. The **Insert Index Entry** dialog box appears, where you can define the entry.

3 Set Up the Index Entry

The typical index you'll be adding is an alphabetical index (click the **Index** list box to select **Alphabetical Index** if you don't currently see it), although you can define another kind of index, called a ***user-defined index***, if you wish.

▶ KEY TERM

User-defined index—An index that is secondary to the primary, alphabetical index, such as a figure index or a list of people index.

If you want to add a slightly different variant of the word to the index, use the **Entry** box. Here, you can reword the index entry (when you define one at a time). Instead, say, of using **micro**, if that's the word you highlighted for the index, you can type microcomputer in the **Entry** box. The entry in the index appears as **microcomputer**, although it refers to the text **micro**.

Use the **1st key** box if you want to create a *multilevel index*. You'd type the highest-level name in the **1st key** box and then Writer adds the selected entry to the next level. if you want a two-tiered entry, type a value in the **2nd key** box, and the selected entry will appear below that in the index.

▶ **KEY TERM**

Multilevel index—An index entry that contains a primary term such as *fruit* and two or more secondary entries, offset to the right under the primary term, such as *apple*, *banana*, and *pear*.

Once you've defined the proper settings for the new entry, click **Insert** to add the entry to the index. The index does not generate when you close the **Insert Index Entry** dialog box. You generate the index once you've added all the entries. Click **Close** to close the **Insert Index Entry** dialog box when you're done with it.

22

4 Generate the Index

Once you've defined all the entries, you're ready to make the request to Writer to generate the index. Writer will compile the index and place it at the cursor's current position. Therefore, place the text cursor at the end of the document and then select **Insert**, **Index and Tables** to display the **Insert Index/Table** dialog box.

▶ **NOTE**

You use the same page of the **Insert Index/Table** dialog box to generate both the index and the table of contents.

Click the **Type** list box to display a list of indexes and tables you can generate. Select **Alphabetical Index** for your index. A preview of your index then appears to the left of the dialog box. Click to uncheck the **Protected against manual changes** option if you want to make edits to the index later (which you almost always want to do, especially to format it to your liking).

Make additional edits to the index options in the **Options** area. For example, you can request that Writer combine index entries by checking the **Combine identical entries** box so that Writer doesn't duplicate the same index entry twice if you happen to select two of the same items for the index on the same page before generating the index.

Click **OK** to generate your document's index.

5 **Make the Final Index Edits**

Once your index appears, you can edit the index to adjust formatting, such as the font and spacing, if you need to so the index matches the format of the rest of the document. If you find that Writer doesn't let you change the index, you didn't uncheck **Protected against manual changes** when you generated the index in the **Insert Index/Table** dialog box. You can regenerate the index with this option unchecked so you then can make any edits you wish.

23 About Writer Tables

✔ BEFORE YOU BEGIN	→ SEE ALSO
5 Edit Text	**24** Create a Table
13 Apply Paragraph Formatting	**25** Format a Table

Writer's table-creation power shines when you see how easily you can compose customized **tables** of information in Writer documents. Tables might contain numbers, text, even graphics, or combinations of any of these. Each row and column intersection is called a **cell**. As you begin to use both Writer and Calc (see **40** **Create a New Spreadsheet**), you might want to embed part of a Calc spreadsheet into a Writer table. Such embedded spreadsheets enable you, for example, to report financial data from within a Writer report.

▶ **KEY TERMS**

Tables—Collections of information organized in rows and columns.

Cell—A row and column intersection in a Writer or Calc table or spreadsheet.

With Writer, you can easily create a new table at any blank point in your document by clicking the **Table** button on the **Standard** toolbar or the **Insert Table** dialog box. For instance, you can request a 12-row, 5-column table, and it will be created at the location of the insertion point. If you create your table using the **Insert Table** dialog box, you can specify additional options and formatting for your table, such as whether to include a header row or to apply an **AutoFormat**. Using the **Table** toolbar button is great for creating a simple table; the **Insert Table** dialog box is best if you want to take advantage of Writer's automatic formatting capabilities and other powerful table tools.

You can format existing text into a table by selecting it and then using either the **Table** toolbar button or the **Insert Table** dialog box. When you format existing text into a table, Writer converts each tab stop to a column divider and each paragraph return to a row divider.

► **TIP**

You can also create a table using your keyboard by typing a series of plus signs and hyphens. If, for example, you type a plus sign (+), followed by 10 hyphens (–), followed by another plus sign and 10 hyphens, and then press **Enter**, Writer converts that text into a 2-column, 1-row table. This is handy if you don't like using a mouse, although it can be more time consuming than using the toolbar or dialog-box method.

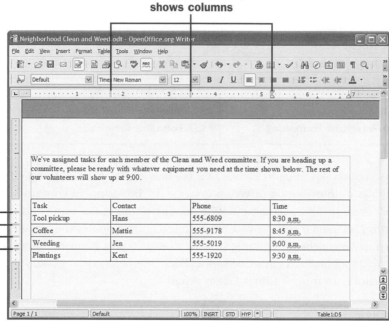

This table contains five rows and four columns.

► **NOTE**

The ruler shows special column markers when you select a table. By adjusting the ruler's columns, you can adjust the table's width.

Once you create a table, you then can easily adjust its height and width simply by dragging one of the edges with your mouse. You can add and delete rows and columns, too. In addition, you can apply formatting attributes to your table to add color, highlighting, special fonts, and other format attributes that make a dull table look good.

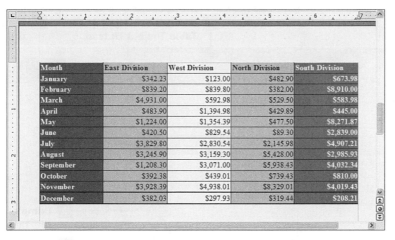

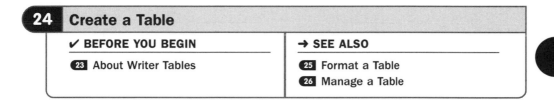

Writer can generate a sophisticated table with automatic formatting, including column shading and lines.

Month	East Division	West Division	North Division	South Division
January	$342.23	$123.00	$482.90	$673.98
February	$839.20	$839.80	$382.00	$8,910.00
March	$4,931.00	$592.98	$529.50	$583.98
April	$483.90	$1,394.98	$429.89	$445.00
May	$1,224.00	$1,354.39	$477.50	$8,271.87
June	$420.50	$829.54	$89.30	$2,839.00
July	$3,829.80	$2,830.54	$2,145.98	$4,907.21
August	$3,245.90	$3,159.30	$5,428.00	$2,985.93
September	$1,208.30	$3,071.00	$5,938.43	$4,032.34
October	$392.38	$439.01	$739.43	$810.00
November	$3,928.39	$4,938.01	$8,329.01	$4,019.43
December	$382.03	$297.93	$319.44	$208.21

24 Create a Table

✔ BEFORE YOU BEGIN	→ SEE ALSO
23 About Writer Tables	**25** Format a Table
	26 Manage a Table

Writer gives you many ways to create, edit, and format tables. Not surprisingly, the simplest ways are usually the most preferred ways.

- Use the **Table** button on the **Standard** toolbar.

- Use the **Insert Table** dialog box to designate rows and columns.

- Select existing text and then use either the **Table** button or the **Insert Table** dialog box.

1 Insert a Table Using the Table Toolbar Button

Open a new document to practice creating tables. Click the **Table** button list arrow on the **Standard** toolbar. A palette of rows and columns opens, allowing you to select the number of rows and columns you want in the table.

2 Determine the Layout

Hover the mouse down to the fourth row, and then across to the fifth column. As you hover the mouse over the palette, the cells are highlighted, indicating the number of rows and columns that will be created. A status area at the bottom of the palette displays the current number of rows and columns selected.

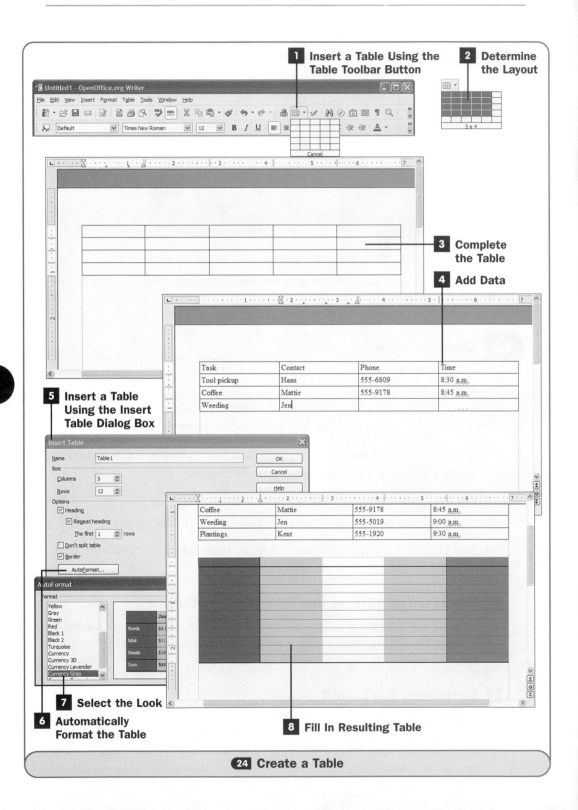

24

3 Complete the Table

Click the cell in the fourth row, fifth column. Writer creates a table that is four rows long and five columns wide.

4 Add Data

Once Writer creates the table, it places your text cursor in the leftmost cell so you can type the table's data. When you finish typing the data, press **Tab** to move to the next cell to the right. If you find you need additional rows after you reach the end of the last row, press **Tab** again and Writer will create another row for you. If you press **Enter** instead of **Tab** at the end of a row, Writer will not add an additional row but simply adds a paragraph return within the cell.

▶ **NOTE**

If your cell is not wide enough to hold what you type, Writer increases the cell height to hold more data. Writer does not widen the cell. To widen the cell, see **26 Manage a Table**.

▶ **TIPS**

If you prefer, you can drag instead of clicking to create a table. Instead of clicking the **Table** button list arrow, press and hold the mouse button, drag in the palette to the table layout you want, and then release the mouse button.

You can request that Writer format the numbers you type in cells as numbers instead of text if you want them to be right aligned. Select **Tools**, **Options**, open the **OpenOffice.org Writer** category, click the **Table** tab, and then click to enable the **Number recognition** check box. If this check box is not enabled, numbers you type will be left aligned and saved in text format.

5 Insert a Table Using the Insert Table Dialog Box

Using the **Insert Table** dialog box gives you more control than when you use the **Table** button. Using this dialog box to generate a table, you can request that Writer format the new table using one of several available AutoFormats, and you can set additional options such as whether to include a heading or add a border.

On a blank line (not inside another table), select **Table** from the **Insert** sub-menu of the Table menu to display the **Insert Table** dialog box. Select the number of columns and rows you want in your table. If you don't know exactly how many columns and rows you need, guess as closely as you can. (See **26 Manage a Table** to learn how to add or remove extra rows and columns.)

Click the **Heading** option if you want the first row of your table to be separated from the rest of the table with a bold line. You can use this row for your heading information, such as titles across the top of the table if you wish. Click the **Repeat heading** option if you want the first row to be repeated on every page, assuming your table will span multiple pages. If you click **Don't split table**, Writer will not begin the table toward the bottom of the page if the page break would split the table; rather, Writer begins the table at the top of the next page.

▶ **NOTE**

Some tables will be so long, the **Don't split table** option will not work. If a table is longer than one page, Writer has to split the table.

6 Automatically Format the Table

Click the **AutoFormat** button to select an initial format for your table. You learn how to apply other kinds of formatting changes to your table in **25 Format a Table**, but you can select an initial format from the list you get when you click **AutoFormat**.

7 Select the Look

Select a format from the list, and when you do, Writer displays a preview of such a table. You can keep selecting from the various formats until you find a format you want to use. Once you've selected a table format, click **OK** to close the **AutoFormat** dialog box. Then click **OK** to close the **Insert Table** dialog box.

8 Fill In the Resulting Table

Writer creates your table and displays its empty cells for you to fill in with data. Be sure to put titles in the first row if you chose an initial first-row heading for your table.

---

25 Format a Table

✔ BEFORE YOU BEGIN	→ SEE ALSO
23 About Writer Tables	**26** Manage a Table
24 Create a Table	

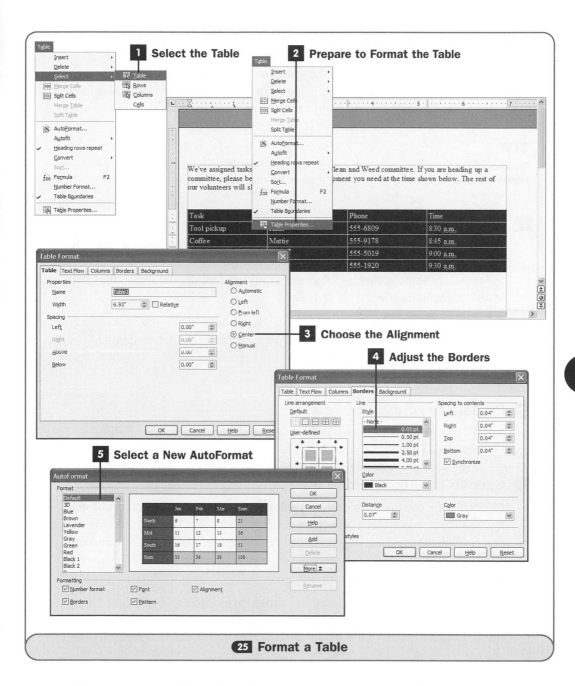

1 **Select the Table**

2 **Prepare to Format the Table**

3 **Choose the Alignment**

4 **Adjust the Borders**

5 **Select a New AutoFormat**

25 Format a Table

If you created a table without choosing an AutoFormat, or if you're unhappy with the table format you chose with AutoFormat, you can change your table's look. A table's primary goal is to present information to its readers in a clear format. If the format detracts from that goal, you should change the format.

Some users initially create very fancy tables from the AutoFormat list that Writer provides. Often, the colors and format take away from the table's effectiveness more than they add to it. Give your table as much time in its formatting as you give other design elements of your documents, perhaps even more, to ensure that your tables clearly say what you want them to say to your readers.

▶ **TIP**

Always print a table onto paper to ensure that the formatting is not too distracting. Tables can look different when printed than when they appear on the screen.

1 Select the Table

To change the overall format of your table, select the entire table. If you only want to change the format of some of your table, select just that portion of the table, such as the first heading row or perhaps all the data rows that fall below the heading row.

You can make selections by highlighting the text with the mouse or by using the **Table, Select** submenu (a more efficient method). The Select submenu contains options for selecting the current row, column, or cell—as well as for selecting the entire table.

2 Prepare to Format the Table

Select **Table Properties** from the **Table** menu. Writer displays the **Table Format** dialog box.

3 Choose the Alignment

Click through the tabs and options in the **Table** tab of the **Table Format** dialog box to change various aspects of your table's design. For example, you can change the way text aligns inside your table's cells from the **Alignment** area in the **Table** tab. Depending on your data, you may want to center or left-justify data beneath a heading.

Click the **Text Flow** tab to display the **Table Format** dialog box's **Text Flow** page. If you want a page break to appear before or after the table, click the **Break** option and designate how you want the page break to appear. You can change the table-splitting option for multipaged tables. The **Vertical Alignment** options enable you to specify where you want text to align to in a tall cell. For example, if your cells are large enough for three rows of text but you type only one row, you can specify whether the text is to appear at the top, center, or bottom of the cell.

25

Click the **Columns** tab to display the **Columns** page. You can enter new values for each column's width.

▶ **TIP**

You can drag a column with your mouse instead of specifying exact column width measurements, as **26** **Manage a Table** shows.

4 **Adjust the Borders**

If you want the borders (the dividing lines between your table cells) to take on a different appearance, click the **Borders** tab. You can elect to change the border thickness, add a shadow to the table's outline, and even determine how far from each cell's edges you want the cell contents to begin.

▶ **NOTE**

Writer's default table options handle things very efficiently. It's rare that you will need to adjust specific measurements such as text inside cell spacing because Writer generally creates appropriate spacing values for you when you create the table.

If you feel that you've changed too much of your table, click the **Table Format** dialog box's **Reset** button in the lower-right corner of the dialog box to reset all measurements back to their original state (before you began changing values inside the **Table Format** dialog box). Once you're happy with the changes you have made, click **OK** to apply those changes and to complete the table's format.

5 **Select a New AutoFormat**

Once you add data to your table's cells, if you don't care for the AutoFormat you chose previously (see **24** **Create a Table**), you can change to another AutoFormat scheme. Select **Table**, **AutoFormat** to display the **AutoFormat** dialog box and select another format to apply.

The **AutoFormat** dialog box shows a **More** button that, when you click it, produces several formatting options. You can elect to include or exclude all the following from the AutoFormat patterns: **Number format**, **Borders**, **Font**, **Pattern**, and **Alignment**. If, for example, you click to uncheck the **Borders** option, all the **AutoFormat** previews change to exclude a border around and between the table cells. Writer does not save your **AutoFormat** dialog box selections, so the next time you insert a table, you may have to select the same AutoFormat again if you want to reuse it.

25

---

26 **Manage a Table**

✔ BEFORE YOU BEGIN	→ SEE ALSO
24 Create a Table **25** Format a Table	**29** Add a Chart or Spreadsheet to a Document

---

Once you're familiar with creating tables and formatting them, you'll still find yourself adjusting them as you work with them. Perhaps you need to add more rows or columns. Perhaps you want to make a quick adjustment to one of the column widths.

Formatting a table and getting data into it is most of the battle, but you also will find that traversing a table differs somewhat from traversing regular text. Table 4.1 shows the keystrokes needed to traverse tables efficiently.

▶ **TIP**

You can insert a table into an existing table cell. This arrangement is known as a **nested table** and is useful when you have complex information to track. Suppose that you're creating a table of monthly sales and want to insert two cells within the *December* cell to include both pre-Christmas and post-Christmas sales. To insert a nested table, click in the cell and then select **Table**, **Insert**, **Table**.

26

TABLE 4.1   Writer's Table-Navigating Keystrokes

Press This...	To Move the Table's Cursor Here
Shift+Tab or left arrow	The preceding cell
Tab or right arrow	The next cell
Up arrow	The cell above the current cell
Down arrow	The cell below the current cell
Ctrl+Home	The first cell in the table
Ctrl+End	The last cell in the table
Enter	Pressing **Enter** in any cell adds a paragraph return within the cell

1 **Resize the Column**

Adjusting a column's size is extremely simple. Move your mouse pointer to the edge of the column you want to resize. The mouse pointer changes to a double arrow. Click the edge of the column and drag left or right to adjust the width of the column. When you release the mouse, Writer resizes the column. If you shrink a column's width too narrow, the text may not all fit on one line, and Writer will be forced to double the height of the rows to hold the extra data.

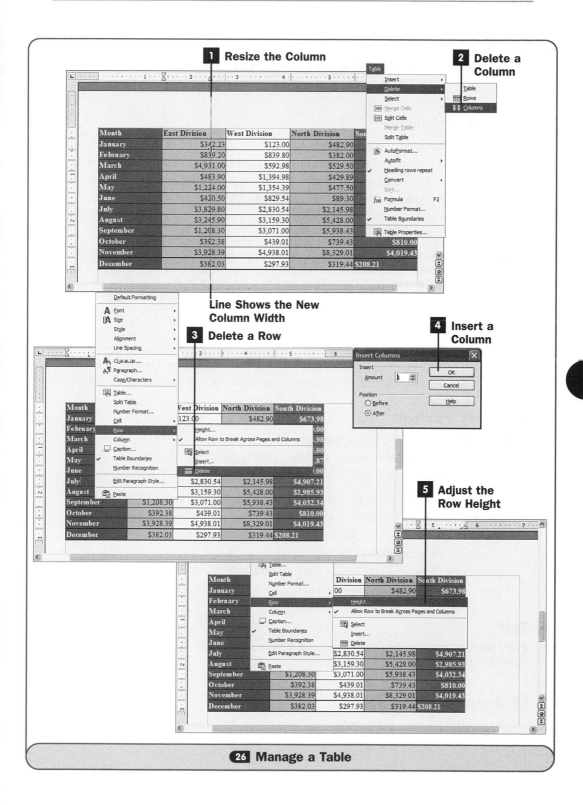

1 Resize the Column

2 Delete a Column

Line Shows the New Column Width

3 Delete a Row

4 Insert a Column

5 Adjust the Row Height

▶ **NOTE**

You can make a column width adjustment by dragging a column's edge on the horizontal ruler atop the document.

② Delete a Column

Select a column you want to delete by right-clicking it. From the submenu that appears, select **Column**, **Delete**. Writer deletes the column and increases the width of the column to the right to maintain the size of the table. If you don't like the wide column that results, drag its edges to adjust its width.

▶ **TIP**

You can change the direction of text flow in a table cell so that the text runs vertically instead of horizontally. To do so, click within the cell, choose **Table, Table Properties** from the menu bar, and then click the **Text direction** list arrow in the **Text Flow** tab.

③ Delete a Row

Deleting a row is similar to deleting a column: Right-click in the row you want to delete. From the submenu that appears, select **Row**, **Delete**. The rows below the deleted column move up to take its place.

④ Insert a Column

Right-click in any cell in a column to insert a column to the right or left of it, and then click **Insert** from the **Column** submenu to open the **Insert Columns** dialog box.

Click **Before** if you want to insert the column in front of (to the left of) the selected column; click **After** if you want the new column to appear after (to the right of) the selected column. You can insert more than one column by adjusting the **Amount** value. When you click **OK**, the new column appears in your table. Now you can fill the new column with data and adjust any column or table widths as necessary.

▶ **TIP**

If you want to insert a new row instead of a new column, select **Row, Insert** from the right-click menu.

⑤ Adjust the Row Height

You can adjust the height of an individual row by dragging the bottom edge of the row or by using the **Row Height** dialog box. The dialog box is your

26

best choice if you want to set the row height precisely or if you want to adjust the height of more than one row at a time.

To adjust one or more rows, select the row or rows you want to adjust and then right-click the selection. Choose **Row, Height** from the menu to display the **Row Height** dialog box. Adjust the **Height** value. If you click the **Fit to Size** option, the row adjusts to match the height of the row's data. If, for example, the row contains text in a large font, the **Fit to Size** option adjusts the row height to accommodate that larger font as well.

---

27 Insert Graphics in a Document

✔ BEFORE YOU BEGIN	→ SEE ALSO
14 Set Up Page Formatting	**28** Draw with Writer
15 Create a Multicolumn Newsletter	

Writer enables you to put pictures in your documents. Those graphic images can have captions and borders, and you can specify how the text around such images wraps.

Writer supports the inclusion of all the following kinds of graphic images:

- Graphic images from a file, such as bitmapped images

- Graphic images from OpenOffice.org's *Gallery*

- Graphic images you scan into your document

- Graphic images produced in OpenOffice.org's other products such as Draw and Impress

- A Calc chart

▶ KEY TERM

Gallery—A collection of graphics supplied by OpenOffice.org programs that you can insert into your documents.

When you insert a graphic image, Writer places an *anchor* at that location. You will see the anchor when editing but not when you print your document. The anchor shows where you inserted the actual image. You can format a graphic image to appear on the left or right of text, or above or below the text in which you insert the graphic. Therefore, the anchor and the actual image may not appear together. When you want to move an image, move its anchor and not the image itself.

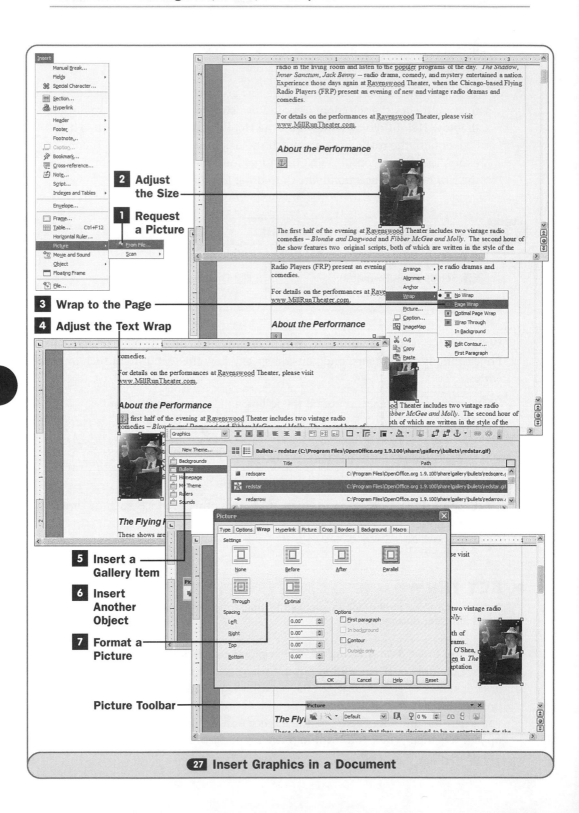

27 Insert Graphics in a Document

▶ KEY TERM

Anchor—A Writer placeholder that shows itself as an icon of a boat anchor. Anchors show the location of objects such as graphic images, footnotes, and endnotes. The anchor shows where you inserted an object. If you move the object, the anchor stays in place.

◼ Request a Picture

To insert a graphic image from a file, first place your text cursor where you want the image to go. Then, select **Insert**, **Picture**, **From File** from the menu. Writer displays the **Insert picture** dialog box, which is nothing more than a file-selection dialog box where you navigate to the file you want to insert. Once you select the graphic image you want to place in your document, click the **Open** button to insert the image.

▶ NOTE

OpenOffice.org supports all popular graphic file formats, including JPG, GIF, and BMP files.

If you want to scan an image directly into Writer, select **Insert**, **Picture**, **Scan** instead and select the scanning method you want to use to scan the picture. (Some scanners support multiple scanning methods.) As long as you have a *TWAIN*-compliant scanner attached to your computer (which most scanners are), Writer will scan the image and bring that image into your document.

The picture is selected so that you can make any adjustments. Whenever a picture is selected, the **Frame** and **Picture** toolbars appear, offering one-click access to many common graphics-related tasks.

▶ KEY TERM

TWAIN—A scanner hardware interface format recognized by all of today's computers.

◼ Adjust the Size

Once Writer brings the graphic image into your document, you can make adjustments to suit your needs. Typically, Writer imports graphic images and centers them at the location you inserted them. No text wraps to either side of the image, and the image often is not sized properly for your document.

To resize the image, drag any of the eight resizing handles inward to reduce the image size or outward to increase the image size.

3 Wrap to the Page

If you want to embed the image inside text, having the text wrap around the image instead of the image consuming space without any text wrapped around it, right-click the image and select **Wrap**, **Page Wrap** from the menu.

▶ TIPS

If you want to add a caption to your image, right-click the image and select **Caption** to display the **Caption** dialog box. You can add a sequential number before your caption so that you can reference all your images from the document by number.

If you want Writer to add a caption automatically whenever you insert an image, choose **Tools, Options** from the menu bar and then select the **AutoCaption** category to specify how you want the caption to look.

If you want to maintain the proportions of a picture as you resize it, press and hold **Shift** while dragging one of the resizing handles. For greater control over how your picture wraps to surrounding text, right-click the image and then choose **Picture**.

4 Adjust the Text Wrap

Once you've elected to wrap to the page, you now can drag the image up or down to the middle of text, and the text will wrap around the image. As you drag the image, a dotted-line placeholder shows where the dragged image will appear when you release your mouse button. When you release your mouse button, the image is anchored into place and surrounding text will wrap around the sides.

You're not limited to keeping the image in the middle of the text. If you'd prefer to move the image over to the left or right margin, you can drag the image or click it and then click the **Align Left**, **Center Horizontal**, or **Align Right** button on the **Picture** toolbar. Often, text is easier to read if it wraps only on the left or right side of an image instead of the image falling directly in the center of the text.

5 Insert a Gallery Item

You may insert one of OpenOffice.org's Gallery images if you wish instead of importing your own graphic image. The Gallery contains a collection of *clip art*, such as fancy numbers, buttons, and graphic borders that you may want to use to spruce up your page.

▶ KEY TERM

Clip art—A collection of low-resolution art, supplied by OpenOffice.org, that you can use to decorate your documents.

You must display the gallery before you can drag items from the gallery into your document. To display the gallery, click the **Gallery** button on the Standard toolbar or select **Tools, Gallery**. The top half of your screen shows the gallery, organized in the following categories: **Backgrounds**, **Bullets**, **Homepage**, **My Theme**, **Rulers**, and **Sounds**. Some of the gallery images are useful for creating and designing web pages. The **Sounds** category contains various sounds you can insert into a document, although this feature is often overused at first and then never used later after its novelty wears off.

To insert a gallery image, click to select that image and drag it to the place in your document where you want the image to go. As with graphic images you insert, once the gallery image appears in your document, you can resize it and align it with text in the way that fits your needs best.

To close the gallery, click the **Gallery** button on the **Standard** toolbar, or choose **Tools, Gallery**. You can also drag the bottom of the gallery up or down to shrink or expand it if you want to leave it open as you work.

6 Insert Another Object

By clicking **Object** on the **Insert** menu, you are given the chance to insert a chart (see **29 Add a Chart or Spreadsheet to a Document**), mathematical expression (see **30 Use Mathematical Formulas in Documents**), *floating frame*, and other kinds of objects into your document.

27

▶ KEY TERM

Floating frame—Used in Web pages to display the contents of files.

▶ TIP

If you plan to insert many objects into a document, display the **Insert Object** toolbar to speed up your work. Choose **View, Toolbars** from the menu bar and then click **Insert Object** to display this toolbar.

7 Format a Picture

You can fine-tune many properties of a picture using the **Picture** dialog box and the **Picture** toolbar. If the **Picture** toolbar does not appear when you select a picture, choose **View, Toolbars, Picture**. Using buttons on the **Picture** toolbar, you can change the graphics mode (for example, from default to grayscale), adjust color and transparency, and even insert another picture. Use the **Picture** dialog box to make even more modifications to the selected picture, such as changing its size, position, spacing from the surrounding text, cropping and borders, and even adding a hyperlink. To open the **Picture** dialog box, right-click the picture and then click **Picture**.

28   Draw with Writer

✔ BEFORE YOU BEGIN	→ SEE ALSO
27 Insert Graphics in a Document	**29** Add a Chart or Spreadsheet to a Document

If you don't have any graphic images to insert into your documents, you can draw your own! Writer supports a drawing toolbar that supplies you with the following drawing tools:

- Line
- Rectangle
- *Ellipse*
- Freeform Line
- Text
- *Callouts*
- Custom Shapes
- Fontwork Gallery
- Insert from File

Custom shapes include the following:

- Basic Shapes
- Symbol Shapes
- Block Arrows
- Flowcharts
- Callout shapes
- Stars

▶ KEY TERMS

Ellipse—A round shape such as a circle or an oval.

Polygon—A multisided shape.

Arc—Half an ellipse, such as a half-moon.

Callout—A caption that points to an item to describe that item.

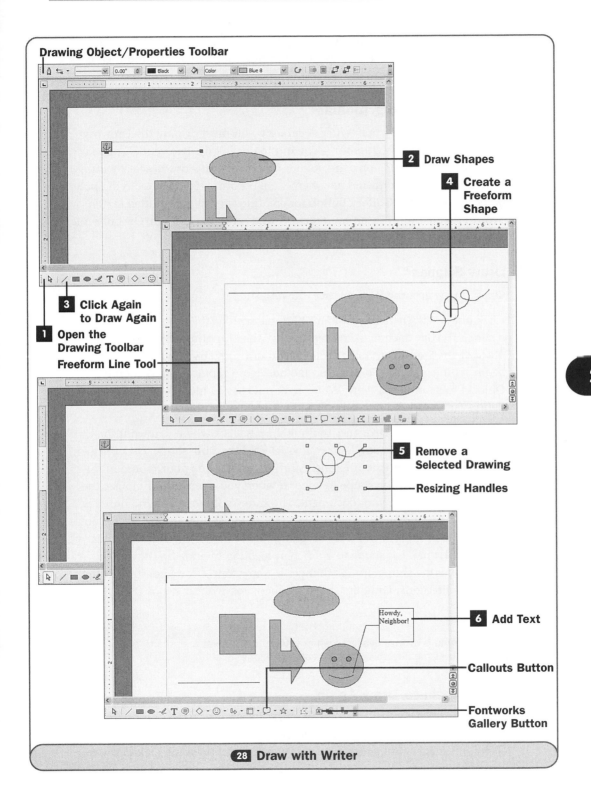

Drawing Object/Properties Toolbar

2 Draw Shapes

4 Create a Freeform Shape

3 Click Again to Draw Again

1 Open the Drawing Toolbar

Freeform Line Tool

5 Remove a Selected Drawing

Resizing Handles

6 Add Text

Callouts Button

Fontworks Gallery Button

Using one of the drawing tools usually requires only that you select the tool you want to use, click your mouse where you want the shape to begin, and then click your mouse where you want the shape to end.

1 Open the Drawing Toolbar

To add a drawing to your Writer document, you must display the Drawing toolbar (choose **View, Toolbar, Drawing** to display it). Twelve tools appear on the **Drawing** toolbar—plus the pointer (for when you want to select within a drawing instead of drawing new elements), a **Points** tool for modifying *polygons*, a **Fontworks Gallery** button for creating specially formatted text, a **From File** button for inserting a picture, and an **Extrusion On/Off** button for working with 3D effects.

2 Draw Shapes

Open a new document to practice drawing shapes.

Click one of the **Drawing** toolbar's buttons, such as the Line button, to draw a shape in your document. Writer displays the **Drawing Objects** toolbar in place of the **Standard** toolbar whenever a drawing shape is selected. If you begin typing text, the **Formatting** toolbar again replaces the **Drawing Objects** toolbar. In this way, Writer makes it easy to modify whichever element you're working on at the time, be it text or graphics.

To create any of the **Drawing Toolbar** shapes, click where you want the shape to begin. For example, if you've selected the **Line** shape, click once on your document to anchor the line's starting point. Drag your mouse in the direction you want the shape to go, and when you release your mouse, the shape will appear in your document. The shape will have resizing handles around it. You may click any handle to resize the shape. For example, you can extend or shorten a line by dragging one of its resizing handles in or out. You can also move a shape to a different location by moving the mouse pointer over the shape until it changes to show four arrows pointing in the compass directions. Drag the shape to where you want it to go.

▶ TIP

A right-click menu is always available when you right-click over a shape to adjust various attributes, such as the line thickness, fill color, size, and location.

3 Click Again to Draw Again

If you want to draw the same shape, click the shape's button on the **Drawing** toolbar and continue drawing. If you ever draw a shape that you don't want, click to highlight that shape's resizing handles and press the **Delete** key to remove the shape.

28

4 Create a Freeform Shape

Click to select a different shape, such as the **Freeform** drawing tool. You can drag the **Freeform** drawing shape to any position, and a line will follow your movement, drawing as you drag your mouse.

▶ **NOTE**

No negative critique of the author's extremely poor drawing talent will be tolerated!

5 Remove a Selected Drawing

If you decide you don't want a drawing or shape you've created, simply click to select it and then press the **Delete** key. If you have drawings that overlap one another, determining exactly what is selected can be tricky; study the resizing handles closely to make sure that you've selected the item you want to delete.

▶ **TIP**

If you change your mind about a deletion, choose **Edit, Undo** from the menu bar or press **Ctrl+Z** to restore the deleted item.

6 Add Text

Callouts are often useful to add to some drawings. You can use a callout as a text balloon showing that someone on your drawing is speaking. For more traditional technical and business drawings, callouts are useful for labeling items on a drawing. To add a callout, select the **Callout** drawing tool, add the callout, and resize and move the callout so it hovers exactly where you want it to land on your drawing. Click inside the callout and type whatever text you wish to use for the callout. All the usual formatting tools work on the callout's text, such as italics and boldface. If the callout is too large for the text you type, resize the callout box.

The **Callout** tool isn't the only way to add text to your drawing. Click the **Text** tool to draw a text box where you can type text inside the box. The primary difference between a text box and a callout is that a callout has a line pointing to another item the text refers to. If you want to get really fancy, you can add animated text to your drawing by selecting the **Fontwork Gallery** tool on the **Drawing** toolbar. When you add animated text to a text box, the text might scroll across the text box area as a marquee does. Right-click animated text that you place and select **Text**; then click the **Text Animation** tab to change the way the text animates.

28

29   Add a Chart or Spreadsheet to a Document

✔ BEFORE YOU BEGIN	→ SEE ALSO
27 Insert Graphics in a Document	**40** Create a New Spreadsheet
	68 Add a Chart to a Spreadsheet

OpenOffice.org's spreadsheet program Calc produces excellent charts and graphs. In many documents, you'll need to include a chart and possibly a spreadsheet to make a point more clear. Business reports, for example, are full of charts, spreadsheets, and text, all working together to demonstrate the financial health of a company.

You'll find that copying charts and spreadsheets into a Writer document is extremely simple to do. Both require that you start in Calc, because Calc is the source of such charts and spreadsheets. All you need to do is select the chart or spreadsheet and drag or copy it into your document. Writer recognizes the copied chart or spreadsheet, and you can resize and format the chart or spreadsheet using Writer's tools.

29

▶ **NOTE**

This task explains how to copy a *static* chart or spreadsheet into Writer—that is, one that will not change if you change the original in Calc after copying to Writer. To keep a link to the original Calc spreadsheet, select **Edit**, **Paste Special**, **DDE Link** to paste the chart or spreadsheet.

1 Select Calc's Chart

Start Calc and load the spreadsheet that has the chart you want to copy to your Writer document. Select the entire chart by clicking it to display its resizing handles.

2 Copy to the Clipboard

Press **Ctrl+C** or click the **Copy** toolbar button to copy the chart to the Windows Clipboard.

3 Paste the Chart into Writer

Return to your Writer document and click where you want the chart to appear. Generally, plan to give the chart plenty of room. In other words, you'll usually give the chart the full margin width.

Press **Ctrl+V** (or click the **Paste** toolbar button) to paste the chart into your Writer document.

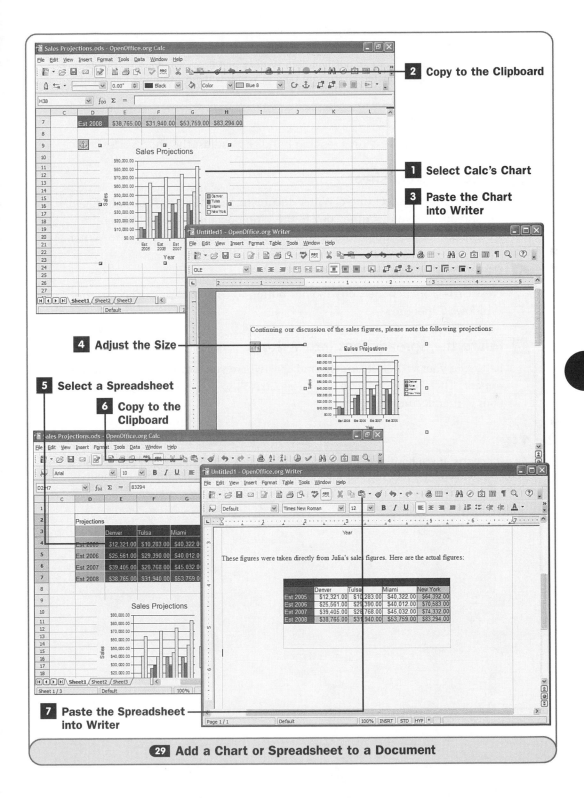

2 Copy to the Clipboard

1 Select Calc's Chart

3 Paste the Chart into Writer

4 Adjust the Size

5 Select a Spreadsheet

6 Copy to the Clipboard

7 Paste the Spreadsheet into Writer

▶ **TIP**

If you have dual monitors or can position both Writer's and Calc's windows on the same screen, you can drag a selected chart from Calc to Writer without using the Clipboard.

4 Adjust the Size

If necessary, drag the chart's resizing handles to adjust the chart's size.

5 Select a Spreadsheet

To bring a spreadsheet into a Writer document, you must start in Calc. Open the spreadsheet you want to copy to the Writer document. Select the entire spreadsheet or just the portion of the spreadsheet you want to copy to Writer.

6 Copy to the Clipboard

Press **Ctrl+C** or click the **Copy** toolbar button to copy the spreadsheet to the Windows Clipboard.

7 Paste the Spreadsheet into Writer

29

Return to your Writer document and click where you want the spreadsheet to appear. Click **Paste** (you can also press **Ctrl+V**) to paste the spreadsheet into your Writer document.

▶ **TIP**

As with charts, if you have dual monitors or can position both Writer's and Calc's windows on the same screen, you can drag the spreadsheet from Calc to Writer without using the Clipboard.

5

Using Writer's Advanced Features

IN THIS CHAPTER:

If you've read some of the Writer tasks that appear earlier, you already know that Writer provides tremendous power and a lot of features. The ability to accept charts and spreadsheets with ease, for example, is enough to turn some Microsoft Word users into Writer users the next time Microsoft releases a "new" Office version for several hundred bucks (see **29** **Add a Chart or Spreadsheet to a Document**).

Writer provides even more advanced features than you've already experienced if you've read tasks that came before. Despite being considered advanced, these features are simple to use. In addition to providing you the ability, for example, to put complex mathematical expressions in your documents (see **30** **Use Mathematical Formulas in Documents**), Writer also can work behind the scenes, automatically making corrections as you type. This chapter provides you with the tools you'll need to take your words to their next level and to create powerful and correct documents.

30

30 Use Mathematical Formulas in Documents

✔ **BEFORE YOU BEGIN**

27 Insert Graphics in a Document
29 Add a Chart or Spreadsheet to a Document

By its very nature, the inclusion of advanced mathematical formulas isn't the simplest to explain. Math experts will understand, and those who cloud up at long division may want to skip the whole thing. Probably, if you have the need to include mathematical formulas, then you understand the math behind what you're including in your document.

This task shows you how to use the formula editor to include a mathematical formula in your document. OpenOffice.org contains a tool called **Math** for creating advanced mathematical equations. Math can be run as a standalone program, but it is often simpler to access its tools while working within another document. Instead of opening Math and then copying and pasting the formula into Writer, you can open a formula editor within Writer to create and insert the formula without ever leaving your document window. Far too many combinations of far too many expressions exist to cover them all in one task. Therefore, this tasks presents some fundamental ways to include such expressions in your document, but it does not present an exhaustive demonstration.

Having said that, you may be amazed at how simple Writer makes it for you to enter such formulas. With Math's *formula editor*, you can build an extremely complex expression.

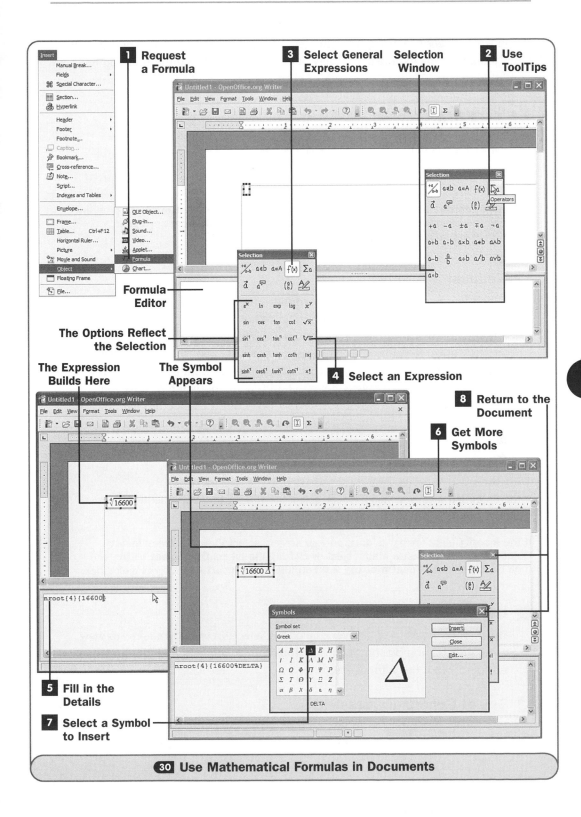

1 Request a Formula

3 Select General Expressions

Selection Window

2 Use ToolTips

Formula Editor

The Options Reflect the Selection

The Expression Builds Here

The Symbol Appears

4 Select an Expression

8 Return to the Document

6 Get More Symbols

5 Fill in the Details

7 Select a Symbol to Insert

30

If you work extensively with mathematical expressions in your documents, you'll want to explore the exhaustive variety of expressions and formula-building tools available to you in Math.

► KEY TERM

Formula editor—A tool with which you can compose complex math equations. OpenOffice.org's formula editing tool is called Math.

► TIP

To open Math as a standalone program, select **Math** from the **OpenOffice.org** program group in the Windows **Start** menu, or select **File, New, Formula** from any open OpenOffice.org program.

1 Request a Formula

When you need a mathematical formula, click **Object** on the **Insert** menu, and then click **Formula** in the submenu. When you do, a new window pane will open in the lower half of your screen to provide a place to build your mathematical formula and the **Tools** toolbar will open to offer one-click access to common Math-related commands. The formula editor is always at work in this lower window pane to build mathematical formulas you request. The **Selection** window appears also. From the **Selection** window, you select the kind of formulas you want to build, such as sums, relations, and functions.

30

► TIPS

If the **Selection** window doesn't appear, select **View, Selection** from the menu to display it.

If the **Insert Object** toolbar is open on your screen (select **View, Toolbars, Insert Object**), you can request a Math object by clicking the **Insert OLE object** button and then double-clicking **OpenOffice.org 2.0 Formula** in the **Insert OLE Object** dialog box.

2 Use ToolTips

Hover your mouse pointer over any of the **Selection** window's items to view more information on that item. The ToolTip that appears provides an explanation of what the symbol stands for.

3 Select General Expressions

When you click a button in the top half of the **Selection** window, the available expressions in the lower half change. Click the **Functions** button (the one that looks like **f(x)**), and the lower half of the window changes to reflect all the functions you can build inside the formula editor.

![4] Select an Expression

Click to select the **N-th Root** button in the lower half of the **Selection** window. As soon as you do, the formula editor displays an expression that represents an nth root.

▶ **NOTE**

You won't see math symbols in the formula editor, but as you build formulas, the symbols will appear above in your document.

![5] Fill in the Details

You now must fill in the details, replacing the placeholder symbols with actual values. To write a formula that represents the 4th root of the number 16,600, for example, you would replace the first placeholder, <?>, with **4** and the second placeholder with **16600**. Have patience, because the formula editor takes its time parsing your expression before producing the formula with all the proper symbols in the document at the top of your screen.

All OpenOffice.org programs support a symbolic mathematical language. When you type the language in the formula editor, the formula editor interprets what you type and builds the formula above in your document. As you work with the formula editor over time, you will get accustomed to the language used there. Once you learn some of the language, you can type the language directly instead of selecting from the **Selection** window if you find that typing the language is easier. For example, instead of selecting the **N-th Root** button, you could have typed nroot{4}{16600}, and the formula editor would have known what you wanted to build.

![6] Get More Symbols

To add more symbols, such as a delta symbol, to your formula, click the **Catalog** button on the **Tools** toolbar. The **Symbols** dialog box appears. You can browse through the available symbols and click the **Symbol set** list arrow to view other available symbol categories. When you find the symbol you want to insert, click the **Insert** button.

▶ **NOTE**

If you double-click a symbol in the **Symbols** dialog box, the symbol is inserted at the location of the insertion point and the dialog box closes. If you select a symbol from the dialog box and then click the **Insert** button, the symbol is inserted but the dialog box remains open.

30

7 Select a Symbol to Insert

When you click a symbol, a description of that symbol, in the formula editor's math language, appears in the lower window pane. The symbol then appears above next to the first part of your formula. You can continue adding symbols (in this case, adding more symbols would represent multiplication of them).

8 Return to the Document

Click the **Close** button to close the **Symbols** dialog box when you're done inserting symbols. You can jump back and forth between the **Symbols** dialog box and the **Selection** window as you build more complicated expressions.

Click the **Selection** window's **Close** button to close this window when you're through building your formula, or simply click anywhere in the document window.

Clicking anywhere in your document hides both the formula editor's window pane and the **Selection** window, so you can get back to work on your document.

31

31	**About Writer's Automatic Correction Tools**

✔ **BEFORE YOU BEGIN**	→ **SEE ALSO**
4 Type Text into a Document **25** Format a Table	**32** Use AutoCorrect to Improve Your Typing

Many of Writer's tools work in the background to make your writing as accurate and as well formatted as possible. If you've read previous chapters already, you've seen the following two automatic helpers:

- **AutoComplete**—Finishes common words before you type them. For example, when you begin typing `following`, Writer's word-completion feature finishes the word for you after you type `follo` (press **Enter** to accept the suggestion or keep typing if you meant something else, such as *follows*). You can keep typing or accept the suggestion. See **4** **Type Text into a Document** for more information.

- **AutoSpellcheck**—As you type words, Writer monitors your progress, and if you type a word incorrectly, such as **wondoes**, the spelling checker corrects the word so you can continue with the rest of the document. See **8** **Check a Document's Spelling** for more information.

Another form of automatic help provided by Writer is the AutoFormat feature you use to format tables. After specifying the number of rows and columns in your table, as **24 Create a Table** explains, you can click the **AutoFormat** button to display a wide range of formats you can choose from to make your table look better than the standard black text on a white background.

Writer provides even more automatic correction tools to help ensure your writing is as accurate as possible. Often, Writer fixes problems without you ever being aware of them, thanks to its *AutoCorrect* feature. As you type, Writer analyzes potential errors and makes corrections or suggested improvements along the way.

▶ KEY TERM

AutoCorrect—The capability of OpenOffice.org programs to analyze what you just typed and replace with a corrected version if needed.

If AutoCorrect recognizes a typing mistake, it immediately corrects the mistake.

Following are just a few of the mistakes AutoCorrect recognizes and corrects as you type:

- AutoCorrect corrects two initial capital letters at the beginning of sentences. For example, "LAtely, we have been gone" becomes "Lately, we have been gone."

- AutoCorrect enables you to enter shortcuts such as your initials, which, when typed into a document, convert to your full name.

- AutoCorrect replaces common symbols with predefined characters. When you type (c), for example, Word converts the characters to a single copyright symbol (©).

- AutoCorrect replaces common spelling transpositions, such as "teh" with "the."

If AutoCorrect corrects something that you don't want corrected, press **Ctrl+Z** and AutoCorrect reverses its action. If you type an entry in the AutoCorrect list that you do not want corrected in the future, such as *QBasic*, which Writer incorrectly changes to *Qbasic*, you can add QBasic to Writer's exception list so that Writer does not make that correction in the future.

▶ TIP

The initial AutoCorrect word list and options are preset, but you can add your own frequently misspelled (or mistyped) words to the list. You will most certainly want to add your initials to the AutoCorrect table, for example, so that you need only type your initials when you want to enter your full name in a document.

---

32 **Use AutoCorrect to Improve Your Typing**

✔ **BEFORE YOU BEGIN**

31 About Writer's Automatic Correction Tools

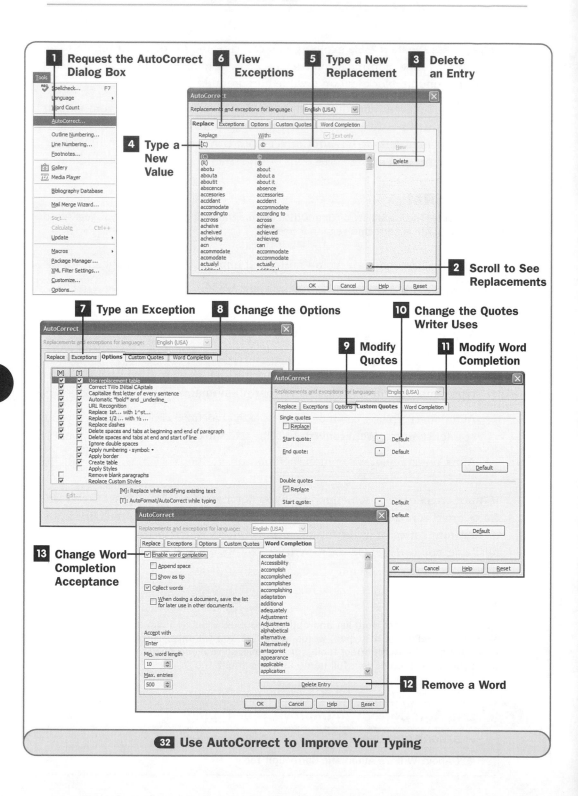

1 Request the AutoCorrect Dialog Box

6 View Exceptions

5 Type a New Replacement

3 Delete an Entry

4 Type a New Value

2 Scroll to See Replacements

7 Type an Exception

8 Change the Options

10 Change the Quotes Writer Uses

9 Modify Quotes

11 Modify Word Completion

13 Change Word Completion Acceptance

12 Remove a Word

32 Use AutoCorrect to Improve Your Typing

Writer gives you complete control over the way it handles AutoCorrect entries. You can modify the correction list, add your own corrections that you want Writer to make, and add to a list of exceptions so that Writer stops correcting things you don't want corrected.

If you find Writer correcting certain words and phrases that you don't want corrected, you can add those words and phrases to Writer's exception list. In addition to autocorrecting words and phrases, the AutoCorrect feature performs some formatting changes for you, most notably changing straight quotes into custom, rounded quotes, sometimes called *smart quotes*.

▶ KEY TERM

Smart quotes—The rounded quotes that curl in or out, depending on whether they begin or end a quoted phrase. Both single quote marks and regular quotations can be smart quotes. The term originally started with Word and applies to a word processor's capability to recognize whether a quote mark should be open or closed.

1 Request the AutoCorrect Dialog Box

Select **Tools**, **AutoCorrect** from the menu to display the **AutoCorrect** dialog box. It is from this dialog box that you control the way AutoCorrect operates on your words. Click the **Replace** tab to display the **Replace** page if it's not already displayed.

2 Scroll to See Replacements

Scroll down the list to see all the replacements that Writer will make on your behalf. Many of the replacements replace common misspellings, such as *believe* for when you accidentally type *beleiv*.

3 Delete an Entry

If you want Writer to stop making one of the replacements, select that entry in the list and click the **Delete** button to the right of the dialog box. For example, you may be writing a book and want to designate your headings using a common format such as A-heads, B-heads, C-heads, and so on, indicating each succeeding level of subheadings throughout the text. If you prefix your third-level headings with (c), Writer immediately replaces the (c) with the copyright symbol, unless you delete that entry from the table.

4 Type a New Value

To add your own AutoCorrect entries, click the **Replace** text box and type your value there. This will be the value you want Writer to replace.

32

5 Type a New Replacement

Type the value you want to replace the other one with in the **With** text box. Click the **New** button that appears to the right of the dialog box when you finish the entry.

▶ **TIP**

You can change any entry in the table by selecting it, changing either the **Replace** or the **With** word, and then clicking the **Replace** button.

6 View Exceptions

Click the **Exceptions** tab to display the **Exceptions** page.

7 Type an Exception

If you regularly use a lowercase abbreviation that you don't want Writer to capitalize, type the exception abbreviation in the **Abbreviations** text box. If you regularly use a word with two initial capital letters, such as *QBasic*, type that exception in the **Words with TWo INitial CApitals** text box.

8 Change the Options

Click the **Options** tab to display the **Options** page. Scroll through the list of options that Writer uses for its AutoCorrect corrections. Instead of entering an exception, for example, for *QBasic* on the **Exceptions** page, you might elect to uncheck the option labeled **Correct TWo INitial CApitals** so that Writer stops trying to correct all such entries.

▶ **TIP**

Two columns appear, labeled **M** and **T**, next to most of the options. Keep the **T** column checked for options you want automatically made as you type. Keep the **M** option checked if you want the option to be applied when you select **Format**, **AutoFormat**, **Apply** from the menu to manually autocorrect a document.

9 Modify Quotes

Click the **Custom Quotes** tab to display the **Custom Quotes** page.

10 Change the Quotes Writer Uses

You can change the quotes that Writer uses when you open or close either single quotes or double quotes (regular quotation marks). To use a different start quote, for example, when you type an opening straight quote mark, click the straight quote button labeled **Start quote** and select a new quote from the symbols that appear. More than likely, you'll be replacing a straight quote with a curly quote. You can replace all four kinds of quotation marks used by Writer on the **Custom Quotes** page.

32

⑪ Modify Word Completion

Click the **Word Completion** tab to display the dialog box's **Word Completion** page. Here, you work with word completion entries to modify the way Writer completes your typing for you (such as offering *additional* when you type add).

▶ **TIP**

If you don't want Writer to complete words automatically as you type, you can turn this feature off. Click to disable the **Enable word completion** check box in the **Word Completion** page of the **AutoCorrect** dialog box.

⑫ Remove a Word

If you want Writer to stop completing a certain word for you, click to select the word and click the **Delete Entry** button.

▶ **NOTE**

When you're typing in a document, the default method for accepting a word completion is by pressing **Enter**. If you don't want to accept the completion, just keep typing.

⑬ Change Word Completion Acceptance

If you want to change the character used to accept a completed word, click to select either **End**, **Enter**, **Space**, or **Right** from the **Accept with** list. For example, if you select **End**, when you type add and Writer replaces the word with *additional*, you'll have to press the **End** key to accept the suggestion; otherwise, Writer erases the suggestion and lets you complete the word.

The other options on the **Word Completion** page enable you to request an automatic space after a completed word and show the suggested word as a ToolTip instead of having Writer complete the word at your cursor's position.

When you finish making changes to the **Word Completion** page, click **OK** to close the dialog box and return to your document.

---

33 | **About Headers and Footers**

✔ **BEFORE YOU BEGIN**	→ **SEE ALSO**
⑭ Set Up Page Formatting	㉞ Add a Header or Footer
⑯ About Styles and Templates	

Headers and *footers* can give your documents a consistent appearance. You can put both a header and a footer on a page or use one or the other. You can select certain pages to receive headers and footers. Writer also supports the use of odd- and even-numbered headers and footers. For example, you might want a page number to appear in the upper-right corner of the header on odd pages and in the upper-left corner of the header on even pages.

▶ **KEY TERMS**

Header—Text and/or graphics that appear at the top of every page in a section or document.

Footer—Text and/or graphics that appear at the bottom of every page in a section or document.

Headers and footers can contain graphics, so you can place your company's logo at the top of every page. Writer also supports the use of *fields*, such as page numbers, the time, the date, and even chapter numbers. When you insert one of these fields, Writer inserts the actual value in the document. If your document, for example, is 50 pages, the pages will automatically display 1 through 50. If you delete a page from your document, Writer instantly renumbers the pages.

33

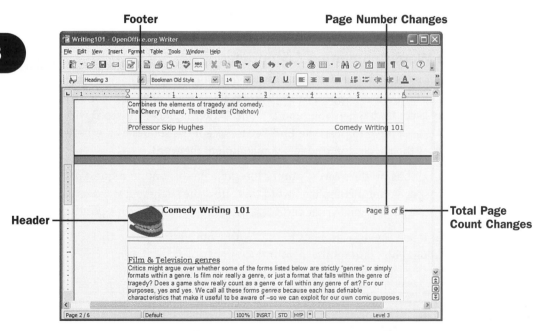

Footer   Page Number Changes

Header

Total Page Count Changes

Headers and footers appear on each page of the section or document.

▶ **KEY TERM**

Fields—Placeholders in your documents that OpenOffice.org fills in with actual values, such as page numbers, the time, and date.

As can paragraphs, pages can also have styles. **14** **Set Up Page Formatting** discusses page styles. You can also use a header or footer that's different from the ones on surrounding pages by setting up a new page style, using the **Format**, **Styles and Formatting**, **Page Styles** list. If you define a new page style anywhere in your document, all pages use the new header or footer until you revert back to the previous page style or switch to a new page style.

► **TIP**

If you write a report that contains several pages of graphical or numerical data, you might want to format a new page style for those pages so they can contain a different header or footer. You might, for example, renumber those pages as **Chart-1**, **Chart-2**, and so on.

If you attempt to insert a header or footer onto a page that already has a header or footer, Writer warns you that the other header or footer exists and lets you verify that you want to delete the contents of the existing header or footer before continuing. Writer won't overwrite a header or footer without you verifying that you really want to do so.

Writer won't overwrite an existing header or footer without you verifying that you really want to do so.

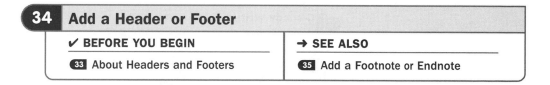

34 Add a Header or Footer

✔ **BEFORE YOU BEGIN**	→ **SEE ALSO**
33 About Headers and Footers	**35** Add a Footnote or Endnote

The **Insert**, **Header** and **Insert**, **Footer** menu options allow you to add headers and footers to your document's pages. Each header and footer is saved in the page's current style. If your document has multiple page styles, your document can have multiple headers and footers, too. The **Insert**, **Fields** menu option inserts placeholder fields that Writer updates as necessary.

► **TIP**

Sometimes you won't want a header or footer to appear on a page. Simply define a new page style for that page and don't add the header or footer.

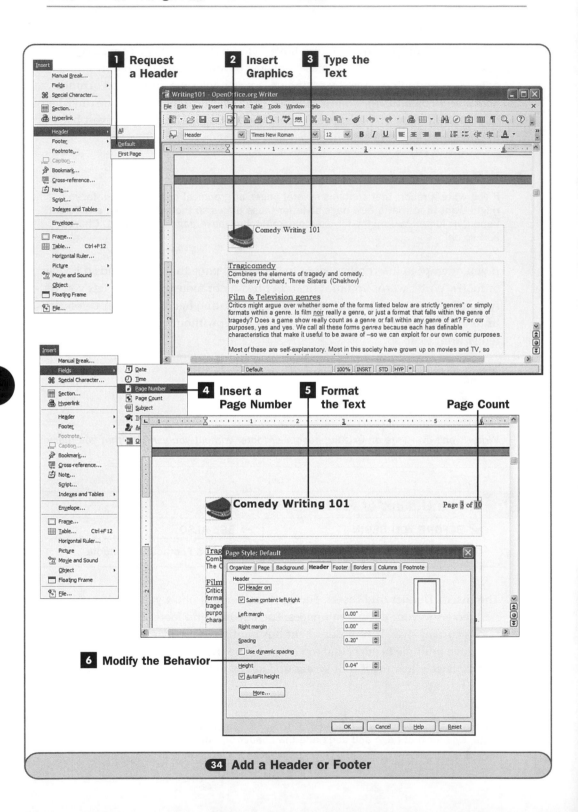

1 **Request a Header**

2 **Insert Graphics**

3 **Type the Text**

4 **Insert a Page Number**

5 **Format the Text**

Page Count

6 **Modify the Behavior**

34 **Add a Header or Footer**

Here are the fields you'll find helpful for headers and footers:

- Date

- Time

- Page Number

- Page Count

- Subject

- Title

- Author

The Page Number and Page Count fields can be combined to create a header or footer that reads, for example, **Page 4 of 17**.

▶ **TIP**

You can create a header or footer that is unique to the first page of a document by clicking **First Page** instead of **Default** in the **Header** or **Footer** submenu on the **Insert** menu.

1 **Request a Header**

Select **Insert**, **Header**, **Default**. Writer inserts a header block at the top of every page in your document of the current page style. If you want to insert a footer instead of a header, you would instead select **Insert**, **Footer**, **Default**. You can insert both a header and footer on the same page.

2 **Insert Graphics**

Feel free to insert a graphic image in your header or footer. You can insert from the gallery, from a graphics file, or you can scan an image into the header or footer (see **27** **Insert Graphics in a Document**).

If the header or footer is not wide enough to display the graphic image, you can change the text's point size or use multiple header or footer text lines to give the graphic image a large enough block in which to appear. Even then, you may want to adjust the size of the image, so click the image and drag the sizing handles inward or outward as needed.

▶ **TIP**

If you don't want any text in the same header or footer that contains a graphic image, but the single line for the header or footer isn't large enough to display the graphic, insert a blank space before or after the image and set the font size for the space to 36 points or another setting that gives the graphic enough room to display.

34

3 Type the Text

Type the text that goes in the header or footer. If you want to end the first line early and start a second line of text, press **Enter** while typing within the header or footer block.

▶ **TIP**

Set a right tab if you want the page number to align with the right edge of the page.

4 Insert a Page Number

Select **Insert**, **Fields**, **Page Number** to insert a page number placeholder in your header or footer. You can set up a page number by typing Page followed by a space before you insert the page number field. You can also insert **Page Count** field that updates as your document grows and shrinks.

5 Format the Text

All the regular character formatting options work on header and footer text, so you can format the text any way you prefer. You can also use the ruler to set tabs if needed.

▶ **TIP**

Clicking the **More** button on the **Header** or **Footer** page allows you to define borders and background colors for your header or footer.

6 Modify the Behavior

Select **Format**, **Page** and click the **Header** tab to display the **Header** page. (There's an identical **Footer** page in the same dialog box.) The **Header** page enables you to control left and right headers for facing pages, margin spacing, and height. By adjusting the **Height** value, you can set the height of a header or footer to be large enough for a graphic image without having to format surrounding text large enough to show the image. As you adjust the header settings, the preview area updates to show you what your header or footer will look like.

---

35 Add a Footnote or Endnote

✔ **BEFORE YOU BEGIN**

33 About Headers and Footers
34 Add a Header or Footer

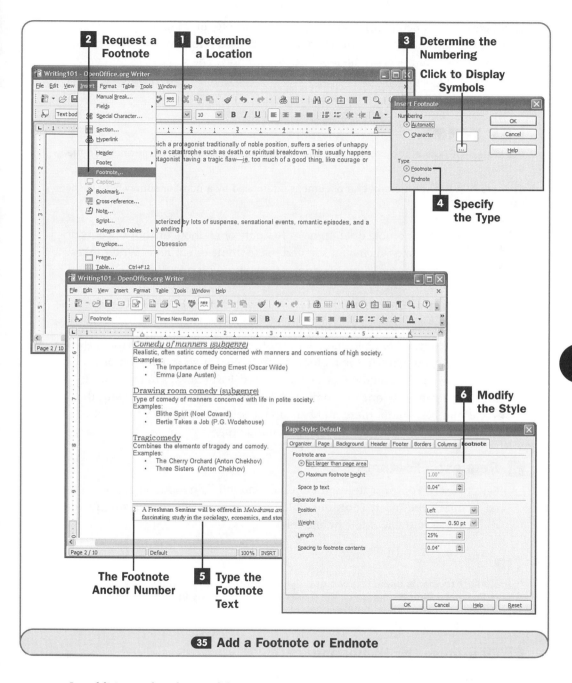

2 Request a Footnote

1 Determine a Location

3 Determine the Numbering

Click to Display Symbols

4 Specify the Type

6 Modify the Style

The Footnote Anchor Number

5 Type the Footnote Text

35 Add a Footnote or Endnote

In addition to headers and footers, Writer supports the inclusion of ***footnotes*** and ***endnotes*** in your documents. A footnote differs from a footer in that it appears only on the page in which it's referenced. An endnote appears at the end of your document, referenced somewhere in the text. You can place both footnotes and endnotes in your documents. Once you set up footnotes or endnotes, Writer takes over the administration of them. Therefore, if you add a footnote between two others, Writer renumbers all the footnotes accordingly. The same goes for endnotes, so if you delete an endnote, Writer renumbers all the other endnotes affected by the deletion.

▶ KEY TERMS

Footnotes—A note at the bottom of a page referenced by a number somewhere on the page.

Endnotes—A note at the end of a document referenced by a number somewhere in the document.

When you insert a footnote or endnote, a footnote or endnote anchor appears at the location in the text where you inserted the footnote or endnote. Writer takes care of numbering footnotes and endnotes for you as you add them.

■1 Determine a Location

Click inside your document where you want the footnote or endnote anchor to go. The anchor will become a sequential number (or some other text that you specify) attached to the footnote or endnote. For your first footnote, the number will be **1**, and the footnote numbered **1** will always apply to that anchor. An endnote anchor numbered **21** will refer to an endnote with the same number. Again, these numbers update automatically if you insert or remove footnotes and endnotes from among others.

■2 Request a Footnote

Select **Insert**, **Footnote** to insert either an endnote or a footnote at the selected location. The **Insert Footnote** dialog box appears, where you can provide the specifics of the footnote or endnote.

▶ TIP

If the **Insert** toolbar is open, you can quickly insert a footnote or endnote by clicking the **Insert Footnote Directly** button or the **Insert Endnote Directly** button. To display the **Insert** toolbar, choose **View**, **Toolbars**, **Insert**.

■3 Determine the Numbering

Generally, you'll leave the **Automatic** numbering option selected. This enables Writer to handle the sequential numbering of your footnotes and endnotes. If you want to use a different character, such as an alphabetic letter, type the letter that will belong to the footnote or endnote. You can use a

35

special symbol, such as a Greek letter if you wish, by clicking the ellipses (…) button.

4 Specify the Type

Click either **Footnote** or **Endnote** to tell Writer where you want the current note handled (either at the end of the page or at the end of the document). Click **OK** to close the **Insert Footnote** dialog box.

5 Type the Footnote Text

Writer drops down to the footnote (or back to the endnote) section after numbering your anchor point and adding the footnote (or endnote) reference number. Type the text for your footnote (or endnote). By default, Writer assigns the **Footnote** style to your text.

▶ NOTE

If you add a footnote to a multicolumned document, the footnote appears at the bottom of the column where you placed the footnote's anchor.

6 Modify the Style

If you want to change the way Writer displays your footnotes or endnotes, select **Format**, **Page** and then click the **Footnote** tab to display the **Footnote** page. Here, you can specify the maximum height of your note as well as determine where the note will go on the page and how thick the dividing line will be between the text on the page and the footnote at the bottom.

36

---

36 Save a Document as a PDF File

✔ BEFORE YOU BEGIN

2 Create a New Document
9 Print a Document

If you need to distribute documents as email attachments or over the Web, you'll be glad to know that OpenOffice.org allows you to create PDF documents quickly and easily.

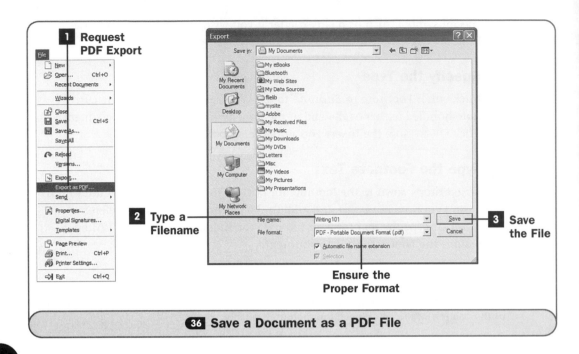

36 Save a Document as a PDF File

36

Adobe Systems, Incorporated designed a special file format called *PDF* that is readable on the Windows, Mac, and Linux platforms. Many electronic books (often called *eBooks*) conform to the PDF format so that Web users can download such books and read them online, save them to their computers for a later reading, or print them on their printers. The problem with the typical file format, such as Microsoft Word's DOC file format, is that web browsers cannot read these files and they are not supportable on some of the major computing platforms in use today (although usually a plug-in utility program is available for most computers that do allow non-Windows users to read PC-based DOC files).

▶ KEY TERM

PDF—The name (and filename extension) given to documents that conform to Adobe Systems' *Portable Document Format*. This format is readable by web browsers and most computers.

Writer (and the other OpenOffice.org programs) supports the PDF format in the following way: When you compose your document, you then can save that document in the PDF format. Once your document is in the PDF format, you can distribute it onto the Web, where most users will be able to read your document.

Almost all computers sold in the past few years support the use of PDF files. For users of older PCs that cannot yet read Adobe's PDF format, the Adobe Reader is available free for download from http://www.adobe.com/products/acrobat/read-step2.html, where the download is quick. Again, almost every computer in use today can read PDF files. So Writer's native capability to save documents in the PDF format gives you the ability to compose documents that most others can read.

PDF documents cannot be edited (at least, not in the traditional sense of the word, although you can add comments and edits if you have Adobe Acrobat), which makes it the format of choice when you want to share a document without allowing the recipient to make changes to it.

Adobe sells Adobe Acrobat, a program that converts documents to PDF format, for several hundred dollars (full retail; wholesale often finds the price still high, at a little more than $300). Writer saves you money!

▶ **TIP**

If you want to convert Microsoft Word documents to PDF, use Writer as your intermediary! Open the Word document in Writer and then save the document using Writer's PDF file-saving feature.

1 Request PDF Export

Select **File**, **Export to PDF** to display the **Export** dialog box, where you save your document to the PDF format.

▶ **NOTE**

Not only are PDF documents readable on virtually every computing platform, but your graphics, tables, headers, footers, multiple columns, and all other formatting remains intact as well.

2 Type a Filename

Type the filename you want to use for your PDF document in the **File name** text box. Make sure the **File format** box reads **PDF—Portable Document Format (pdf)**. Leave the **Automatic file name extension** check box selected to ensure that your exported document retains the proper .pdf filename extension.

▶ **TIP**

If you want to give someone a file in the OpenOffice.org file format but don't want to allow them to make changes to the document, use the **File sharing options** section in the **Security** page of the **Options** dialog box to designate the document as read-only.

36

3 **Save the File**

Click the **OK** button to save the file.

Don't confuse the common web page format (HTML) with PDF files. You'll often make PDF files available on a web page for your users to download and read, but the web page itself, the page that delivers your PDF document, must be in the standard HTML format. So when creating documents for others to download from the Web, always use PDF, not HTML.

---

37 **Use the Mail Merge Wizard**

✔ BEFORE YOU BEGIN	→ SEE ALSO
1 Create a New Document	**5** Edit Text
3 Open an Existing Document	

37

Writer provides a Mail Merge Wizard you can use to create form letters or email messages addressed to many recipients. If you want to send a mass mailing yet want each letter to be personalized with the recipient's name, address, or other information, you'll appreciate the speed and simplicity of *mail merge*.

The Mail Merge Wizard involves several steps, which vary depending on whether you have already created a *starting document* or a set of *Address data* to use for this mailing.

▶ **KEY TERMS**

Mail merge—The process of merging a text document with address or other information to create personalized mass mailing.

Starting document—A document containing text that will stay the same in each letter in the mail merge.

Address list—A data source, such as an address book or list you create in the Mail Merge Wizard, that contains addresses and other information that changes for each recipient in the mail merge.

1 **Request the Mail Merge Wizard**

You can start the Mail Merge Wizard either before or after creating the document you plan to personalize.

If you have created a letter you want to use as the form letter in a mail merge, open that document. Then choose **Tools, Mail Merge Wizard**. The first page of the Mail Merge Wizard opens. The list on the left side of the dialog box helps you navigate through each step in the process.

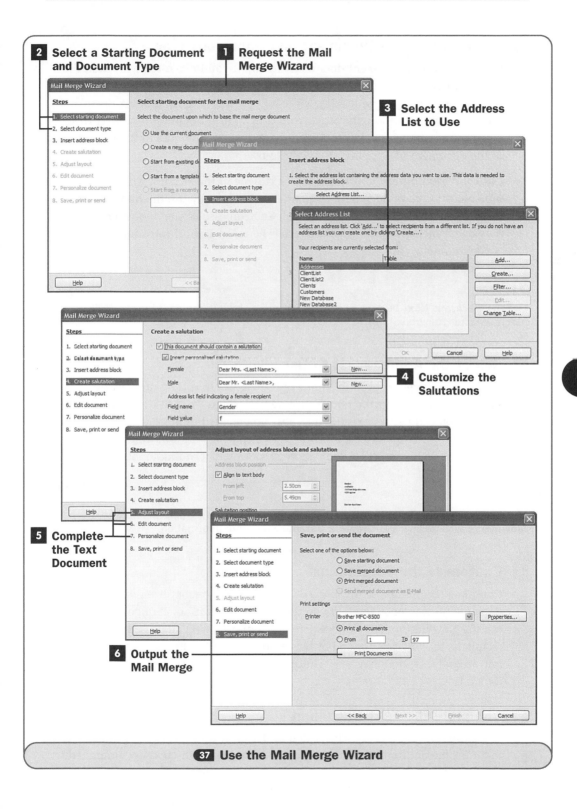

2 Select a Starting Document and Document Type

1 Request the Mail Merge Wizard

3 Select the Address List to Use

4 Customize the Salutations

5 Complete the Text Document

6 Output the Mail Merge

37 Use the Mail Merge Wizard

2 Select a Starting Document and Document Type

Enable the **Use the current document** option if you have already opened the document you want to use as the basis for your letter. Enable the **Create a new document** if you want to type the text for this letter in a blank document now. If you choose the **Start from an existing document** or **Start from a template** option, you can use a **Browse** button to navigate to the location of the document or template you want to use.

Click the **Next** button to move to the next page in the Wizard, where you indicate the type of document to create. You'll typically use the Mail Merge Wizard to create a form letter, although you can also create a mass email message. When you have specified either **Letter** or **E-mail message**, click the **Next** button.

▶ TIP

Use the **Back** and **Next** buttons at any time to move through the pages in the Mail Merge Wizard dialog box.

3 Select the Address List to Use

Use the numbered steps in this page of the Wizard to specify an existing address list or to enter the names and addresses you want to use in the mail merge. You can use an existing database you created in Base, your address book file from Thunderbird, Mozilla, or Netscape, a Windows system address book (such as Microsoft Outlook Express), or any external database.

▶ TIP

You may want to create your address book in Base rather than typing the data in the Mail Merge Wizard. See **135 Create a Database** for more information.

4 Customize the Salutations

Complete the options in this page of the Wizard to personalize the salutations included in each letter. If you don't like a salutation, change it by clicking the **New** button. For example, if you want all letters addressed to female recipients to show **Ms.** instead of **Mrs.** in the salutation line, click the **New** button and then define a new salutation in the **Customize Salutation** dialog box.

5 Complete the Text Document

Continue working through each page in the Wizard to prepare your document for the mail merge. You can adjust the layout of the text document, edit the text, and further personalize each proposed document in the mass mailing.

6 Output the Mail Merge

In the last page of the Mail Merge Wizard, you can choose to save, print or email the document.

If you choose to save the document, you must decide exactly what you want to save. You can choose the **Save starting document** option to save only the starting document. You can choose the **Saved merged document** to save either one large document containing every personalized letter or individual files for each personalized letter.

If you choose **Print merged document**, you can print any or all of your letters immediately.

37

PART II

Crunching Numbers with Calc

IN THIS PART:

6

Getting to Know Calc

IN THIS CHAPTER:

This chapter introduces topics related to Calc, OpenOffice.org's *spreadsheet* program. A spreadsheet is a collection of one or more *sheets*. OpenOffice.org's Calc is to numbers what Writer is to text; Calc has been called a "word processor for numbers." With Calc, you can create numerically based proposals, business plans, business forms, accounting spreadsheets, and virtually any other document that contains calculated numbers. If you've heard of, or have seen, Microsoft Excel, OpenOffice.org's Calc is OpenOffice.org's answer to Excel...only without the price tag.

▶ KEY TERMS

Spreadsheets—OpenOffice.org documents that hold one or more sheets (called *workbooks* in Microsoft Excel).

Sheets—Numerical information presented in a tabular row and column format with text that labels and discusses the data (also, loosely, called *spreadsheets*).

If you are new to electronic spreadsheets, you may have to take a little more time learning Calc's environment than you have to take to learn other programs such as Writer. Calc starts with a grid of cells in which you place information, not unlike Writer's tables (see **23 About Writer Tables**). This chapter orients you to Calc by offering tasks that explain how to enter and edit data in Calc spreadsheets as well as how to navigate them.

38

---

38 | **About Sheets and Spreadsheets**

→ SEE ALSO

39 Set Calc Options
40 Create a New Spreadsheet
46 Edit Cell Data

Calc enables you to create and edit one or more sheets that you store in spreadsheets. Generally, people work with a single sheet for simple applications, such as a worksheet that an investor might use to analyze a single stock investment.

Typically, Calc helps users prepare financial information, but you can manage other kinds of data in Calc, such as a project timeline. Calc even supports simple database routines (see Chapter 10, "Using Calc as a Simple Database"), although you'll want to use OpenOffice.org's Base program for in-depth database projects (see Chapter 18, "Organizing Your Data with Base"). If your project requires multiple closely linked financial sheets, you'll keep these sheets in one large spreadsheet file.

Row numbers

Name of active cell

Active cell   Column headings

Formula bar   Formatting toolbar

Standard toolbar

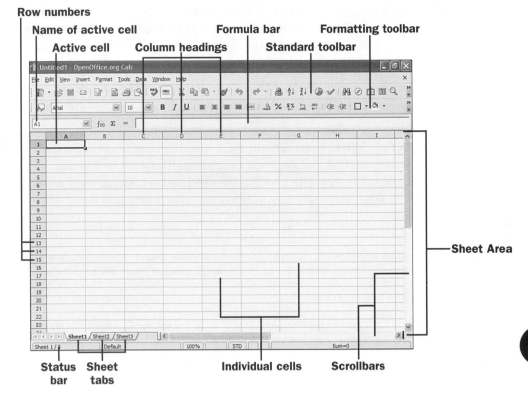

Sheet Area

Status   Sheet
bar   tabs

Individual cells   Scrollbars

38

A sheet is a collection of rows and columns that holds text and numbers.

▶ NOTE

Many people loosely use the term *spreadsheet* for single sheets inside a Calc *spreadsheet*. This lax term is used because Excel's sheets are called *spreadsheets*, but a Calc *spreadsheet* is technically the name for multiple sheets. It gets confusing! You'll often know by the context whether *spreadsheets* refer to a single sheet or a collection of sheets.

A simple example may help solidify the difference between a *spreadsheet* and a *sheet* in your mind. A company with several divisions might create a spreadsheet with annual sales for each division, and each division might be represented with its own tabbed sheet inside the spreadsheet. Any time you create, open, or save a Calc file, you are working with a spreadsheet. Often, that spreadsheet contains only one sheet. When that's the case, the terms *spreadsheet* and *sheet* really are basically synonymous.

All Calc files end in the .ods (Open Document Spreadsheet) filename extension. (Older Calc files end in the file extension .sxc and are completely compatible with OpenOffice.org.) Your spreadsheet name is the Calc name you assign when you save the file. You can save Calc sheets and spreadsheets in HTML and other spreadsheet formats, such as Microsoft Excel and Star Calc. When you save your sheet as an HTML file, you can embed your sheet data inside a web page. To save your work for the first time, select **File, Save As**; then name your Calc spreadsheet, specify the location, and select the format if you want to save the spreadsheet in a non-Calc format. To load an existing Calc or compatible spreadsheet file, use **File, Open**.

A sheet is set up in a similar manner to a Writer table (see **23 About Writer Tables**), except that Calc sheets can do much more high-end, numeric calculating than Writer tables can.

Initially, blank Calc spreadsheets contain three sheets, named **Sheet1**, **Sheet2**, and **Sheet3**. When you click a sheet's tab, Calc brings that sheet into view. Initially, you'll probably stay with one sheet per spreadsheet, so you may never have to click the secondary sheet tabs to bring the other sheets into view.

▶ TIPS

You can insert additional sheets into a spreadsheet. Choose **Insert, Sheet** from the menu bar to open the **Insert Sheet** dialog box. Specify whether you want to add the sheet before or after the currently selected sheet, and whether it should be a new sheet or a copy of a sheet from an existing file.

Give your sheet a name other than **Sheet1**. Doing so helps you keep track of what data is on each sheet. Right-click the sheet tab labeled **Sheet1**, select **Rename Sheet** from the menu, and enter a different name, such as 2005 Payroll.

38

Each sheet column has a heading; heading names start with **A**, **B**, and so on. Each row has a heading, starting with **1**, **2**, and so on. The intersection of a row and column, called a *cell*, also has a name, which comes from combining the column number and row name, such as **C4** or **A1**. **A1** is always the top-left cell on any sheet. The gridlines throughout the sheet help you to distinguish between cells. The **Standard** toolbar, **Formatting** toolbar, and **Formula** bar offer quick access to common spreadsheet commands and options. Every cell in your spreadsheet contains a unique name or address to which you can refer when you are tabulating data. This name is called the ***cell reference***, and it is unique for each cell in the sheet. The active cell or cells are always highlighted with a dark border (**46 Edit Cell Data** shows how to select multiple cells). A cell's location, also known as its *reference*, appears in the Name Box.

▶ KEY TERM

Cell reference—The name of the cell, composed of its column and row intersection, such as **G14**. This is also called the *cell address*.

▶ NOTE

No matter how large your monitor is, you see only a small amount of the **Sheet Area**. Use the scrollbars to see or edit information in the off-screen cells, such as cell **M200**.

39 Set Calc Options

✔ BEFORE YOU BEGIN	→ SEE ALSO
38 About Sheets and Spreadsheets	**41** Open an Existing Spreadsheet
	46 Edit Cell Data

Not everybody works the same way, so not every Calc user wants to use Calc the same way. By setting some of Calc's many options, you will make Calc conform to the way you like to do things. For example, you may want Calc to hide the grid lines that normally distinguish between rows and columns to reduce onscreen clutter. If so, Calc has an option to display or hide the grid lines.

As a matter of fact, Calc has an option for just about anything! Table 6.1 describes Calc's options. You'll learn a lot about what Calc can do just by looking through the options available to you.

▶ **NOTE**

A Calc spreadsheet can contain up to 65,536 rows, the same number available in a Microsoft Excel sheet.

39

TABLE 6.1   Calc Spreadsheet Options

Calc Option Category	Explanation
General	Describes general Calc settings, such as the default unit of measurements and data-entry settings (see **42** **Enter Simple Data into a Spreadsheet**).
View	Describes how Calc appears on the screen and which Calc special elements (such as grid lines) appear by default.
Calculate	Describes how Calc displays dates and interprets search criteria when you search for data inside your spreadsheet (see **48** **Find and Replace Data**).
Sort Lists	Describes the sorting order for Calc's various lists of data, such as days of the week.
Changes	Describes how Calc interprets revisions that you or someone else makes to spreadsheets.
Grid	Describes the grid Calc uses so you can accurately place objects in your document exactly where you want them.
Print	Describes how Calc handles the printing of empty sheet pages (you can either print blank sheets or omit their printing). You can also control whether Calc can print only selected sheets or the entire spreadsheet.

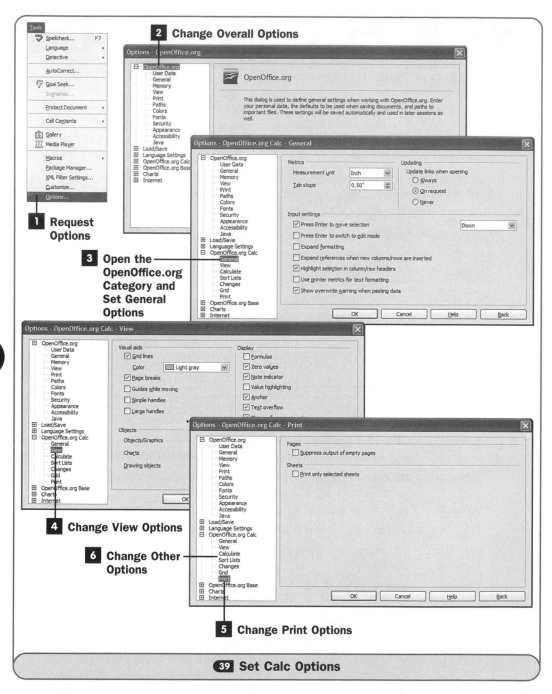

39 Set Calc Options

▶ **NOTE**

The placement grid described by the **Grid** option is not the row and column grid that you see in a sheet's background. The placement grid helps you accurately put objects such as graphics in a sheet exactly where you want them.

1 Request Options

Select **Options** from Calc's **Tools** menu. The **Options** dialog box appears. From the **Options** dialog box, you can change any of Calc's options as well as the options for the other OpenOffice.org programs.

▶ TIP

Often, you'll work in one OpenOffice.org program and realize that you need to change an overall option. For example, if you want to print several kinds of OpenOffice.org documents to a file (instead of to your printer) to send to others via email, you can change the **OpenOffice.org** option labeled **Print**, from within Calc, to apply that setting to all OpenOffice.org programs.

2 Change Overall Options

Select any option in the **OpenOffice.org** category to modify OpenOffice.org-wide settings, such as pathnames. For example, if you don't like the pathname you see when you open or save a file, click the **Paths** option and change it to a different default file path.

If you're new to OpenOffice.org, consider leaving all the OpenOffice.org options "as is" until you familiarize yourself with how the OpenOffice.org programs work.

3 Open the OpenOffice.org Calc Category and Set General Options

Click the plus sign next to the **OpenOffice.org Calc** option to display the seven Calc-specific options listed in Table 6.1, at the beginning of this task.

Click the **General** options category; the dialog box changes to show options you can select to make changes to the general Calc options. The **Metrics** section enables you to specify how you want to handle measurements and tab stops, such as in inches or metrically. The **Updating** section enables you to specify when Calc is to update links you put in a sheet, such as to a web page. The **Input settings** section enables you to specify how you want to enter data into spreadsheets, such as whether to move to the next cell when you press **Enter** or stay in the current cell.

4 Change View Options

Click the **View** category under the **OpenOffice.org Calc** category; the dialog box changes to show options that handle Calc's onscreen display. For example, you can hide and change the color of Calc's grid lines in the background of sheets from within the **Visual aids** section. The **Display** section determines how special values such as zeros, formulas, and anchors are to be shown. The

Objects section determines how Calc shows objects such as charts and graphics. The **Window** section specifies the display of various Calc screen elements, such as the scrollbars and sheet tabs, that contain the name of the sheets in the current spreadsheet.

5 Change Print Options

Click to select the **Print** category under the **OpenOffice.org Calc** category. Only two options appear: **Suppress output of empty pages** and **Print only selected sheets**. With a judicious use of these options, you can save a lot of paper in some documents if you don't print every blank page or all sheets in the spreadsheet.

6 Change Other Options

Continue viewing and changing the remaining options in the **OpenOffice.org Calc** category by first selecting the category and then looking at the individual options.

When you're done specifying Calc options, click the **OK** button to close the **Options** dialog box.

---

40 Create a New Spreadsheet

✔ BEFORE YOU BEGIN	→ SEE ALSO
38 About Sheets and Spreadsheets	**41** Open an Existing Spreadsheet
	42 Enter Simple Data into a Spreadsheet

Calc offers two ways to create new spreadsheets: You can create a completely blank, new spreadsheet (if you choose this approach, you must decide what to put in the spreadsheet and where that information should go), or you can use a spreadsheet template to open a preformatted spreadsheet. **16 About Styles and Templates** explains what templates are.

▶ NOTE

Unlike Writer, Wizards offer no help for creating spreadsheets.

▶ TIP

A quick way to start OpenOffice.org is to use the **QuickStarter** icon on the taskbar. Right-click this icon; from the context menu, choose any OpenOffice.org program to launch it, use a template, or load an existing document. The **QuickStarter** icon is available only if the **Load OpenOffice.org during system startup** option is enabled. To enable this option, select the **Memory** category in the **OpenOffice.org** options list in the **Options** dialog box of any OpenOffice.org program.

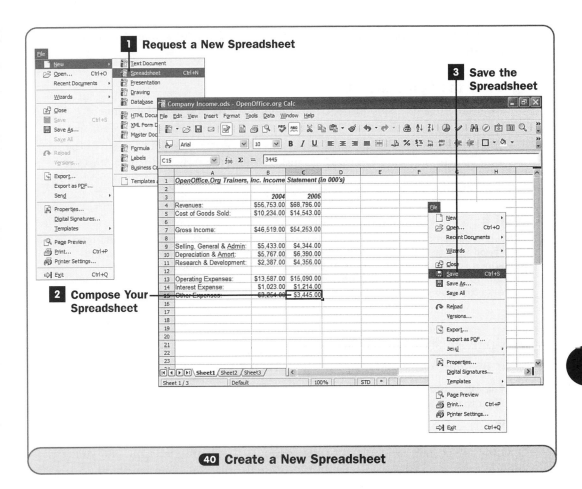

40 Create a New Spreadsheet

Although Calc does not come with templates when you first install OpenOffice.org, you can easily create a template to reuse later. This task shows you how to open a blank spreadsheet. **18** **Use a Template** explains how to create a new spreadsheet based on a template you may have created and saved previously.

1 Request a New Spreadsheet

Select **Spreadsheet** from the **File**, **New** menu option. Calc creates a blank spreadsheet. Alternatively, click the **New** toolbar button to open a new blank Calc spreadsheet quickly.

2 Compose Your Spreadsheet

Create your spreadsheet in the blank work area of cells that Calc gives you. You'll enter text, numbers, and formulas, depending on the needs of your spreadsheet. You can print your spreadsheet (see **46 Print a Spreadsheet**) at any time.

3 Save the Spreadsheet

After creating your spreadsheet, select **File, Save As** and type the name of your spreadsheet. Calc uses the filename extension `.ods` for your spreadsheet. You can select another file format, such as Microsoft Excel; doing so saves the spreadsheet with the `.xls` Excel extension. Other file formats include StarCalc (`.sdc`), Text CSV (`.csv`), and HTML (`.html`).

▶ **NOTE**

Although you can also use the **File, Save** command to save a new file for the first time, it's a good idea to use the **Save As** command. If you have already saved a file, using **Save** does not open the **Save As** dialog box but instead automatically saves any changes to the existing file—a problem if you were planning to save the file with a new name so that you could preserve the original file.

---

41 **Open an Existing Spreadsheet**

✔ **BEFORE YOU BEGIN**	→ **SEE ALSO**
38 About Sheets and Spreadsheets **40** Create a New Spreadsheet	**46** Edit Cell Data

Opening an existing spreadsheet to edit in Calc is simple. You tell Calc that you want to open a spreadsheet file and then locate the file. Calc then loads the spreadsheet into the editing area.

One important Calc feature is its ability to open documents you create in other spreadsheet programs. Most notably, Calc opens Microsoft Excel spreadsheets (called *workbooks* in Excel) with ease. Although Calc might not fully support 100% of Microsoft Excel's advanced features, Calc does a super job of loading Excel spreadsheets into Calc's workspace so that you can edit the spreadsheets using Calc's interface.

▶ **NOTE**

Microsoft Excel uses the `.xls` file extension. You'll see any Excel spreadsheets that reside in the folder you open from within Calc along with any other files that also appear in that folder.

1 Request a Spreadsheet

Select **Open** from the Calc **File** menu to display the **Open** dialog box.

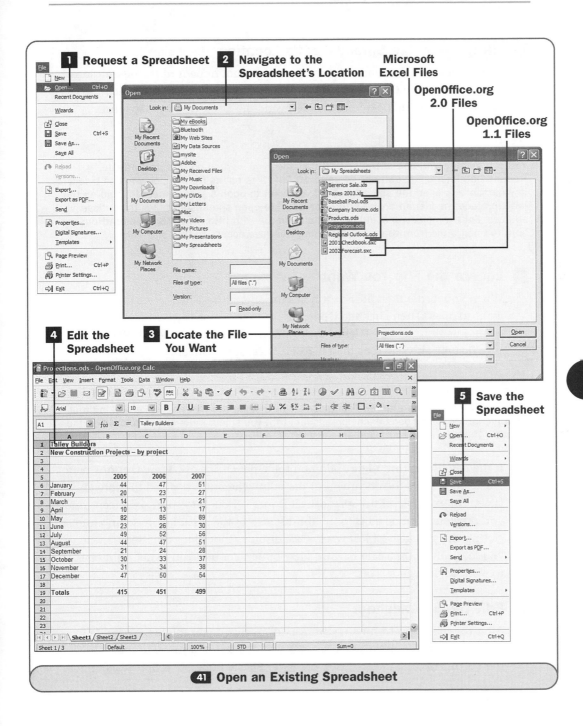

1 Request a Spreadsheet

2 Navigate to the Spreadsheet's Location

Microsoft Excel Files

OpenOffice.org 2.0 Files

OpenOffice.org 1.1 Files

4 Edit the Spreadsheet

3 Locate the File You Want

5 Save the Spreadsheet

41

41 Open an Existing Spreadsheet

2 Navigate to the Spreadsheet's Location

The spreadsheet that you want to open might not appear at the default location shown in the **Open** dialog box, so navigate to the folder in which the spreadsheet you're looking for resides using the **Look in** drop-down list.

▶ **TIP**

You can quickly load one of the last 10 Calc files you worked on by selecting **File, Recent Documents**; a submenu of up to 10 Calc files opens from which you can select any filename to open the spreadsheet. If you want to open a spreadsheet located on the Web, preface the filename with http:// or ftp:// to open spreadsheet files from those sources. For example, you could preface a filename with http://www.SimpleRentHouses. com to open a file from that site (assuming you have access to that site's files).

3 Locate the File You Want

When you locate the folder that holds the spreadsheet file, select the file you want to open. Then click the **Open** button to open the selected file in Calc's editing workspace. The **Files of type** option enables you to select files of a specific type only, such as the Microsoft Excel spreadsheets.

▶ **TIP**

Feel free to open more than one spreadsheet by holding the **Ctrl** key while clicking multiple filenames. Calc opens each spreadsheet that you select in its own window. Use the **Window** menu to select an open spreadsheet to edit.

If the default **Editing view** option on the **OpenOffice.org View Options** page is set, Calc opens the document at the point where it last saved the spreadsheet. For example, if the spreadsheet is large enough to span six screens and you previously made edits to the third screen of the sheet before saving and closing the spreadsheet last week, Calc displays that place on screen 3 where you last quit editing. The **Editing view** option enables you to get right back to work where you left off.

4 Edit the Spreadsheet

After the file opens in the Calc workspace, you can edit the file. Navigate to where you wish to make edits (see **46 Edit Cell Data**) or move to the end of the document and add to it (see **42 Enter Simple Data into a Spreadsheet**).

5 Save the Spreadsheet

Once you've made all the changes you wish to make, select **File, Save** to save your spreadsheet. Your recent changes will be saved in the spreadsheet file for your next editing session.

42   Enter Simple Data into a Spreadsheet

✔ BEFORE YOU BEGIN	→ SEE ALSO
40 Create a New Spreadsheet	**46** Edit Cell Data
41 Open an Existing Spreadsheet	**47** Print a Spreadsheet

Often, entering worksheet data requires nothing more than clicking the correct cell to select it and then typing the data. The various kinds of data behave differently when entered, however, so you should understand how Calc accepts assorted data.

Calc works with the following kinds of data:

- **Labels**—Text values such as names and addresses, as well as date and time values.

- **Numbers**—Numeric values such as 34, –291, 545.67874, and 0.

- **Dates and times**—Calc accepts date and time values that you type in virtually any format.

- **Formulas**—Expressions that compute numeric results. (Some formulas work with text values as well.)

This task walks you through a short editing session just to give you a feel for entering data into a Calc sheet. Keep in mind that Calc's interface is different from most other programs you may have worked with, unless you've worked with electronic spreadsheet programs before. Having said that, some of the editing skills you acquire in one OpenOffice.org program apply to the other OpenOffice.org programs as well. For example, both Calc and Writer offer the capability to display or hide the **Standard** toolbar. The **Standard** toolbar changes slightly depending on which program you use, but most of its functions are similar across the OpenOffice.org programs.

1   Move the Active Cell

Click cell **D5** to make **D5** the active cell. The cell's dark outline indicates that the cell is selected. Also, the cell name appears in the **Sheet Area**.

2   Type Text in the Cell

Type `ABC Co.` into cell **D5**. To enter the text, simply type the text, and it appears both in the cell as well as in the **Input** line toward the top of the screen. When you press **Enter**, the active cell moves down one row. Instead of **Enter**, you can press the **right arrow** button or **Tab**, and the cell to the right of the cell becomes active next.

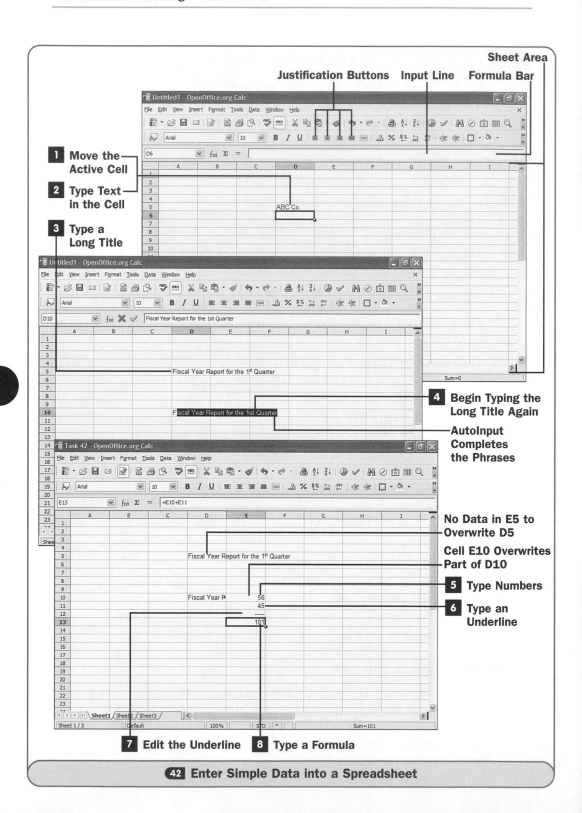

42

1 Move the Active Cell

2 Type Text in the Cell

3 Type a Long Title

4 Begin Typing the Long Title Again

AutoInput Completes the Phrases

No Data in E5 to Overwrite D5

Cell E10 Overwrites Part of D10

5 Type Numbers

6 Type an Underline

7 Edit the Underline

8 Type a Formula

Sheet Area

Justification Buttons   Input Line   Formula Bar

42 Enter Simple Data into a Spreadsheet

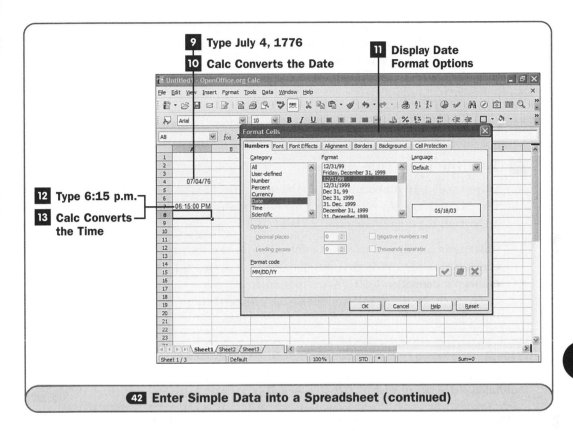

9 Type July 4, 1776

10 Calc Converts the Date

11 Display Date Format Options

12 Type 6:15 p.m.

13 Calc Converts the Time

42 Enter Simple Data into a Spreadsheet (continued)

By default, text always appears left-justified in a cell, although you can click one of the justification buttons to center or right-justify text in a cell. To correct a mistake, press **Backspace** and type the corrected text.

▶ **NOTE**

You can change the action of the **Enter** key from the **Options, OpenOffice.org Calc, General** dialog box page.

If you press the **Esc** button at any point during text entry but before you move to another cell, Calc erases the text you typed in the cell and restores the original cell. In addition, you can press **Ctrl+Z** (for undo) or click the **Undo** button to back up to a cell's previous state.

3 **Type a Long Title**

Replace the text in cell **D5** by typing Fiscal Year Report for the 1st Quarter. As you type, the text spills into cells **E5**, **F5**, and finally ends in **G5**. The important thing to note is that only cell **D5** holds the text value Fiscal Year Report for the 1st Quarter. Although it *looks* as though pieces of the title spill into the cells to the right, Calc is showing the full text in cell **D5** because no values appear to the right of **D5**. If any data resided in cells **E5**, **F5**, or **G5**, Calc would *not* have shown the full value in **D5**.

▶ **TIP**

You'll see that when you type 1st, Calc's AutoCorrect feature converts it to 1ˢᵗ.

4 **Type the Long Title Again**

Move to cell **D10** and begin typing the same title, Fiscal Year Report for the 1st Quarter. As with cell **D5**, the full text shows because nothing appears in the cells to the right of **D10**.

Calc automatically completes the entry thanks to a feature called **AutoInput**, which is similar to Writer's AutoComplete feature (see **31** **About Writer's Automatic Correction Tools**). AutoInput matches your text to input found elsewhere in the column. You can accept the proposed completion by pressing **Enter** or ignore the suggestion and continue typing.

42

▶ **TIPS**

To turn the AutoInput feature on and off, choose **Tools**, **Cell Contents** and then click the **AutoInput** check box to enable or disable the option.

Instead of typing the title twice, you could select the title and click **Copy** (or press **Ctrl+C**). You then could paste the title where you want it by clicking the cell and then clicking **Paste** (or pressing **Ctrl+V**).

If you ever want to see the full content of a cell that contains more data than can be displayed, click the cell and view its contents in the Formula bar.

5 **Type Numbers**

Type the following numeric values into cells **E10** and **E11**, respectively: **56** and **45**. You'll see that as soon as you type cell **E10**'s value, the long text in cell **D10** no longer displays. The long text is still in cell **D10**, but Calc doesn't display the text because then you would be unable to see the number in cell **E10**. Instead, it displays a small red triangle at the end of the cell to indicate that the cell contains more data than there is room to display.

Calc usually recognizes any entry that begins with an alphabetical character as text. Some textual data, such as price codes, telephone numbers, and ZIP Codes can fool Calc into thinking you are entering numeric data because of the initial numeric value. Calc treats numeric data differently from text data when you type the data into cells. If you want Calc to treat a number (such as a ZIP Code) as a text entry so that it does not perform calculations on the cell, precede the contents with a single apostrophe ('). For example, to type the ZIP Code 74137, type '74137; the apostrophe lets Calc know to format the value as text. Knowing this enables you to enter text-based numbers such as ZIP Codes and product codes that require a leading zero. Without the quote, Calc interprets a value with a leading zero as a number and removes the zero and right-justifies the number.

Also notice that, unlike text values, Calc right-justifies numeric values. You'll also see when you enter formulas that Calc right-justifies the results of those formulas.

6 Type an Underline

You can put a line, composed of dashes, below the two numbers you just entered. Type — — · in cell **D7** and press **Enter**. The dashed line doesn't look correct because Calc left-justified the line since the line is not numeric but text.

7 Edit the Underline

Click cell **D7** to make it active. Then click the **Align Right** button that resides in the group of justification buttons and Calc right-justifies the underline.

8 Type a Formula

Type =E10+E11 in cell **E13**. You've just typed your first formula in Calc. The moment you press **Enter**, Calc displays the formula's answer instead of the formula itself.

Click cell **E13** to make it active again. You'll see the formula in the **Input** line. So when you click a formula's cell, Calc shows you both the formula and the value. If you want to change the formula, either press **F2** to display the formula once again inside the cell itself or click to edit the formula in the **Input** line.

▶ **NOTE**

For now, do not make changes to the formula but rather click cell **E13** and press **F2**. Calc colorizes the formula and highlights each formula value's cell so you can easily see the cells that comprise the formula. Press **Enter** to keep the current value.

9 Type July 4, 1776

Type July 4, 1776 in cell **A4**.

42

🔟 Calc Converts the Date

Press **Enter** and Calc converts your date to a different format. Calc converts the date to **07/04/76**. Calc does retain the date's full value inside the cell, and only the date's display appears in the *mm/dd/yy* format.

🔟 Display Date Format Options

Calc supports almost every national and international date and time format. To determine which format Calc is to display dates (and times) in, select **Format**, **Cells**, click the **Numbers** tab, and then click the **Date** entry under **Category**. You can change the way Calc displays any cell's date by modifying its format. **60 Format Cells** goes into detail about how to format cells. Click OK to close the dialog box.

🔟 Type 6:15 p.m.

Type 6:15 p.m. in cell **A7**.

🔟 Calc Converts the Time

Press **Enter** and Calc converts your time to a different format. Calc converts the time to **06:15:00 PM**, the time's full value in the *hh:mm:ss AM/PM* format.

▶ **NOTE**

Type the **am** or **pm** designation when entering time values or enter the time using a 24-hour clock. Either **6:15 pm** or **18:15** work to enter the same time in the cell.

---

43 About Moving Around Calc

✔ BEFORE YOU BEGIN	→ SEE ALSO
41 Enter Simple Data into a Spreadsheet	**43** About Calc Formulas

---

Your mouse and arrow keys are the primary means of navigating keys for moving from cell to cell in sheets. Unlike Writer, which uses an insertion point, Calc uses its active cell, the highlighted cell, to indicate your current position in the sheet.

▶ **NOTE**

If you select multiple cells, the selection is considered to be a single set of active cells.

The active cell has a darkened border around it and accepts whatever data you enter. As you press an arrow key, Calc moves the cell pointer in the direction of the arrow to a new cell, making the new cell the active one. Once you begin typing inside a cell, the insertion point appears.

If you're working with a rather large sheet, you might find the **Navigator** dialog box useful. Press **F5** to display the **Navigator** dialog box, where you can select a range of cells that you might have previously named or enter a cell address, such as **C141**, to jump to that cell. You may also click any object in the **Navigator** dialog box, such as a sheet name, or select a range name to jump to.

**Click to Display
Specific Items**

Use the Navigator dialog box to move around a spreadsheet efficiently.

Table 6.2 lists the most commonly used navigational keystrokes within Calc. Use your mouse to scroll with the scrollbars.

TABLE 6.2   Using the Keyboard to Navigate Calc

Press This Key...	To Move
Arrow keys	The direction of the arrow, one cell at a time
Ctrl+up arrow, Ctrl+down arrow	The topmost or bottommost cell that contains data or, if at the end of the range already, the next cell that contains data or, if no cells above or below contain data, the top or bottom cell in the column
Ctrl+left arrow, Ctrl+right arrow	The leftmost or rightmost cell that contains data or, if at the end of the range already, the next cell that contains data, or, if no cells to the left or right contain data, the leftmost or rightmost cell in the row
PageUp, PageDown	The previous or next screen of the worksheet
Ctrl+Home	The upper-left corner of the worksheet (cell A1)
Ctrl+PageUp, Ctrl+PageDown	The next or previous sheet within the current spreadsheet
Ctrl+End	The bottom-right corner of the current range containing data

43

44   About Calc Formulas

✔ BEFORE YOU BEGIN	→ SEE ALSO
38 About Sheets and Spreadsheets	**45** Copy and Move Formulas

Without *formulas*, Calc would be little more than a simple row-and-column-based word processor. When you use formulas, however, Calc becomes an extremely powerful timesaving, planning, budgeting, and general-purpose financial tool.

▶ KEY TERM

Formulas—Equations composed of numeric values and often cell addresses and range names that produce a mathematical result.

On a calculator, you typically type a formula and then press the equal sign to see the result. In contrast, all Calc formulas begin with an equal sign. For example, the following is a formula:

=4*2-3

The asterisk is an operator that denotes the times sign (multiplication). This formula requests that Calc compute the value of 4 multiplied by 2 minus 3 to get the result. When you type a formula and press **Enter** or move to another cell, Calc displays the result and not the formula on the worksheet.

When you enter =4*2-3 in a cell, the answer 5 appears in the cell when you move away from the cell. You can see the formula in the Input line atop the sheet if you click the cell again to make it active. When entering a formula, as soon as you press the equal sign, Calc shows your formula in the **Input** line area as well as in the active cell. If you click the **Input** line first and then finish your formula there, the formula appears in the **Input** line as well as in the active cell. By typing the formula in the **Input** line, you can press the **left-** and **right-arrow** keys to move the cell pointer left and right within the formula to edit it.

Table 6.3 lists the primary math operators you can use in your worksheet formulas. Notice that all the sample formulas begin with the equal sign.

TABLE 6.3   The Primary Math Operators Specify Math Calculations

Operator	Example	Description
^	=7 ^ 3	Raises 7 to the power of 3 (called *exponentiation*)
/	=4 / 2	Divides 4 by 2
*	=3 * 4 * 5	Multiplies 3 by 4 by 5
+	=5 + 5	Adds 5 and 5
−	=5 - 5	Subtracts 5 from 5

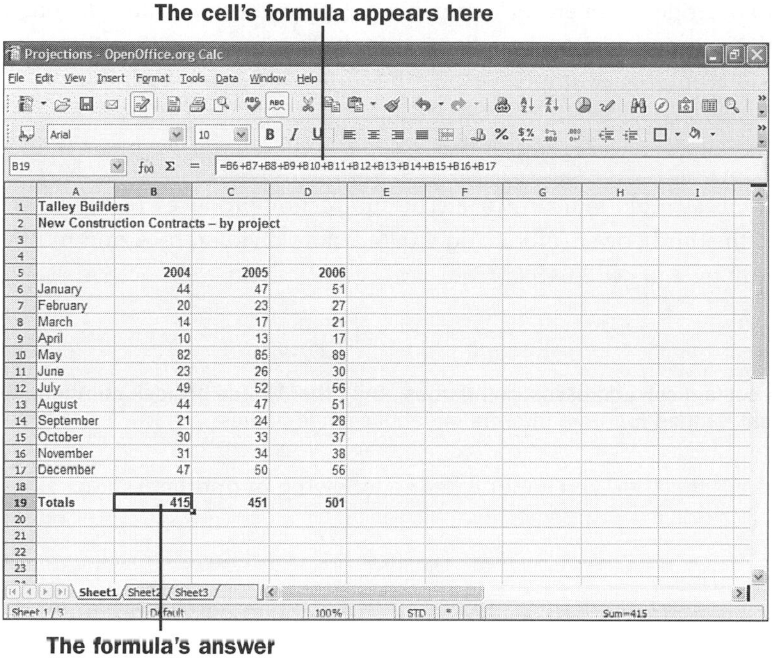

The cell's formula appears here

The formula's answer

Calc displays a formula's result in the cell.

44

You can combine any and all the operators in a formula. When combining operators, Calc follows the traditional computer (and algebraic) *operator hierarchy model*. Therefore, Calc first computes exponentiation if you raise any value to another power. Calc then calculates all multiplication and division in a left-to-right order (the first one to appear computes first) before addition and subtraction (also in left-to-right order).

▶ KEY TERM

Operator hierarchy model—A predefined order of operators when equations are being calculated.

The following formula returns a result of 14 because Calc first calculates the exponentiation of 2 raised to the third power and then divides the answer (8) by 4, multiplies the result (2) by 2, and finally subtracts the result (4) from 18. Even though the subtraction appears first, the operator hierarchy forces the subtraction to wait until last to compute.

`=18 - 2 ^ 3 / 4 * 2`

If you want to override the operator hierarchy, put parentheses around the parts you want Calc to compute first. The following formula returns a different result from the previous one, for example, despite the same values and operators used:

```
=(18 - 2) ^ 3 / 4 * 2
```

Instead of 14, this formula returns 2,048! The subtraction produces 16, which is then raised to the third power (producing 4,096) before dividing by 4 and multiplying the result by 2 to get 2,048.

▶ NOTE

Formulas can contain cell addresses, cell names, and other values besides numbers. See **49 About Calc Ranges** for more information about range names.

To add three cells together, you could type the following in another cell:

```
=D3+K10+M7
```

Calc adds the values in **D3**, **K10**, and **M7** and shows the result in place of the formula. The cells **D3**, **K10**, and **M7** can also contain formulas that reference other cells.

45

45	**Copy and Move Formulas**

✔ BEFORE YOU BEGIN	→ SEE ALSO
44 About Calc Formulas	**50** Create a Range

You can copy, move, and paste one cell into another using standard copy-and-paste tools such as the Windows Clipboard. When you copy formulas that contain cell addresses, Calc updates the cell references so they become *relative references*. For example, suppose that you enter this formula in cell **A1**:

▶ KEY TERM

Relative reference—A cell that is referenced in relation to the current cell.

```
=A2 + A3
```

This formula contains two cell references. The references are relative because the references **A2** and **A3** change if you copy the formula elsewhere. If you copy the formula to cell **B5**, for example, **B5** holds this:

```
=B6 + B7
```

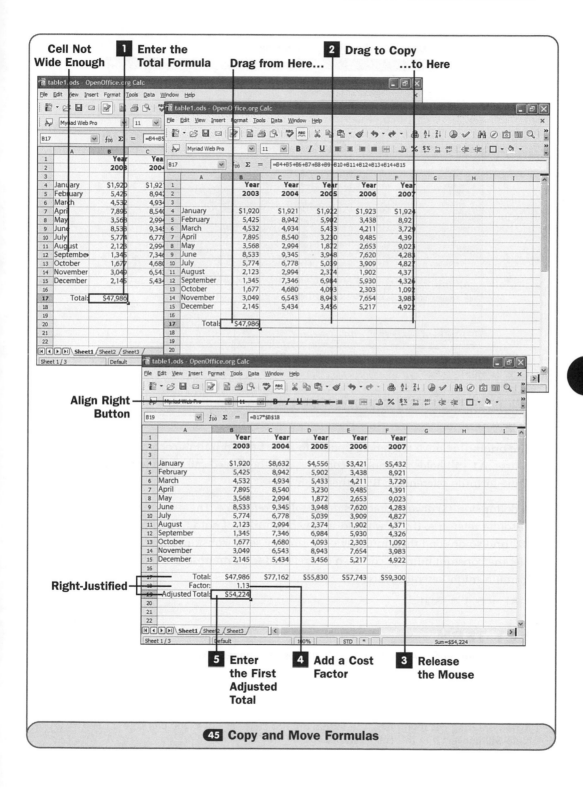

Cell Not Wide Enough

1 Enter the Total Formula

Drag from Here...

2 Drag to Copy

...to Here

Align Right Button

Right-Justified

5 Enter the First Adjusted Total

4 Add a Cost Factor

3 Release the Mouse

45 Copy and Move Formulas

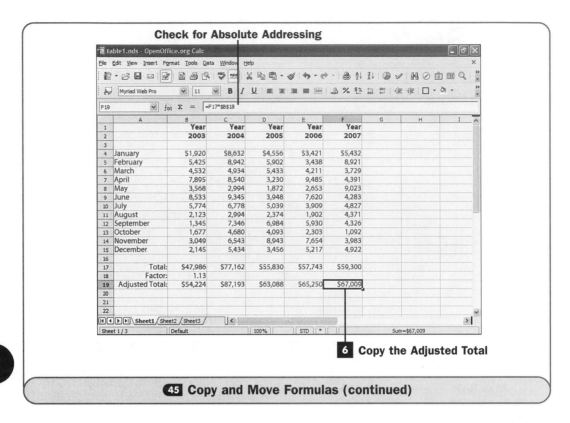

Check for Absolute Addressing

6 Copy the Adjusted Total

45 Copy and Move Formulas (continued)

45

The original relative references update to reflect the formula's copied location. Of course, **A1** still holds its original contents, but the copied cell at **B5** holds the same formula referencing **B5** rather than **A1**.

A dollar sign ($) always precedes an *absolute reference*. The reference **B5** is an absolute reference. If you want to sum two columns of data (**A1** with **B1**, **A2** with **B2**, and so on) and then multiply each sum by some constant number, for example, the constant number can be a cell referred to as an *absolute reference*. That formula might resemble this:

```
=(A1 + B1) * $J$1
```

▶ KEY TERM

Absolute reference—A cell reference that does not change if you copy the formula elsewhere.

▶ TIP

When entering cell references, the letters are not case-sensitive. You can type **a3** and Calc will convert it to the cell reference **A3**.

In this case, **J1** is an absolute reference, but **A1** and **B1** are relative. If you copy the formula down one row, the formula changes to this:

```
=(A2 + B2) * $J$1
```

Notice that the first two cells changed because when you originally entered them, they were relative cell references. You told Calc, by placing dollar signs in front of the absolute cell reference's row and column references, not to change that reference when you copy the formula elsewhere.

$B5 is a partial absolute cell reference. If you copy a formula with **$B5** inside the computation, the **$B** keeps the **B** column intact, but the fifth row updates to the row location of the target cell. For example, if you type the formula

```
=2 * $B5
```

in cell **A1** and then copy the formula to cell **F6**, cell **F6** holds this formula:

```
=2 * $B10
```

You copied the formula to a cell five rows and five columns over in the worksheet. Calc did not update the column name, **B**, because you told Calc to keep that column name absolute. (It is always **B** no matter where you copy the formula.) Calc added five to the row number, however, because the row number is relative and open to change whenever you copy the formula.

▶ **TIP**

Most of the time, you'll use relative referencing. If you insert or delete rows, columns, or cells, your formulas remain accurate because the cells that they reference change as your worksheet changes.

1 **Enter the Total Formula**

For this sheet, assume you want a formula for each past year and projected year into the future. You would type the formula to total the first year in cell **B17**. One formula that would total this year would be

```
=B4 + B5 + B6 + B7 + B8 + B9 + B10 + B11 + B12 + B13 + B14 + B15
```

▶ **TIP**

There are several better ways to total a column. The most tedious but easiest to understand is this step's way. One better way would be to type this formula: =Sum(B4:B15). **52** **About Calc Functions** explores Sum() and other Calc functions.

45

Notice that cell **A12** does not display all of the month of September's name. The column is not wide enough to display the full month. Calc warns you that this cell's contents aren't fully displayed with a small triangle along the right side of the cell. You can widen cells like this that you find are too narrow by dragging the dividing line between the name of column **A** and column **B** to the right to give every month name enough room to display properly.

A quick way to resize a column to ensure that it is wide enough for all its data is to double-click the column divider between the column you want to widen and the one on its right. Calc automatically resizes the column width to hold the widest value in the column.

2 Drag to Copy

Once you type a formula in cell **B17**, you can copy that cell to the Windows **Clipboard** with **Ctrl+C** and then paste the cell into **C17**, then **D17**, then **E17**, and finally **F17**. Calc offers an easier way though. Drag the lower-right corner of cell **B17**, where you'll see a small square, to the right, and Calc highlights each empty cell along the way as you copy.

45

▶ **NOTE**

When you drag your mouse across multiple cells, you are indicating a range that you want to work with.

3 Release the Mouse

Once you release your mouse button over cell **F17**, you will see that Calc totals all five columns for you where you copied the total formula.

▶ **NOTE**

Look at the Input line for cell **F17**. You'll see that Calc copied the formula from **B17** using relative addressing. It wouldn't make sense to put the total for column **B** in cell **F17**. When Calc saw that you wanted to copy the formula, and because the formula contains relative cell references, Calc copied the formula as though it referred to cells relative to **B17**.

4 Add a Cost Factor

To demonstrate absolute cell addressing, add a cost factor of 1.13 below **Year 2002**'s total. You then can multiply the total to create an adjusted total in cell **B19**. If you also want to multiply the remaining totals by the adjustment factor, you *cannot* use relative addressing for the cost factor. In other words, if you multiply cell **B17** by cell **B18** and store the result in **B19** with the formula =B17*B18, and then copy that formula to cell **C19**, cell **C19** would hold this formula: =C17*C18. However, **C18** is blank! So Calc would multiply **C17** by zero, which is not the correct adjustment factor.

▶ **NOTE**

The figure's cells are formatted to display dollar signs in some places and not in others. **60** **Format Cells** explains how to format cells the way you want them to look. The labels for **Factor** and **Adjusted Total** are right-justified (with the **Align Right** button); however, they first enter their respective cells left-justified because they contain text.

5 Enter the First Adjusted Total

To enter the correct adjusted total in cell **B19**, you would type =B17 * B18.

By using absolute addressing in cell **B18** (that is, **B18**), when you copy it to the remaining years, all the cells you copy to will also use **B18** instead of a different cell for the factor.

▶ **TIP**

You don't need to leave spaces between operators such as multiplication (*) in formulas. Doing so makes them easier to read and to check for errors, however.

45

6 Copy the Adjusted Total

To copy the adjusted total to the other years, you can use **Ctrl+C** and then paste with **Ctrl+V** into each year's adjusted total cell, but it's simpler just to drag the small square in the first cell's lower-right corner (the mouse pointer changes to a plus sign when you point to this square) across through the cells that are to receive the copied formula.

When you release your mouse after making such a copy with one or more absolute cell addresses in the range, the absolute address remains the same and the relative addresses inside the cells change. This sounds less obvious than it is. In other words, when you copy the formula =B17 * B18 to cell **C19**, cell **C19** gets this formula: =C17 * B18. Cell **D19** gets =D17 * B18, and so on.

▶ **NOTE**

You can make only the row or only the column of a cell address absolute. In the cell reference **M$15**, the column named **M** is relative and will change if you copy a cell that contains this reference elsewhere, but the absolute row number, **$15**, will not change.

46   Edit Cell Data

✔ BEFORE YOU BEGIN	→ SEE ALSO
42 Enter Simple Data into a Spreadsheet	**49** About Calc Ranges

Entering numeric data is error-prone at its best; the faster you edit cell values accurately, the faster you compose accurate sheets. If you have already moved to another cell when you recognize that you have entered an error, you can quickly correct the mistake as follows:

1. Move the cell pointer to the cell you need to correct. (Click the cell to move the pointer there.)

2. Double-click in the cell, or press **F2** (the standard Windows editing shortcut key). You know Calc is ready for your edit when you see the insertion point appear in the cell. You can also click and edit the **Input** line to change the cell's contents.

3. Use the **arrow keys** to move the insertion point to the mistake.

4. Press the **Insert** key to change from Overtype mode to Insert mode, or vice versa. As with Writer, Overtype mode enables you to write over existing characters, whereas Insert mode shifts all existing characters to the right as you type the correction.

5. Press **Enter** to anchor the correction in place.

▶ **TIP**

If you want to reverse an edit, click the **Undo** button. To reverse an undo, select **Edit**, **Redo**.

Inserting cells, as opposed to inserting data inside a cell, requires that the existing sheet cells move to the right and down to make room for the new cell. Perhaps you created a sheet of employee salaries and failed to include the employees who work at another division. You can easily make room for those missing entries by inserting new cells. You can insert both new rows and new columns in your sheets.

Use the **Delete Contents** dialog box not only to delete cells but also to delete entire rows and columns.

▶ **TIP**

If you want to delete multiple rows or multiple columns, select cells from each column or row you want to delete before displaying the **Delete Contents** dialog box.

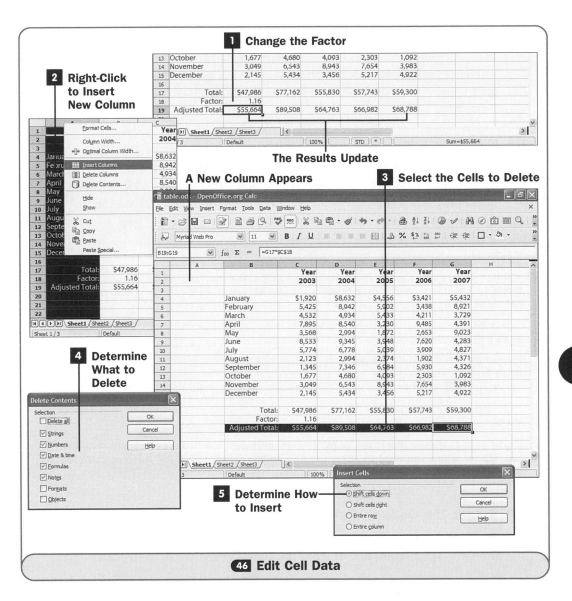

1 Change the Factor

2 Right-Click to Insert New Column

The Results Update

A New Column Appears

3 Select the Cells to Delete

4 Determine What to Delete

5 Determine How to Insert

46 Edit Cell Data

46

Deleting rows and columns differs from deleting specific contents inside cells. When you want to erase a cell's specific contents, the other cells to the right and below that cell don't shift to fill in the empty space. To erase a cell's contents, click the cell to move the cell pointer there and press **F2** to edit the cell's contents. Press **Backspace** to erase the cell. Even quicker, you can press **Ctrl+X** or select **Edit**, **Cut** to remove the contents and send them to the Clipboard, where you can paste them elsewhere or ignore them.

1 Change the Factor

To change the factor, you click cell **B18** and press **F2** to enter editing mode. You'll see the insertion point at the end of the cell's contents. Press **Backspace** once to erase the 3 and then type 6. Press **Enter**. You have just changed the factor from **1.13** to **1.16**.

2 Right-Click to Insert New Column

To insert a column before another, click a column name that is to *follow* the new column. Then right-click your mouse and a menu appears. Select **Insert Columns** (even if you want to insert only one column). Calc moves the sheet's contents to the right by one column.

▶ **TIP**

You can just as easily insert more than one column. For example, if you want to insert three new columns, select three column names that are to *follow* the new columns before selecting the **Insert Columns** option. Calc inserts three columns.

▶ **NOTE**

46

If a column contains any merged cells, you will not be able to insert a new column. You must first reverse the merge, insert the desired columns, and then merge the cells again. See **71** **Combine Multiple Cells into One** for more information on merging cells.

▶ **TIP**

If you want to quickly insert two or more columns, select the two (or more) columns *to the right* of where you want to insert the new columns. Right-click the selected columns. Calc inserts that same number of new columns.

3 Select the Cells to Delete

To delete the contents of one or more cells, click to select the cell or drag your mouse to select multiple cells. Press the **Delete** key to delete the contents.

4 Determine What to Delete

Calc opens the **Delete Contents** dialog box. You can select what from the cell you want to delete. Usually, you'll immediately press **Enter** or click **OK** to delete the data from the cells you selected. Doing this maintains any formatting in the cells you deleted.

You can remove the formatting as well by clicking **Formats** in the **Delete Contents** dialog box before clicking **OK**. Or, you can remove only the formatting but keep all the data. The options you select before performing the deletion determine exactly what you want to delete.

5 Determine How to Insert

To insert a cell before another, you must first consider the implications of what you're doing. Other cells reside in the sheet. If, for example, you wanted to insert a cell before the final **Adjusted Total** value, how is Calc supposed to handle the value that's in the cell? Should Calc delete it, move it to the right, or move it down?

If other data were to appear to the right of a cell you try to insert, you must tell Calc how to handle the insertion. When you click to select a cell (or drag to select a range of cells) and select **Insert**, **Cells**, the **Insert Cells** dialog box appears. From the dialog box, you tell Calc whether you want the cells to the right of the newly inserted cell to shift down or to the right, or if you want the entire row or the entire column moved so that all the data in the affected row or column moves.

▶ **TIP**

If you were to insert four quarter values after each year in this sample sheet, you would want to shift the entire columns to the right as you insert the quarterly data to retain all the year information appropriately.

47	**Print a Spreadsheet**
✔ **BEFORE YOU BEGIN**	→ **SEE ALSO**
40 Create a New Spreadsheet **41** Open an Existing Spreadsheet	**62** Set Up Calc Page Formatting

Once you're done creating your spreadsheet, you'll want to print it to paper. Calc supports the standard printing options that most Windows programs support. If your document has color charts and you have a color printer, the charts will print just fine. Otherwise, the charts will print in shades of black and gray (and still look fine!).

Be sure to save your spreadsheet before you print it. Actually, it's a good idea to select **File**, **Save** to save your work throughout the editing of your sheets. If your printer jams or the Windows print queue messes up during the printing process (rare, but it can happen), you could lose the changes you made to the spreadsheet before you printed it.

▶ **TIP**

If you select **File**, **Export as PDF**, Calc saves your document in the common PDF format, which you can send to any computer that has Adobe Acrobat Reader installed. See **36** **Save a Document as a PDF File** for more information about PDF files.

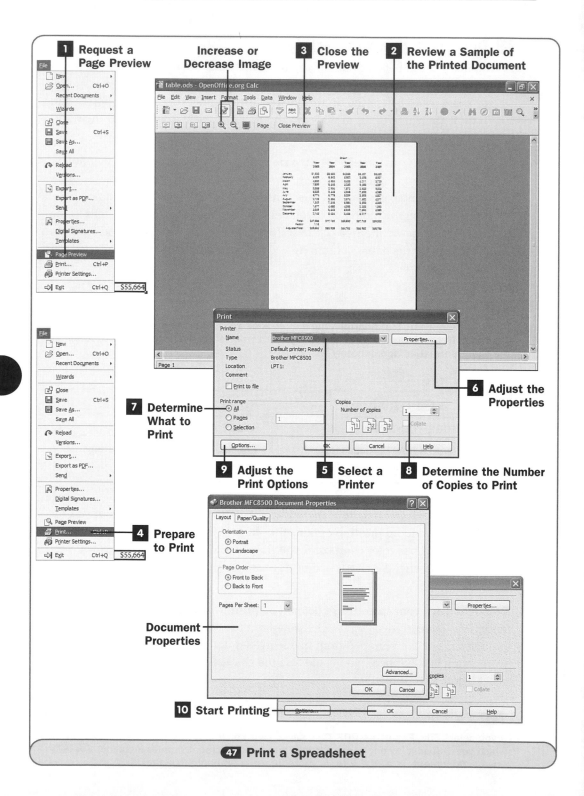

1 Request a Page Preview

Increase or Decrease Image

3 Close the Preview

2 Review a Sample of the Printed Document

6 Adjust the Properties

7 Determine What to Print

9 Adjust the Print Options

5 Select a Printer

8 Determine the Number of Copies to Print

Document Properties

4 Prepare to Print

10 Start Printing

47 Print a Spreadsheet

Before you print, consider looking at the **Page Style** dialog box by selecting **Format, Page** and then clicking the **Sheet** tab. From the **Sheet** page, you can specify whether you want to print using any of the following options:

- **Top to bottom, then right**—Prints the sheet down one column at a time.

- **Left to right, then down**—Prints the sheet across one row at a time.

- **Spreadsheet elements**—Requests the printing of any or all of the following: column and row headers, the sheet's grid, notes, graphics, charts, formulas (instead of their results), and zero values (instead of blanks).

- **Scaling**—Use this option to reduce the size of the printout to fit on one page (if the sheet is small enough) and to specify exactly how many pages you want Calc to attempt to print the sheet to. The scaling options often enable you to squeeze a sheet that's larger than a single page onto one printed page.

▶ **TIP**

If your sheet produces errors, you might want to print it with the formulas showing so you can more easily locate the problem in the sheet.

1 Request a Page Preview

Select the **Page Preview** option from the **File** menu. Calc shows you the current sheet. A **Page Preview** toolbar opens, offering one-click access to common previewing tasks such as zooming in or out, viewing the **Page Style** dialog box, and closing this view. If you want to print a different sheet, you need to click that sheet name before selecting **File, Page Preview**. It's easy to forget that a spreadsheet can have multiple sheets. When one does, you'll preview (and print) each sheet individually.

2 Review a Sample of the Printed Document

Look over the preview of the sheet to see if it appears to be properly formatted. Click the **Zoom In** or **Zoom Out** button to increase or decrease the preview.

3 Close the Preview

Once you've previewed what your sheet will look like printed, click the **Close Preview** button on the Page Preview toolbar. If you need to make further edits to your sheet, do so now.

4 Prepare to Print

Once you're satisfied that the sheet is ready to print, select the **Print** option from the **File** menu. The **Print** dialog box appears.

▶ **TIP**

To print immediately, click the **Print** button on the **Standard** toolbar. Calc does not open the **Print** dialog box but instead prints the document immediately using the current default print settings.

5 Select a Printer

Select the printer you want to print to using the **Name** drop-down list.

▶ **TIP**

If you have a fax modem, you can select your fax from the **Name** list to send your document to a fax recipient.

6 Adjust the Properties

If you want to adjust any printer settings, click the **Properties** button. The dialog box that appears when you click **Properties** varies from printer to printer. Close the printer's **Properties** dialog box once you've made any needed changes.

7 Determine What to Print

Click to select either **All** or **Pages** to designate that you want to print the entire sheet or only a portion of it. If you clicked **Pages**, type the page number or a range of page numbers (such as **2-5** or **1-10, 15-25**) that you want to print.

8 Determine the Number of Copies to Print

Click the arrow button next to the **Number of Copies** option to determine how many copies you want to print.

9 Adjust the Print Options

Click the **Options** button to display the **Printer Options** dialog box. From the **Printer Options** dialog box, you can adjust several print settings, such as whether you want graphics, tables, and drawings printed or omitted from the printed sheet.

47

► **NOTE**

Although it's called the **Printer Options** dialog box, this dialog box is not printer specific but rather controls the way your document appears when printed. If, for instance, you want to print for a binder, you can click to select the **Left pages** and **Right pages** options to leave an extra middle margin on every other printed page.

Click the **OK** button to close the **Printer Options** dialog box.

10 Start Printing

Once you've determined how many pages and copies to print, click the **OK** button to print your sheet and close the **Print** dialog box.

7

Working with Calc Data

IN THIS CHAPTER:

This chapter teaches you how to manage and organize your Calc spreadsheets to make them really work for you. You'll be surprised how Calc follows and updates formulas as you modify worksheet data. If you really want to master Calc, you must understand how to set up and work with cell ranges. Therefore, this chapter's material will greatly enhance your Calc expertise. You will learn to use range names and references to produce more powerful Calc formulas and functions.

In addition to learning about Calc's range features, you'll also see how Calc's built-in *functions* save you many steps when you need to perform calculations. By using functions, you'll leverage the use of common calculations such as averages and advanced calculations such as trigonometric calculations.

▶ KEY TERM

Functions—Built-in mathematical and logical routines that perform common calculations.

48	**Find and Replace Data**

✔ BEFORE YOU BEGIN	→ SEE ALSO
41 Open an Existing Spreadsheet	**53** Enter Calc Functions
43 About Moving Around Calc	

You'll find yourself working with small, single worksheets quite a bit in Calc because each sheet usually represents one aspect of a financial analysis, such as weekly sales figures for a division. Nevertheless, you'll also work with large spreadsheets quite often too. Many times, a company needs to consolidate numbers from several different regions, companies, or departments into a single spreadsheet. Therefore, you'll combine numerous smaller sheets into a spreadsheet and consolidate them, report totals from them, and analyze them against one another.

Whether you have one large sheet or multiple smaller ones, being able to locate numbers and text easily is important. Calc provides powerful find and replace tools you can use to locate and change the data you want.

▶ NOTE

Unlike Writer's find and replace tools, when you search for Calc data, Calc highlights the entire cell that contains the data. So, if you were to search for the number 1 in a large spreadsheet, Calc locates and highlights the first cell (searching from left to right, row to row) that contains a 1, even if other numbers and text are in that cell.

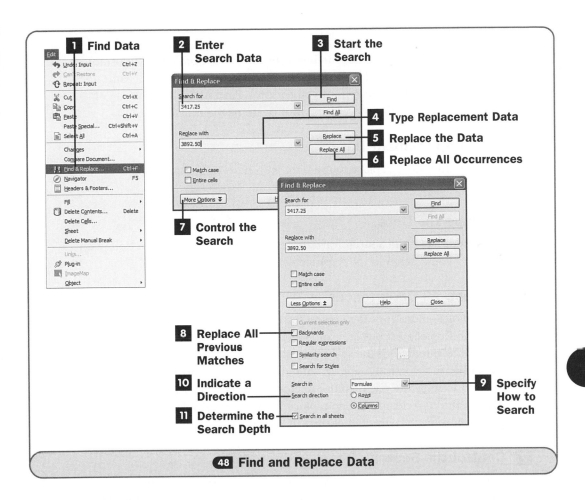

48 Find and Replace Data

1 Find Data

Select the **Find & Replace** option from the **Edit** menu to display the **Find & Replace** dialog box. You can also click the **Find** button on the **Main** toolbar or press **Ctrl+F** to display the **Find & Replace** dialog box.

2 Enter Search Data

Type the data you want to find in the **Search for** text box.

▶ TIP

If you've searched for the same data before, you can click the down arrow to open the **Search for** drop-down list box and select the data to search for it once again.

3 Start the Search

Click the **Find** button. Calc searches from the current cell cursor's position in the sheet to the end of the sheet. If Calc finds the data anywhere within a cell, Calc highlights that cell. (If you click the **Find All** button instead of **Find**, Calc will highlight every cell that contains the matched data.)

4 Type Replacement Data

If you want Calc to replace found data with new data, type the new data into the **Replace with** text box.

5 Replace the Data

Click **Replace**. If the **Search for** data is found, Calc replaces that data with the data you entered in the **Replace with** text box.

6 Replace All Occurrences

Instead of **Replace** (or after you perform one or more replacements), if you click the **Replace All** button, Calc replaces all the matches with your replacement data throughout the sheet. Such a change is more global and possibly riskier because you may replace data you didn't really want replaced. By clicking **Find** before each replace operation, you can be sure that the proper data in the correct cell is being replaced, but such a single-occurrence find and replacement takes a lot of time in a long spreadsheet.

7 Control the Search

To control the way Calc searches the current sheet, or to enable Calc to search all sheets within the current spreadsheet, click the **More Options** button. Calc expands the **Find & Replace** dialog box with additional options.

8 Replace All Previous Matches

Click to select the **Backwards** option before doing a find or replacement if you want to find or replace from the current cursor's position back to the start of the sheet.

9 Specify How to Search

Perhaps you only want Calc to search formulas for calculated results that match your search term. If so, select **Formulas** from the **Search in** list. If you want Calc to search only in values and text you've typed, but not formulas, click to select **Values**. (The **Notes** option is available if you want to search for text inside notes you've attached to cells within the sheet.)

48

▶ NOTE

Selecting **Formulas** enables Calc to locate your search term in either formulas or results. Selecting **Values** only returns a match if your search term is found in an actual number or text and not if it's the result of a formula.

⑩ Indicate a Direction

Although Calc normally searches from left to right and from the top row down, you can specify that Calc search completely down the first column of data before moving to the next column. Click to select the **Columns** option if you want to search down entire columns before searching the next one.

⑪ Determine the Search Depth

If you want Calc to search throughout all sheets inside the current spreadsheet, click to select the **Search in all sheets** option. Unless you check this option, Calc only searches the currently active sheet (the one displayed) within the current spreadsheet.

When you finish finding and replacing all the data for this search session, click the Find & Replace dialog box's **Close** button to close the dialog box and return to the sheet's work area.

---

49   **About Calc Ranges**

✔ BEFORE YOU BEGIN	→ SEE ALSO
45 Copy and Move Formulas	**50** Create a Range

A selected group of cells comprises a *range*. A range is always rectangular, and it might be a single cell, a row, a column, or several adjacent rows and columns. The cells within a range are always contiguous, but you can select multiple ranges at the same time. You can perform various operations on ranges, such as moving and copying. If, for example, you want to format a row of totals in some way, you first select the range that includes the totals and then apply the format to that range.

▶ KEY TERM

Range—One or more cells, selected adjacent to each other in a rectangular manner, that you can name and treat as a single entity or group of cells in formulas.

49

The next figure shows three selected ranges on a sheet. You can describe a range by the cell reference of the upper-left cell of the range (the **anchor point**) and the cell reference of the lower-right cell of the range. As you can see from the figure, multiple-celled ranges are designated by listing the anchor point, followed by a colon (:), followed by the range's lower-right cell reference. Therefore, the range that begins at C8 and ends at E12 has the range of C8:E12. To select more than one range, in case you want to apply formatting or calculations to different areas of your worksheet at once, hold **Ctrl** while selecting the ranges.

▶ KEY TERM

Anchor point—One corner of a range of cells; typically, the upper-left cell in a range is considered the anchor point, although any of the four corner cells can be considered an anchor point also.

49

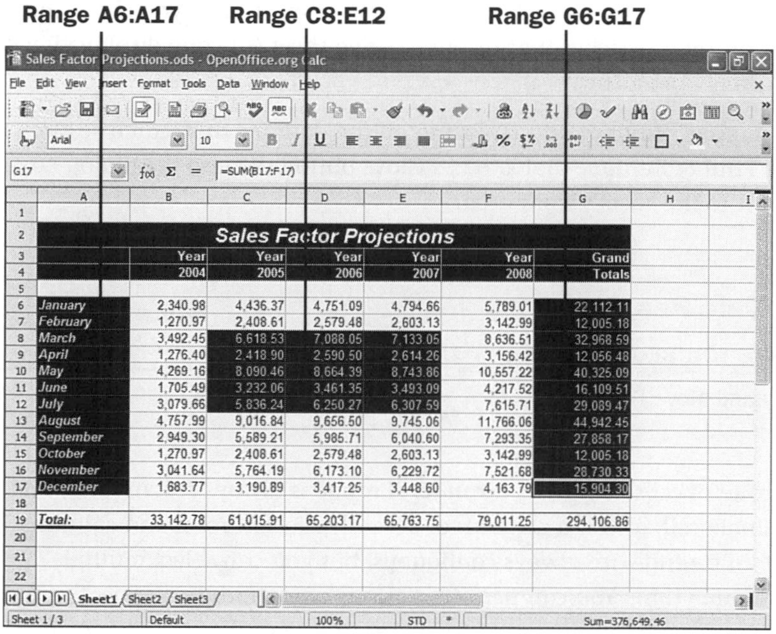

Range A6:A17   Range C8:E12   Range G6:G17

A sheet can have multiple ranges selected at one time.

Keep in mind that a single cell, if selected, can be considered a range. So, D5:D5 is a range composed solely of the cell D5. In this case, the anchor point is the entire range, which is only one cell.

The true power of Calc shows when you use ranges of cells, as opposed to specifying every individual cell, in formulas. (**50 Create a Range** explains how to name ranges.) Instead of referring to the range F2:G14, you can name that range MonthlySales and then refer to MonthlySales in your formulas by name.

All the following are valid formulas. Cell references or range names appear throughout the formulas:

```
=(SalesTotals)/NumOfSales
=C4 * 2 - (Rate * .08)
=7 + LE51 - (Gross - Net)
```

When you enter formulas that contain range references, you can either type the full reference or point to the cell reference. If you want to include a complete named range in a formula (formulas can work on complete ranges), select the entire range, and Calc inserts the range name in your formula. Often, finding and pointing to a value is easier than locating the reference and entering it exactly.

If, for example, you are entering a formula, when you get to the place in the formula that requires a cell reference, don't type the cell reference (such as G23); instead, point to and click on the cell you want to use in the formula, and Calc adds that cell reference to your formula. If you enter a formula such as =7 +, instead of typing a cell reference of LE51, you can point to that cell and press **Enter** to end the formula or type another operator to continue the formula. Immediately after typing the cell reference for you, Calc returns your cell pointer to the formula (or to the Formula bar if you are entering the formula there) so that you can complete the formula.

▶ **TIP**

Range names are absolute. If a formula in one cell refers to a range named Commission, **Calc considers the reference to be absolute (see** **45** **Copy and Move Formulas). Also, you don't use the dollar sign as you would when making cell addresses absolute (such as** B10**).**

After you assign a name to a range, you don't have to remember that range's address, such as R31, when you use it in formulas. Suppose that you are creating a large worksheet that spans many screens. If you assign names to cells when you create them—especially to cells that you know you will refer to later during the worksheet's development—entering formulas that use those names is easier. Instead of locating a cell to find its address, you need only type its name when entering a formula that uses that cell.

50 **Create a Range**

✔ **BEFORE YOU BEGIN**	→ **SEE ALSO**
49 About Calc Ranges	**51** Fill Cells with Data

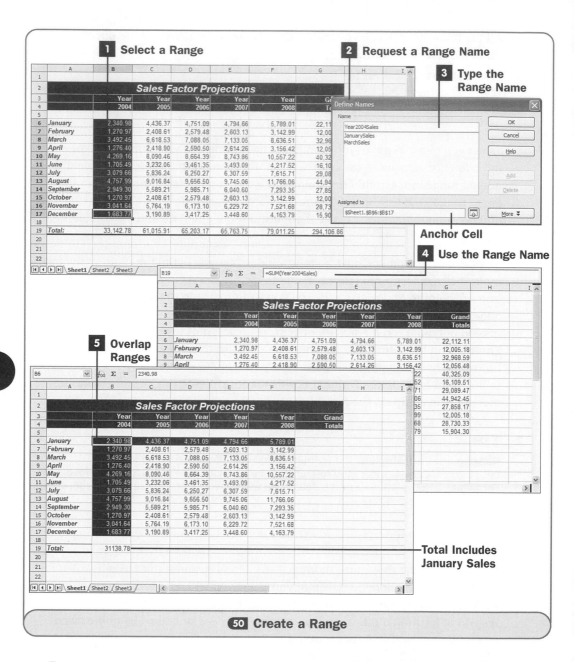

50 Create a Range

To name a range, you only need to select a range and assign a name to it. The name of the range then appears instead of the range address in the Formula bar's **Name Box** whenever you select that range. Calc supports the naming, renaming, and deleting of range names. Once you've named a range of cells, you no longer have to refer to that group of cells by their cell addresses.

▶ **TIP**

Give your ranges meaningful names. The name `Payroll05` is obviously a better name than `XYZ` for payroll data in the year 2005. The better you name ranges, the fewer errors you'll type in your sheets because you'll more accurately refer to cells.

Calc keeps track of your ranges and changes them as needed. If you insert a cell in the middle of a range, or even entire rows and columns somewhere inside a range, Calc reassigns the range name to the new cell range. This holds true if you delete cells from a range as well. (If you delete only cell contents, the range is unaffected.)

1 Select a Range

Click the anchor cell in a range you want to define. While holding down your mouse button, drag your mouse to the last cell in the range. Calc highlights the cells within the range as you drag the mouse.

2 Request a Range Name

Select **Insert, Names, Define** from the menu. (You can also press the shortcut **Ctrl+F3**.) The **Define Names** dialog box appears. This is where you name ranges and manage them.

3 Type the Range Name

Type a name for your selected range in the **Name** text box. Do not include spaces in the range name. Click **Add** to add the name to your sheet. A spreadsheet can contain as many names as you need, and you can define more than one range at a time in the **Define Names** dialog box. After you've added the current name to your sheet, you can select another range without closing the dialog box. If you can't see the cells you want to select, drag the dialog box out of the way or click the **Shrink** button to temporarily shrink the dialog box so that you select what you need. When you are finished, click OK to close the Define Names dialog box. You can now use your range name in formulas.

▶ **TIP**

To create a range name even more quickly, select the range and then replace the range address in the **Name** text box with the name you want to use. When you press **Enter**, the new name appears in the **Name** box.

4 Use the Range Name

Where you would otherwise use cell addresses—such as in a `Sum()` function—use the range name instead. The **Formula** bar always displays the range name inside formulas, and the **Name** box displays the range name when it is selected.

▶ NOTE

AutoComplete keeps track of your range names and inserts them when you are creating a formula; press **Enter** to accept the suggested insert or continue typing if that's not the range name you want to include.

▶ TIP

52 **About Calc Functions** explains how to use functions such as the Sum( ) function.

5 Overlap Ranges

Two or more cells can appear in different ranges. Depending on the kind of sheet you're creating, overlapping range names can be common. Multiple rows might comprise one range, whereas columns within some of those rows might define a different range. You can name any range you wish, regardless of whether part or all of that range appears in other range names.

Name as many ranges as you can because the more range names you create, the less error-prone your sheets will be. By referring to ranges by name, you are less likely to make a mistake than if you reference the cells within that range by their addresses.

---

51 Fill Cells with Data

✔ BEFORE YOU BEGIN	→ SEE ALSO
40 Create a New Spreadsheet	**53** Enter Calc Functions
46 Edit Cell Data	

Calc often predicts what data you want to enter into a sheet. By spotting trends in your data, Calc uses educated guesses to fill in cell data for you. Calc uses data *fills* to copy and extend data from one cell to several additional cells.

▶ KEY TERM

Fills—The automatic placement of values in sheet cells based on a pattern in other cells.

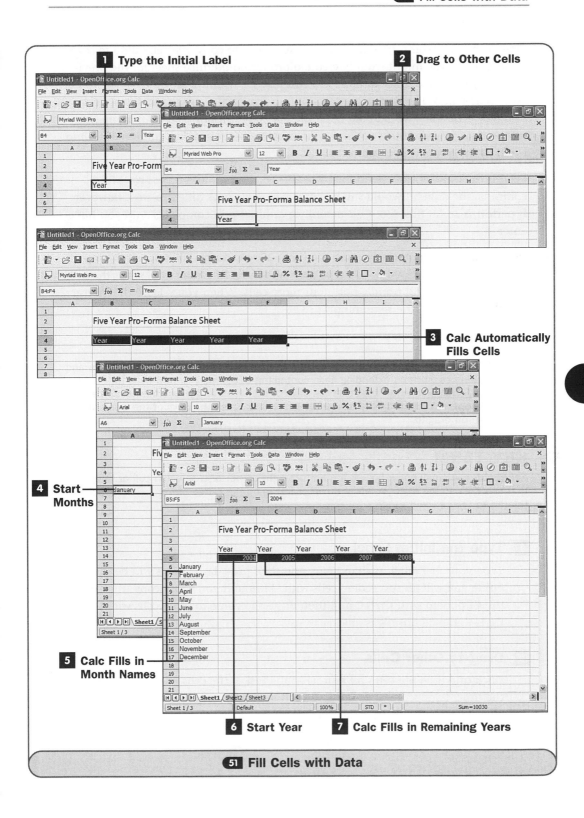

1 Type the Initial Label

2 Drag to Other Cells

3 Calc Automatically Fills Cells

4 Start Months

5 Calc Fills in Month Names

6 Start Year

7 Calc Fills in Remaining Years

51 Fill Cells with Data

One of the most common data fills you perform is to copy one cell's data to several other cells. You might want to create a pro forma balance sheet for the previous five-year period, for example. You can insert a two-line label across the top of each year's data. The first line would contain five occurrences of the label **Year**, and the second line would hold the numbers **2004** through **2008**. After entering all the data in year 2004's column, you only need to select that column and drag to fill in the remaining columns.

Even if the only fill Calc performed was this copying of data across rows and columns, the data fill would still be beneficial. Calc goes an extra step, however: It performs smart fills, too. Calc actually examines and completes data you have entered.

Using Calc's fill capability to enter the years 2004 through 2008 across the top of the sheet requires only that you type 2004 under the first Year title, select the cell, and then drag the fill handle right four more cells. When you release the mouse button, Calc fills in the remaining years.

▶ **TIP**

51

Calc fills in not only numbers in sequences but can also determine sequential years and other sequences (such as extending cells containing 3, 6, and 9 to new cells that hold 12, 15, 18, and so on). Calc also extends days of the week and month names. Type Monday in one cell and drag the *fill handle* to let Calc finish the days of the week in every cell you drag to.

▶ **KEY TERM**

Fill handle—A small black box, at the bottom-right corner of a selected cell or range, that you drag to the right (or left or down or up) to fill the range of data with values related to the selected range.

▮ Type the Initial Label

Type your first label, such as Year, and then press **Enter**. This will be the value you will fill succeeding cells with. Although you could copy the value to the Clipboard with **Ctrl+C** and then paste the value to other cells with **Ctrl+V**, the fill handle is quicker to use.

▮ Drag to Other Cells

Click and drag the cell's fill handle to the rest of the cells in which you want the label to appear. As you drag the fill handle to the right, Calc highlights each cell that will receive the filled data.

3 Calc Automatically Fills Cells

When you release your mouse button, Calc fills the remaining cells in the range with your label. Calc fills with numeric data, too, not just text inside cells. When you drag *integers*, Calc extends the range by increasing the integer by one.

▶ **NOTE**

Combine text and numbers for more advanced fills. For example, if you extend Qtr 1 with the fill handle, Calc continues with Qtr 2, Qtr 3, and so on.

▶ **KEY TERM**

Integers—Numbers without decimal points such as 0, –52,164, and 435 (also called *whole numbers*).

4 Start Months

To see Calc's smarter fill capability, you can type a month name and drag that month's fill handle across or down the sheet to fill in the rest of the months.

5 Calc Fills in Month Names

When you release your mouse, Calc fills in the remaining month names for you.

▶ **NOTE**

If you drag the fill handle fewer than 11 additional months, Calc only fills in those months. Therefore, you would drag the **January** cell's fill handle down only five more cells if you wanted to show the months January through June only.

6 Start Year

Type the initial year. Any single number, such as a year or any other number without a decimal point, whose fill handle you drag will increment by one in each cell you drag the fill handle to.

7 Calc Fills in Remaining Years

When you release your mouse, Calc fills in the remaining years by incrementing the years for you throughout the range.

51

52   About Calc Functions

✔ BEFORE YOU BEGIN	→ SEE ALSO
44 About Calc Formulas	**53** Enter Calc Functions

Entering individual formulas can get tedious. Suppose you want to add all the values in a column of 100 cells. You would type a formula such as =F2+F3+F4+... and would likely run out of room—and patience!—before you complete the formula. In addition, such long formulas are likely to produce errors when you have to type so much.

Fortunately, Calc includes several built-in functions that perform many common mathematical calculations. Instead of writing a formula to sum a row or column of values, for example, you would use the Sum() function.

Function names always end with parentheses, such as Average(). A function accepts zero or more **arguments**. A function might use zero, one, or more arguments, depending on how much information the function needs to do its job. When using multiple arguments in a function, separate the arguments with semicolons. If a function contains only a single argument, do not use a semicolon inside the parentheses. Functions generally manipulate data (numbers or text), and the arguments inside the parentheses supply the data to the functions. The Average() function, for example, computes an average of whatever list of values you pass in the argument. Therefore, all the following compute an average from the argument list:

```
=Average(18; 65; 299; $R$5; 10; -2; 102)
=Average(SalesTotals)
=Average(D4:D14)
```

▶ KEY TERM

Arguments—Values appearing inside a function's parentheses that the function uses in some way to produce its result.

▶ TIP

When you begin to enter a formula, ToolTips pop up after you start to type the formula's name to help guide you through the formula's required contents. When you type =A into a cell, a ToolTip pops up that reads =AVERAGE. You can take advantage of Calc's AutoComplete feature by pressing **Enter** when you see the ToolTip if that's the function you're entering and not another, such as =Abs().

When you type a function name, whether you type it in uppercase or lowercase letters, Calc converts the name in your formula to all uppercase letters.

As with some functions, Average() accepts as many arguments as needed to do its job. The first Average() function computes the average of seven values, one of which is an absolute cell reference. The second Average() function computes the average of a range named SalesTotals. No matter how many cells comprise the range SalesTotals, Average() computes and displays the average. The final Average() function shows the average of the values in the range D4 through D14 (a columnar list).

Functions improve your accuracy. If you want to average three cell values, for example, you might type something such as this:

```
=C2 + C4 + C6 / 3
```

However, this formula does not compute an average! Remember that the operator hierarchy forces the division calculation first. If you use the Average() function, as shown next, you don't have to worry as much about the calculation's hierarchy:

```
=Average(C2; C4; C6)
```

The Sum() function is perhaps the most common function because you so often total columns and rows. Instead of adding each cell individually, you could more easily enter the following function:

```
=Sum(F2:F101)
```

▶ **TIP**

When you insert rows within the Sum() range, Calc updates the range inside the Sum() function to include the new values.

You can use functions inside other formulas. The following formula might be included in a cell that works on sales totals:

```
=CostOfSales * Sum(Qtr1; Qtr2; Qtr3; Qtr4) / SalesFactor * 1.07
```

Table 7.1 describes common built-in functions for which you'll find a lot of uses as you create spreadsheets. Remember to start every formula with an equal sign and to add your arguments to the parentheses, and you are set.

TABLE 7.1   Common Calc Functions

Function Name	Description
Abs()	Computes the absolute value of its cell argument. (Good for distance- and age-difference calculations.)
Average()	Computes the average of its arguments.

TABLE 7.1   Continued

Function Name	Description
Count()	Returns the number of numerical arguments in the argument list. (Useful if you use a range name for the argument list.)
Max()	Returns the highest (maximum) value in the argument list. (Useful if you use a range name for the argument list and you need to pick out the highest value.)
Min()	Returns the lowest (minimum) value in the argument list. (Useful if you use a range name for the argument list and you need to pick out the lowest value.)
Pi()	Computes the value of mathematical pi (requires no arguments) for use in math calculations.
Product()	Computes the product (multiplicative result) of the argument range.
Roman()	Converts its cell value to a roman numeral.
Sqrt()	Computes the square root of the cell argument.
Stdev()	Computes the argument list's standard deviation.
Sum()	Computes the sum of its arguments.
Today()	Returns today's date (requires no arguments).
Var()	Computes a list's sample variance.

▶ **NOTE**

Calc supports many functions, including complex mathematical, date, time, financial, and engineering functions. Select **Help** to get more details on all the functions you can use.

---

53   Enter Calc Functions

✔ BEFORE YOU BEGIN	→ SEE ALSO
52 About Calc Functions	**54** Use the Function Wizard

Computing totals is so common, Calc makes the Sum() function even easier to use by placing the **Sum** button on the **Formula** bar. Just click a blank cell below or to the right of a range of values, click the **Sum** button, and Calc computes the sum and writes the proper Sum() function for you. If Calc guesses incorrectly at which cells you want to include in the function, you can edit the cell addresses in the **Formula** bar.

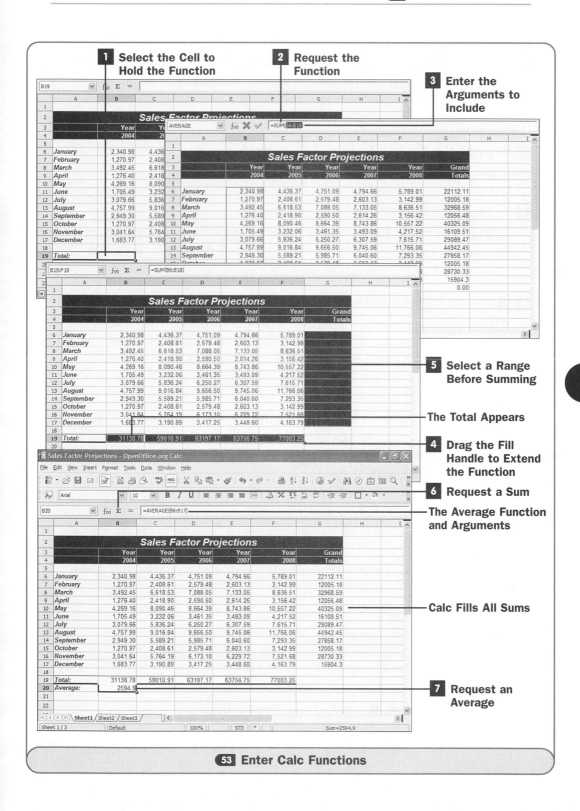

1 Select the Cell to Hold the Function

2 Request the Function

3 Enter the Arguments to Include

5 Select a Range Before Summing

The Total Appears

4 Drag the Fill Handle to Extend the Function

6 Request a Sum

The Average Function and Arguments

Calc Fills All Sums

7 Request an Average

You'll have to type the remaining functions yourself when you want to use them, but doing so is far from a chore. **52** **About Calc Functions** lists some of the most common functions you'll use. For the rest, use Calc's **Help** feature to find the function you want to use and then type that function and its arguments to get the result you want.

▮1▮ Select the Cell to Hold the Function

Click to select the cell you want to contain the results of the function.

▮2▮ Request the Function

Type an equals sign (=) followed by the name of the function. For the Sum() function, you can bypass this step and simply click the **Sum** button on the **Formula** bar.

▮3▮ Enter the Arguments to Include

Type an open parenthesis (() and then type or select the values you want to include in the function, followed by a closing parenthesis ()). A border appears around the cell or range to be included in the equation. For the Sum() function, your task is simplified once again because Calc proposes a range as soon as you click the **Sum** button. If it guesses wrong, drag to adjust the selection.

If the range is correct, press **Enter** to accept the sum; otherwise, type a different range inside the Sum() function's argument list and then press **Enter**. The sum then appears in the cell.

▶ **TIP**

The **Status** bar at the bottom of the work area provides a quick way to see the result of common functions on-the-fly. Simply select a range, and the status bar automatically displays the range's sum until you select a different cell or range. You can right-click in the **Status** bar to automatically display other common functions such as **Average** or **Count**, or to display no results at all if you don't want this quick reference available as you work.

▶ **NOTE**

As with formulas, you can select a cell containing a function and press **F2** to change the function, its arguments, or a formula that uses the function.

▮4▮ Drag the Fill Handle to Extend the Function

As with any other formula or cell label, you can drag the formula's fill handle, whose cell contains a function such as Sum(), to another cell to extend that formula.

5 **Select a Range Before Summing**

Calc doesn't make you request one sum at a time. Just select all the cells at the end of a set of rows or columns before clicking **Sum**.

6 **Request a Sum**

When you click the **Sum** button, Calc automatically sums the preceding rows or columns for the cell you selected.

7 **Request an Average**

Although other functions aren't represented on the **Formula** bar, you can easily request them as well. To get a yearly sales average, for example, you can type =Average(B6:B17) in cell B20 to learn your average monthly sales in 2004.

---

54 **Use the Function Wizard**

✔ **BEFORE YOU BEGIN**	→ **SEE ALSO**
52 About Calc Functions	**56** Work with Dates and Times
53 Enter Calc Functions	

54

Some functions require more arguments than a simple cell or range. Calc contains many financial functions, for example, that compute loan values and investment rates of return. If you want to use one of the more advanced functions, or if you're unsure exactly which arguments are required for a function you're about to use, be sure to take advantage of Calc's **Function** Wizard.

With this wizard, you can

- Select from a list of functions organized by category

- Build your functions one argument at a time

From the Function Wizard dialog box, you don't need to memorize long function argument list requirements. This wizard helps you create your functions.

If you need only a reminder of what a function is named or what it's for, just request the *Function List*.

▶ **KEY TERM**

Function List—A window pane that lists all functions, organized by type.

54

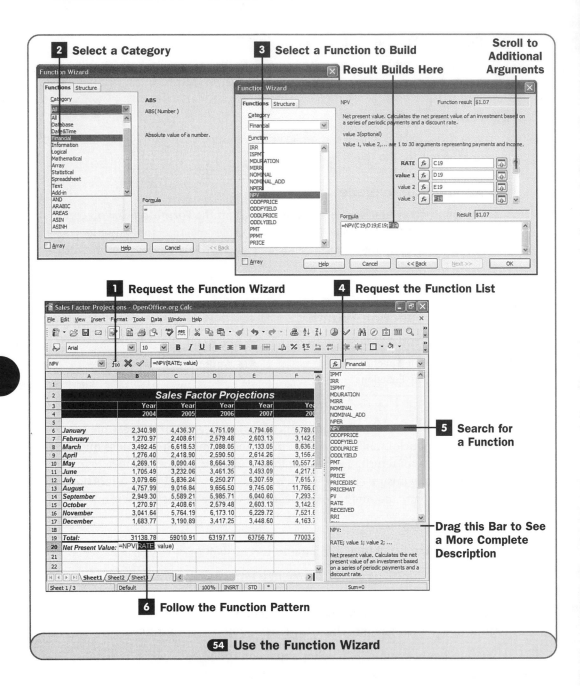

54 Use the Function Wizard

1 Request the Function Wizard

Click the cell you want to hold the function and then click the **Function Wizard** button on the **Formula** bar. Alternatively, choose **Insert, Function** from the menu bar. The **Function Wizard** dialog box opens to guide you through each step in this process. As with any wizard, you can use the **Next** and **Back** buttons to move among the steps.

2 Select a Category

Select the category from which you wish to write a function. For example, if you are wanting to compute the net present value of a series of cash flows, you would first select the **Financial** category and scroll down until you reach the **NPV** function entry.

3 Select a Function to Build

When you see the function you wish to use in the **Functions** list, double-click to select that function name. Calc displays a list of fields to match every argument that function needs.

For example, if you selected the **NPV** function, Calc would display the fields that match the NPV() argument list: rate of return and one or more values representing the cash flow. As you add arguments, Calc displays the current result in the **Function** Wizard's **Result** area. You can type the arguments into the fields or click the appropriate cells in the worksheet. If you can't see the cell you want to include as an argument, click the **Shrink** button for the desired field, click the cell or select the range, and then click the **Maximize** button to enter the argument and restore the dialog box. Click **OK** when you finish the function.

▶ TIP

In the **Function** Wizard, you can type either specific values, cell addresses, or ranges (by name or by their address), or you can click to select cells from the current sheet. Click to scroll the scrollbar if more arguments are needed than will show on the current **Function Wizard** dialog box.

4 Request the Function List

If you don't need the **Function** Wizard's help, select **Insert**, **Function List** from the menu to display the **Function List** pane at the right of your screen.

5 Search for a Function

Open the function category list to select the function category you want to choose from. Scroll the list of functions in that category to find the one you want to use. Click any function to see the types of arguments it requires and a description of its purpose at the bottom of the task pane.

54

▶ **TIPS**

You can hide the Function List at any time by clicking its **Hide** button. Also, you can turn the **Function List** pane into a floating toolbar that you can move to any location on your screen by dragging the pane's title bar into the work area.

If the area at the bottom of the **Function** list is too small to provide a useful description of the selected function, drag its top edge up for a better view.

If you're working on a complex formula or function and want to see the results of only part of it, select only the arguments whose result you want to see and press press **F9**. The result appears in a ScreenTip which disappears when you continue typing or press **F9** again.

6 **Follow the Function Pattern**

If you double-click the function in the **Function List**, Calc inserts the function's format in your cell and highlights each argument (such as RATE) while you fill in each argument with a value, cell, or range.

After entering the arguments, press **Enter**. Calc then completes the function and displays the results.

55 **Reference Data Outside This Sheet**

✔ **BEFORE YOU BEGIN**	→ **SEE ALSO**
42 Enter Simple Data into a Spreadsheet	**64** Conditionally Format Data
46 Edit Cell Data	

If all your data resided in the current sheet, referencing other cells would be simple. You'd only need to know the other cell's address, such as D4. What if the cell is in another sheet inside the current spreadsheet? If Sheet1 needs to reference cell G6 in a sheet named Sheet3, you cannot use the simple G6 reference.

▶ **TIP**

If you use a spreadsheet with multiple names, consider renaming the default sheet names of Sheet1, Sheet2, and Sheet3 to names that are more meaningful, such as Division1Sales, Division2Sales, and Division3Sales. Right-click the sheet name's tab and select **Rename** to rename, insert, or delete any sheet.

Perhaps the data you need isn't even in another sheet but resides across your network somewhere. Or, perhaps, the data resides across the world, accessible from the Internet. That's no problem for Calc. You can insert network addresses and web address links anywhere in a spreadsheet to display data from that location.

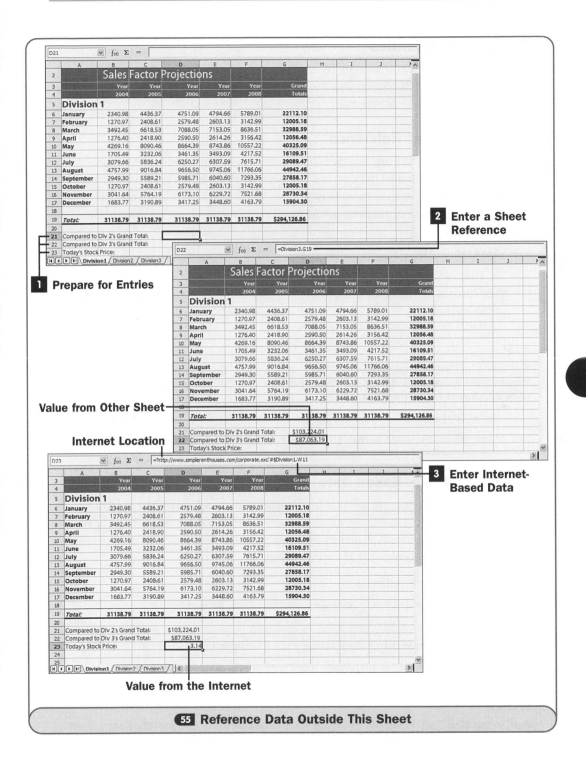

2 Enter a Sheet Reference

1 Prepare for Entries

Value from Other Sheet

Internet Location

3 Enter Internet-Based Data

Value from the Internet

1 Prepare for Entries

Set up your sheet so it's ready for entries from other sheets and even from other locations. Of course, you can always add the labels after you reference data from other locations too.

2 Enter a Sheet Reference

To reference a cell from another sheet, preface your cell address with the sheet's name followed by a period, followed by that sheet's cell you want to reference. For example, to display in the current sheet the value from cell G19 of a sheet named Division2, you'd type the following value in the current sheet's cell:

=Division2.G19

Calc locates the value in cell G19 of the sheet named Division2 and places it in the current cell.

▶ **TIP**

55

You aren't limited to displaying values from other sheets. You may also want to use those values in calculations and functions. For example, the following duration function uses arguments from three other sheets:

```
=Duration(Region1.G45, Accounting.PValue, Finance.FutValue*.9)
```

Two of the values are range names given to individual cells: PValue and FutValue.

3 Enter Internet-Based Data

If you want to reference a value from a spreadsheet stored on the Internet, feel free to do so. Obviously, an always-on Internet connection is best for such a reference. Otherwise, Calc will dial your modem connection to get the value every time you recalculate the spreadsheet.

Use the following pattern:

```
='http://www.YourDomain.com/Spreadsheet.sxc'#Sheet1.Cell
```

That's quite a mouthful! Here is one such example:

```
='http://www.simplerenthouses.com/corporate.sxc'#Division1.W11
```

▶ **NOTE**

Remember that .sxc is the file extension for previous versions of OpenOffice.org spreadsheets. Calc can also reference data from Excel workbooks that use the .xls file type.

To read such a long reference, it helps to begin at the right. This references cell W11 in the sheet named Division1 in a spreadsheet named Corporate.sxc on a website named www.SimpleRentHouses.com; keep in mind that you must enclose the web page reference inside single quote marks.

Calc adds a dollar sign ($) to your external sheet name to keep it an absolute reference. Also, Calc will rename your web page reference to all lowercase letters if you type any in uppercase.

56 Work with Dates and Times

✔ BEFORE YOU BEGIN	→ SEE ALSO
42 Enter Simple Data into a Spreadsheet	**60** Format Cells
53 Enter Calc Functions	

Calc supports almost every national and international date and time format. Calc converts date and time values that you type to a special internal number that represents the number of days since midnight January 1, 1900. Although this strange internal date representation of days since 1-1-1900 might not make sense at first, you'll use these values to compute time between two or more dates. You can easily determine how many days an account is past due, for example, by subtracting the current date from the cell in the worksheet that contains the due date.

If you enter a date in a longer format, such as July 4, 1776, Calc usually converts the date to another format (such as 7/4/76 18:15). You can enter a date, a time value, or both. You can format the date and time values you enter (see **60** **Format Cells**) to take on any format you wish.

▶ **TIP**

The date and time functions are useful for calculating durations for past due and other calculations related to date and time values.

1 Enter This Moment

Type =Now() in a cell. When you press **Enter**, Calc converts the function to the computer's currently set date and time. You may have to widen the column in which you're working to see the result. You can use this to calculate values based on this moment, such as the number of days old you are.

56

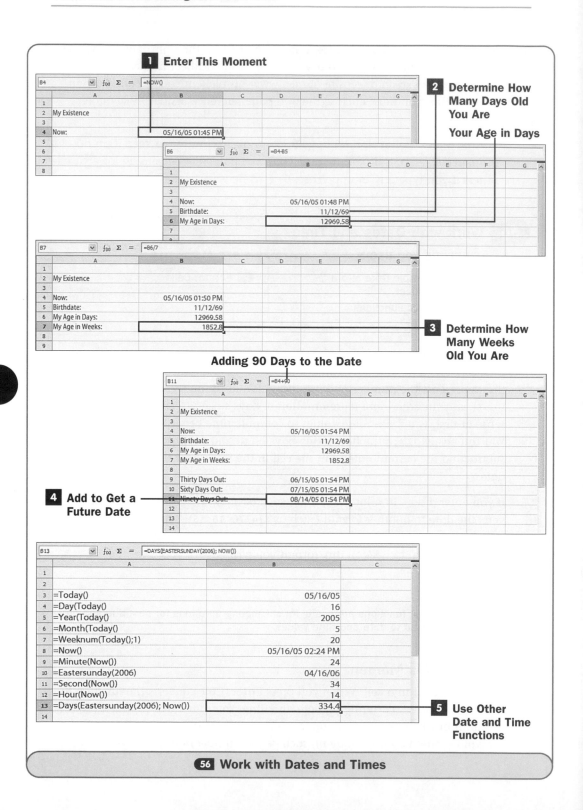

1 Enter This Moment

2 Determine How Many Days Old You Are

Your Age in Days

3 Determine How Many Weeks Old You Are

Adding 90 Days to the Date

4 Add to Get a Future Date

5 Use Other Date and Time Functions

56 Work with Dates and Times

▶ **TIP**

Remember that Now() and the other date functions operate as number of days since January 1, 1900. Therefore, when you add or subtract dates with or without using Calc's date functions, the result is always a number of days.

2 Determine How Many Days Old You Are

Enter your birth date. Type the date in any format. Although you can format the date using the **Format** menu, don't worry about the format now; concentrate on what occurs when you use date arithmetic.

Subtract your birth date from the current date to determine how many days old you are. Digits to the right of the decimal indicate partial days since midnight of your birth date.

3 Determine How Many Weeks Old You Are

Because the dates work in days, you can divide your age in days by seven to determine approximately how old you are in weeks.

4 Add to Get a Future Date

What will be the date one month from today? Sure, it's simple to look at a calendar, but when you write general-purpose spreadsheets, you've got to be able to apply such formulas to dates to age accounts receivables and other calculations.

By adding **30**, **60**, and **90** to today's date, you can display the date when future payments will come due. Calc understands how many days different months have in them, so adding **60** to April 12th properly returns June 11th and not June 12th.

▶ **NOTE**

Generally, you'll use date formats to hide the time when you work with date arithmetic. When working with time values, a day has 24 hours in it, so you'll need to multiply by 24 to obtain the number of hours represented by the value. When you subtract two date and time values, if you multiply by 24 you'll get the number of hours represented. For example, if you subtract a cell containing your birth date from a cell containing today's date, then multiply the result by 24, you'll learn how old you are in hours.

5 Use Other Date and Time Functions

Several date and time functions are available to make working with dates and times simpler. Today() returns the date only (without the time, unlike Now()). Day() returns today's day of the month of whatever date you use as its argument. Weeknum() returns the week number (within the year, from 1 to

56

52) of the date inside its argument list. Weeknum() requires two arguments: a date and either 1 or 2 to indicate that the start of the week is Sunday or Monday, respectively. Month() returns the month number of its date argument. Year() returns the year of the date given as its argument. You'll use these functions to pick off what you want to work with in another formula or label: either the day, month, or year by itself instead of working with the complete date.

Eastersunday() returns the date of Easter given the year of its argument. You can add to or subtract from Eastersunday() to get the days around the holiday, such as Good Friday, which displays for any year with the following calculation: =Eastersunday(yearCell) - 2.

Second() returns the second number of its time argument. Minute() returns the minute number of its time argument, and Hour() returns the hour number of its time argument.

▶ **TIP**

You can enter a time value, a date value, or both. If you don't enter a date with a time value, Calc displays only the time in the cell.

57

Days() requires two date arguments and returns the number of days (and partial days) between two dates. Therefore, to determine the number of days between today and Easter, you could enter the following:

=Days(Eastersunday(Year); Now())

Although at first glance this appears convoluted, it's a simple set of arguments.

57 About Names as Addresses

✔ **BEFORE YOU BEGIN**

49 About Calc Ranges
50 Create a Range

The makers of OpenOffice.org designed Calc to be watching over your shoulder, ready to help you when possible. One way that Calc does this is to look at the labels you place in your spreadsheets and use them as range names when appropriate.

Consider the sheet in the following figure. The totals do not align well with any specific row or column. In other words, cell B4 is going to hold the total of the four Miami estimates, not G7, where the total could easily be placed by selecting G7 and clicking the **Sum** button. To compute the total projections of Miami, for example, requires more than clicking the **Sum** button, because the total entry for Miami does not fall right below the column of Miami-related data. As you see in **53 Enter Calc Functions**, the **Sum** button is useful when you are totaling a column or a row and the total is to appear directly at the end of that column or row.

Totals do not always fall at the end of a row or column.

Of course, you could type the Sum() function in the appropriate cells of column B, but doing so (especially if the table were much larger) is time-consuming and error-prone. To total the Miami sales projections, for example, you would enter this into cell B4:

`=Sum(H4; H10)`

Likewise, you would have to enter every other range for the rest of the totals.

One improvement would be to create and name the following ranges from the sheet: Est2005, Est2006, Est2007, Est2008, Denver, Tulsa, Miami, and New York. At least entering the Sum() functions would be simpler. For Miami's total, you would type =Sum(Miami) into cell B4. If you added data to the table, your range names would expand appropriately, keeping the totals accurate.

▶ **TIP**

You rarely can name too many ranges. If you create a spreadsheet that you plan to add to quite a bit, create range names as you go so that subsequent formulas you enter will be able to rely on those names. For very small sheets, though, sometimes naming ranges is more trouble than its worth.

In spite of some advantages to the range names, naming six ranges for this small table is a lot of work. It's simpler and quicker—although, as just stated, more error-prone and more difficult to maintain—if you create the ranges individually for totals.

Fortunately, Calc is smart. Notice the headings over the columns of data: Denver, Tulsa, Miami, and New York. These are not range names; rather, they are just labels typed over the columns to label the data. The same is true for the rows with these labels: Est 2005, Est 2006, Est 2007, and Est 2008.

Although the column labels are not range names, you can often treat such column and row headings as though they are range names! Therefore, you can enter the following formula into Denver's total cell B2:

=Sum(Denver)

57

Denver's total computed correctly without range names.

Calc did *not* generate a new range named Denver. All Calc did was make an educated guess that you wanted to calculate the column under the heading Denver. Calc did not confuse the labels Denver in the table with Denver: in column A because column A's Denver: has a colon following it.

You won't want to rely on Calc's capability to calculate from labels in large and complex sheets because you'll be rearranging such sheets occasionally, and range names are better suited for sheets that you edit often. For smaller sheets, though, using the labels as column and row headings for summing and performing other routine functions makes a lot of sense.

▶ **NOTE**

If you copy or move a cell that uses a heading or row name to another place in the sheet, Calc moves the cell using absolute addressing (see **45** **Copy and Move Formulas**).

One thing you must keep in mind when using cell labels inside functions and calculations is to enclose the labels in single quote marks if they contain a space. For example, the following two cell entries would produce errors in this sheet:

```
=Sum(New York)
=Sum(Est 2007)
```

To correct these entries, you must use quotes like this:

```
=Sum('New York')
=Sum('Est 2007')
```

If a label is nothing more than a number, as the year 2005 would be if used as a label in the table, you would not be able to use that label in such calculations, even if you enclosed it inside quotes.

The next figure shows the completed sheet with all the totals. As you can see, all the totals work fine, even though no range names exist.

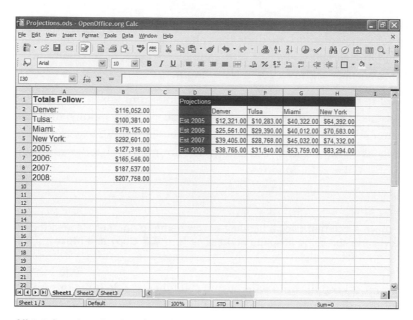

All totals entered using the table's column and row labels.

57 ▶ **NOTE**

Make sure that you use single quotes (') rather than double quotes (") in a label entry, or Calc will not be able to interpret the cell label.

8

Formatting Spreadsheets with Calc

IN THIS CHAPTER:

Calc makes it easy to make even simple spreadsheets look professional. *AutoFormat* quickly formats your sheets within the boundaries you select. If you want to format your spreadsheet by hand, the formatting commands you learn in this chapter will enable you to pinpoint important data and highlight that data. Others can then look at your spreadsheets and easily find your highlighted information.

▶ KEY TERM

AutoFormat—The process that Calc uses to format spreadsheets from a collection of predetermined styles.

During this chapter, you'll learn how to change the appearance of your spreadsheets so they look as good as possible. First you'll learn how to freeze row and column headers to improve a large spreadsheet's readability. Then you'll move on to learn how to select from a list of AutoFormats styles, how to format selected cells and ranges, and how to leverage your spreadsheet designs so you can reuse them again with little trouble.

58 | Freeze Row and Column Headers

✔ BEFORE YOU BEGIN	→ SEE ALSO
42 Enter Simple Data into a Spreadsheet	**61** Center a Heading over Multiple Columns

Often, you'll enter lots of data into a spreadsheet—perhaps daily sales figures, for example. As you add more and more data, your sheets will grow to be quite large. Perhaps at the end of each month, quarter, or fiscal year, you close your books so that you can consolidate the data and begin anew the next time period.

Until you restart the data entry for the next time period, the data can consume many rows and columns as time goes by. Eventually your data will take more than one screen, which can lead to a problem: If you initially put labels across the top of the sheet to label the columns and put labels down the left column to label the rows of data, when you page down or move too far to the right, the column and row headings will scroll off the screen. In order to keep track of what the purpose of your sheet's values are, you can freeze the scrolling of row and column headers so that those headers remain on the screen while the rest of the data scrolls under or to the right of them.

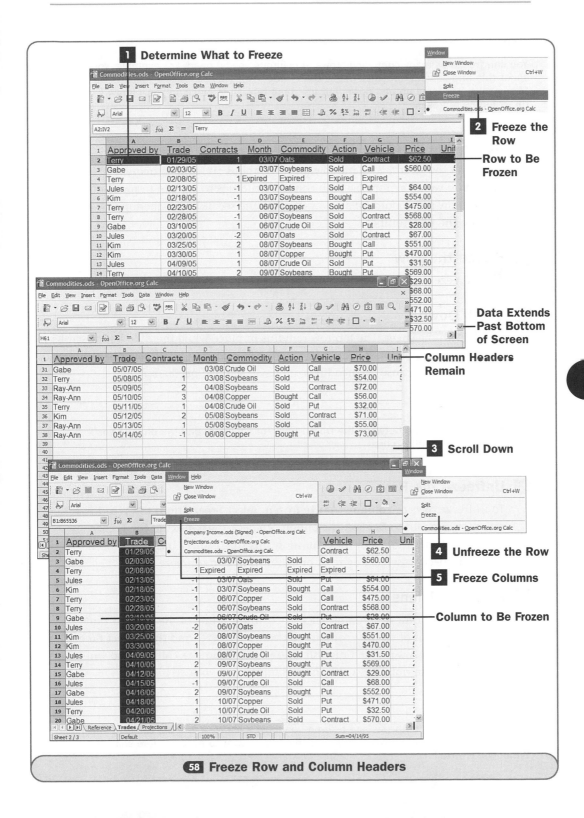

1 Determine What to Freeze

2 Freeze the Row

Row to Be Frozen

Data Extends Past Bottom of Screen

Column Headers Remain

3 Scroll Down

4 Unfreeze the Row

5 Freeze Columns

Column to Be Frozen

58 Freeze Row and Column Headers

► **TIP**

You can freeze as many contiguous rows or columns as you need. For example, your sheet title and column headings might span three rows. All rows below those three frozen rows will scroll up and down, but the three remain in place so you'll know what the columns represent.

1 **Determine What to Freeze**

Select the row that *follows* the row (or rows) that you want to freeze. For example, if you want the top row with column headings to remain in place no matter how much data falls below it, select the second-from-the-top row by clicking the row number.

2 **Freeze the Row**

Select **Freeze** from the **Window** menu to freeze the row or rows above the top row.

3 **Scroll Down**

Scroll down the sheet. The top row remains in place while the data below scrolls upward. No matter where you are in the worksheet, you know the labels that go with the data because the headings are never scrolled off the screen.

58

► **TIP**

Calc inserts a thick line between the frozen rows (or columns) and the data so you'll know where the break occurs.

4 **Unfreeze the Row**

To unfreeze rows or columns you've frozen, select **Freeze** from the **Windows** menu once again to deselect the option. A check mark next to the **Freeze** option indicates that a row or column in this spreadsheet has been frozen. You don't need to select any rows or columns first to unfreeze them.

5 **Freeze Columns**

To freeze one or more columns, click the column name of the column that falls to the right of the last column you want to freeze, and then select **Freeze** from the **Windows** menu. Calc will freeze the column (or columns) so when you scroll to the right, the column titles remain on your screen.

► **TIP**

If you want to freeze both row and column headings, click to select the cell that intersects the row and column following the headings you want to freeze before selecting **Windows, Freeze**.

59 AutoFormat a Spreadsheet

✔ BEFORE YOU BEGIN	→ SEE ALSO
42 Enter Simple Data into a Spreadsheet	**60** Format Cells **62** Set Up Calc Page Formatting

Although you can format individual cells to make them look the way you want, many Calc users take advantage of Calc's AutoFormat feature to apply formatting to an entire spreadsheet. If you enter straight text, numbers, formulas while building your sheets, without regard to the formatting as you go, when you finish with the data, you can apply one of several AutoFormats that Calc offers. Many times, you will have to do nothing more because AutoFormat works so well to make your spreadsheets look good.

Calc offers several AutoFormat styles from which you can choose. The AutoFormat feature analyzes your spreadsheets looking for data that is probably heading information. With only a few mouse clicks, your entire spreadsheet changes its appearance.

▶ **TIP**

Calc also offers AutoFormat for charts so your charts can take on one of several pre-designed looks (see **68** **Add a Chart to a Spreadsheet**).

1 Select the Area to Format

AutoFormat works best after you have created an entire spreadsheet to format. Create your spreadsheet, but for now don't worry about formatting it to look any certain way. Once you create your spreadsheet, select the area you want to format.

▶ **NOTE**

You'll often select your entire sheet, with **Ctrl+A**, to format with AutoFormat.

2 Request AutoFormat

Once you've selected the area you want to format, select **AutoFormat** from the **Format** menu. The **Main** toolbar also has an **AutoFormat** button that you can click to request AutoFormat.

59

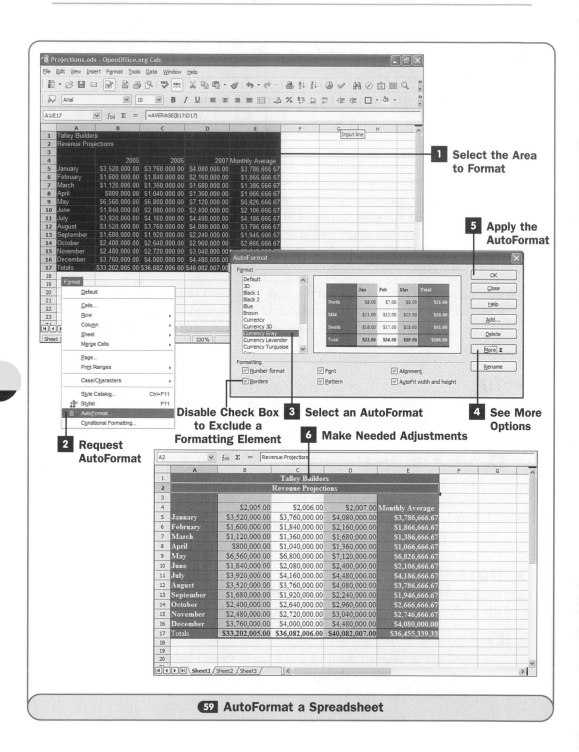

59 AutoFormat a Spreadsheet

▣ Select an AutoFormat

The **AutoFormat** dialog box scrolls to show numerous formats from which you can choose. As you click each sample AutoFormat, Calc displays a preview of it to give you an idea of what your spreadsheet will look like if you were to go with that AutoFormat option.

► **NOTE**

The **AutoFormat** dialog box's preview image does not contain a preview of your data. To really see what your spreadsheet looks like with the current AutoFormat applied, you'll have to click **OK** to see the actual results of your selected AutoFormat. You can always select another AutoFormat or click **Undo** to get rid of an AutoFormat you dislike.

▣ See More Options

Click the **AutoFormat** dialog box's **More** button to see additional formatting options. You can limit whether AutoFormat applies a number format, font format, alignment format, borders, grid pattern, or *AutoFit* by selecting from those six options, which appear at the bottom of the **AutoFormat** dialog box.

► **KEY TERM**

AutoFit—The capability of AutoFormat to keep the original widths and heights of the cells it formats.

▣ Apply the AutoFormat

Click **OK** to apply the AutoFormat to your spreadsheet.

▣ Make Needed Adjustments

Keep in mind that AutoFormat does a lot of formatting, and often you'll be completely satisfied with the format you choose. Other times, you'll want to make some minor adjustments. For example, if your heading takes more than one row, AutoFormat may not have realized that when formatting your sheet. Therefore, you'll have to manually apply cell formatting to that extra row (see **60** Format Cells).

---

60 Format Cells

✔ **BEFORE YOU BEGIN**	→ **SEE ALSO**
59 AutoFormat a Spreadsheet	**61** Center a Heading over Multiple Columns
	62 Set Up Calc Page Formatting

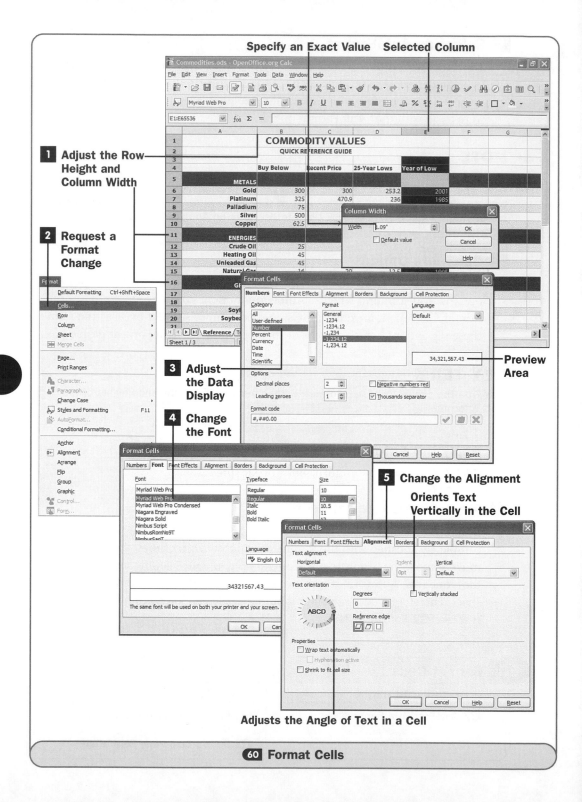

1 Adjust the Row Height and Column Width

2 Request a Format Change

3 Adjust the Data Display

4 Change the Font

5 Change the Alignment

Orients Text Vertically in the Cell

Specify an Exact Value   Selected Column

Preview Area

Adjusts the Angle of Text in a Cell

Now you see how to pretty things up, one cell at a time, if that's what you want. Calc offers many ways to change the look of your spreadsheets, such as enabling you to do the following:

- Align data inside cells (such as left- and right-justification)

- Modify row and column heights and widths

- Change the font

- Format data values such as currency, date, and time values

If you've used other OpenOffice.org programs such as Writer, you'll feel at home with many of Calc's formatting tools because the menus and options are similar to those of the other OpenOffice.org programs.

■ Adjust the Row Height and Column Width

If you want to increase or decrease the height of a row, just drag the row divider for that row up or down. To increase or decrease the width of any column, drag the column divider to the left or right. For more accurate control, right-click a column letter or row number and select **Column Width** or **Row Height** from the context menu. In the dialog box that appears, specify an exact value for the height or width of that row or column.

► **NOTE**

If you increase the size of the characters in a row, Calc increases the row's height to match the new character height.

If you make a column too narrow, Calc displays the characters #### to let you know that there's not enough room to display the data. Your data is still stored in the cell, but the value can't display until you increase the width of the column.

The **Format** menu contains **Row** and **Column** options that you can choose to specify an exact height or width of selected rows or columns. By selecting the **Optimal** option on either menu, Calc will adjust to include the tallest or the widest data value within the selected rows or columns.

► **TIP**

You can change the height or width of multiple rows or columns by selecting several cells in the rows or columns before making your adjustments. Press and hold the **Ctrl** key and click to select multiple rows or columns that are not adjacent to one another.

60

☑ Request a Format Change

To change a selected cell's font, alignment, display format, or background, select **Format**, **Cells** from the menu. The **Format Cells** dialog box will then appear. You can also right-click over any selected cell or range to display the **Format Cells** dialog box, where you can modify the cell's formatting, such as alignment, font, background, and colors.

☒ Adjust the Data Display

The **Numbers** tab on the **Format Cells** dialog box enables you to change the way data appears on the sheet. For example, if you want a dollar sign and cents to appear in cells that contain currency amounts, you would click the **Currency** category and then select the currency format you want to see from the **Format** list. Various **Number** and **Percent** formats are available so you can control how numbers appear. For example, some people prefer to display negative amounts with parentheses around them, whereas others prefer to see the minus sign. You control how your sheets display numbers with the **Number** formats.

60 ▶ **NOTE**

No matter how you change the display with **Format Cells**, the actual data inside each cell never changes—only the display of the data changes.

If you use dates or times inside your spreadsheets, you'll almost always want to change the format of those values by using the **Date** and **Time** categories. Often, companies have standards they enforce for published reports that indicate how date and time values are to display, and you'll want to format yours accordingly. You'll also see scientific and other formats available to you for many different data displays.

The **Format Cells** dialog box shows a preview of how your selected data will look as you select from the various formatting options.

You can control the number of decimal places displayed as well as whether you want leading zeros to appear (such as **012.31**). The **Thousands separator** option determines whether a comma (or decimal, depending on your country) separates digits to show the places of the thousands, such as **34,321,567.43**, and the **Negative numbers red** option ensures that negative values stand out when you need them to.

☐ Change the Font

Click the **Font** tab to select the **Font** page in the **Format Cells** dialog box. You can choose from various fonts and typefaces (such as bold and italics), and you can specify a font size, in points, to use. See **12** **Apply Character Formatting** for information on fonts, typefaces, and point sizes.

Many of these font-related options, such as bold and italics, as well as various number formats, are also available on the **Formatting** toolbar.

▶ **TIP**

Additional font-related options are available if you click the **Font Effects** tab. You can change the color of text and data that you display as well as control a shadow effect, which may be beneficial to make your titles stand out.

5 Change the Alignment

Not only can you left-justify, center-justify, and right-justify data within cells from the **Alignment** page of the **Format Cells** dialog box, you can also orient text vertically or to whatever angle you prefer.

When you select the **Vertically Stacked** check box, Calc changes all selected cells to vertical orientation.

If you want to angle text, such as titles at the tops of columns, select a different **Degrees** value or click the rotating text pointer to the angle you desire. When you click **OK**, Calc rotates the selected text to your chosen degree. Although you don't want to overdo this text-slanting capability of Calc's, a 45-degree angle for certain column headings really makes them stand out. All the text within the selected cells that you choose to slant prints at the angle you choose.

Although not as common in spreadsheets as they are in Writer documents, you can add special borders to certain cells from the **Borders** tab of the **Format Cells** dialog box. The **Background** tab controls the background color of selected cells, and the **Cell Protection** tab controls the protection of data to ensure that it cannot be changed (see **70** **Protect Spreadsheet Data**).

61	**Center a Heading over Multiple Columns**
✔ **BEFORE YOU BEGIN**	→ **SEE ALSO**
60 Format Cells	**62** Set Up Calc Page Formatting

If you want to center a title over multiple columns, you might find that you have trouble adjusting the title just right. Your first instinct is probably to type the title into the most central column over the sheet below. When the title usually doesn't align properly, you go back and edit the column, inserting spaces, until the title is just right.

61

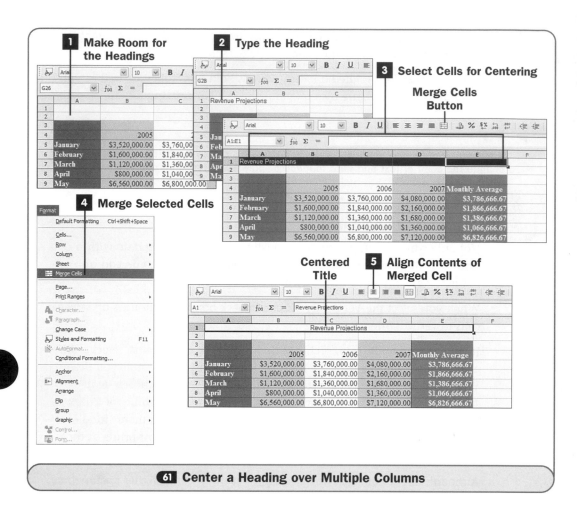

61 Center a Heading over Multiple Columns

This problem occurs because, when we think about centering text in a document, we usually think about centering in the entire width of the document. But Calc handles text cell by cell. If you center text in a cell, it's centered within that cell and not within the entire document. Another challenge in creating a heading is adjusting the data below the heading so that it doesn't look crowded. Those who learned about formatting with a word processing program might expect Calc to make room for the heading by adding some extra space. But Calc doesn't work that way.

Formatting headings in Calc is just as easy as it is in Writer, but you have to take a couple extra steps to accomplish it. To create space above the data (to display the heading attractively), you must add one or more blank rows or modify the size and alignment of the heading row.

To center a heading so that it spans multiple cells of data, you must *merge* the cells. Merging two or more cells lets you align text across those cells. If, for example, your spreadsheet contains eight columns, you can create a heading and merge it across eight cells so that the heading is centered over the entire sheet.

▶ **NOTE**

The **Align Center** button does not accomplish what you want by itself when you attempt to center a title over multiple columns. The alignment (or justification) buttons only align text within single cells, not across multiple cells.

▶ **KEY TERM**

Merge cells—To combine two or more cells into one so that the contents of the cells can be centered or otherwise aligned across the width or length of all the cells.

1 Make Room for the Headings

When you create your spreadsheet, leave room atop the columns for the title. It's best to create the columns, enter some or all the data, and adjust the column widths before worrying with the title. You can also type a title atop these columns as a placeholder and then perform the actual centering once you finish the spreadsheet's columns. Many users prefer to add the title after completing the rest of the sheet, which makes a lot of sense. Often, I'll add a placeholder title first and find that I must adjust it some later once I've completed the rest of the sheet.

▶ **TIP**

When you insert a new row, it takes on the formatting of the row below it. To quickly remove any formatting, press **Delete**; in the **Delete Contents** dialog box that opens, enable the **Formats** check box.

2 Type the Heading

Type the title that you want to center over the columns. Type the title atop the first column only.

3 Select Cells for Centering

Select the title and the columns to the right within which you want to center the title. In other words, if you want to center the title over five columns, select all five of those columns on the row that contains the title.

▶ **TIP**

If you merge cells that contain data in more than one cell, Calc asks whether you want to merge into the first cell the data from the cells that will be hidden. If you answer **No**, Calc deletes the content in those cells following the first row; if you answer **Yes**, all the content is moved into the first row and treated as one entry.

4 Merge Selected Cells

Select **Format**, **Merge Cells** or click the **Merge Cells** button on the **Standard** toolbar to request that Calc merge the selected cells into a single cell.

5 Align Contents of Merged Cell

Now that you've merged all five cells into a single wide cell, you can click the **Align Center** button to center the title. In fact, any formatting changes you make, such as changing the font, background, etc, affect the merged cells as if they were one single cell.

▶ **NOTE**

Once you've centered a title over multiple columns correctly, if you adjust the width of the columns that fall below the title, the centered title will adjust to remain centered without your intervention.

62

62 | Set Up Calc Page Formatting

✔ BEFORE YOU BEGIN	→ SEE ALSO
60 Format Cells	64 Conditionally Format Data
	33 About Headers and Footers

You will often need to make format changes to your entire spreadsheet. Perhaps you want to change the printed margins on the page. You may want to add a background color or a header or footer, or even put a border around the sheets.

The **Page Style** dialog box contains all of Calc's options that enable you to modify your document's format. Any changes you make to the current page apply to all pages in your sheets.

1 Open the Page Style Dialog Box

Select **Page** from the **Format** menu to open the **Page Style** dialog box.

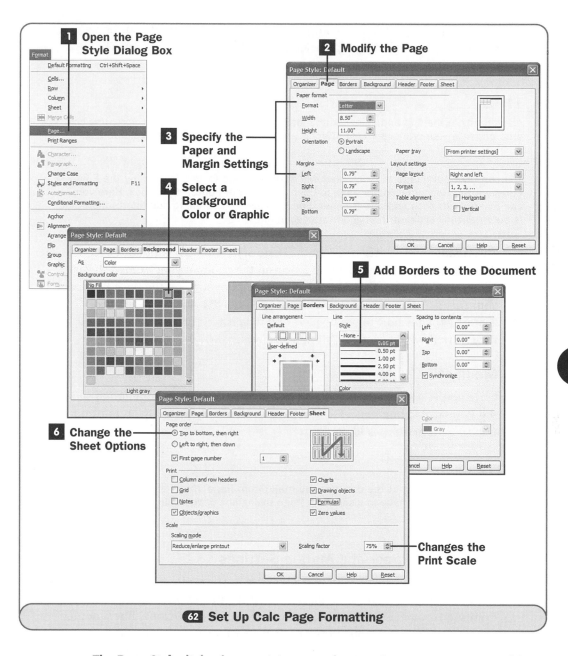

The **Page Style** dialog box contains several categories you can use to modify the pages in your document. Click each tab across the top of the **Page Style** dialog box to select from the dialog box pages. The **Organizer** page determines the default style currently used and enables you to select a different style. See **65** **About Calc Styles and Templates** for help with understanding and using styles. Clicking the **Page** tab enables you to format your paper's settings, such as selecting a page length as well as margin settings. The **Background** page enables you to place a background color on the page.

▶ **TIPS**

As with any formatting and color commands, don't overuse background colors. Use colored paper in your printer for best effect if you want to print on a single-colored background.

You can take advantage of Calc's predefined headers and footers by clicking the **Edit** button in the Header or Footer page to open a **Header** or **Footer** dialog box. Here you can insert fields such as **Page Number**, **Sheet Name**, and so on, to add information that is automatically updated throughout the document.

The **Header** and **Footer** pages in the **Page Style** dialog box provide you with the ability to place a header and footer on the pages of your printed sheets. For example, you might want to place a company logo on the page header of your first page, and you'd do so inside a header. **33** **About Headers and Footers** explains how to use headers and footers in Writer documents, and they work the same way in Calc spreadsheets.

62

② Modify the Page

Once you've displayed the **Page Style** dialog box, click the **Page** tab to show the **Page** dialog box page. From here you will modify page-layout information such as margins and paper size.

▶ **NOTE**

You cannot undo many of the changes you make from **Page**. If you apply a change and want to undo it, you'll have to display the **Page** dialog box page again and change the incorrect setting back.

③ Specify the Paper and Margin Settings

When you change the type of paper you use in your printer, such as going from letter size to legal, you'll need to select the proper option, such as **Legal**, from the **Format** list. If you use a nonstandard paper size, one that is not letter, legal, or one of the other options in the **Format** list, you can click to adjust the **Width** and **Height** settings to the unique settings of your paper.

You also may want to change the orientation of your printed page from portrait to landscape. Many spreadsheets are wide, and the landscape mode is perhaps used more for spreadsheets than for any other documents. In addition, you can give your margins more or less room by adjusting the **Left**, **Right**, **Top**, and **Bottom** measurements. If you have multiple paper trays in your printer, such as one with your letterhead and one with blank paper in it, you may want to select a different tray from the **Paper tray** option. Finally, the **Layout settings** options enable you to control how the pages print in relation to one another; for example, if you plan to bind your output into a booklet, you may want the left and right margins to be mirrored to leave more room in the middle for the binding or hole punching.

4 Select a Background Color or Graphic

Click the **Background** tab to add a background color or graphic to your sheet. Although you may want to use colored paper for extensive coloring, you might want to lightly highlight a report page that appears inside your document with a highlighted background color.

To add a background graphic instead of a color, choose **Graphic** from the **As** list and click the **Browse** button to open the **Find graphics** dialog box. Navigate to the location of the graphic file. In the **Type** area, you can enable the **Position**, **Area**, or **Tile** option to specify how you want the graphic to appear. If you want to place it in the top-right corner of the sheet, for example, select the **Position** option and then click the top-right option button.

▶ **TIP**

You can link the background graphic if you want it to update automatically in the spreadsheet (for example, if you edit the image in a graphics program, the linked graphic in the sheet will update automatically). To link the graphic, select the picture in the **Find graphics** dialog box and then enable the **Link** check box before clicking **OK**. The picture will be updated any time the source file is modified.

5 Add Borders to the Document

Click the **Borders** tab to display the **Borders** page. Here, you can specify which edges you want to use as a border (one or two sides, the top and bottom, or all four sides) and the line thickness of the border (from the **Line** list). If you want to add an additional effect to your border, you can adjust the position and color of shading. Shading a border softens the border's look.

6 Change the Sheet Options

Click the **Sheet** tab to display the **Sheet** page. Here, you specify the elements from your spreadsheet that you want to print as well as the order of those printed elements. For example, you specify whether you want Calc to print your spreadsheet from top to bottom (an entire column) before printing the next column, or print from left to right (an entire row) before moving down to print the next row.

62

You can change the **Scaling** options if you want to resize the spreadsheet to suit your printing needs. Use the **Scaling mode** list to specify whether you want to reduce or enlarge the spreadsheet by a given percentage, fit a width or height, or span a certain number of pages. After you specify the mode, the options to the right of the **Scaling mode** list change to let you enter the necessary details, such as the percentage by which to reduce or enlarge the sheet or how many pages the sheet should span. Calc does the work of figuring out how to size individual elements of the spreadsheet; all you have to decide is what you want the final size or page count to be.

▶ **NOTE**

All large spreadsheets will consume multiple printed pages. By specifying "by column" or "by row" order printing, you determine where the page breaks are likely to fall.

The **Print** section of the **Sheet** page specifies exactly what you want to print. You may elect to print the spreadsheet's grid lines, headers, graphics, or any combination of the three. Also, you can request that zero values print as blanks or as zeros.

Finally, the **Scale** section enables you to change the scale of your spreadsheet when you print it so that you might be able to fit a large spreadsheet on fewer pages. Calc will squeeze your sheets as much as possible in an attempt to honor your request. For example, if your spreadsheet takes a page and a half to print, you can almost always click the **Fit printout on number of pages** option and change the setting to 1 so that Calc reduces the size of the spreadsheet's output to one page.

63

63	**Attach a Note to a Cell**
✔ **BEFORE YOU BEGIN**	→ **SEE ALSO**
47 Print a Spreadsheet	**65** About Calc Styles and Templates
48 Find and Replace Data	

You've seen the yellow sticky notes that some people plaster all over their desks. The reason for their popularity is that these notes work well for reminders. You can put them on just about anything, and although they stick for a while, they come right off without removing what's underneath and without leaving sticky gunk behind.

Calc offers the electronic equivalent of these notes. You can attach notes to cells inside your spreadsheets. The notes can remain yours alone, meaning they don't print when you print the sheets, or you can print the notes for others to see when you print the spreadsheet's contents.

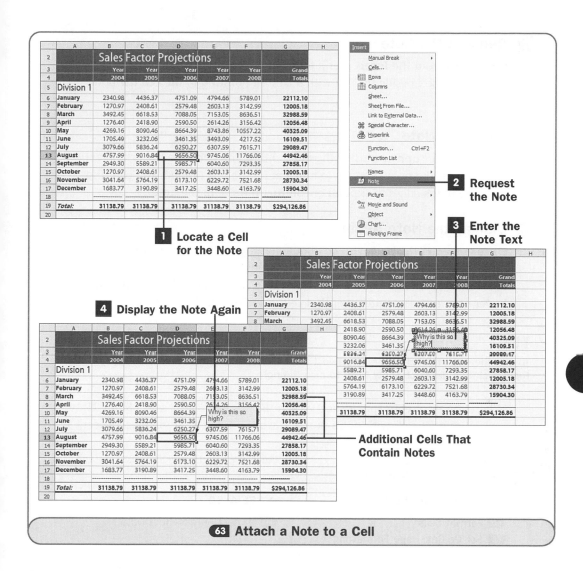

63 Attach a Note to a Cell

▶ **TIP**

Suppose you notice an anomaly in a report, such as a division's forecast is lower than expected. You can attach a note to that cell to follow up and find out where the problem lies.

1 Locate a Cell for the Note

When you want to attach a note to a cell, click to select the cell.

▶ **NOTE**

You can attach a note to a single cell only, not a range of cells.

2 Request the Note

Select **Note** from the **Insert** menu to request a note. Calc then displays the yellow note box beside the cell with a callout pointing to the cell the note goes with.

3 Enter the Note Text

The text cursor appears inside the note so that you can type the note's text. As you type, the note expands to make more room if needed. You can also drag the note's edges to expand or contract the size of the note.

4 Display the Note Again

Once you enter the note, you go about working in your spreadsheet as usual. Calc indicates which cells contain notes by displaying a small red box in each cell's upper-right corner that contains a note. To see the note in any cell, hover your mouse pointer over that cell, and Calc displays the note.

▶ TIP

64

To edit the note, right-click the cell, select **Show Note**, and edit the text that appears. Right-click and deselect **Show Note** to hide the note.

When you print your spreadsheet, you must right-click and select **Show Note** on any and all cells with notes that you want printed with the spreadsheet.

---

64 | Conditionally Format Data

✔ BEFORE YOU BEGIN	→ SEE ALSO
60 Format Cells	**70** Protect Spreadsheet Data
62 Set Up Calc Page Formatting	

Conditional formatting enables you to make your spreadsheets respond to the data they contain. When certain conditions arise, you can draw attention to particular cell entries by automatically making those cells display differently from the cells around those exceptions.

▶ KEY TERM

Conditional formatting—The process of formatting cells automatically, based on the data they contain. When the data changes and triggers a predetermined condition, Calc automatically changes the cell's format.

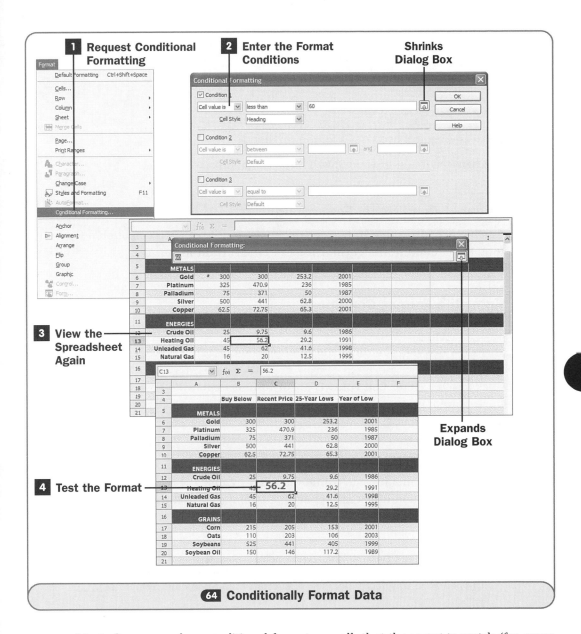

1 Request Conditional Formatting

2 Enter the Format Conditions

Shrinks Dialog Box

3 View the Spreadsheet Again

4 Test the Format

Expands Dialog Box

64 Conditionally Format Data

Most often, users place conditional formats on cells that they want to watch (for example, for extraordinarily high or low conditions that might require special attention).

The way you indicate if a condition is met is to specify a value and a condition that must become true before the format takes place. Here's a list of the available conditions:

- Less than
- Greater than

- Equal to

- Not equal to

- Less than or equal to

- Greater than or equal to

- Between (requires two values for the condition)

- Not between (requires two values for the condition)

1 Request Conditional Formatting

Click to select the cell or range on which you want to apply a conditional format. Select **Conditional Formatting** from the **Format** menu. The **Conditional Formatting** dialog box appears.

2 Enter the Format Conditions

You can apply up to three conditions for the cell you've selected to format conditionally. Most often, you'll probably only need to use a single conditional format.

Click to select either **Cell value is** or **Formula is** to indicate how the conditional format is to apply. If the format depends on a value, as it usually will, select **Cell value is**. If the format depends on a formula, select **Formula is** and enter a cell reference for that formula to the right of the option.

Select the **Cell Style** setting that you want Calc to use for the data's display if the condition is met by data within the cell. Any time the data changes to make the condition true, Calc applies the format style to the cell.

▶ **NOTE**

The available formats are **Default**, **Heading**, **Heading1**, **Result**, and **Result2**. If you want to display a different format, you'll have to select one of these styles and change its format so it appears the way you prefer (see **65** About Calc Styles and Templates).

Select the condition, such as **Less than**. If the cell's value ever goes below the value you enter next to the condition, Calc changes the cell's format to match the style you select. Two of the conditions, **Between** and **Not between**, require two values for the condition to be matched. If you select either of these conditions, Calc provides two text boxes so you can enter both values that define the condition.

3 **View the Spreadsheet Again**

The **Conditional Formatting** dialog box consumes quite a bit of space, and while you're filling it in, you may need to see your data on the sheet beneath the dialog box. If so, click the **Shrink** button. Calc temporarily shrinks the **Conditional Formatting** dialog box to a thin line so you can view the spreadsheet once again.

Click the **Shrink** button once again to return the **Conditional Formatting** dialog box to its original size so that you can complete the formatting. After setting up the conditional format, click **OK** to apply it.

4 **Test the Format**

If the cell never matches the condition, the cell's format will remain unchanged. If, however, the cell does pass the condition, Calc applies the format so it becomes noticeable to anyone looking at the spreadsheet.

▶ **NOTE**

Calc constantly monitors cell contents. Every time you enter a new value or the spreadsheet recalculates, Calc tests all the conditional formats and applies any of those formats if needed.

65

65 **About Calc Styles and Templates**

Templates enable you to create a spreadsheet that has a prearranged look. Styles enable you to format a cell (or, more commonly, a range of cells) with a predefined format. By reusing templates and styles, you reduce the amount of work you have to do to create a spreadsheet and to make your existing spreadsheets look the way you want them to look.

▶ **NOTE**

16 **About Styles and Templates** describes how to use templates and styles in Writer documents. If you need to review terminology, you can review that task because the background is the same whether you're applying templates and styles to Calc spreadsheets or to Writer documents.

Suppose you find yourself producing a spreadsheet of weekly payroll figures. Management requests that you format out-of-town payroll figures in a sheet different from the corporate office's payroll numbers. Each goes on its own sheet inside the same spreadsheet, although management requests that you lightly shade the background on the noncorporate payroll figures and use a different table format for them.

If your spreadsheet takes on the same general look each week, even though it contains two very different sheets, you can create a template that acts like a pre-formatted, fill-in-the-blank spreadsheet. In the future, you start with that template so you no longer have to worry with formatting the same spreadsheet each week. You also can create styles for individual sections within each sheet so you can quickly apply those styles to ranges of cells that are to take on that appearance.

▶ TIP

Templates are more global than styles. A template is a model for a spreadsheet, and a style is a model for a cell or range of cells. Often, a template contains several cell styles that you can choose from.

A template is to an entire spreadsheet what a style is to selected cells. When creating a spreadsheet that's to look like another you often create, such as a weekly payroll report or invoices, you can start with a template that you've already set up, and you only need to fill in the details.

▶ NOTE

In reality, you always use a template when you create new Calc spreadsheets. Calc uses a default template named **Default** unless you specify another template. The font, margin, and cell-formatting settings offered when you create a new spreadsheet come from this default template.

A template may contain several styles. When you want to use a style that's available to your current template, you can easily select that style and apply it to existing cells or cells you're about to fill in.

The **Styles and Formatting** window, available from the **Format** menu or by pressing **F11**, lists every style available in the current spreadsheet. Each style has a name. If you create a new spreadsheet using **File**, **New**, **Spreadsheet**, the list will display the default template's styles. If you create a new spreadsheet using a predefined template, the styles in the **Styles and Formatting** window come from the styles defined in that template.

Shows Page Styles

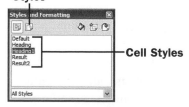

The **Styles and Formatting** window displays the current styles available to you.

When you want to use a template, you'll select **File**, **New**, **Templates and Documents** to choose the template you want to work from.

▶ **NOTE**

When you first install Calc, you won't find any preexisting Calc templates. OpenOffice.org comes with several templates for Writer and Impress but none for Calc. You can build your own templates and save them in the template area (see **67** **Create a Calc Template**).

---

66   **Create a Calc Style**

✔ **BEFORE YOU BEGIN**	→ **SEE ALSO**
65 About Calc Styles and Templates	**67** Create a Calc Template

---

Using a style is simple. You can apply a style to selected cells to format those cells with the style's formatting. Calc comes with several styles, and you can add your own.

Suppose you routinely create income statements for various departments. You might develop three separate sets of character formats that work well, respectively, for the title of the income statements, the data that comprises the body of the income statements, and the profit or loss line at the bottom of the income statement.

Instead of defining each of these cell formats every time you create the income statement, you can create three styles and store the styles under their own names (such as **IS Heading**, **IS Data**, and **IS ProfitLoss**). The next time you create the income statement, you need only to select a style such as **IS Title** before typing the title. When you then type the title, the title looks the way you want it to look.

One of the easiest ways to apply a style is to keep the **Styles and Formatting** window visible at all times by pressing **F11** (or by choosing **Format, Styles and Formatting**). If you don't have enough room on your screen to keep the **Styles and Formatting** window displayed, you can choose to show it only when you need it.

▶ **TIP**

The Styles and Formatting window provides existing styles, and you can define your own from text you select before displaying the Styles and Formatting window.

66

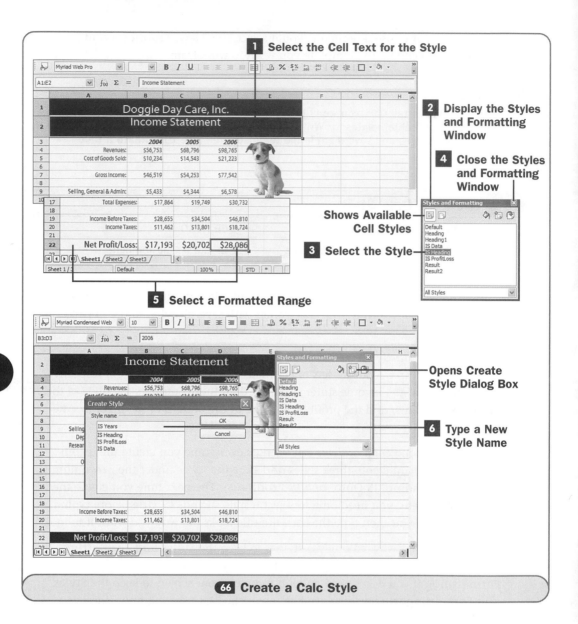

66 Create a Calc Style

1 Select the Cell Text for the Style

When you want to apply a predefined style to text, first select the cell or range. The format of the cell will completely change depending on which style you apply, but the data inside the cell will not change.

2 Display the Styles and Formatting Window

Press **F11** to display the **Styles and Formatting** window. If you see the page styles and not the cell styles, click the **Cell Styles** button. The style names will then appear that you can apply to your selected cells.

3 Select the Style

Double-click the style in the list that you want to apply to the selected range. Depending on the arrangement of your screen and windows, you can usually see the style immediately applied to your selected text. If you want to try a different style, double-click another in the list. Feel free to keep the **Styles and Formatting** window dialog box showing or click **Close** to hide it, depending on how much you plan to use the Style list during the rest of your editing session.

4 Close the Styles and Formatting window

Once you've applied the styles, close the **Styles and Formatting** window to return to your formatted spreadsheet.

5 Select a Formatted Range

You can easily add your own styles. You add styles to Calc's list by example. In other words, format a cell or range to match a style you want to create and then tell Calc to create a new style based on that format.

To add the new style, press **F11** to display the **Styles and Formatting** window after selecting the formatted range in the sheet.

6 Type a New Style Name

Click the **New Style from Selection** button, the second button from the right atop the **Styles and Formatting** window. Calc displays the **Create Style** dialog box.

Type a name for your style (one that does not already exist in the list, unless you want to replace one). When you click **OK**, Calc creates the new style based on your selected text. The next time you select that kind of cell and select the new style, Calc applies the new style's formatting to the cell without you having to worry about the formatting details for that cell ever again.

66

67 Create a Calc Template

✔ BEFORE YOU BEGIN

65 About Calc Styles and Templates
66 Create a Calc Style

→ SEE ALSO

73 Import and Export Sheet Data

Templates contain formatting for complete spreadsheets. Think of a template as a model for a spreadsheet. All the OpenOffice.org programs support templates. If you create a new spreadsheet without specifying a template, Calc uses the **Default** template style to create the empty spreadsheet and to set up initial font, margin, and other formatting-related details.

The **Template Management** dialog box, available from the **File**, **Templates**, **Organize** menu option, lists all templates currently available to you. You work with templates, selecting and adding them, from the **Template Management** dialog box.

▶ NOTE

Calc templates use the filename extension .ots.

67

1 Request a Template

Select **File, New, Templates and Documents** to open the **Templates and Documents** dialog box. The buttons along the top and left side of the dialog box let you navigate among different folders and view information about the selected template. Click the **Templates** icon on the left to see folders of templates such as **My Templates** (used for Impress; see **86 Use an Impress Template**). To open a template folder, double-click it to see all the available templates in that folder. Double-click the **My Templates** folder to see its contents.

2 Choose a Template

Decide which template you want to work with.

▶ NOTE

If you've recently installed Calc or have not added new templates, you may only see a Writer template named **letter**.

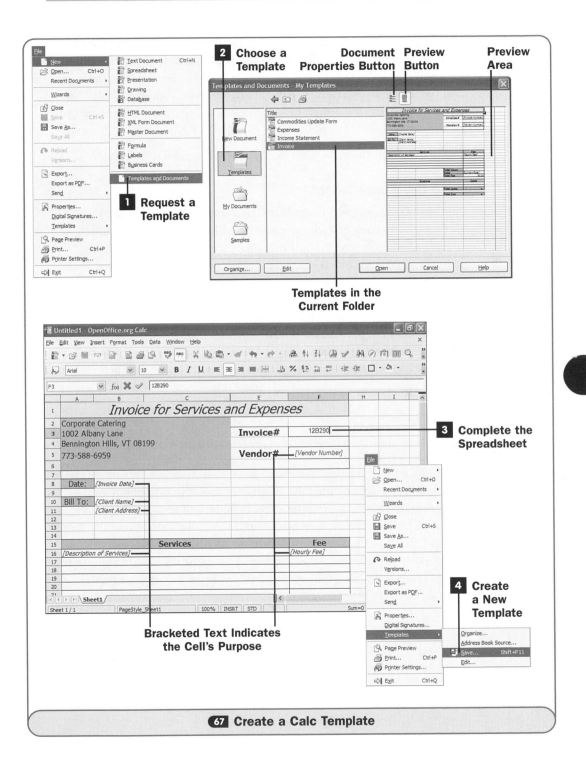

2 Choose a Template

Document Properties Button

Preview Button

Preview Area

1 Request a Template

Templates in the Current Folder

3 Complete the Spreadsheet

4 Create a New Template

Bracketed Text Indicates the Cell's Purpose

67

67 Create a Calc Template

After clicking to select a template, you can click the **Preview** button to see a preview of the template at the right of the **Templates and Documents** dialog box. If you then click the **Document Properties** button, the preview goes away and the template's properties will display, showing you who created the template, how long ago the template was created, the template's size, and the last time the template was modified.

Click the **Open** button to create a spreadsheet based on the template.

3 Complete the Spreadsheet

Once Calc creates a new spreadsheet based on the template, you then fill in the specific details to complete the spreadsheet. When designing templates, you can add placeholder text for names, titles, years, and other common data to be requested from inside brackets. The placeholder text indicates that you should fill in those cells with more specific data. Bracketed text is not a requirement in any way; it simply serves to tell you what is expected in those cells. When you develop your own templates, remember to add bracketed text so whoever uses the template in the future will know what is expected. Not all cells in a spreadsheet template will need these bracketed placeholders, though. Many cell contents require data that is obvious from the labels around those cells.

67

▶ **TIP**

Templates are easier to maintain as models of spreadsheets than storing actual spreadsheets that you reuse over and over.

You might wonder what the difference is between creating a template and creating a spreadsheet and saving the sheet to be reused as a starting point later. If you start a new spreadsheet based on a template, when you save the spreadsheet, Calc knows to save the spreadsheet in a new spreadsheet file and will not overwrite the template. The template is always ready to be used. If you were to start with an actual spreadsheet that you use as your model, you can easily overwrite that model by performing a **File**, **Save** operation.

▶ **TIP**

If your template spreadsheet contains formulas, you should protect those cells so that anybody who creates a spreadsheet from the template doesn't inadvertently overwrite those formulas with data (see **70** **Protect Spreadsheet Data**).

▶ **NOTE**

You can also save a template using the **Save As** dialog box. To do so, choose **File, Save As** and then choose a folder location, type a filename, and change the file type to the .ots filename extension. If you use this option, make sure that you either navigate to the **My Templates** folder to save your template to this location, or remember its folder location so that you can navigate to it when you want to create a new spreadsheet based on this template.

4 **Create a New Template**

Feel free to create your own templates! Remember to include placeholder instructions to the user of your template, such as [**Type Discount Rate Here**].

After you create and format a spreadsheet that you may need to re-create in the future, save the spreadsheet and then remove all the data specific to that particular spreadsheet, keeping all the formulas and formatting intact.

When you select **File**, **Templates**, **Save**, Calc opens the **Templates** dialog box, where you can assign a name and folder for your template (the default location is the **My Templates** folder). The next time you create a new document from a template, your new template will appear in the **My Templates** folder.

67

9

Creating Advanced Spreadsheets

IN THIS CHAPTER:

A picture is worth a thousand words—and worth even more numbers! Your spreadsheet data might contain a ton of numbers, but many times you can present data better with a chart or graphic. The actual raw data supplied by a worksheet is accurate and vital information for analysis, but for trends and overall patterns, charts demonstrate the data's nature quickly and effectively. After you create and format your worksheets, use Calc to quickly create a chart that depicts your data graphically. After Calc generates the chart, you then can customize the chart to look exactly the way you want.

You can easily import graphics into your spreadsheets, as you might do, for example, with a graphic logo for your company or pictures of inventory items. The distinction between numbers, text, and graphics is blurred these days thanks to modern technology, and Calc handles virtually any data you want to store in a spreadsheet.

Once you create spreadsheets with data, charts, and graphics, you'll want to protect the contents so you (or another user of your spreadsheet) don't accidentally overwrite something you shouldn't. You can protect cells to maintain their integrity. Calc's other capabilities, such as being able to check certain cells for accuracy, are explored in this chapter.

68

▶ **NOTE**

Data integrity is vital. If you enter bad data, the results will be wrong because Calc works with what you give it. As you create and design spreadsheets, protect cells with formulas and try to use data-entry validation for cells where data is typed to help ensure your calculations are as accurate as possible.

68	**Add a Chart to a Spreadsheet**

✔ **BEFORE YOU BEGIN**	→ **SEE ALSO**
51 Fill Cells with Data	**69** Insert Graphics into a Spreadsheet

Although Calc can produce professional-looking graphs from your spreadsheet data, you don't need to know a lot about graphing and charting unless you want to create extremely sophisticated graphs. Instead, you'll simply tell Calc what data you want to see in the chart and select the type of chart you want Calc to produce, and Calc does the rest.

Table 9.1 describes each of Calc's chart types. Different charts reflect different kinds of data. If you create one chart and realize it's not the best type of chart to use, you can request that Calc switch to a different type.

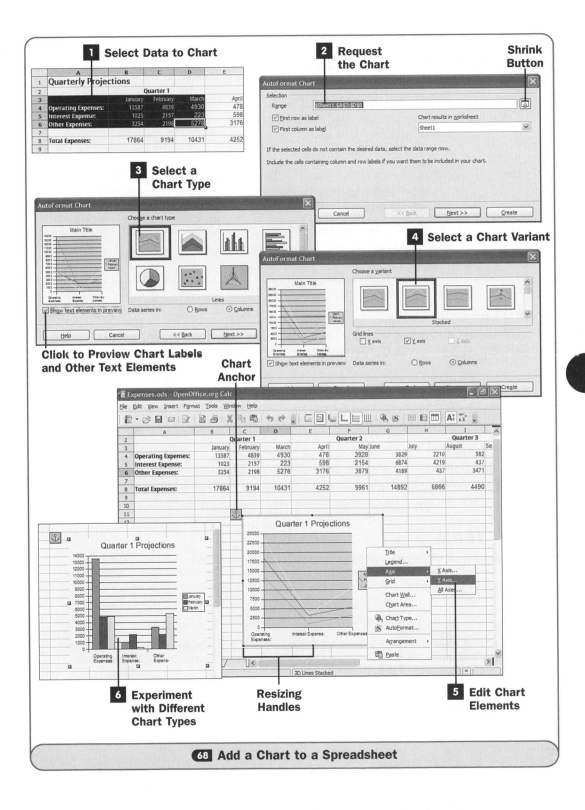

1 Select Data to Chart

2 Request the Chart

Shrink Button

3 Select a Chart Type

Cliok to Preview Chart Labels and Other Text Elements

4 Select a Chart Variant

Chart Anchor

6 Experiment with Different Chart Types

Resizing Handles

5 Edit Chart Elements

TABLE 9.1   Calc Chart Options

Chart Type	Description
Areas	Emphasizes the magnitude of changes over time.
Bars	Compares data items. A bar chart is a column chart with horizontal lines.
Columns	Shows changes over time and compares values. A column chart is a bar chart with vertical bars.
Lines	Shows trends and projections.
Net	Puts in each category an *axis* that radiates from the center of the graph (useful for finding the data series with the most penetration, as needed in market research statistical studies).
Pies	Compares the proportional size of items against the parts of the whole.
Stock	Illustrates a stock's (or other investment's) high, low, and closing prices.
XY (Scatter)	Shows relationships of several values in a series.

▶ NOTE

Calc supplies 3D versions of these chart types for use when you must chart data in multiple time periods or from multiple perspectives.

68

1 Select Data to Chart

You must first tell Calc exactly what you want to chart. To do this, you must select one or more **data series** to use in the chart. A data series might consist of a time period such as a week or year. One person's weekly sales totals (from a group of several salespeople's weekly totals) could form a data series. Some charts only graph a single series, such as a pie chart, whereas other charts can graph one or more data series, such as a line chart.

▶ KEY TERM

Data series—A single group of data that you might select from a column or row to chart. Unlike a range, a data series must be contiguous in a row or column with no empty cells in between.

▶ TIP

You can also request a chart by clicking the **Insert Chart** button on the **Standard** toolbar and then clicking in the sheet where you want the chart to appear. If the **Standard** toolbar is not open, choose **View**, **Toolbars**, **Standard** to display it.

When you select a data series, include labels if available next to the series. Calc can use those labels on the chart itself to label what is being charted.

2 Request the Chart

Select **Insert, Chart** from the menu to display the **AutoFormat Chart** dialog box. Calc analyzes your selected data and automatically puts that range in the **Range** text box (using an absolute range reference, including the sheet name). If you decide to use a different range, either type the range in the **Range** box or click the **Shrink** button to select a different range before clicking the **Shrink** button once again to restore the **AutoFormat Chart** dialog box and continuing with the chart.

Calc will probably have already checked the **First row as label** option and/or the **First column as label** option. In doing so, Calc wants to use either the first row or column in your selection for the labels on the data points that will be graphed. If you don't want labels, or if your selected data series doesn't include labels, click to uncheck either of these options. If you selected multiple data series, you still could select the row or column that precedes the series to be used for the labels.

▶ **TIP**

Calc will display the chart you build next to the data in the current sheet. If you would prefer the chart to appear in a sheet by itself, click the **Chart results in worksheet** option and select a different sheet. Doing so keeps your data and chart separated into different sheets.

Click **Next** to continue with the chart building so you can select the type of chart you want to build.

3 Select a Chart Type

Scroll through the various charts offered and select the chart you wish to build. The preview area updates as you select different chart types to give you a good idea of what your chart will look like. Use the preview area to determine as early as possible the best chart type for the data series you selected. For example, if you selected only a single data series, such as 12 monthly gross sales figures, you would want to select a simple chart type and most likely a line chart. The line will show the direction and trend of the sales over the year. A chart type that compares multiple data series against others, such as an area chart, would make little sense when charting a single series.

Click the **Next** button once you've selected a chart type.

4 Select a Chart Variant

Each chart type includes several variables. You'll now want to choose one of those variants that displays your selected data the best. You may also want to hide or display grid lines on both axes of the chart, or only on one or the other. As you select from the options and variants, Calc updates the preview to show you what your chart will look like.

▶ **TIPS**

During the chart-building process, you can generate the chart immediately without having to click **Next** to run through each of the possible steps. Click **Create** at any point to generate the chart with the options you've selected so far.

If you want the preview window to show text elements such as chart labels, enable the **Show text elements in preview** check box. The chart itself appears smaller in the window, but you'll see a more complete preview of your work.

Click **Next** to continue building the chart. Calc displays one more dialog box where you enter a title for your chart, indicate if you want a *legend* to display, and type labels for the two (or three, depending on whether the chart is a regular 2D or a 3D chart) chart axes. You can type a title to appear above the chart by enabling the **Chart title** check box and then typing a title in the **Chart title** text box. When you're finished, click **Create** to complete the chart.

68

▶ **KEY TERM**

Legend—Tells a chart's audience what series each colored line or bar represents.

▶ **TIP**

If you create a 3D chart (or edit your chart to change it to a 3D chart), you can customize all 3D aspects of it, such as its shading and rotation angle, by right-clicking the chart and selecting **3D Effects** from the context menu. Note that this option appears only if you have chosen a 3D chart type.

5 Edit Chart Elements

Once Calc displays your chart (next to the data or in its own sheet, depending on your selection when you built the chart), you are free to edit any and all the elements in the chart. The resizing handles that appear when you click the chart enable you to resize the chart to any proportion you prefer. The chart's anchor appears anytime you select the chart, in case you want to move the chart or delete it (by moving or deleting the anchor).

If you want to change individual elements within the chart, such as the chart title, legend, or chart type, double-click the chart to open it for editing. A gray border around the chart indicates that it is open for editing. You can then right-click the chart to open a context menu of editing and formatting choices.

You can also edit many elements by simply double-clicking them. By double-clicking the title, for example, you can edit and format the title just as you would any other text box. By double-clicking the chart area, you open the **Chart Area** dialog box, where you can change the look of the chart's background.

6 Experiment with Different Chart Types

When first mastering the nuances of Calc's charting capabilities, start with a single data series to get a feel for the charting dialog boxes and to learn the terminology. Then, you can experiment with charting additional data series within the same chart to make data comparisons that sometimes are easier to study in chart form as opposed to lists of numbers inside a large worksheet.

---

69 Insert Graphics into a Spreadsheet

✔ BEFORE YOU BEGIN	→ SEE ALSO
62 Set Up Calc Page Formatting	**74** About Advanced Spreadsheet Printing
68 Add a Chart to a Spreadsheet	

69

Calc enables you to put pictures in your spreadsheets. Perhaps you'll want to accent a motivational message next to sales figures or perhaps insert your logo at the top of the sheet.

▶ NOTE

Calc supports all popular graphic file formats including JPG, GIF, and BMP files.

When you insert a graphic image, Calc places the image's anchor at that location. You will see the anchor when editing but not when you print your spreadsheet. The anchor shows where you inserted the actual image, but you can adjust the placement of the image. For example, you might adjust the image so that it appears right-justified; the anchor will remain where you last placed it, even when you change the position of the picture. When you want to move an image, move its anchor and not the image itself.

1 Request a Picture

To insert a graphic image from a file, first select the cell where you want the image to go. Then, select **Insert**, **Picture**, **From File** from the menu. Calc displays the **Insert Picture** dialog box, which is nothing more than a Windows file-selection dialog box where you navigate to the file you want to insert.

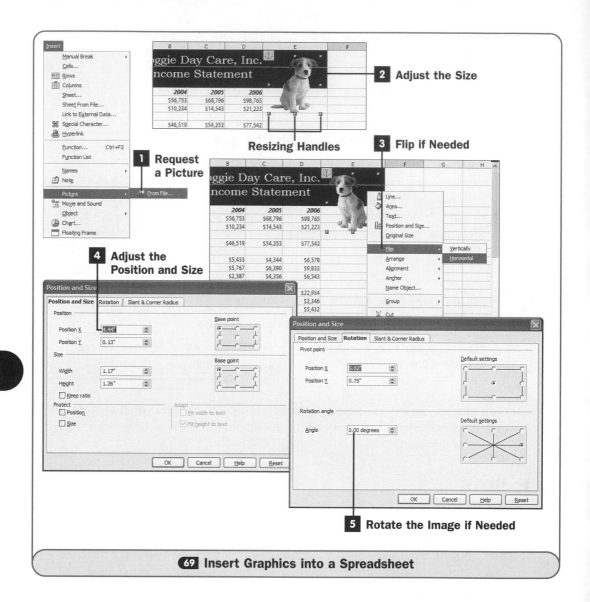

69 Insert Graphics into a Spreadsheet

► TIPS

Click the **Insert Graphics** dialog box's **View** button and select **Thumbnails** to see pre-views of your graphics before you import them.

You can also request a picture by clicking the **From File** button on the **Formatting** toolbar.

Once you select the graphic image you want to place in your document, click the **Open** button to insert the image. The image appears in your spreadsheet at the location you first selected.

2 Adjust the Size

Once Calc brings the graphic image into your spreadsheet, you can make adjustments to suit your needs. Typically, Calc imports graphic images and centers them at the location where you inserted them. No text wraps to either side of the image because, unlike a word processed document, a spreadsheet relies on the exact placement of data inside the rectangular grid. Therefore, you'll usually have to move the image so that it doesn't overwrite any important data in your spreadsheet.

Often, your imported image is not sized properly for your spreadsheet. To resize the image, drag any of the eight resizing handles inward or outward to reduce the image size.

3 Flip if Needed

Depending on your image and your data, you may want to flip, or reverse, the image so it points the other direction, either vertically or horizontally. Right-click over the graphic and select the **Flip** menu to flip the image so it faces differently. Be sure to check your image after reversing it because if any text appears in the image, it will also be reversed.

▶ **TIP**

If you insert multiple graphics, they can overlap each other. By right-clicking an image and selecting **Arrange**, **Send Backward** or **Bring Forward**, you can control which image gets the top spot when layered with other images.

69

4 Adjust the Position and Size

Right-click the image and select **Position and Size** to display the **Position and Size** dialog box. From this dialog box, you can resize, move, or slant the graphic image using exact measurements. The **Position X** and **Position Y** values determine where the image appears on the page from the upper-left corner. The **Size** values determine how large your image will appear. If you do resize an image, be sure that you click to select the **Keep ratio** option so that Calc resizes the width in proportion to any height changes you make (or so Calc resizes the height in proportion to any width changes you make) to keep your image clear and in the correct ratio as the original. If you fail to maintain the ratio, your image can look skewed and stretched. Checking the **Protect** area ensures that you don't inadvertently move the image with your mouse later.

5 Rotate the Image if Needed

Click the **Position and Size** dialog box's **Rotation** tab to display the **Rotation** page. Here, you can rotate the image any angle by specifying a value in the **Angle** field. The image rotates around the center of your image.

▶ TIP

If you rotate or resize the image too much and want to begin again with the original position and size, click the **Position and Size** dialog box's **Reset** button to restore the values to the original image state.

---

70 Protect Spreadsheet Data

✔ BEFORE YOU BEGIN	→ SEE ALSO
60 Format Cells	72 Ensure Valid Data Entry
67 Create a Calc Template	

70

When developing spreadsheet templates (see 67 **Create a Calc Template**) or creating spreadsheets that others less savvy in Calc will work with, you may want to protect certain cells from being changed. This protection helps ensure that formulas do not get changed and that fixed data remains fixed.

In addition to protecting individual cells and ranges, you can password-protect entire spreadsheets to keep them secure and to limit access to them.

▶ NOTE

Cells you designate as protected are only protected if you also protect the spreadsheet.

1 Select Cells to Protect

Select the cell or the range of cells you want to protect. (Hold **Ctrl** and click to select multiple cells in a range.) These cells can contain data, be empty, or contain formulas. Also, if you've stored a graphic image in a cell, you can protect that image from being moved or overwritten.

2 Request Cell Protection

Select **Format**, **Cells** from the menu. The **Format Cells** dialog box appears.

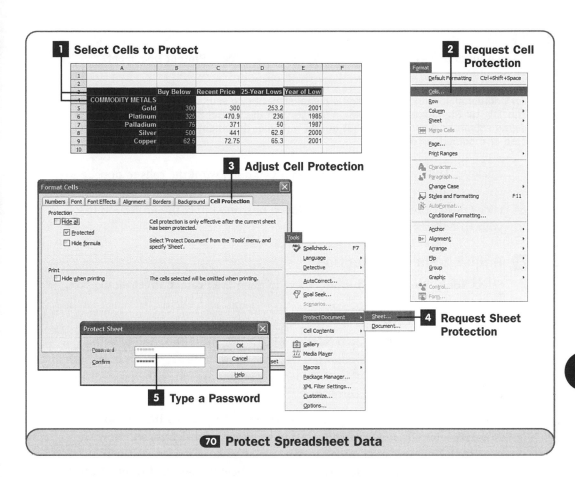

1 Select Cells to Protect

2 Request Cell Protection

3 Adjust Cell Protection

4 Request Sheet Protection

5 Type a Password

70 Protect Spreadsheet Data

3 Adjust Cell Protection

Click the **Cell Protection** tab to display the **Cell Protection** page within the **Format Cells** dialog box. If you click to select the **Hide all** option, the contents of the selected cells will not appear when the spreadsheet is viewed. The **Protected** option keeps the selected cells from being changed. The **Hide formula** option hides any formulas in the protected cells, if any formulas reside there.

▶ NOTE

When you hide formulas, the user cannot see them but can still see the cell values that result from the formulas.

▶ **TIPS**

If you want to protect all the sheets in the file, choose **Tools, Protect Document, Document**.

For additional security, you can add a digital signature to your spreadsheet by choosing **File, Digital Signatures** and adding a signature in the **Digital Signatures** dialog box. A *digital signature* is information that travels with your document and verifies that you created or modified the document.

Click the **Hide when printing** option if you don't want the cells to appear when the user prints the spreadsheet. Once you've indicated the protection, click **OK** to close the **Format Cells** dialog box and apply the protection to your spreadsheet.

4 Request Sheet Protection

Select **Tools, Protect Document, Sheet** to open the **Protect Sheet** dialog box.

5 Type a Password

In the **Protect Sheet** dialog box, type a password, press **Tab**, and type the password once more. The password does not show on the screen in case someone is looking over your shoulder. The second typing of the password ensures that you typed it correctly the first time.

Once you type the password and click **OK**, you've protected the spreadsheet. Any cells that you now designate as protected (or have before) will now be protected. No user can change the contents of those protected cells without first removing the protection from the entire sheet by selecting **Tools, Protect Document, Sheet** once again and entering the correct password.

---

71 **Combine Multiple Cells into One**

✔ **BEFORE YOU BEGIN**

58 Freeze Row and Column Headers
61 Center a Heading over Multiple Columns

Sometimes you'll need to merge multiple cells into a single cell. Perhaps you want to pad a label with several surrounding blank cells to add spaces that can't be easily removed from the label. This gives you greater flexibility when formatting a sheet for attractiveness or easier readability.

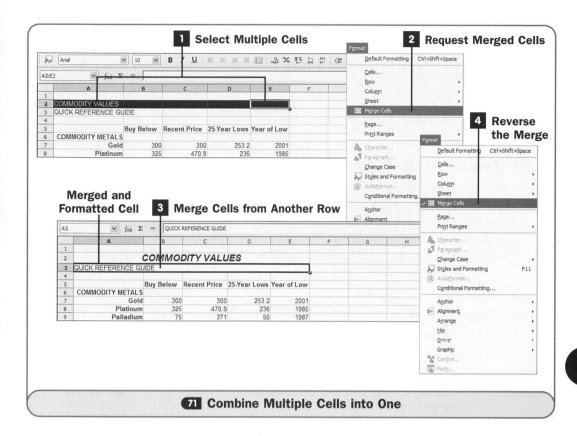

71 Combine Multiple Cells into One

▶ **TIP**

One of the most common reasons to merge two or more cells into a single cell is to center titles over multiple columns (see **61** **Center a Heading over Multiple Columns**).

Not only can Calc merge multiple cells into a single cell, but it can also turn a single cell with multiple values back into multiple cells once again.

1 Select Multiple Cells

Select the cells that you want to merge into a single cell. Generally, this requires that you select empty cells to the right or to the left of one or more labels.

2 Request Merged Cells

Select **Format**, **Merge Cells** from the menu. Calc merges the cells into a single cell for you. You can now format the merged cell just as you would a single cell—changing its alignment, size, or the formatting of the text—to create a bolder or more useful label.

▶ **NOTES**

If you select cells from two or more rows to merge, Calc merges those cells' contents into a single cell on a single row. Usually, you'll want to merge only adjacent cells from the same row.

The **Merge** button on the **Standard** toolbar is a toggle button; clicking it once requests the merge, clicking it again removes the merge.

3 Merge Cells from Another Row

If you have other cells from a subsequent row that you want to merge into one, continue selecting adjacent cells in each row and merging them from the **Format**, **Merge Cells** menu. You might do this, for example, if your spreadsheet uses a multiline title atop the data; by merging the title's cells into a single cell, you can more easily center the title over the data.

4 Reverse the Merge

To reverse the merge, select **Format**, **Merge Cells**, **Remove**, or simply click the **Merge Cells** button on the **Standard** toolbar.

72

72	Ensure Valid Data Entry

✔ **BEFORE YOU BEGIN**

64 Conditionally Format Data
70 Protect Spreadsheet Data

Not only can you conditionally format data so that the format changes based on the data (see **64** **Conditionally Format Data**), you can also set up *data validity* rules to help maintain accurate spreadsheets. Once you set up data validity rules, you or those who use your spreadsheets are limited on what they can enter into certain cells.

▶ **KEY TERM**

Data validity—A check to determine whether data entered into a cell is valid, defined by a set of criteria that you set up.

Without data validity checks, anybody can enter any value into any cell (assuming the cell is not protected). Once you set up data validity checks, if someone violates any criterion you set up, such as entering a negative payroll amount, that you deem impossible, Calc flags the entry as an error. If a user types a value that violates any data validity check you've set up, Calc displays an error message you define for that situation.

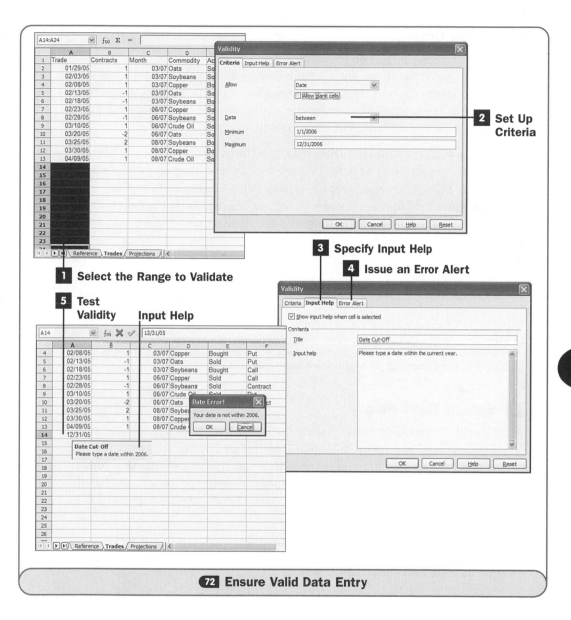

1 Select the Range to Validate

2 Set Up Criteria

3 Specify Input Help

4 Issue an Error Alert

5 Test Validity   Input Help

72 Ensure Valid Data Entry

1 Select the Range to Validate

Select the cell or range that you want to create a data validity check for. For example, you may want to create a range of dates and disallow any entry into the range that is not a valid date.

To add the data validity check, select **Data**, **Validity** to display the **Validity** dialog box.

2 Set Up Criteria

On the **Criteria** page, you set up the criteria to which the range must conform before the user can enter a value. For example, if you require a date that falls after January 1, 2006, you would select **Date** from the **Allow** field. Keep the **Allow blanks** option checked if you want to allow blanks in the range without the blanks violating the criteria.

Select a condition from the **Data** field that the range must meet. For example, to allow the entry of dates January 1, 2006 and after, you would select **greater than**. Then, you'd type 1/1/2006 in the **Minimum** field. The **Maximum** field appears if you select either **between** or **not between** so that you can define the two fields that limit the input range.

▶ NOTE

The **Allow** field enables you to set up criteria for dates, times, whole numbers, or decimals. You can also limit the number of characters that can be typed into a text cell.

▶ TIP

If you want to clear all the options you've selected in the **Validity** dialog box and start again, click the **Reset** button to quickly restore the defaults.

3 Specify Input Help

Click the **Input Help** tab to display the **Input Help** page in the **Validity** dialog box. Here, you set up a floating ToolTip that appears whenever the user selects the cell. The title and message that you type in the **Title** and **Input help** fields appear when the cell becomes active. The purpose of the **Input help** field is to let your users know the kind of data you allow in the cell.

▶ TIP

Usually, cells don't require both a title and input help if the criteria is simple. A title such as **Must be more than 0** is usually sufficient.

4 Issue an Error Alert

The **Error Alert** page describes what happens if and when the user violates the criteria you set up on the **Criteria** page. The **Action** field can be set to **Stop**, **Warning**, **Information**, or **Macro**, depending on what you want to happen when the violation occurs. When you select **Stop**, Calc disallows any entry into the cell until the user enters data that conforms to the criteria. **Warning** or **Information** allows the data but shows a pop-up dialog box with the title and error message you enter in the **Title** and **Error message** fields of the **Error Alert** page.

72

▶ **NOTE**

The **Macro** option starts a macro program that you or someone else may have written. See **128** About OpenOffice.org Macros for more information about macros.

5 Test Validity

Test your data validity check by typing data in the cell. When you select the cell, the **Input Help** message should appear, telling you what data the cell expects. If you enter a value that violates the criteria, Calc responds with a warning or a pop-up dialog box, depending on how you set up the error alert.

---

73 **Import and Export Sheet Data**

✔ BEFORE YOU BEGIN	→ SEE ALSO
47 Print a Spreadsheet	**74** About Advanced Spreadsheet Printing
	140 Access an Existing Database

As with all the OpenOffice.org programs, Calc works well with data from similar programs such as Microsoft Office and StarOffice. Most of the time, you can load an Excel spreadsheet directly into Calc and work with the spreadsheet as though you had originally created it in Calc. When you load a spreadsheet from another program into Calc, you are using Calc's automatic *import* feature to bring that data into Calc's workspace. If you want to use Calc data in a program that does not support the **OpenDocument** format, you must *export* the spreadsheet data.

▶ **KEY TERMS**

Import—To load data from a non-Calc program into Calc.

Export—To save data from Calc so another program can use the data.

▶ **NOTES**

All spreadsheet programs that support the OASIS standard use the same file extensions. Therefore, any spreadsheet created in StarOffice 8 or KOffice shares Calc's native file extensions: .ods for spreadsheets and .ots for spreadsheet templates.

If you want to use a database you create in Calc in the Base component of OpenOffice.org, you must first register the Calc database with OpenOffice.org. See **140** **Access an Existing Database** for more information.

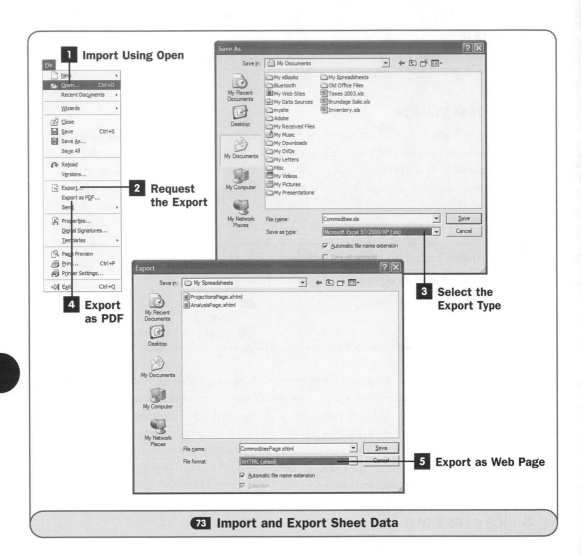

73 Import and Export Sheet Data

Although Calc imports virtually all Excel spreadsheets, Calc may have problems importing the following Excel items. If your imported spreadsheets contain any of these items, you may need to adjust the imported spreadsheet manually to eliminate the sections with these items or make a note that the items will not be appearing:

- AutoShapes
- OLE objects
- Advanced Office form fields
- Pivot tables

- Non-Calc-supported chart types
- Excel's conditional formatting
- Esoteric Excel functions and formulas

Like OpenOffice.org 2.0, StarOffice 8 and KOffice use the new file format developed by the Organization for the Advancement of Structured Information Standards (OASIS), so exchanging documents with StarOffice is virtually seamless. Working with Microsoft Excel files is not quite as transparent but is usually simple enough.

In addition to exporting Calc files to other spreadsheet programs, you can export them as *PDF* or *XHTML* files. PDF files are useful for eBooks and for offering as downloads to web page visitors because PDF files can be read on many kinds of computer systems. A primary advantage of PDF files is that they look the same no matter what kind of computer you view them on. The XHTML format is useful for saving a spreadsheet as a web page so that it can be opened in a web browser.

Like a PDF file, an XHTML file cannot be directly edited. People viewing the page in a Web browser can select and copy data, but cannot change it.

▶ KEY TERMS

Portable Document Format (PDF)—A file format developed by Adobe Systems, Inc., that enables you to electronically send formatted documents and have them appear onscreen exactly as they would if they were printed.

eXtensible Hypertext Markup Language (XHTML)—A nonproprietary file format that lets you save a file as a Web page and ensure that the content and formatting remain intact.

73

1 Import Using Open

To import an Excel or other non-OpenDocument format spreadsheet into Calc, simply use **File**, **Open** to request the file. Browse the files from the **Open** dialog box until you find the spreadsheet you want to import and then click **OK** to import the file into Calc. Almost always, assuming the spreadsheet doesn't contain some advanced or esoteric feature, such as those listed in this task's introduction, the spreadsheet imports perfectly, and you can continue editing and printing it as though you had created the sheet originally in Calc.

▶ NOTE

If you open a spreadsheet created in an earlier version of OpenOffice.org Calc (such as version 1.1), notice that not only do earlier Calc files have a different file extension (.sxc.), they also display a different icon in the **Open** dialog box. Like Excel files, these files open seamlessly in OpenOffice 2.0 and retain most formatting and content.

▶ TIP

After importing a spreadsheet, save the spreadsheet with **File**, **Save As** and select the OpenDocument Spreadsheet extension .ods from the **Save as type** list box to convert the spreadsheet to Calc's native format. This also preserves the file's original Excel format.

2 Request the Export

Although Calc's **File** menu contains an **Export** command, you should only use this command when you want to export your current spreadsheet data to a PDF file (see **36 Save a Document as a PDF File**).

To export your spreadsheet in a non-OpenDocument format, select **File, Save As**.

3 Select the Export Type

The **Save As** dialog box opens, and you select the type of file you want Calc to convert your spreadsheet to in the **Save as type** list box.

You can export the file to a Data Interchange Format with the .dif extension, a dBASE file with the .dbf extension, one of several versions of Excel (most commonly, the .xls extension is used for Excel spreadsheets), one of several pre-version 8 versions of StarCalc (with the .sdc extension), a SYLK file with the .slk extension, a text-based comma-separated values file (known as a *CSV* file) with the .csv or .txt extension, or an HTML document with the .html extension, which you would use if you wanted to display your spreadsheet as a Web page.

73

▶ **TIP**

The dBASE file format is useful when you use Calc as a database, as you learn in **75 About Calc Databases**.

When you click **Save**, Calc converts the spreadsheet to the format you selected and saves the file under the name you typed in the **File name** field. A warning dialog box may open if there is any danger of losing content or formatting in the selected format.

4 Export as PDF

Calc's **File, Export as PDF** command converts your spreadsheet to Adobe's PDF format (see **36 Save a Document as a PDF File**) and saves the file with the .PDF filename extension. After you save the file, an **Options** dialog box opens where you can set options such as choosing a range within the document print, or raising or lowering the quality of JPEG images contained in the document. You can customize your new PDF document or accept the defaults and click **OK**.

You can also use the **Export Directly As PDF** button on the **Standard** toolbar instead of the menu command to save a spreadsheet as a PDF document, but you will not be able to choose additional options for saving the file if you go this route.

5 **Export as Web Page**

Calc's **File**, **Export** command offers two choices: You can export to PDF format (as described in step 4) or you can export to XHTML format. The default file format in the **Export** dialog box is PDF, so use the **File format** list arrow to change to the XHTML format.

▶ **NOTE**

If you try to save an existing Calc spreadsheet in an earlier version of Calc (such as the OpenOffice 1.0 Spreadsheet file format), a dialog box opens to warn you that some formatting or content might be lost. Although you can choose to save in the older format if necessary, it's hard to imagine why anyone would decide not to upgrade to the newer version of the software.

▶ **TIPS**

An XML (eXtensible Markup Language) format is also available for Excel 2003 XML documents, as well as a PXL (Pocket Excel) format if you want to export to Microsoft's Pocket PC operating system.

Calc's **File**, **Export** command also offers the option of converting a file to PDF format, but the **File**, **Export to PDF** command offers quicker access to this option.

74

74 **About Advanced Spreadsheet Printing**

✔ **BEFORE YOU BEGIN**

47 Print a Spreadsheet
62 Set Up Calc Page Formatting

Printing Calc spreadsheets offers some challenges that other kinds of documents, such as Writer documents, do not require. For example, once you develop a comprehensive spreadsheet, you may want to print the spreadsheet with all its notes showing, perhaps even with formulas showing instead of values. Such reports serve as documentation to the spreadsheet and can help you pinpoint errors in the spreadsheet that might be more difficult to locate searching and scrolling around the screen.

▶ **TIP**

Before printing, be sure to view a preview with **File**, **Page Preview**. The preview ensures that your printed spreadsheet will look exactly the way you want it to look before you send the spreadsheet to paper.

The **Format**, **Page** menu option displays the **Page Style** dialog box. The **Sheet** tab displays the **Sheet** page, where you can specify the kinds of items you wish to print or to suppress during printing. For example, if you want to print formulas instead of the values they equate to, you would click to select the **Formulas** option in the **Print** area of the **Sheet** page.

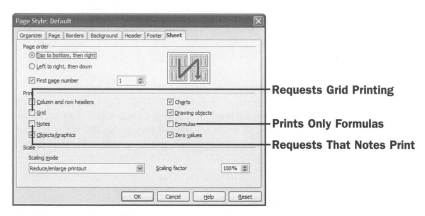

Requests Grid Printing

Prints Only Formulas

Requests That Notes Print

The Sheet page specifies how you want your spreadsheet to print.

74

Normally, the gridlines that separate cells are suppressed during printing, but to help with your row and column alignment when studying large spreadsheets, you may opt to select the **Grid** option so that Calc prints the gridlines to paper. In addition, Calc normally suppresses notes that you've attached to cells but will print those notes along with the rest of the spreadsheet if you click to select the **Notes** option.

▶ **TIP**

If your spreadsheet contains one or more charts along with data, you can print just the charts by unchecking every option in the **Print** section except the **Charts** option.

The **Print** dialog box itself enables you to print only a selected range. If, for example, you wanted to print only certain rows in your spreadsheet, select those rows and then select **File**, **Print** from the menu. Click the **Print** dialog box's **Selection** option before clicking **OK** to start printing.

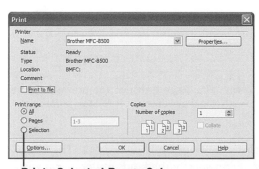

Prints Selected Range Only

Calc can print only selected ranges if you wish.

10

Using Calc as a Simple Database

IN THIS CHAPTER:

Although OpenOffice.org includes a full-featured *database* program called Base, it also supports the use of Calc-based database tables from which you can store, edit, sort, and report from the data.

If your data management needs are simple, you can use Calc's database features to store and organize lists of information without leaving the friendly confines of your Calc spreadsheet.

If your needs are more complex, however, you'll want to explore OpenOffice.org Base, a *relational database* program comparable to Microsoft Access that lets you create tables, forms, reports, queries, and views. You can also use Base to define relationships between different sets of data. That being said, you might still want to start working with databases in Calc so that you can learn some simple database concepts that will support *all* your data management needs.

▶ KEY TERM

Database—A collection of data that is often organized in rows and columns to make searching and sorting easy to do.

75

Everyone trudges through a lot of data at work and at home. With the proliferation of computers, information overload seems to be the norm. Calc's database features enable you to turn raw facts and figures into meaningful information. Calc processes data details so you can spend your valuable time analyzing results. Suppose that your company tracks thousands of parts in a Calc database, and you need to know exactly which part sold the most in Division 7 last April. Calc can supply the answer for you.

This chapter introduces you to the world of databases with Calc. The nature and use of databases are not difficult to master, but you must understand something about database design (see **75** About Calc Databases) before you can fully master Calc's capability to process database data.

75 About Calc Databases

✔ BEFORE YOU BEGIN	→ SEE ALSO
40 Create a New Spreadsheet	**76** Create a Calc Database
	77 Import Data into a Calc Database
	135 Create a Base Database

Before using a database, you need to learn how a database management system organizes data. With Calc, you can create, organize, manage, and report from data stored in your Calc spreadsheet.

▶ **NOTE**

Calc's row-and-column format makes it a useful tool as a database program and as a spreadsheet program. The difference between the two is how you access, change, and sort the data in the spreadsheet.

A database typically contains related data. In other words, you might create a home-office database with your household budget but keep another database to record your rare-book collection titles and their worth. In your household budget, you might track expenses, income, bills paid, and so forth, but that information does not overlap the book-collection database. Of course, if you buy a book, both databases might show the transaction, but the two databases would not overlap.

Technically, a database does not have to reside on a computer. Any place you store data in some organized format, such as a name and address directory, could be considered a database. In most cases, however, the term *database* is reserved for organized, computerized data.

When you design a database, consider its scope before you begin. Does your home business need an inventory system? Does your home business often need to locate a single sales contact from a large list of contacts? If so, a Calc database works well. Only you can decide whether the inventory and the sales contacts should be part of the same system or separate, unlinked systems. The database integration of inventory with the sales contacts requires much more work to design, but your business requirements might necessitate the integration. For example, you might need to track which customers bought certain products in the past.

If you need your database tables to relate to each other, so that you can create reports that, for example, compare your spending on rare books printed before 1750 and after 1750, and to see contact information for all dealers who sold you books that have appreciated in value in the past 12 months, you probably need a relational database such as Base. See Chapter 18, "Organizing Your Data with Base."

▶ **NOTE**

Not all database values relate to each other. Your company's loan records do not relate to your company's payroll, but both might reside in your company's accounting database. You probably would keep these in separate Calc spreadsheets, although for a small company, one spreadsheet with multiple sheets representing separate databases might be manageable.

To keep track of data, you can break down each database sheet into ***records*** and ***fields***. A database's structure acts just like a Calc worksheet because the rows and columns in a worksheet match the records and fields in a database. This similarity between databases and spreadsheets is why Calc works well for simple database management.

► KEY TERMS

Records—The rows in a database representing all the data for a single item. A single employee record would consist of one employee's data, such as employee number, first name, last name, address, birth date, hire date, and so on.

Fields—The columns in a database representing individual descriptions of the records. A field in an employee database might be the last name field or the hire date.

Relational database—A powerful type of database program that stores data in a series of related tables and allows you to view the data in different ways.

In the following figure, the database's records are the sheet's rows, and the fields are the columns. This database is a simple checkbook-register database; you usually organize your checkbook register just as you would organize a computerized version of a checkbook, so you will have little problem mastering Calc's concepts of records and fields.

76

Six Fields

	A	B	C	D	E	F	G
1			Checkbook Register Database				
2	Date	Number	Description	Amount	Deposit	Balance	
3	10/01/05		Starting Balance		$904.11	$904.11	
4	10/02/05	2561	Horizons Yoga	-$350.00		$554.11	
5	10/03/05	2562	Allied Internet Service	-$74.11		$480.00	
6	10/05/05	2563	North Center Cleaners	-$12.40		$467.60	
7	10/06/05	2564	Oasis Foods	-$48.53		$419.07	
8	10/10/05		Southern U. Paycheck		$897.31	$1,316.38	
9	10/11/05	2565	Jenna Beckman	-$25.00		$1,291.38	
10							
11							

Seven Records

A database contains records and fields that associate to Calc's rows and columns.

---

76 **Create a Calc Database**

✔ BEFORE YOU BEGIN	→ SEE ALSO
75 About Calc Databases	**77** Import Data into a Calc Database

You already know how to create a Calc database if you know how to create a Calc spreadsheet. A database consists of records and fields (see **75 About Calc Databases**), and a sheet inside a spreadsheet consists of rows and columns that perform the same purpose as records and fields when you type data into them.

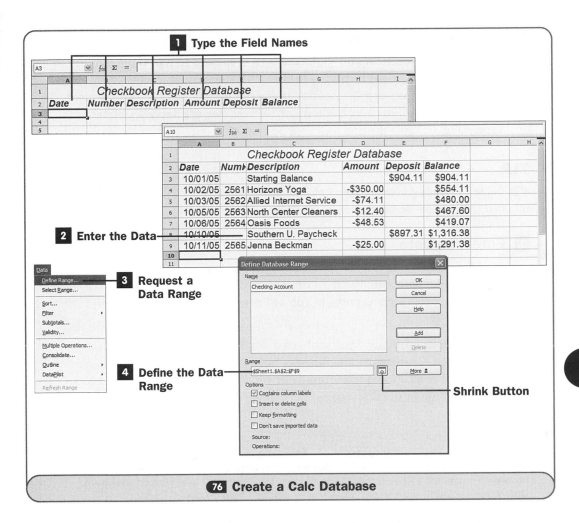

76 Create a Calc Database

Each field in your database must have a name. The simplest way to designate a field name is to type a label atop each column in your database. That label, such as **Address** or **DateHired**, becomes the name of that field. A field contains as many values as you have records in the database. For example, if your database has 100 rows, your database has 100 records, and each field in the record contains 100 values (some may be blank).

▶ **NOTE**

A field can consist of a calculated value that contains a formula based on other data in the record.

1 Type the Field Names

To create field names for your database, you only need to type a one-line label atop each column in your spreadsheet's database. First, label your spreadsheet with an appropriate title that describes the database you're creating. Use the standard character-formatting tools (see **12** **Apply Character Formatting**) to make the title and field names stand out.

▶ **TIP**

61 **Center a Heading over Multiple Columns** shows you how to center your database title in a wide column across the top of the fields.

2 Enter the Data

Type the data that falls beneath the field names. Reserve one row for each record in your database. Use the standard data-entry techniques you'd use for any spreadsheet (such as pressing **Tab** or **Enter** at the end of a value, and so on).

You may enter formulas if you wish. In a database that represents a checkbook register, for example, the **Balance** field (column) should be calculated and consist of a running total from your very first deposit that you used to set up the account in the first record.

▶ **NOTE**

You can sort database records into many different orders. For example, you can sort a checkbook record into alphabetical order based on whom you wrote checks to. This, however, makes the calculated **Balance** field nonfunctional for that view of your data. Only when sorted by date would a calculated balance field be useful.

If you want to use a database you create in Calc in the Base component of OpenOffice.org, you must first register the Calc database with OpenOffice.org. See **140** **Access an Existing Database** for more information.

3 Request a Data Range

Once you've entered some or all of your database records (you can always add more later), you must define a *data range* for the data so that Calc will know which rows and columns hold database data. Select your database rows and columns that will make up your database. If you include the column titles above each column, Calc makes those titles the field names that you can refer to later when accessing the database.

76

▶ **KEY TERM**

Data range—A range you define that specifies exactly which rows and columns comprise the records and fields of your database. If you include column title cells, Calc makes those titles the field headings in your database.

Select **Data**, **Define Range** from the menu to display the **Define Database Range** dialog box.

4 Define the Data Range

Type a name for the data range in the **Name** text box. Choose a simple name that you associate with this collection of data (don't include any spaces). Click the **Define Database Range** dialog box's **More** button to display extra options you'll often need to define the data range. If you've included column titles and you want Calc to make them field names, make sure to select the **Contains column labels** option. Calc fills in your selected range for you (using absolute addressing with the sheet name preceding the range), but you can change the range if you wish to. The **Shrink** button collapses the **Define Database Range** dialog box in case you want to look at your sheet once again without closing the dialog box (click **Shrink** again to restore the dialog box to its original size).

Click **Add** to add the data range to Calc's stored databases. You can define multiple data ranges per sheet, but generally you'll be able to track your data better if you keep each sheet a separate database range. If you ever want to remove a defined data range, display the **Define Database Range** dialog box once again but click the **Delete** button instead of the **Add** or **OK** button to remove the data range from Calc's database collection.

▶ **TIP**

If you plan to add data later to the database, click to check the **Insert or delete cells** option so that Calc automatically updates the data range when you append data to the end of it or remove rows from within the range. The **Keep formatting** option maintains the cell formats with the data.

77	**Import Data into a Calc Database**
✔ **BEFORE YOU BEGIN**	→ **SEE ALSO**
75 About Calc Databases	**78** Sort Calc Database Data
76 Create a Calc Database	

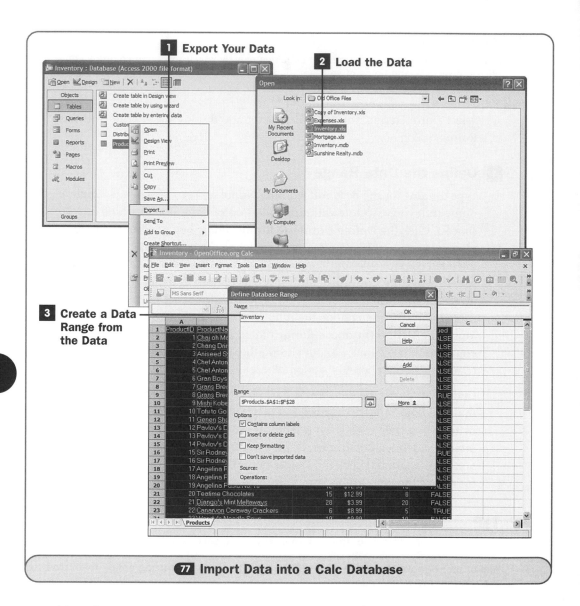

77 Import Data into a Calc Database

Although you can type data into a Calc database, if you already have that data stored elsewhere, you can usually import that data directly into Calc by first saving the data in a format that Calc can read. For example, suppose your company uses an Access database for its records and you want to import the customer table into Calc's database so that you can work with the data more easily. You would first export that customer table's data in Excel's XLS spreadsheet format and then open that spreadsheet in Calc.

Once the table is open, you must define the data range and save the file as a Calc spreadsheet. See **73** **Import and Export Sheet Data** for help with importing non-Calc spreadsheets into Calc and **76** **Create a Calc Database** for help with converting your imported data to a Calc spreadsheet data range.

▶ NOTE

A spreadsheet can have multiple data ranges, and they can overlap. Depending on how you want to sort or filter your data (see **79** **Filter Data That You Want to See**), you might overlap several columns, or fields, in several different range names.

1 Export Your Data

In Access, or wherever your data resides, export that data to an Excel spreadsheet or an OpenDocument spreadsheet (if this option is available). In Access, you can right-click over a table name, select the **Export** option, select the Excel XLS spreadsheet format, and click **Export All** to export the entire table.

2 Load the Data

Select **File**, **Open** and then select the file to load into Calc.

3 Create a Data Range from the Data

Select all the data including the column headings. Once you've selected all the data that is to reside in the database, select **Data**, **Define Range** to define the data as a data range and to name the data range. This name becomes your database name for this data.

▶ TIP

If column headings didn't import from the original source, you should take the time to add them. The column names will serve as field names for your data.

Click **Add** to save the data range and return to your spreadsheet. If you don't perform any database-related tasks, such as sorting or filtering, you can work with the data just as you would any spreadsheet data. The data, when defined in a data range, however, is also available to you for analysis as a database.

77

78 | **Sort Calc Database Data**

✔ BEFORE YOU BEGIN	→ SEE ALSO
77 Import Data into a Calc Database	**79** Filter Data That You Want to See
	80 Compute Table Totals and Subtotals

One of the reasons some people create a database data range from their spreadsheet data is to sort the data using Calc's database-related sorting tools. Once you set up the database, you can sort on amounts or text *ascending* or *descending*.

▶ KEY TERMS

Ascending—The sort method where lower values are sorted early in the list and higher values fall at the end of the list, as is the case with an alphabetical list of names.

Descending—The sort method where higher values are sorted early in the list and lower values fall at the end of the list, as would be the case where payroll amounts are sorted from highest to lowest.

By sorting your data, you can often gain insights into it, such as where the top and bottom values lie, without having to resort to extra work to find those values (such as writing **Max()** or **Min()** functions in cells outside your database's data range). Also, you can print parts of the list in ZIP Code order as you might do when printing a list of names and addresses for a mailing.

▶ NOTE

When you sort a data range, you sort on one or more fields (columns), but all the data in all the rows of the data range sort along with your key sorting fields.

1 Request the Sort

Once you've defined the data range for the data you want to sort, select **Data**, **Sort** from the menu to display the **Sort** dialog box.

2 Specify Sort Criteria

Set up your sorting criteria by selecting a field name from the **Sort by** list box. The field names will be those fields you designated as field names (the labels atop the columns) when you created the data range.

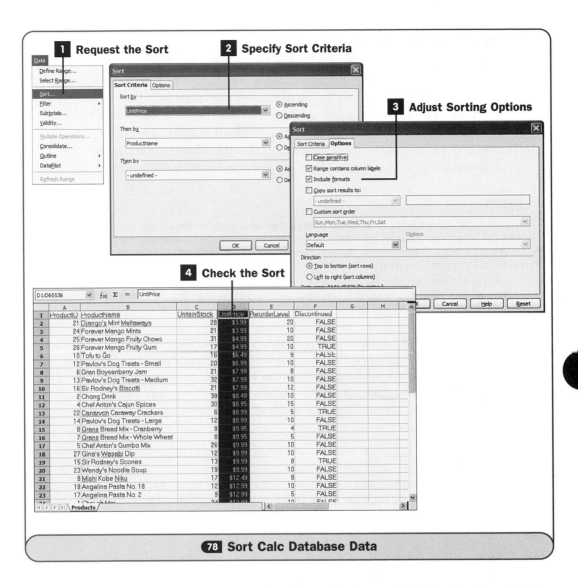

78 Sort Calc Database Data

You can select optional second and even third sort criteria by selecting a field name from the next two **Then by** list boxes. For example, if you sort initially by **UnitPrice**, then by **ProductName**, if two or more products in your data range have the same unit price, they will be listed together and sorted alphabetically within that price, as long as you keep the **Ascending** options selected. If you change **Ascending** to **Descending** on any of the sort criteria field names, that criteria will sort from high to low instead of from low to high values.

3 Adjust Sorting Options

Click the **Options** tab to display the **Options** page in the **Sort** dialog box. The **Options** page enables you to adjust the way Calc sorts your data. You can make the sorts case sensitive so that lowercase letters are distinguished from (and considered to follow) uppercase letters. Therefore, eBay would follow Zsoft if you sort on company names. (Without the **Case sensitive** option checked, eBay would be listed before Zsoft because eBay precedes Zsoft in the alphabet.)

▶ TIPS

You'll almost always want to keep the **Range contains column labels** option checked so that Calc does not consider your field names at the top of the columns to be part of the data that it sorts. Also, keeping **Include formats** selected ensures your sorted data remains formatted properly.

To sort on one field at a time, you can also use the **Sort Ascending** and **Sort Descending** buttons on the Standard toolbar.

If you specify a range after **Copy sort results to**, Calc will sort the data but place it at that range, keeping your original data range intact. Otherwise, Calc sorts your original data. The **Custom sort order** option enables you, if you've created a *custom sort list*, to change the way Calc sorts your data from the normal alphabetical or numerical order to an order based on a different ranking system you define.

▶ KEY TERM

Custom sort list—A predefined list of values (such as month names and the days of the week), or a list you define from the **Tools, Options, Spreadsheet, Custom Lists** option, that determines a special sorting rank that differs from the normal alphabetic or numerical sorts.

Because Calc databases are almost always stored with the rows representing records and the columns representing fields, keep the option labeled **Top to bottom (sort rows)** selected so that Calc sorts all rows properly. If you select the **Left to right (sort columns)** option, Calc sorts an entire column's data before looking at the next column, which can really mess up your data unless your original data imported was transposed for some reason.

When you click the **OK** button, Calc sorts your data in the order you requested.

4 Check the Sort

Once Calc finishes the sort, check the data to ensure that Calc sorted properly. For example, if you sorted by **UnitPrice** and then by **ProductName** fields in ascending order, you would make sure that the table is sorted from lowest priced products to highest, and that product names at the same price point appear in alphabetical order.

---

79 **Filter Data That You Want to See**

✔ BEFORE YOU BEGIN	→ SEE ALSO
77 Import Data into a Calc Database	**75** Create a Calc Database
78 Sort Calc Database Data	**80** Compute Table Totals and Subtotals

---

Databases can grow to be enormous. Without some way to filter the data, finding what you want is tedious. Calc's **Find and Replace** command works well enough to locate values that you want to find, but by being able to apply a filter to your database, you can actually hide data that does not currently interest you without removing that data from your database. When you're done with the filtered data, you can easily return to the full database view.

Calc supports two kinds of filters, both of which are related:

- *AutoFilter* filters, where you specify values to filter by

- Standard dialog box filters, where you can specify a range of values to filter by

▶ **KEY TERM**

AutoFilter—A Calc database filter where you select from a list of values to filter by and view.

▶ **NOTE**

If you delete or format cell ranges that include rows currently hidden by an auto-filter, those rows are not affected by the deletion or formatting. For more information on formatting cells, see **60** **Format Cells**; for more information on deleting cells, see **64** **Edit Cell Data.**

1 **Request a Standard Filter**

Once you define your data range, you can request a filter by selecting **Data, Filter, Standard Filter**. Calc displays the **Standard Filter** dialog box.

2 **Specify the Filter Criteria**

Select from the **Field Name** dialog box. All the fields defined by the data range's column names will appear when you open the **Field Name** list box. Select a condition in the **Condition** list box, such as an equal sign or less-than sign, and then enter a quantity (you can also click the **Value** list box's

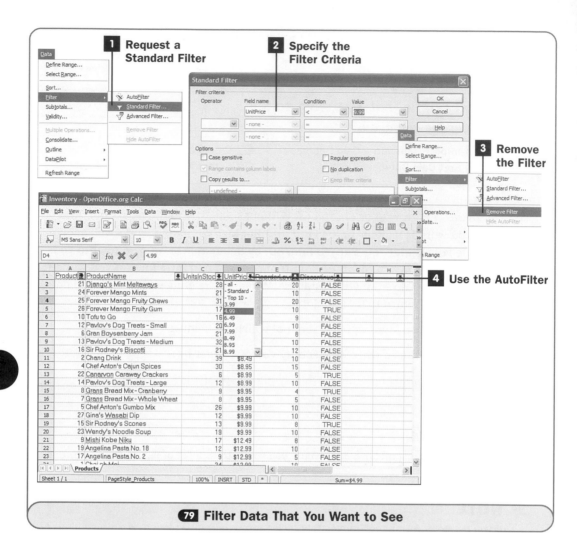

79 Filter Data That You Want to See

down arrow to see a list of possible values) stating what you want to filter by. For example, if you enter UnitsPrice, <, and 9.99, you are requesting that you only want to see the products that are priced less than $9.99.

You may add additional criteria to filter down your data even further by selecting **AND** or **OR** from the **Operator** column and entering second and even third criteria.

▶ **TIP**

Click the **More** button to see additional filter options, such as the ability to make your criteria case sensitive so a match is made against text fields only if the uppercase and lowercase letters match your criteria's uppercase and lowercase letters. Also, you can request that the filtered data be copied to a range you specify instead of the filtering taking place right in your data range itself.

Click **OK** to apply the filter and view the results.

③ Remove the Filter

To restore your data to its original state once you've viewed, printed, stored, or saved the filtered data, select **Data**, **Filter**, **Remove Filter** to remove the filter and return your complete data range to your spreadsheet.

④ Use the AutoFilter

To use the AutoFilter feature, select **Data**, **Filter**, **AutoFilter**. Arrows appear to the right of each field name.

When you click one of the field name arrows, a list of values opens to display all possible unique values in that field, with scrollbars if needed to display the entire list. When you select any value in that list, Calc immediately filters on that value, displaying only those records that match that criteria. For example, if you click the **UnitsInStock** field name arrow and select **12**, only the products with an inventory of **12** will appear in the list.

Once you create the filter, you can print, sort, save, or copy the filtered data and return to the full database by selecting **Data**, **Filter**, **AutoFilter** once again to remove the check mark next to the command.

80

▶ TIPS

For quick filters when you want to filter based on exact matches, use the AutoFilter feature, which is faster than displaying the **Standard Filter** dialog box every time you want to filter the database.

If the **Tools** toolbar is open, you can access the AutoFilter feature by clicking the **AutoFilter** button. To open the **Tools** toolbar, choose **View**, **Toolbars**, **Tools**.

Use the **Top 10** option in the **AutoFilter** list to see the 10 records with the highest value in the field name column you chose—for example, the 10 highest prices or the 10 top sales amounts.

---

80 | **Compute Table Totals and Subtotals**

✔ **BEFORE YOU BEGIN**

77 Import Data into a Calc Database
78 Sort Calc Database Data
79 Filter Data That You Want to See

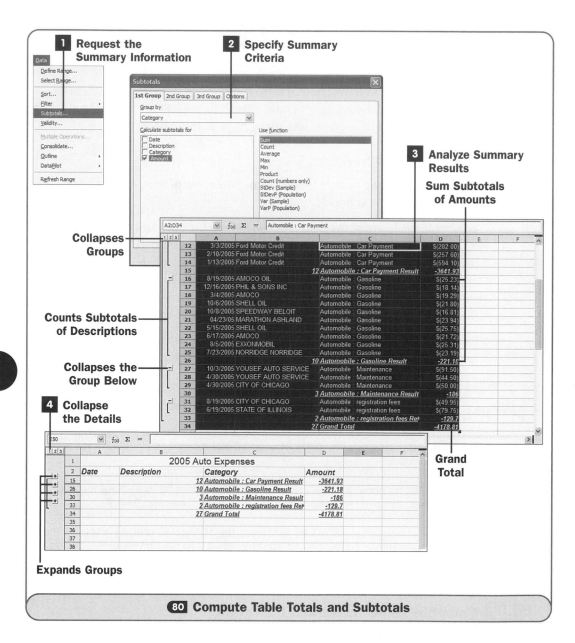

80 Compute Table Totals and Subtotals

When working with any kind of financial database information, the ability to calculate subtotals and totals, based on sorted data, becomes necessary. For example, you might want to see all the total sales from a given region or ZIP Code. If any sales are down in one area, you can get your Marketing Department to step up their efforts in that area.

Calc can summarize database data for you based on any of the following criteria:

- **Sum**—The added total of data

- **Count**—The number of items in the data range

- **Average**—The calculated intermediate value in a range of data

- **Min or max amounts**—The lowest or highest value in the data

- **Product**—The multiplied result of the data values

- **Standard deviation (of a sample or population)**—A statistic that measures how well dispersed values in a data range are

- **Variance (of a sample or population)**—The square of the standard deviation used for statistical measurements

❶ Request the Summary Information

Click anywhere within the data range that you want to summarize. Select **Data**, **Subtotals** to open the **Subtotals** dialog box.

❷ Specify Summary Criteria

The **Subtotals** dialog box opens with the **1st Group** tab displayed. This is where you specify the first grouping you want to see. Often, you'll select only one group, even though Calc supports up to four subtotal groups. Specify the **Group by** value (such as expense category), followed by a selection of the field you want a subtotal for (such as **Amount**). You then must tell Calc how the subtotals are to be calculated (such as by **Sum**). In this case, you are requesting a sum for each category of expense so that you can see what you spent in each area (such as gasoline and maintenance). If you also enable the **Description** field and then click the **Count** function, Calc will tell you how many transactions are contained in each category grouping.

▶ NOTE

The 2nd Group and 3rd Group tabs are for performing statistical analysis, which you may want to do when you have multiple divisions in multiple areas, or countries, and want to group first by area, then by division, and then by an individual field, such as sales per customer. The resulting summarized groups would show a subtotal of each customer, then each division, and finally each area, with a grand total at the bottom.

❸ Analyze Summary Results

Calc produces a summarized version of your data range. At first, the summary may look confusing because Calc inserts counts (or sums or averages or other summary items, depending on your selection) throughout your data.

80

The count totals, for example, might show by each category in your data what the expenses were for that category and how many individual expenses there were for each category. At the end of the report, Calc provides a grand total of all the counts.

4 Collapse the Details

You can click the minus sign to the left of a row number to collapse that group's detail. The minus sign then becomes a plus sign. By collapsing various types of detail in your summary (by clicking the **1**, **2**, or **3** button to the left of the row number), you can get a count of the grand total only, of each group, of each group with all the details shown, respectively.

80

PART III

Impressing Audiences with Impress

IN THIS PART:

11

Learning About Impress

IN THIS CHAPTER:

Have you wanted to wow your audiences with professional *presentations*? You can with Impress. This chapter introduces you to Impress. You'll soon be designing and creating effective presentations. By using the predefined presentation tools of Impress, you generate good-looking presentations without needing to worry about design, format, and color specifics. After Impress generates a sample presentation, you need only follow a few simple procedures if you want to modify and tweak the presentation into your own unique version.

▶ KEY TERM

Presentation—A set of screens, called *pages* or *slides*, that you present to people in a room or over the Internet.

The primary purpose of Impress is to help you design, create, and edit presentations and printed handouts. Because Impress provides a wide variety of predefined templates, you don't have to be a graphics design specialist to create good-looking presentations.

▶ NOTE

Remember, the term *presentation* refers to an entire Impress collection of slides (or pages), whereas the term *slide* or *page* refers to an individual screen within that presentation. *Slide* is more common than *page* due to Microsoft Office PowerPoint's use of the slide terminology.

Impress slides can hold many kinds of information. Here are a few of the things you can add to an Impress presentation:

- Data you insert into Impress, including text, charts, graphs, and graphics
- Writer documents
- Live data from the Internet, including complete web pages
- Calc worksheets
- Multimedia content such as video and sound files
- Graphics from graphics programs such as Draw

81 Create a New Presentation

✔ BEFORE YOU BEGIN	→ SEE ALSO
82 Set Impress Options	**83** Open an Existing Presentation
	84 Run a Presentation

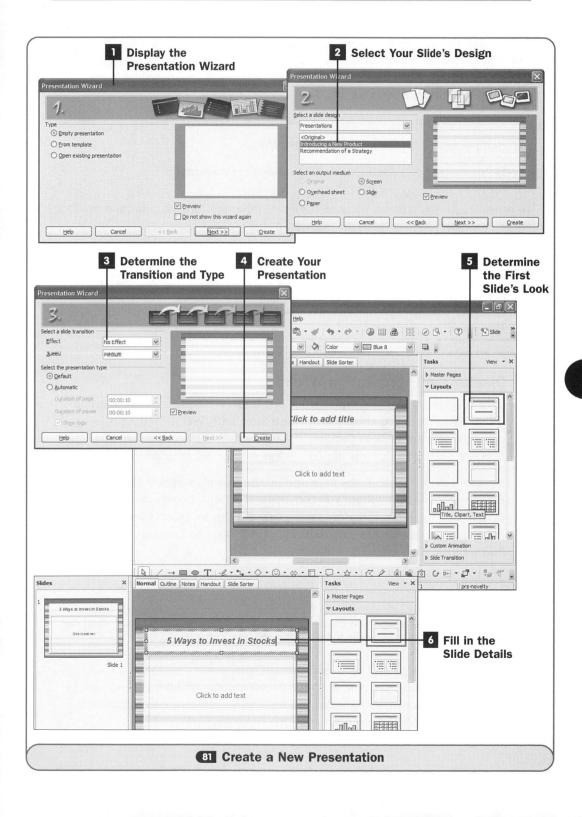

1 Display the Presentation Wizard

2 Select Your Slide's Design

3 Determine the Transition and Type

4 Create Your Presentation

5 Determine the First Slide's Look

6 Fill in the Slide Details

You'll almost always begin a new presentation the same way—you'll start Impress, follow the **Presentation Wizard**, and build an initial but empty presentation. Perhaps you'll build an empty presentation based on a template supplied with Impress or from a template you built before and saved for reuse.

The creation of a presentation does take two steps:

1. Build your initial presentation with the Wizard.

2. Fill in details by designing each slide inside the presentation.

In other words, you'll create an overall presentation that forms a collection of slides and then you'll work on the individual slides.

▶ **TIP**

Plan your presentations! Think about your target audience. Presenting identical information to two audiences might require completely different approaches. A company's annual meeting for shareholders requires a different format, perhaps, from the board of director's meeting. After determining your target audience, create a slide outline before you begin.

81

1 Display the Presentation Wizard

Start **Impress** by selecting **OpenOffice.org Impress** from the program group on the **Start** menu. Assuming the default **Start with Wizard** setting is in effect (see **81 Set Impress Options**), the **Presentation Wizard** dialog box appears. You can follow the dialog box's steps to create your presentation.

You can elect to create a new presentation that is empty by selecting the **Empty presentation** option, you can create a presentation from a template by selecting the **From template** option (see **86 Use an Impress Template**), or you can open an existing presentation (see **83 Open an Existing Presentation**).

▶ **TIP**

Although most Impress users prefer the Wizard's help, you can click the option labeled **Do not show this dialog again** on the initial **Presentation Wizard** dialog box to keep the Wizard from running automatically the next time you start Impress.

If starting a new presentation from scratch, you would click to select the **Empty presentation** option. Keep the **Preview** option checked so you can see a preview of your presentation as you build it. To continue creating the new presentation, click the **Next** button.

2 Select Your Slide's Design

The next step in the Wizard enables you to select your slide's design. By selecting either **Presentations** or **Presentation Backgrounds**, you are actually selecting from a short list of templates that come with Impress. For example, by selecting **Presentations** and then selecting **Introducing a New Product** from the list that appears below, you inform the Wizard that you want to create a new presentation based on the stored template for introducing a new product. Even though you may have elected to create an empty presentation in step 1, Impress still offers these templates from which you can choose. The templates provide background colors and some default slide effects, but in reality, the templates are not that impressive… even though they belong to Impress! Impress does not come presupplied with scores of sample template presentations, only a couple. If you're just beginning to use Impress, you might want to use a template guide to create your first presentation so you won't have to supply as many color, screen, and design elements as you would if you began with a completely blank presentation. Having said that, if you select <Original>, Impress creates a blank presentation without any background color or assumptions of any kind. **86 Use an Impress Template** explains more about the templates that you can use and create with Impress.

Generally, you'll be creating a presentation for the screen. For example, if you plan to give your presentation as a speech, you might display your presentation from a laptop's projection system to a large screen that the audience can follow. Rarely will you want to create a presentation for printed paper only. So unless you plan to present your presentation on a medium other than a screen, leave the **Screen** option checked. Click **Next** to move to the next Wizard screen.

81

▶ NOTE

If you plan to print your presentation for audience handouts, even though you will be giving the presentation on the screen during your talk, keep the **Screen** option selected. You can always print a screen-based presentation to paper without rerunning the Presentation Wizard.

3 Determine the Transition and Type

You now can select the kind of *transition* you want Impress to make as your presentation moves from slide to slide. If you leave **Effect** at its default setting of **No Effect**, Impress simply replaces each slide with the next as you move forward in your presentation. The **Speed** option determines the transitional speed. You can always change the speed later, so generally, unless you're familiar with the transition speeds, you should leave the default speed (**Medium**) as is until you see whether you need a faster or slower setting.

▶ KEY TERM

Transition—The way one slide leaves the presentation screen and the next slide appears. You can select from a variety of Impress transitional effects, such as fading from one slide to another or having the new slide fly in from the side or from the top, overwriting the previous slide.

▶ NOTE

Be sure to save your presentation when you finish building it. Even better, save your presentation after you complete each slide to ensure that the presentation is safely stored on your disk drive in case your computer has a problem of some kind and you must reboot. Impress presentation files use the `.odp` (OpenDocument presentation) file-name extension.

Your presentation type might be an automatic slide show, as might be the case if you want to set up your presentation in a kiosk-style setting where your presentation plays by itself. You might prefer an automatic presentation for a sales screen that advertises products as customers walk by. If you want an automatic presentation such as this, adjust the duration settings that determine how long each slide page remains on the screen and how long you want Impress to pause between presentations before repeating the presentation once again. See **101 Make an Automatic Presentation** for help with creating and presenting automatic presentations.

▶ TIP

If the **Layouts** task pane does not appear, choose **Slide Layout** from the **Format** menu to display it. If the task pane takes up too much room on your screen, you can close it when it's not in use or drag it into the document area to turn it into a smaller, floating window.

For presentations you give and control yourself, leave the presentation type set to **Default** so that you control when each slide changes to the next as you give your presentation.

4 Create Your Presentation

When you're ready to create the presentation, click the **Create** button.

5 Determine the First Slide's Look

Once the **Presentation Wizard** ends, your presentation is far from over! What you accomplished with the **Presentation Wizard** is creating the backgrounds, default transitions, and time durations of your overall presentation. Not one slide is finished yet because you have yet to add text or graphics to any slide. Actually, only one slide even exists—the very first one. Your job is to determine the kind of slide you want to modify the first default slide into by selecting an *AutoLayout* from the Layouts task pane to the right of the work area.

▶ KEY TERM

AutoLayout—A predesigned slide layout for Impress presentation slides. Some AutoLayouts contain both text and graphics, whereas others are more suitable for title screens with large titles or for charts with very little to no text.

▶ TIP

If the **Layouts** task pane does not appear, choose **Slide Layout** from the **Format** menu to display it. If the task pane takes up too much room on your screen, you can close it when it's not in use or drag it into the document area to turn it into a smaller, floating window.

Select an AutoLayout slide layout by double-clicking it in the Layouts pane. Impress changes the first slide in your presentation to the selected AutoLayout format so that you can continue filling in the details and continue inserting new slides until you finish the presentation.

6 Fill in the Slide Details

AutoLayout slides provide you with placeholders for text and sometimes for graphics and charts. To add text, click a placeholder and replace the placeholder text with your own text. You'll continue inserting new slides, modifying the new slides by selecting an AutoLayout for them, and filling in their details as you build your presentation.

82　Set Impress Options

→ SEE ALSO

81 Create a New Presentation
84 Run a Presentation

Not everybody works the same way, so not every Impress user wants to use Impress the same way. By setting some of Impress's many options, you will make Impress conform to the way you like to do things. For example, you may want Impress to create all new presentations using the **Presentation Wizard** (see **81** **Create a New Presentation**) or you might always want to begin with a completely empty presentation and add all the initial elements. The Impress options you set control these and many other Impress aspects.

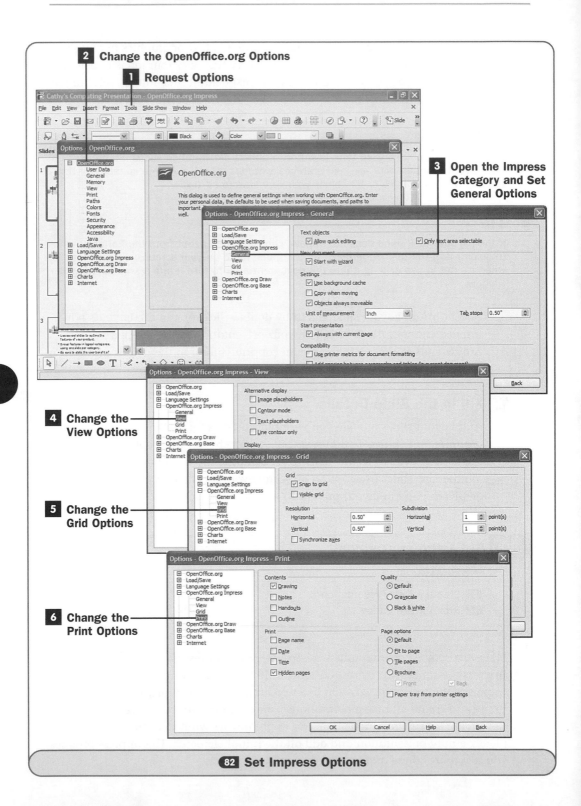

82 Set Impress Options

▶ **TIP**

Even if you're familiar with Calc or another OpenOffice.org set of options, initially learning about Impress's options helps you see a preview of what Impress is able to do.

As a matter of fact, Impress has an option for just about anything! Table 11.1 describes Impress's options. You'll learn a lot about what Impress can do just by looking through the option categories available to you.

TABLE 11.1 Impress Presentation Options

Impress Option Category	Explanation
General	Describes general Impress settings, such as the initial use of the Presentation Wizard when you create new presentations, and sets the default unit of measurement for elements within a presentation.
View	Describes how Impress appears on the screen and which Impress special elements, such as rulers and text placeholders, are shown.
Grid	Determines whether Impress displays a grid for you on your presentation slide backgrounds, to help you place elements on your slides more accurately and consistently.
Print	Describes how Impress handles the printing of presentations, such as printing presentation notes along with the presentation.

82

1 **Request Options**

Select **Options** from Impress's **Tools** menu. The **Options** dialog box appears. From the **Options** dialog box, you can change any of Impress's options as well as overall options for all OpenOffice.org programs. Click the plus sign next to OpenOffice.org to display the categories.

2 **Change the OpenOffice.org Options**

Select any option in the **OpenOffice.org** category to modify OpenOffice.org-wide settings such as pathnames. For example, if you don't like the pathname you see when you open or save a file, click the My Documents option in the **Paths** category, and then click **Edit** and change the file path to a different location.

▶ **TIPS**

If you're new to OpenOffice.org, consider leaving all the OpenOffice.org options "as is" until you familiarize yourself with how the OpenOffice.org programs work.

If you change a file path and want to restore the original path, select the path again and click **Default**.

3 Open the Impress Category and Set General Options

Click the plus sign next to the **Impress** option to display the four Impress-specific options listed in Table 11.1 at the beginning of this task.

Click the **General** options category; the dialog box changes to show options you can select to make changes to the general Impress options. The **Text Objects** section enables you to specify how you wish to edit text objects inside your presentations—either quickly when they're available by clicking them or only after you double-click the text object (or click the **Option** bar's **Allow Quick Editing** button, if the Options toolbar is displayed). The **New Document** section determines whether you want the Presentation Wizard to start when you first create a new presentation. The **Settings** section describes how you want Impress to use its *background cache* when displaying objects in a presentation (without the cache, Impress runs more slowly, although on recent computers you'll hardly notice the difference). In addition, you can specify how you wish to handle copying and moving presentation objects, and you may also specify how you want to handle measurements and tab stops, such as in inches or metrically. The **Start Presentation** section determines whether you want Impress to jump to the most-recently edited slide or the first slide when you open a new presentation. The **Compatibility** section determines how you want Impress to handle the printing and paragraph-spacing capabilities of Impress.

▶ KEY TERM

Background cache—A memory area that Impress can use to speed some operations. Instead of waiting for Impress to load all objects needed in a presentation from the disk drive, you can have Impress preload certain presentation objects into the background cache memory area so those objects more rapidly appear when it becomes time for them to display.

4 Change the View Options

Click the **View** options category under the **Impress** category; the dialog box changes to show options that handle Impress's onscreen display. The **Alternative display** section determines how and when Impress shows slide elements such as text and images or shows only placeholders or contours. If you choose to show **Image placeholders** or **Text** *placeholders*, Impress will not display actual text and graphics but rather will show placeholders for them to speed your screen's display. If your slides contain drawings, you may want to display them in **Contour mode** or **Line contour only** to speed their display as well. During the editing of a large presentation, you can often speed up the editing process by electing to show placeholders and contours instead of actual text and graphics. When running your presentation for others, of course, Impress will show the actual text and graphics during the presentation. The **Display** section determines how special elements such as the rulers are to show while you work within Impress.

▶ **KEY TERM**

Placeholders—Fast-loading graphic or text objects that take the place of slower-loading graphic images and long spans of text.

5 Change the Grid Options

Click to select the **Grid** category under the **Impress** option category. The **Grid** section allows you to determine whether you wish to display a nonprinting grid to help align objects, and whether you want to use the **Snap to** feature so that items automatically align with the nearest gridline. The **Resolution** section specifies the width between each grid point measurement (decrease the width for detailed slides). If you click to check the **Synchronize axes** option, when you change the *X-axis*, the *Y-axis* adjusts symmetrically at the same time, instead of changes to one axis not affecting the other. The **Snap** section allows you to determine what you want objects to snap, or align, to and just how precisely. If you plan to produce many freeform presentation slides, you'll want to turn off all snap-to items. If you create commercial presentations, such as for business meetings, advertisements, and education classes, that show relationships and textual backgrounds and layouts, you may wish to require that some objects move toward the closest snap-to grid for consistency and alignment of objects.

▶ **KEY TERMS**

X-axis—The horizontal axis on a slide (or drawing) with the lower-left corner of your slide having an X-axis value of 0 and increasing as you move up the slide.

Y-axis—The vertical axis on a slide (or drawing) with the lower-left corner of your slide having a Y-axis value of 0 and increasing as you move to the right on the slide.

6 Change the Print Options

Click to select the **Print** category under the **Impress** option category. The **Contents** section lets you specify whether, when you're printing, Impress should include graphic objects, notes, handouts, and an outline. The **Quality** section allows you to determine whether you want your slides printed in the default screen colors, in a more efficient grayscale, or in black and white (both printed without colors, thus saving color printer ink and toner). The **Print** section specifies what you want printed, such as the page name (if

82

you've assigned one), date, time, and pages you've hidden within the presentation but may want to print. The **Page options** section allows you to determine how you want your presentations to fit the final page—whether they take up the actual size specified by the ruler on your drawing or whether you want Impress to shrink the slides enough to fit on the current page. You can use the **Brochure** option if you want to print on the front and back of the page and you can opt to use the printer's own paper tray settings instead of the default settings.

▶ **TIP**

If you are new to presentations, perhaps it's best to accept Impress's default option settings. Read through them now to familiarize yourself with Impress terminology, however. Once you've created some presentations, you'll better understand how these options impact your work.

---

83 **Open an Existing Presentation**

✔ **BEFORE YOU BEGIN**	→ **SEE ALSO**
82 Set Impress Options	**84** Run a Presentation
81 Create a New Presentation	

83

When you open a document in most programs, such as Writer or Calc, you usually start the program and then select **File**, **Open** from the menu. Opening a presentation from within Impress usually differs somewhat due to the importance of the Presentation Wizard and its appearance every time you start Impress.

▶ **NOTE**

Obviously, if you've turned off the option to begin with the **Presentation Wizard** (see **82** **Set Impress Options**), Impress starts without the Wizard. Whenever you're inside Impress and want to open an existing presentation, you do use the **File**, **Open** menu command to open an existing presentation.

The **Presentation Wizard** dialog box gives you the option to open an existing presentation instead of creating a new presentation. If you want to open an existing presentation, Impress's the **Presentation Wizard** dialog box helps by displaying a list of presentation files from which you can choose.

▶ **NOTE**

Microsoft PowerPoint uses the .ppt file extension.

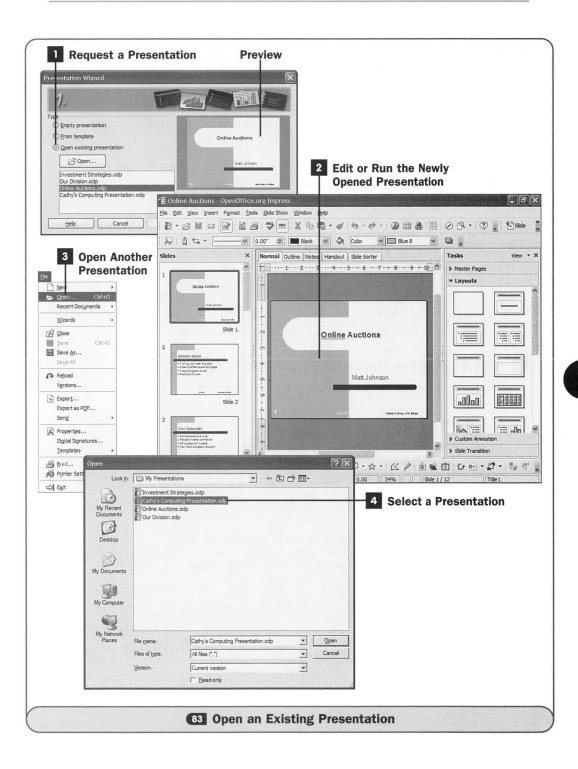

1 Request a Presentation

Select **Presentation** from the **OpenOffice.org** Windows menu. Impress opens the **Presentation Wizard** dialog box from which you can start a new presentation or, in this case, select an existing presentation. Click the option labeled **Open existing presentation** to see a list of Impress presentations in your default folder.

You can also open Microsoft PowerPoint presentations in Impress, although these files are not listed in the Presentation Wizard. To view any Microsoft PowerPoint files in your default folder, or to browse to other folders for additional Impress files, click **Open** to display the **Open** dialog box, where you can browse to any folder location and select a file. Impress also shows a graphic preview of the first slide in any Impress presentation in the **Presentation Wizard**'s preview area when you click to select the presentation.

Although you would think Impress would give you an **Open** button, instead you must click the **Create** button to open your selected presentation.

83

2 Edit or Run the Newly Opened Presentation

Once Impress loads the presentation, you are free to run or edit it.

3 Open Another Presentation

Once inside Impress, if you want to open a second presentation, select **File**, **Open** from the menu. Impress displays the **Open** dialog box from which you can select a presentation to open.

▶ TIP

If you want to close your existing presentation before opening another one, select **File**, **Close** to do so. If you've made changes since you last saved the presentation, Impress gives you the opportunity to save the presentation before closing it.

4 Select a Presentation

From the **Open** dialog box, select the presentation you wish to open and click the **Open** button. Impress opens the presentation, and you can edit or run the presentation.

84 **Run a Presentation**

✔ BEFORE YOU BEGIN	→ SEE ALSO
81 Create a New Presentation	**85** Print a Presentation
83 Open an Existing Presentation	

Unlike a Writer document or a Calc spreadsheet or a Draw drawing, your Impress presentation is active from the beginning. That is, your presentation is meant to move, from slide to slide, from beginning to end, and possibly back and forth, depending on the exact order you desire.

Therefore, your audience doesn't just read a static document or spreadsheet when they view your presentation. When you want to show your audience an Impress presentation, you *run* the presentation. In Impress terminology, when you run a presentation, you show your audience a *slide show*.

▶ KEY TERMS

Run—The act of showing your Impress presentation to an audience so the presentation moves from slide to slide.

Slide show—Your running presentation, given this name due to its slide-by-slide format.

You'll want to master some common presentation-controlling keystrokes before you give a presentation. When you master these keystrokes, you'll be able to step through your presentation, jump around the presentation, and control the entire presentation live. Table 11.2 lists the keystrokes you should know before running your presentation.

▶ TIP

If you use your mouse pointer in your presentation, it's simple to move forward one slide at a time by clicking anywhere on your slide with your left mouse button.

TABLE 11.2　Using the Keyboard to Navigate Through Presentations

Press This Key...	To Move...
PageDown	Forward through your presentation one slide each time you press PageDown
PageUp	Backward through your presentation one slide each time you press PageUp
Home	To the first slide in your presentation
End	To the last slide in your presentation

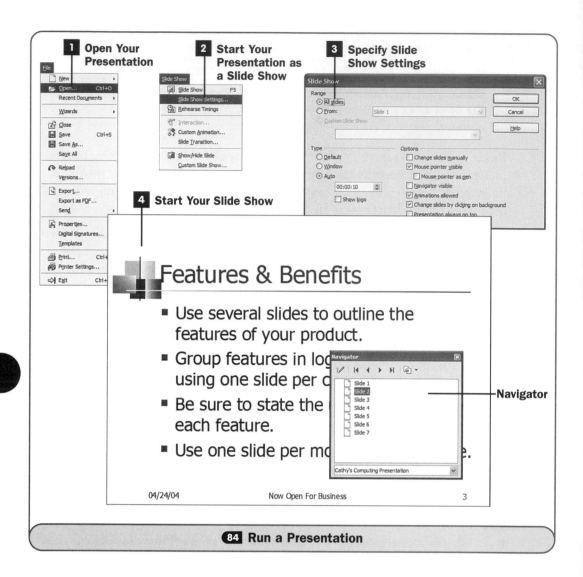

84 Run a Presentation

1 Open Your Presentation

Select **File**, **Open** from the menu and select the presentation you want to run.

▶ TIP

Most presentations are given in front of an audience, often from a laptop plugged into an overhead projector. Walk through this task of running your presentation before your audience arrives to ensure that you have the overhead connected properly to your laptop.

▣ Start Your Presentation as a Slide Show

You now can select **Slide Show, Slide Show Settings** from the menu to prepare for your presentation. Impress displays the dialog box.

▣ Specify Slide Show Settings

Many of your **Slide Show** dialog box settings are determined when you create your presentation, although you can always change them here at the **Slide Show** dialog box. You'll be able to select all or just a range of slides (from the **From** list box) as well as determine how your slide show will display (either in the default full-screen mode or in a smaller window). You can display the OpenOffice.org logo (assuming you'd want to do that) by clicking the **Show logo** option. Also, you can set the pause time between presentations that show from the **Auto** option.

▶ **TIP**

Most presenters prefer to keep their mouse pointer showing during a presentation, although the **Mouse pointer visible** option can hide your mouse pointer if you wish. During your presentation, you can use your mouse pointer to point out items of interest to your audience.

84

For example, if the **Change slides manually** option is unchecked, you originally created this presentation to display automatically, without intervention. If you're speaking and using the presentation to support your speech, you'll probably not want the automatic changing of slides that occurs. Instead, you will want to move from slide to slide when you're ready to do so. If your audience has questions along the way or if you decide to cover a topic longer than you originally planned, you need full control over your presentation. So in such a case, ensure that **Change slides manually** is checked.

▶ **TIP**

Using the **Navigator visible** option, you can display the **Navigator** dialog box during your presentation so you can more easily navigate between pages and graphic elements instead of moving sequentially through your slide show.

Once you've set the options that suit your current presentation, click the **OK** button to close the **Slide Show** dialog box.

▣ Start Your Slide Show

To start your slide show, select **Slide Show** from the **Slide Show** menu (or press **F9**) when you're ready to begin your presentation.

85 Print a Presentation

✔ BEFORE YOU BEGIN	→ SEE ALSO
81 Create a New Presentation **83** Open an Existing Presentation	**94** Change a Presentation's Background

Unlike the other OpenOffice.org programs, such as Writer, Calc, and Draw, Impress offers no print preview. You cannot see a print preview of a presentation due to the slide-by-slide nature of presentations.

▶ TIP

If you want a preview of a simple printed copy of your presentation, one slide per printed page, just press **F9** and page through your presentation. You are, in effect, seeing a preview of what will appear on the printed page.

Although you learn some about Impress printing options in **82** **Set Impress Options**, it's critical to delve into the things you may want to print through Impress. In other words, Impress was not designed to be printed but presented. Having said that, you'll still make use of the printer on occasion with Impress as you see here.

1 Request the Print Dialog Box

Select **File**, **Print** from the menu.

2 Request Print Options

Click the **Options** button to display the **Printer Options** dialog box.

3 Specify Printer Options

Until now, setting up print options is routine and the same as the other OpenOffice.org programs. You now are at the place, at the **Printer Options** dialog box, where you determine the Impress settings you need.

The **Contents** area determines what you want to print. In today's modern world of fast, low-cost color printers, printing both graphics and text isn't as big of a deal, and your audience will appreciate it very much if you print a copy of your presentation to hand out. They will be able to concentrate on your speech and not worry about taking copious notes. Click to select the **Handouts** option to print multiple slides on one page. Your audience will be able to read the slides, but you won't waste as much paper as you would if you printed one slide per page. **103** **Create Presentation Handouts** explains how to produce effective audience handouts.

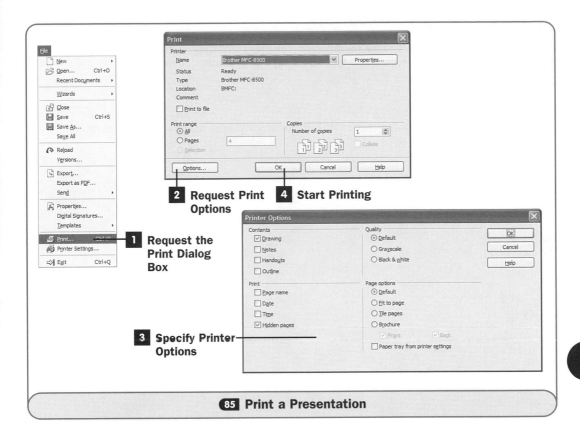

2 Request Print Options

4 Start Printing

1 Request the Print Dialog Box

3 Specify Printer Options

85 Print a Presentation

You may want to print only your speaker's notes by clicking to select the **Notes** option (see **103** **Add Notes to a Presentation**). The notes will print beneath the slides you've attached them to. You might choose to print your presentation's outline. To do that, click to select the **Outline** option.

▶ **TIP**

By selecting multiple **Contents** options, Impress prints everything sequentially. For example, you might want to print notes, handouts, and the outline at once.

If you're printing a large presentation, you might want to save some color ink by printing a grayscale or black-and-white version of your presentation for your audience. Use the **Grayscale** and **Black & white** options in the **Print** dialog box to print using only black ink.

The **Print** section determines whether the date and time appear as well as whether you want to print slides you've set up as hidden. Click **OK** to close the **Print Options** dialog box.

85

▶ **TIP**

You can also use hidden pages for different audiences, unhiding certain pages for audiences those pages were designed for and hiding them for other audiences.

4 Start Printing

Click the **Print** dialog box's **OK** button when you're ready to begin printing.

85

12

Adding Flair to Your Presentations

IN THIS CHAPTER:

When you first learn Impress, you should get a general overview of what presentations are all about and how to create them. Chapter 11, "Learning About Impress," covers all those topics, and if you have not ever worked with Impress, you may want to review the tasks in that chapter.

This chapter covers details, such as how to add text to your presentation slides. No matter how graphical you want your presentation to be, the presentation's words are what usually convey your information to your audience. You must enter and format text on the slides in a way that informs your audience without overwhelming them.

▶ **NOTE**

Not only will too much text be difficult to read, presentation slides aren't designed to convey lots of textual information. That's your job as the presenter! Design your presentation to support and enhance the message you convey as you give your presentation.

---

86 | **Use an Impress Template**

✔ **BEFORE YOU BEGIN**

81 Create a New Presentation
84 Run a Presentation

→ **SEE ALSO**

90 Format Presentation Text

When you use a template as a model for a presentation, you have to do less work because the template already has the backgrounds and slide information arranged for the initial presentation. Impress does not come fully loaded with lots of presentation templates. Actually, Impress only comes loaded with two templates—one named **Introducing a New Product** and another named **Recommendation of a Strategy**. Surprisingly, these are extremely limited, but they do get you started with templates you can use for your own presentations.

Creating a presentation using templates requires little more than selecting a few options using the Presentation Wizard when you first start Impress.

▶ **NOTE**

If you want to create your own Impress template, create the presentation skeleton to use as your template and save the file by choosing **File, Save As** and then selecting **OpenDocument Presentation Template (.otp)** as the file type. All Impress templates use the filename extension .otp (with the exception of Impress templates from earlier versions of OpenOffice.org, which use the filename extension .sti but still can be used in OpenOffice.org 2.0).

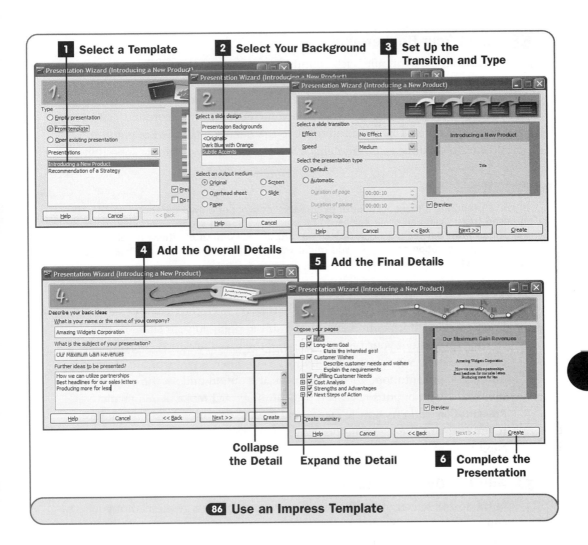

1 Select a Template

2 Select Your Background

3 Set Up the Transition and Type

4 Add the Overall Details

5 Add the Final Details

Collapse the Detail

Expand the Detail

6 Complete the Presentation

86 Use an Impress Template

1 Select a Template

Select **OpenOffice.org Impress** from the **OpenOffice.org** program group on your Windows Start menu to start the Presentation Wizard. Click to select the **From template** option. When you do, Impress lists the Impress templates available to you. As long as you've checked the **Preview** option, a preview image of the template appears in AutoPilot's preview area.

Select the template you want to use as the basis for your presentation and click **Next** to move to the next page in the Presentation Wizard.

2 Select Your Background

Select from the available backgrounds. Choose a background that will not overwhelm your audience. (With only two backgrounds available for your initial Impress installation, you don't have a lot to choose from.) Click to select the background you desire, and you can see that background's effect in the preview area. Click **Next** to move to the next page in the Presentation Wizard to continue selecting items from the template's available collection.

▶ NOTE

If you're preparing a presentation for overhead slides, paper only, a computer screen (as opposed to an overhead projector), or to be placed on 35mm slides, select the appropriate option from the section titled **Select an output medium**. Often, these media produce the same presentation anyway, so you might want to start with the default **Original** option and change it if needed.

3 Set Up the Transition and Type

Select the kind of transition effect you want to apply to your slides as they change throughout your presentation and the speed at which you want the change to occur when one slide changes to another. If you want to create an automatic presentation, select the **Automatic** option and set the page duration and length of pause between presentations. **101 Make an Automatic Presentation** explains how to create and present an automated presentation. If you're giving the presentation, leave the **Default** option selected. Click **Next** to move to the next page.

4 Add the Overall Details

In the fourth screen of the Presentation Wizard, Impress requests that you enter information that Impress will place throughout your presentation. You'll enter your company name, the subject of your presentation, and some additional ideas that you want to cover in the presentation. Impress scatters these details at appropriate places in the presentation it generates, based on the template's design. Click **Next** to move to the final page.

5 Add the Final Details

In the final page of the Presentation Wizard, Impress offers a list of details that you may or may not want in your presentation. The list changes depending on which of the two templates you chose when you first started the presentation. The new product details relate to the introduction of a new product, and the strategy template details relate to introducing a new strategy into your company plans.

86

Click the plus sign next to each group to see the details in that group. For example, you would click the plus sign next to **Fulfilling Customer Needs** to see the two lines that will appear at that point in the presentation. Although the details are general, you'll be able to change them to your company's specific details once Impress generates your initial presentation.

Initially, all groups are selected (indicated by a check mark), but you can click to uncheck any group that you don't want to appear in your presentation. For instance, you may not want to discuss cost analysis in this presentation; if not, uncheck the group labeled **Cost Analysis** so that Impress won't include that group in this presentation.

6 Complete the Presentation

Click the **Create** button to generate the presentation based on the information you supplied as you went through the screens in the Presentation Wizard. Once Impress generates the presentation, you can change the general details to those that match your specific company needs. For example, you would replace the template-produced text that reads **Compare quality and price with those of the competition** with your own specifics in that area. You can also add and remove slides throughout the presentation, depending on your specific needs. The template did its job by designing a general presentation that you now can make specific.

▶ NOTE

The first slide that Impress generates from the template will show your company name, presentation subject, and further ideas to be presented based on your answers in the fourth Presentation Wizard step.

87	**About Impress Views**	
✔ **BEFORE YOU BEGIN**		→ **SEE ALSO**
82 Open an Existing Presentation		**88** Enter Text into a Presentation
		96 Insert Graphics into a Presentation

87

Views are important in Impress because of the nature of presentations. Impress makes it easy to switch among a variety of views with the click of a button, so that you can work efficiently. You can choose from the following five views:

- **Normal view**—This is the default view in Impress, and the one you will likely work in most often. It displays three panes at once—a **Slide** pane, a drawing pane, and a **Task** pane—and you can further customize it to suit your preferences. The drawing pane in the middle of the screen shows one slide at a time, and is best for editing your slides and paging back and forth among them. The **Slide** pane on the left displays your presentation in slide sorter view so that you can see your entire presentation at a glance and quickly navigate among all the slides. The **Task** pane on the right displays one of four panes depending on the task you're currently engaged in. When you first create a presentation, it displays the **Layouts** pane because you're most likely to want to use this pane to change the layout of your slides. You can hide or move the **Slide** pane and the **Task** pane if you want, although the advantage of this view is that you can work all three panes at once.

- **Outline view**—Shows the title and secondary text of slides. You can easily and quickly scroll through your presentation, looking through the text. By default, the **Task** pane does not appear in this view because you are not likely to use it when working exclusively on text.

87

The Outline view shows text from several slides at once so you can focus on composing your thoughts.

▶ TIPS

The **Task** pane switches automatically when you initiate a task it can help with, but you can also display a different **Task** pane manually. To do so, click the **View** list arrow, and then select a different task.

You can further customize any view if you want. To display or hide the **Task** pane at any time, choose **Task Pane** from the **View** menu from any view. To display or hide the **Slide** pane at any time, choose **Slide Pane** from the **View** menu from any view.

► **TIP**

To change the number of slides displayed at once in **Slide Sorter** view, click the **Up** or **Down** arrow of the **Slides Per Row** button on the **Slide View** toolbar.

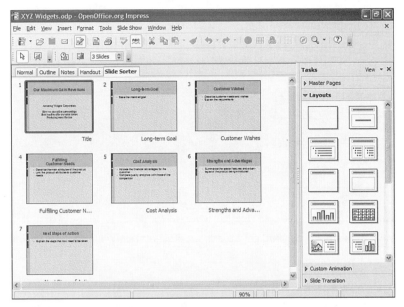

The Slide Sorter view shows several slides at once, allowing you to rearrange your presentation by dragging slides from one place to another.

- **Notes view**—When you add speaker notes to your slides, you can view those notes, along with the slides the notes go with, in this view. The notes appear at the bottom of the slide, with one slide and its notes showing at a time as you move through your presentation with **PageUp** and **PageDown**. See **102 Add Notes to a Presentation** for help with adding notes.

- **Handout view**—If you want to print your presentation as a handout for your audience (see **85 Print a Presentation** and **103 Create Presentation Handouts**), you can get a preview of the presentation handout by displaying the **Handout** view. The **Handout** view shows four slides per page.

- **Slide Sorter view**—Shows multiple slides in a thumbnail form so that you can get a general overview of your slides, as many as 12 or more at a time. Depending on your monitor, you can probably make out most of the text and graphics on each slide. You can drag any slide from one location in your presentation to another while viewing the slides, making it simple to rearrange your presentation.

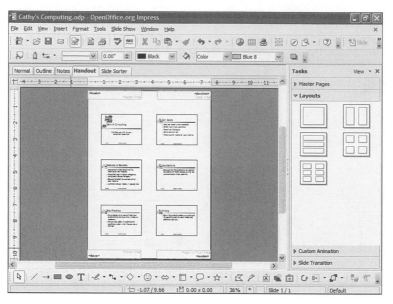

The Handout view shows how your audience's printed presentation will appear on each printed page.

87

▶ **NOTE**

With four slides per page, your audience will be able to read your slides on their handouts, yet you use far less paper than if Impress printed one slide per page.

To change from view to view, click the tab of the view you want to work with. You can also display the appropriate view by choosing options from the **View** menu. For example, if you're viewing notes at the top of the work area in **Notes** view and decide you want to change a slide's graphic, you can return to **Normal** view to make the edits more easily to your slide by clicking the **Normal** tab or by choosing **View**, **Normal** from the menu bar.

Generally, you work in **Normal** view, but if you want to see a different view of the current slide, you can click another tab. The toolbars above the work area adjust to provide quick access to the most commonly used tools for the current view. For example, when you are working in **Slide Sorter** view, the **Slide Sorter** toolbar and **Slide View** toolbar appear in addition to the **Standard** toolbar (which always appears by default). When you are working in **Outline** view, the **Slide Sorter** and **Slide View** toolbar do not appear by default, but the **Text Formatting** toolbar does.

▶ **KEY TERMS**

Master slide—Also called a *master page* and refers to a page that determines the background and formatting styles in the current presentation. If you change the master slide, you change the entire presentation's format.

Notes master—A page that determines the background and formatting for any notes pages.

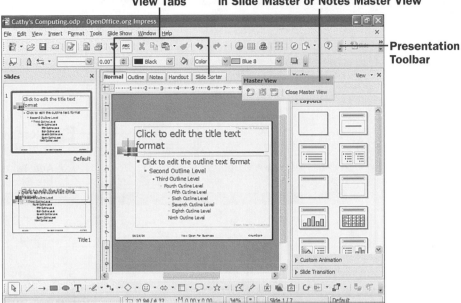

Slide Master view shows you the contents of the master slide.

88

The **View** menu contains viewing options in addition to the five tabbed views. If you choose **View, Master, Slide Master**, you can view and edit the *master slide*. If you select **Notes Master** on the **Master** submenu, you can view and edit the *Notes master*. The **View** menu also contains commands to start **Slide Show** view so that you can run a presentation. If you have room on your screen to display the **Presentation** toolbar, you can also access **Slide Show** view by clicking the **Slide Show** button.

▶ **TIP**

The **Presentation** toolbar is displayed by default in Impress, but if there is no room on your screen to display it, it might not be very helpful. You can drag the toolbar to different location, such as under the **Standard** toolbar, to access its buttons more easily.

88 **Enter Text into a Presentation**

✔ BEFORE YOU BEGIN	→ SEE ALSO
81 Create a New Presentation	**89** Format Presentation Text

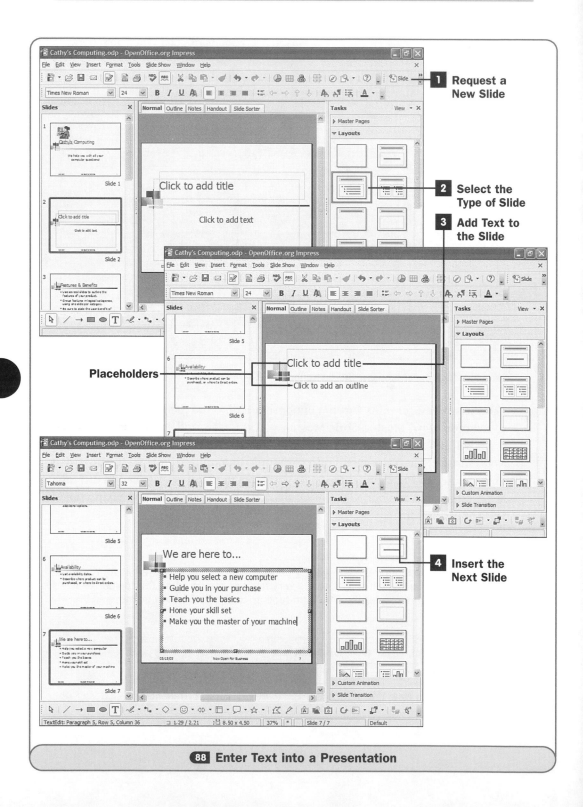

1 Request a New Slide

2 Select the Type of Slide

3 Add Text to the Slide

Placeholders

4 Insert the Next Slide

88 Enter Text into a Presentation

Generally, you'll add text and edit your slides in Normal view. (See **86** **About Impress Views** for a discussion of Normal view.) You can make edits directly on the slide and see the results of those edits as you make them.

First, you must insert a new slide in your presentation. The new slide will hold the text you want to type. The format of the new slide determines how your text appears and whether graphics might appear with the text. When you want to edit some text, you'll actually be editing text within a text box that lies on a slide. To edit text in a text box, click that text box to activate the text box and to place the text cursor inside it.

Impress displays the text box surrounded by sizing handles. Impress treats a slide's title as a single object and the slide's bulleted set of items as another object. Both of these objects are text objects, and they will appear inside an editable text box when you click them.

▶ **NOTE**

If you've inserted an element other than text onto the slide, such as graphic image, sound, or video clip, you can click that object and move, edit, or delete it as well.

1 **Request a New Slide**

To insert a brand new slide, click the **Slide** button from the **Presentation** toolbar. If you don't see the **Presentation** toolbar, you can display it by selecting **View**, **Toolbars**, **Presentation**.

A new slide appears at the location, with the layout of the preceding slide. Placeholders will let you know where text is expected.

2 **Select the Type of Slide**

You can change the layout of the new slide using the **Layouts** task pane. If you want to insert a slide with text and no graphics, you would select either the blank slide or one of the title slides in the pane.

3 **Add Text to the Slide**

Click any placeholder. If the placeholder rests in a title area, you'll be able to add a title to the slide. If the placeholder resides in an outline area, you will be able to add multiple lines of bulleted text to that area.

▶ **TIP**

You can request that the current date or time appear anywhere on a slide by selecting **Insert**, **Field** and selecting one of the **Date** or **Time** options. If you choose a **variable** date or time, the current date or time appears at that location when you run your presentation. If you choose a **fixed** date or time, the field reflects the date or time you inserted in the presentation.

88

4 **Insert the Next Slide**

Once you finish with one slide, you can insert the next slide by clicking the **Slide** button on the **Presentation** toolbar, or by selecting **Insert, Slide**.

▶ **TIP**

The **Duplicate Slide** option on the **Insert** menu makes an exact copy of your current slide in case you want a duplicate. Sometimes, it's faster to duplicate and then edit a copy of the current slide than to start with a brand-new slide.

---

89 **Find and Replace Text**

✔ **BEFORE YOU BEGIN**	→ **SEE ALSO**
82 Open an Existing Presentation	**90** Format Presentation Text
	91 Animate Text

When you work with large presentations, being able to locate text quickly, either to edit the text or to verify its accuracy, is vital. You don't want to step through a presentation slide by slide until you find text you want to see.

As with all of the OpenOffice.org programs, Impress offers a powerful find-and-replace command that enables you to locate text you want to find. Once Impress locates the text, you can request that Impress automatically replace it. If, for example, you realize that your company's Vice President's name is spelled *McGuire* instead of *MacGuire*, you can quickly make Impress change all the misspelled instances of the name, even if you're about to start your presentation in the next minute. (Just make sure you don't pass out those preprinted handouts of your slides!)

1 **Find Text**

Select the **Find & Replace** option from the **Edit** menu to display the **Find & Replace** dialog box. You can also press **Ctrl+F** to display the **Find & Replace** dialog box.

2 **Enter the Search Text**

Type the data you want to find in the **Search for** text box. If you've searched for the same data before, you can click the down arrow to open the **Search for** drop-down list box and select the data to search for it once again.

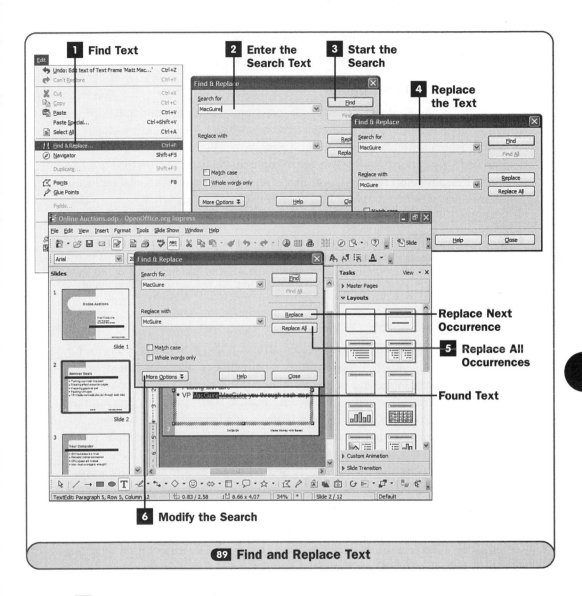

89 Find and Replace Text

3 Start the Search

Click the **Find** button. Impress searches from the current position in the presentation to the end of the presentation and then prompts you to continue the search from the beginning of the document. If Impress finds the text anywhere in the presentation, it displays the first slide that holds that text.

4 Replace the Text

If you want Impress to replace found text with new text, type the new text into the **Replace with** text box.

If the **Search for** text is found, Impress replaces that text with the text you entered in the **Replace with** text box.

5 Replace All Occurrences

If you click the **Replace All** button, Impress replaces all the matches with your replacement text throughout the slide. Such a change is more global and possibly riskier because you may replace text you didn't really want replaced. By clicking **Find** before each **Replace**, you can be sure that the proper text is being replaced, but such a single-occurrence find-and-replacement operation takes a lot of time in a long presentation.

▶ TIP

You can use the **Whole words only** option if you don't want Impress to find words that are contained within other words. If, for example, you want to find instances of the word *in*, you probably don't want to find every word that contains the letter combination *in*.

6 Modify the Search

Click the **More Options** button to expand the dialog box so that you can further refine your search. For example, you can click to select the **Backwards** option before doing a find or replacement if you want to find or replace starting from the insertion point and looking back to the start of the presentation. If you want to search for an approximate match instead of an exact one, select the **Similarity** option and then click the ... button. For example, if you think you might have misspelled vice president McGuire's name even beyond *MacGuire*, you can use the **Similarity Search** dialog box to search for words that differ from *MacGuire* by two letters; the Similarity Search will then find words such as *MagGuire* and *McaGuire*.

When you finish finding and replacing all the text for this search session, close the **Find & Replace** dialog box and return to the presentation by clicking the dialog box's **Close** button.

90

90	**Format Presentation Text**

✔ **BEFORE YOU BEGIN**	→ **SEE ALSO**
88 Enter Text into a Presentation	**91** Animate Text
	93 Use a Style

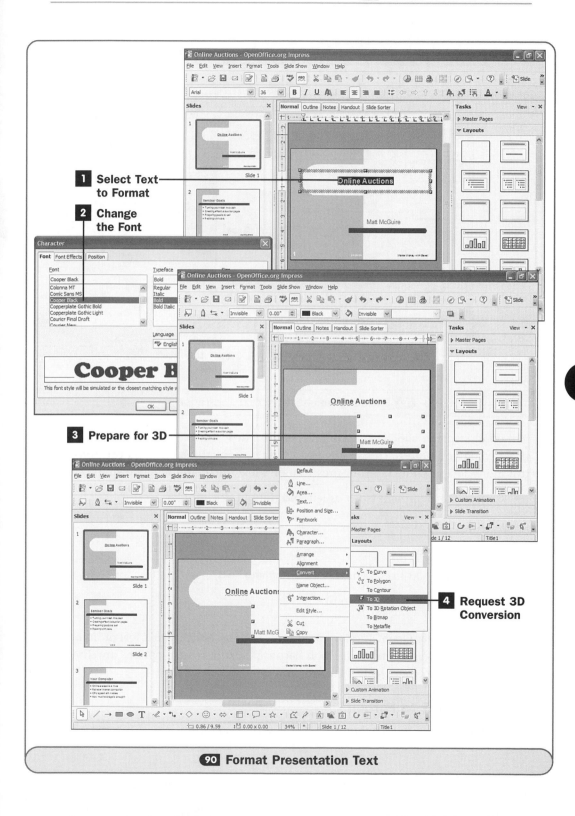

1 Select Text to Format

2 Change the Font

3 Prepare for 3D

4 Request 3D Conversion

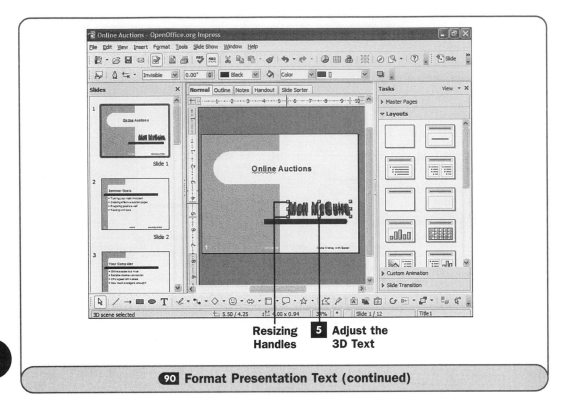

Resizing Handles

5 Adjust the 3D Text

90 Format Presentation Text (continued)

90

Although Impress's slide Layouts define preformatted text, there will be many times when you want to change the text format to something else. You can control many factors related to your presentation's text, including the following:

- Choose the alignment (such as left and right justification)
- Change the text size
- Change the font
- Animate the text (as described in **91** **Animate Text**)
- Change the text to a 3D format

If you've used other OpenOffice.org programs, such as Writer, you'll feel at home with some of Impress's formatting tools because the font-related options are similar to those of the other OpenOffice.org programs.

■ Select Text to Format

Locate the slide that contains the text you want to format. Select the text.

2 Change the Font

To change the selected text's font, alignment, display format, or background, select **Format**, **Character** from the menu. The **Character** dialog box appears. You can also right-click over the selected text to display the **Character** dialog box. Other right-click options are more specific, such as **Font**, **Size**, **Style**, and **Alignment**, in case you want to change one of those specific aspects of the text.

From the **Character** dialog box's **Font** page, you can change the font, the typeface (such as bold or italic), and the size of the text. A preview updates at the bottom of the **Font** page, showing you how your changes will affect your text. Click to select the **Font Effects** tab to change other aspects of the text, such as underlining and the text color. The **Position** tab determines how the text appears on the line (as normal, *superscript*, or *subscript* text). Click the **OK** button to close the dialog box and view your formatted text.

▶ KEY TERMS

Superscript—Small text that begins above the text baseline, as is often used to indicate the square of a number.

Subscript—Small text that begins below the text baseline, as is often used to indicate numbers that drop below the line in chemical formulas.

90

3 Prepare for 3D

If you want to convert your text to 3D, you often can, depending on whether Impress can convert the font used to 3D. As appealing as 3D text sounds, the result may not meet your expectations. The text is often too dark and thick to work well. You can experiment and decide whether you like the 3D effect.

Click to select the text box that holds the text you want to convert to 3D. Impress selects the text and places the resizing handles around it.

4 Request 3D Conversion

Press the **Esc** key once. The resizing handles will stay around the text, but the selection outline goes away. Right-click the text to display the menu and then select **Convert**, **To 3D**. Impress converts the text to 3D.

▶ NOTE

When converting text to 3D, Impress changes the text to a graphic image. If a text placeholder, such as **Type name here**, originally appeared where the text was, it may return once the 3D effect occurs. You may need to type a space over the placeholder to hide the placeholder text behind the 3D image.

5   Adjust the 3D Text

Once the text converts to 3D, drag the resizing handles up and down to make the text appear as clear as possible. Right-click the 3D text and select **3D Effects** to adjust the way Impress applies the three-dimensional style to your text.

---

91   Animate Text

✔ BEFORE YOU BEGIN	→ SEE ALSO
90 Format Presentation Text	**93** Use a Style

One of the more interesting features of Impress is its capability to animate the various text elements of your slides, producing an animated effect as the slide appears during the presentation. Consider how captivating your presentation could be when any of the following occurs:

- The title and then the rest of the text flies onto the slide from the side.

- The title falls down from the top while the bottom half of the slide rises up from the bottom edge.

- The slide's graphics appear and the text slowly fades into view. (**99** **Impress with Special Effects** describes how to animate graphics.)

- Each bulleted item in the list comes onto the slide by each letter cartwheeling into view.

- Paragraphs of text fade in at different moments.

- The title of your slide bounces into view, and when it finally comes to rest at its anchored location, the rest of the slide appears.

▶ NOTE

The biggest problem with animation is not getting it to work but getting it to work far too well. Don't overdo animation. The animated effects are so fun to work with that it's tempting to add all sorts of fades, cartwheels, wipes, and bounces to the slides. After so many, your presentation will become so top-heavy with animation that the importance of the content will be lost on your audience and the presentation will take on an overdone appearance.

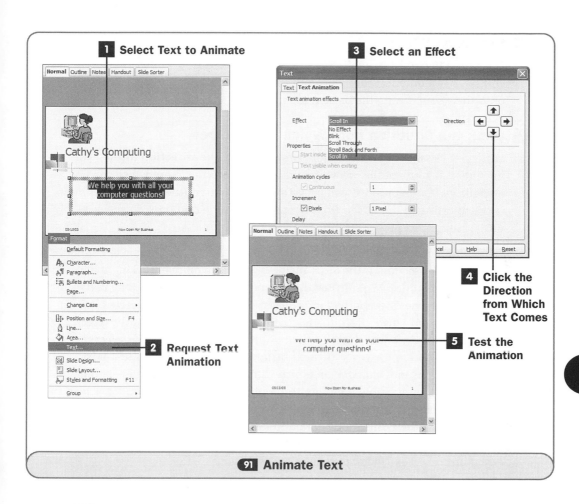

91 Animate Text

▮ Select Text to Animate

Click to select the text you wish to animate. Opening titles make good candidates for animated text, perhaps with some music in the background as your presentation's title flies in from the side of the screen. Self-running presentations should have slightly more animation than presentations that you give simply to keep the presentation from becoming stagnant. But even self-running presentations shouldn't overdo the effects at the expense of the content.

▮ Request Text Animation

With the text still selected, click to open the **Format** menu and select **Text**. This displays the **Text** dialog box. Click the **Text Animation** tab to display the **Text Animation page** in the **Text** dialog box.

3 Select an Effect

Click the **Effect** list box to display the possible effects from which you can choose. Select an effect that you want Impress to use when bringing the text onto the screen during the presentation.

4 Click the Direction from Which Text Comes

Once you've selected an effect from the **Effect** list, the **Direction** arrows will activate. Click one of the arrows to indicate the direction from which the text is to arrive. For example, if you click **To Bottom** button (the down arrow), the text will arrive on the screen from the top of the slide and drop downward until it rests in its proper position in the text box.

Depending on which effect you chose, you may or may not be able to change the **Properties** section. If the **Start inside** option is available, clicking it will make the animation begin inside the text box instead of entering the text box first from the direction you indicate. In other words, if you selected the **Scroll Back and Forth** effect, the text will first enter its area from the direction you chose and then shake back and forth. If you've clicked to select the **Start inside** option, however, the text instantly appears inside its text box area and begins moving back and forth without any entrance. If available, click to select **Text visible when exiting** option to keep the text on the screen after the animation completes (for when you don't request a continuous animation). Click the **Continuous** option to keep the animation going after it has performed its first cycle. The **Continuous** option keeps the animation going until the next slide appears on the screen.

▶ **NOTE**

You're sure to lose your audience's attention if you keep the animation continuous as you talk! Leave the **Continuous** option unchecked for presentations you'll be controlling while speaking. You can keep the **Continuous** option checked for any animations that take place on automatic presentations that run on their own.

The **Increment** value determines how many *pixels* the animation moves at each step. The smaller the number, the slower the animation moves; the larger the number, the faster the animation moves. The **Delay** option determines how long Impress waits before repeating the animation if you've elected to use continuous animation. Click the **OK** button to close the dialog box.

▶ **KEY TERM**

Pixels—An abbreviation for *picture elements*, which refers to the smallest addressable dot, or graphic element, on a screen or printer.

5 **Test the Animation**

You don't have to run your entire presentation to test each text animation effect. Once you set up text for animation, click anywhere outside the text area (to remove the resizing handles) to see the effect immediately. To edit the effect, click the text once again and select the **Format**, **Text** menu option to adjust the animation.

92	**About Impress Styles**
✔ **BEFORE YOU BEGIN**	→ **SEE ALSO**
90 Format Presentation Text	**93** Use a Style

Styles enable you to format text or graphics on your presentation's slides using a predefined format. By reusing styles, you reduce the amount of work you have to do to create and format a slide and to make your existing slides look the way you want them to look.

▶ **NOTE**

16 **About Styles and Templates** describes how to use styles in Writer documents. If you need to review terminology, you can review that task because the terminology is the same whether you're applying styles to Impress slides or to Writer documents.

The terminology of styles is similar across all the OpenOffice.org products. Impress, however, uses styles in a more limited manner. With Writer, for example, you can select a word, sentence, or paragraph and select a new style from the **Style** dialog box to apply to that text. As soon as you do, the text takes on all the formatting that the style defines.

Impress limits your use of styles in the following ways:

- You must use styles applicable to the current slide Layout. In other words, if you insert a blank, empty slide into your presentation, you will not be able to apply any styles to that slide. Instead, you must format the slide using the **Format** menu instead of the Styles and Formatting window. If you insert a new slide using a slide Layout, such as the **Title, Text Layout**, the presentation styles defined by that Layout are available to you.

- You can only modify a style by changing one of the Layout element's format and then changing the style. All existing slides that use that style, and all slides you add in the future to that presentation, use that modified style. In other words, if you add a slide with a title using a Layout from the Layout Task pane, as shown in the following figure, and you change the title's style, if you add a similar slide later, the new slide's title will take on the modified style, too.

92

Formatted by Slide Layout

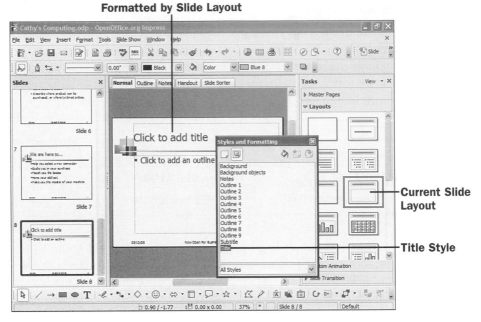

You can easily control your presentation's overall set of styles.

93

When you insert a new slide, you'll select a layout from the Layouts Task pane that most closely matches the slide you want to insert. All styles for that Layout are then available to you when you press **F11** or select **Format, Styles and Formatting** from the menu.

93 Use a Style

✔ **BEFORE YOU BEGIN**	→ **SEE ALSO**
92 About Impress Styles	**94** Change a Presentation's Background

Using styles inside Impress differs from the other OpenOffice.org programs, as **91** **About Impress Styles** explains. The styles are linked to the Layouts that you use when you insert new slides into your presentation. You can only modify existing styles, and once you modify a style, all slides that use that style also change.

▶ NOTE

Impress's graphics styles are more lenient than the presentation text styles, although you'll probably use them less often. You can modify a style and apply it directly to a single graphic image, whereas any text style you modify (listed as *presentation styles* in the Style Catalog) causes all text that uses that style to change format.

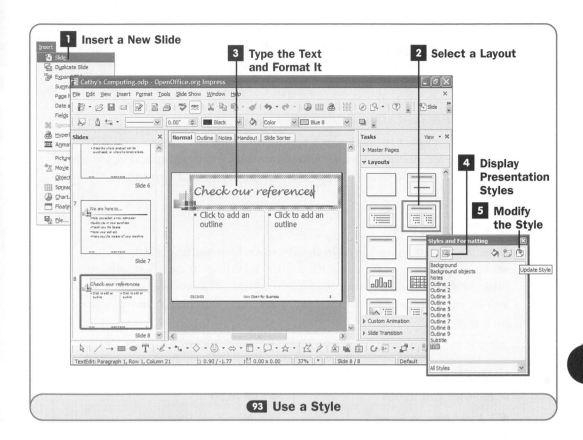

93 Use a Style

1 Insert a New Slide

Select **Insert**, **Slide** to insert the next slide into your presentation. The **Insert Slide** dialog box lists the Layout slides available to you. If you are creating a new presentation, the **Insert Slide** dialog box appears when you begin working on the first slide in the presentation.

2 Select a Layout

Click in the **Layouts** task pane to change the new slide layout to one that best suits the slide you want to insert. After you click the layout, its presentation styles are applied to the new slide.

3 Type the Text and Format It

If you want to change a style in the Style list, first type the text that uses that style, such as a title on the slide, and then format the text any way you want the style to look.

▶ **TIP**

If you only want this single occurrence changed, don't change any styles! You only want to modify the style used by this element of the slide if you want all other like elements to change too.

4 **Display Presentation Styles**

Press **F11** to display the **Styles and Formatting** window. Impress automatically highlights the style used by your selected text. For example, if you modified a title, the **Title** style will be selected in the **Styles and Formatting** window.

5 **Modify the Style**

Click the **Update Style** button in the **Styles and Formatting** window. The selected style takes on the formatting of the text inside the current style. All future slides you add to your presentation with that same style (such as when you insert a new slide with a similar Layout form) will take on the attributes of that style.

94

94	**Change a Presentation's Background**

✔ BEFORE YOU BEGIN	→ SEE ALSO
92 About Impress Styles	**100** Add a Slide Transition
93 Use a Style	

The background of your slide provides the overall tone of your presentation. If your presentation's background appears in cool blue tones, your presentation will feel far more relaxed than if you use bright orange and red tones in the background of your slides.

You can change the background of a single slide or of your entire presentation. Often, presenters prefer to use the same background on all their slides. Doing so keeps their presentations consistent and maintains a similar mood throughout. All slides in a presentation use the same background specified by the *master slide*'s background. If you want to change a single slide's background, you'll have to hide the master slide's background elements.

▶ **NOTE**

Click the **Master view** button to change your entire presentation's background. Click the **Slide view** button to change only a single background.

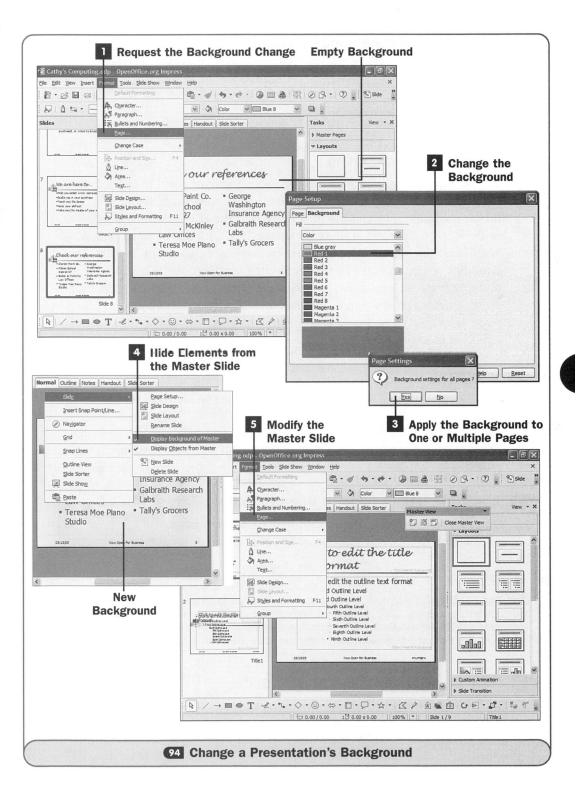

94 Change a Presentation's Background

1 Request the Background Change

If you want to change only one slide's background, display that slide in Normal view. Then, select **Format**, **Page** to display the **Page Setup** dialog box.

Click the **Background** tab to display the **Background** page.

2 Change the Background

The **Background** page determines the background you want to apply to the current slide or to your entire presentation. First you select how you want to fill the background by clicking the list arrow in the **Fill** section. You can elect to show no background (a white background) by clicking the **None** option. The **Color** option enables you to select from a list of colors that appears. The **Gradient** option enables you to select from a list of *gradients* that you want to apply to the background. The **Hatching** option enables you to select from a list of various crosshatching patterns. The **Bitmap** option enables you to select from a list of background graphics, such as a brick wall or a sky pattern with clouds.

94 ▶ **KEY TERM**

Gradient—A transition from one color or pattern to another on the same slide.

Click to select the type of fill you want and then select the specific fill from the choices that appear. Click **OK** to apply the fill and close the **Page Setup** dialog box.

3 Apply the Background to One or Multiple Pages

Impress asks whether you want to apply the background to a single page (the page you were on when you changed the background) or all pages.

▶ **NOTE**

The **Page Settings** dialog box can apply the background to all pages in your presentation, except for the first slide. If you had first clicked the **Master view** button before changing the background, all slides, including the first one, would change. No matter what you do, the original background, determined by the master slide, shows also.

4 Hide Elements from the Master Slide

If the master slide's background or graphic objects interfere with the look of a particular slide (assuming that the master slide has a specified background you can see) you can hide these elements from view. Right-click any blank area of the slide whose background you have modified and choose **Slide** from the context menu. From the submenu that appears, click to the remove the check mark next to **Display Background of Master** if you want to hide the background color or fill of the master. You can also click to remove the check mark next to **Display Objects from Master** if you want to hide any graphic objects such as decorative icons or logos. These elements are removed from only the current slide.

⁵ Modify the Master Slide

If you want to hide some or all of the background elements on *all* the slides in a presentation, you can modify the master slide. First open **Slide Master** view by choosing **View, Master, Slide Master**. When **Slide Master** view opens, follow the same steps you did for modifying an individual slide: Choose **Page** from the **Format** menu and then choose a fill and color or color combination.

When you are finished, click **OK** to close the dialog box and apply the new background to all slides except those you have designated *not* to display the master slide's background

▶ **TIP**

If you change your mind about a slide and want the slide master's background to be applied to it, right-click a blank area of that slide, choose **Slide** from the context menu, and then click to restore the check mark next to the **Display Background of Master** option.

94

13

Making More Impressive Presentations

IN THIS CHAPTER:

Impress can help you drive home your point with several advanced features. You can add flair and pizzazz so your presentations won't be boring. You can add charts and import graphics to spruce up your presentations. You can also animate graphics and determine special slide transitions so the movement from slide to slide matches the tone of your presentation.

The Notes feature enables you to add your own private speaker's notes to your slides so you always remember important points you want to make. Your audience will also appreciate it when you print a copy of your presentation for them to take. Impress doesn't stop with live presentations; you can create automated presentations that repeat themselves, and you can easily put your Impress presentations on the Web for the world to view.

95   Insert a Chart into a Presentation

✔ BEFORE YOU BEGIN	→ SEE ALSO
94 Change a Presentation's Background	**96** Insert Graphics into a Presentation

95

A chart can summarize your presentation, and audiences often glean information from charts that they might not otherwise get from long lists of data or from you listing scores of numbers for them. So often you'll want to use charts in your presentations to make your data more available to your audience.

Impress (as does Writer) includes its own Calc-like charting capability. Impress accomplishes this by supporting the use of a mini-version of Calc right inside Impress. In other words, when you want to place a chart on an Impress slide, you can build the chart from within Impress, entering data into a spreadsheet as though Calc were inside Impress, ready to build your charts.

▶ TIP

68 **Add a Chart to a Spreadsheet**, although a Calc-based lesson, describes charts and terminology related to them. If you are unfamiliar with OpenOffice.org charts, take a few minutes to review this task.

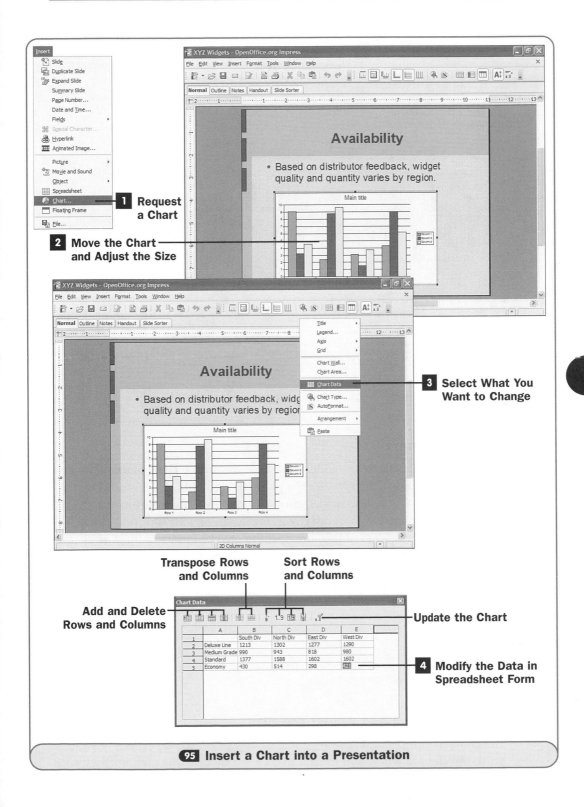

1 **Request a Chart**

2 **Move the Chart and Adjust the Size**

3 **Select What You Want to Change**

Transpose Rows and Columns

Sort Rows and Columns

Add and Delete Rows and Columns

Update the Chart

4 **Modify the Data in Spreadsheet Form**

95 Insert a Chart into a Presentation

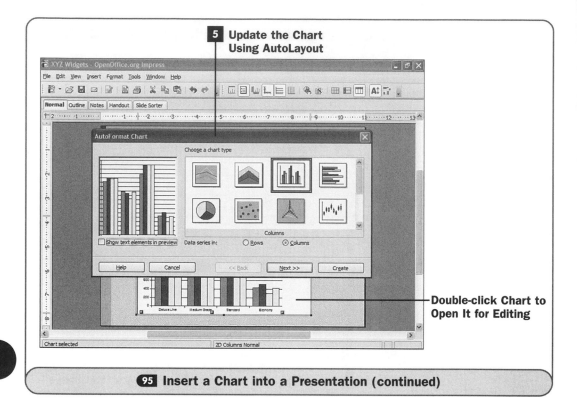

5 Update the Chart Using AutoLayout

Double-click Chart to Open It for Editing

95

95 Insert a Chart into a Presentation (continued)

1 Request a Chart

You can insert a chart in any slide. If the slide contains a chart placeholder (a small icon of a chart), double-click the placeholder to add the chart. If the slide doesn't contain a placeholder, choose **Chart** from the **Insert** menu. Impress places a sample chart directly in the center of your slide and closes the **Slide** and **Task** panes (if they are open) to give you more room to work with the chart. You now must position the chart where you want it and change the data values used in the chart to match the data you want to portray in the presentation. In addition, you can change the chart type as well as all its labels.

▶ **NOTE**

Remember, Impress generates a sample chart for you, and you must change the chart's data and labels to suit your purpose.

2 Move the Chart and Adjust the Size

The chart that Impress places on your slide appears in the center of the slide. Move the chart to where you want it to go. Even though this sample chart is not the chart you want to present, you can go ahead and position as well as resize the chart to make it easier to see later, along with the rest of your slide's contents. You now must enter data and edit the chart so it reflects the information you need in the slide.

3 Select What You Want to Change

Right-click the chart to display a menu showing all the chart-related elements you can now change. You'll certainly want to modify the chart data because you don't want to use the chart's sample data for your presentation. In addition, you'll always want to modify the title so that your chart is labeled on your slide as well as on any printed handouts you might make from your presentation. Generally, the legend and the axis labels need to be changed. Finally, the chart type might very well need to be changed to reflect your data's intent.

▶ **TIP**

68 Add a Chart to a Spreadsheet describes each chart type and the best use for each one.

95

4 Modify the Data in Spreadsheet Form

When you select **Chart Data** from the right-click menu, a small spreadsheet appears in the center of your slide. This is a Calc-like spreadsheet add-in program. Although all of Calc's features aren't represented in Impress's spreadsheet, you can easily enter the data needed to create your chart in the rows and columns there.

Replace the sample row and column labels with your own data's label information. Replace the data inside the spreadsheet's body with your own data. You can add or delete rows or columns, simply by selecting a row or column that precedes the one you want to add or by selecting a row or column to delete. You may sort by rows or columns, as you might do if you wanted data to appear alphabetically in the chart.

5 Update the Chart Using AutoLayout

After editing the spreadsheet, click the **Apply to Chart** button to update the chart on your slide and close the Chart Data window. Once you update the chart, you must double-click the chart to display the editing options again. This is because as soon as you update your chart with your data, Impress converts the chart to an *OLE object*. You must tell Impress that you want to edit that object when you want to make additional changes, such as changing the title or legend rather than simply moving or resizing it.

▶ **KEY TERM**

OLE object—Abbreviation for *Object Linking and Embedding.* This term refers to an object that can be placed inside documents of different types, such as a Writer word processing document and an Impress presentation. You can place charts in Impress and Calc because OpenOffice.org converts the charts to OLE objects that both programs accept.

Once you've entered your specific data into the chart, the **AutoFormat** dialog box is the simplest place to update all the chart's details, such as titles and legends. After double-clicking the chart, select **AutoFormat** from the right-click menu to modify the other chart features, including changing the chart's type, such as from a bar chart to a pie chart.

| **96** | **Insert Graphics into a Presentation** |

✔ **BEFORE YOU BEGIN**	→ **SEE ALSO**
95 Insert a Chart into a Presentation	**99** Impress with Animation Effects

---

96

Impress enables you to put pictures throughout your presentation slides. Perhaps you'll want to stress your point when giving a motivational speech, for example, by showing a runner winning a race.

▶ **NOTE**

Impress supports all popular graphic file formats, including JPG, GIF, and BMP files.

When you insert a graphic image, Impress places the image's anchor at that location. You will see the anchor when editing but not when you present your presentation. The anchor also does not show if you print your slides as handouts. The anchor shows where you inserted the actual image. The anchor and the actual image may not appear together, depending on how you format the image, but they will appear on the same slide. When you want to move an image, move its anchor and not the image itself.

1 Request a Picture

To insert a graphic image from a file, first select the slide where you want the image to go. If the slide contains a picture placeholder (a small icon showing a house), double-click the placeholder to add the picture. If the slide doesn't contain a placeholder, select **Picture** from the **Insert** menu and then click **From File** in the submenu. Impress displays the **Insert Graphics** dialog box, which is nothing more than a Windows file-selection dialog where you use to navigate to the file you want to insert.

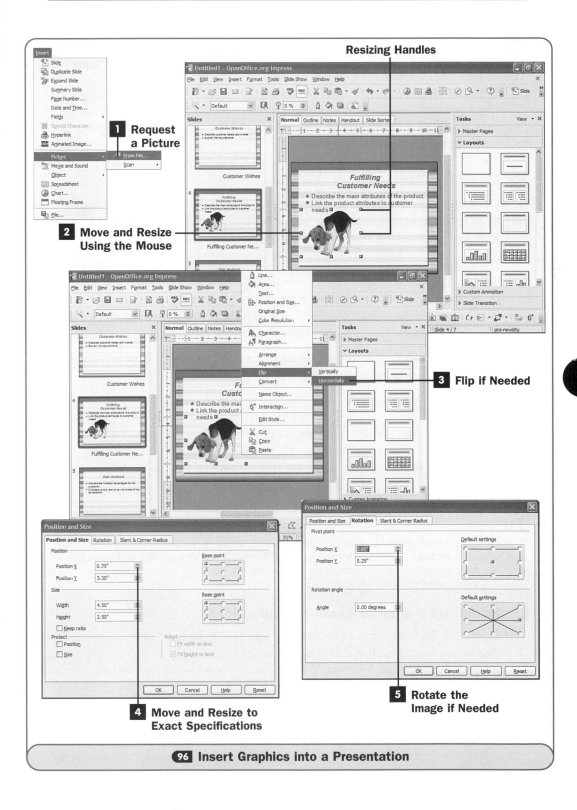

Resizing Handles

1 Request a Picture

2 Move and Resize Using the Mouse

3 Flip if Needed

96

4 Move and Resize to Exact Specifications

5 Rotate the Image if Needed

96 Insert Graphics into a Presentation

▶ **TIP**

Click the **Insert Graphics** dialog box's **View** button and select **Thumbnails** to see a pre-view of your graphic before you insert it.

Once you select the graphic image you want to place in your presentation, click the **Open** button to insert the image. The image appears in your presen-tation at the location you first selected.

2 Move and Resize Using the Mouse

Once Impress brings the graphic image into your presentation, you usually need to make adjustments so the image suits your needs and rests on the slide in the proper position and with the correct size.

Typically, Impress imports a graphic image and centers it at the location you inserted it. No text wraps to either side of the image because, unlike a word processed document, a presentation relies on the exact placement of text and data on your slide. Therefore, you'll usually have to move the image so that it doesn't overwrite any important information on your slide.

To resize the image, drag any of the eight resizing handles inward to reduce the image size or outward to increase the image size.

3 Flip if Needed

Depending on your image and your data, you may want to flip, or *reverse*, the image so it points the other direction, either vertically or horizontally. Right-click over the graphic, select the **Flip** menu, and then select **Vertically** or **Horizontally** to flip the image so it faces differently.

▶ **TIP**

If you insert multiple graphics, they can overlap each other. By right-clicking an image and selecting **Arrange, Send Backward**, or **Bring Forward**, you can control which image gets the top spot when layered with other images.

4 Move and Resize to Exact Specifications

Right-click the image and select **Position and Size** to display the **Position and Size** dialog box. From this dialog box, you can resize, move, or slant the graphic image using exact measurements. The **Position X** and **Position Y** values deter-mine where the image appears on the page from the upper-left corner. The **Size** values determine how large your image will appear. If you do resize an image, be sure you click to select the **Keep ratio** option so that Impress resizes the width in proportion to the height changes you make (or so Impress resizes the height in proportion to any width changes you make) to keep your image clear and in the

96

correct ratio as the original. If you fail to maintain the ratio, your image can become stretched out of proportion. Checking the options in the **Protect** area ensures that you don't inadvertently move the image with your mouse later.

5 Rotate the Image if Needed

Click the **Position and Size** dialog box's **Rotation** tab to display the **Rotation** page. Here, you can rotate the image any angle by specifying a value in the **Angle** field. The *pivot point*, which remains at the center of your image unless you change the pivot point, determines where the imaginary spindle lies while the image rotates.

▶ **TIP**

If you rotate or resize the image too much and want to begin again with the original position and size, click the **Position and Size** dialog box's **Reset** button to restore the values to the original image state.

---

97 | Add a Presentation Header and Footer

✔ **BEFORE YOU BEGIN**	→ **SEE ALSO**
81 Create a New Presentation	**103** Create Presentation Handouts

97

You must add headers and footers to your slides through the master slide (see **87 About Impress Views**). Each header and footer is saved in the presentation's master slide so that the header and footer (you can have one or the other or both) reside on all slides throughout your presentation. You cannot add a different header or footer on different slides, although you can hide the header or footer from individual slides.

You may add the date, time, or slide number (referred to as the *page number*) in a header or footer area. When that slide appears during your presentation, the current date or time at that moment appears in the header or footer area.

1 Change the View

Technically, Impress does not support headers and footers (except in Handouts view). You can, however, use text boxes to insert text at the top or bottom of your slides that acts just like Writer, Calc, or Base headers and footers. To add a text box, you must work in **Normal**, **Notes**, or **Handout** view. You'll generally find it's easier to work in **Normal** view because you'll have a larger view of the slide.

▶ **NOTE**

This task refers to text that appears at the top or bottom of every slide in the presentation as *header and footer text*, even though such text is just normal text in these particular locations.

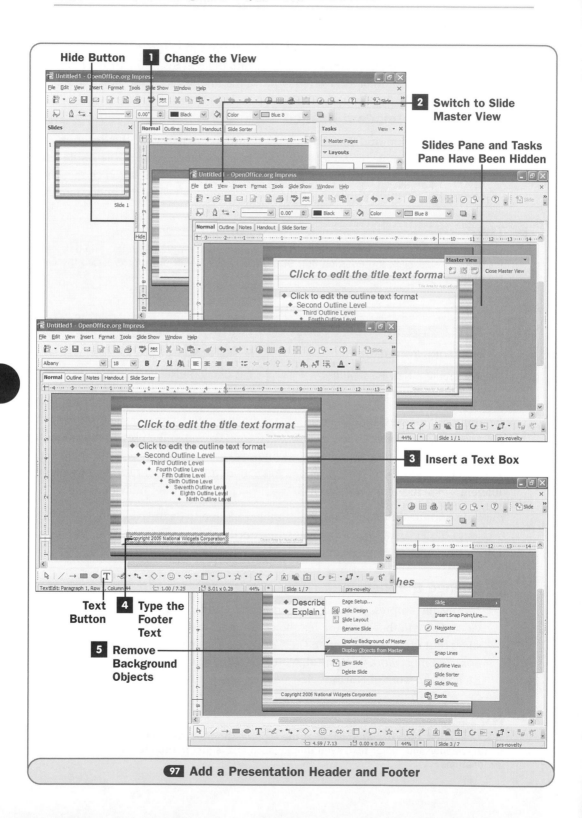

To increase your view of the current slide, you can hide or resize the **Slides** pane or the **Task** pane by dragging the inner edge of the pane or by clicking the **Hide** button.

2 Switch to Slide Master View

Usually, you'll want the header or footer to appear on all slides throughout the presentation, so you should add the header or footer text to the master slide. Choose **View, Master, Slide Master** to display the presentation's master slide.

3 Insert a Text Box

Your header and footer text must reside inside a text box. Click the **Text** tool in the **Drawing** toolbar; the mouse pointer changes to a crosshair, indicating that you can now place a text box anywhere on the slide.

▶ **TIPS**

If the Drawing toolbar is not open on your screen, choose **View, Toolbars, Drawing**.

See **102** **Add Notes to a Presentation** for more information on working with headers and footers in **Handout** view.

97

Click the upper-left corner of your footer's (or header's) text box and drag your mouse down and to the right to draw the text box. When you release your mouse button, Impress places the text box in that position and inserts the text cursor inside it so you can type the header or footer text.

4 Type the Footer Text

Type the text that you want to appear in the footer (or header). If you want to display the time or date, you may want to insert a field instead of a text box. Generally, you'll want to insert the date or time that's current when you give your presentation, so select **Insert, Fields, Date (variable)** or **Time (variable)** to insert either the *variable date* or *variable time*. (In a similar manner, you can insert a *fixed date* or *fixed time* also.) Click the **Close Master View** button on the **Master View** toolbar to return to the previous view.

▶ **KEY TERMS**

Variable date—The current presentation date as opposed to the fixed date.

Variable time—The current presentation time as opposed to the fixed time.

Fixed date—The date you created the slide as opposed to the variable date.

Fixed time—The time you created the slide as opposed to the variable time.

▶ **TIP**

If you want to remove the header or footer from multiple slides within your presentation, you must change each slide's layout one at a time.

5 Remove Background Objects

Move to the slide you want to modify. Right-click the slide and then click **Slide** in the context menu to open the submenu. Click to uncheck the **Display Objects from Master** option to hide the header or footer. (This action might remove other items as well.) Impress removes your header or footer from that one slide but not from the other slides in the presentation.

See **94** **Change a Presentation's Background** for more information on adjusting the background elements in a presentation.

▶ **TIP**

Click the **Select** button atop the **Main** toolbar to stop adding text boxes to the slide and to return the mouse cursor to its normal pointing cursor shape.

---

98   Add Sound to a Presentation

✔ BEFORE YOU BEGIN	→ SEE ALSO
96 Insert Graphics into a Presentation	**100** Add a Slide Transition **99** Impress with Animation Effects

---

You can add sound to your presentations to accent an effect or to get your audience's attention during slide transitions. Impress supports the following sound file extensions and formats:

- AU and SND files (SUN/NeXT)

- WAV (Microsoft Windows)

- VOC (Creative Labs SoundBlaster)

- AIFF (SGI/Apple)

- IFF (Amiga)

Surprisingly, there appears to be no way to provide timed narration throughout an entire presentation, as you might want for an automatic presentation. Nevertheless, Impress does support enough sound techniques to pique your audience's attention.

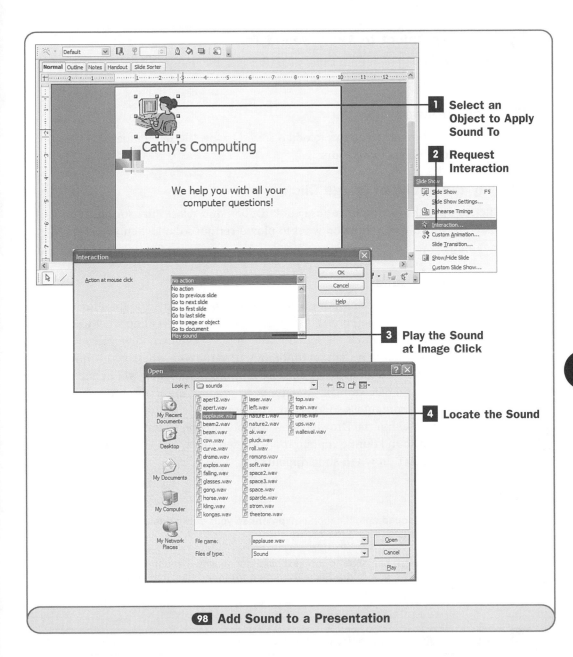

1 Select an Object to Apply Sound To

2 Request Interaction

3 Play the Sound at Image Click

4 Locate the Sound

98 Add Sound to a Presentation

▶ NOTES

As with all special effects, don't overdo the use of sound; otherwise, it will distract from your presentation.

You can insert a sound file at any place in a slide by selecting **Insert**, **Object**, **Sound** and navigating to the sound file you want to insert. However, the sound only plays when you double-click it, so this method is not very useful for most presentation purposes.

1 Select an Object to Apply Sound To

Click to select an object on a slide, such as a graphic image or text box. You can attach a sound to this item for a special effect.

2 Request Interaction

Select **Slide Show**, **Interaction** to add a sound to the selected image. The **Interaction** dialog box appears.

3 Play the Sound at Image Click

Click to open the **Action at mouse click** list box and select **Play sound**. You have just told Impress that you want to play a certain sound when you click the image.

4 Locate the Sound

Browse your hard disk or network to locate the sound to play. Use the **Play** button in the Open dialog box to listen to a sound before deciding whether to insert it. Click **OK** to attach the sound to the image. When you give your presentation (assuming it's not an automatic presentation, where you cannot add sound linked to a mouse click because no human presenter will be there to click the mouse), you can click the image to produce the sound through the presentation computer's sound card. You can test the sound effect by clicking it from within the Drawing view without having to run your presentation. (To add sound during an automatic presentation, you can select an action such as **Action when slide appears**.)

99

▶ **NOTES**

Obviously, you'll need sound amplification equipment so your entire audience can hear the sound when you trigger it with the mouse click.

When you transition from one slide to the next, you can specify a sound that will play during the transition. See **99** **Add a Slide Transition** for more information on setting up slide transitions.

---

99 | **Impress with Animation Effects**

✔ BEFORE YOU BEGIN	→ SEE ALSO
96 Insert Graphics into a Presentation	**100** Add a Slide Transition
98 Add Sound to a Presentation	

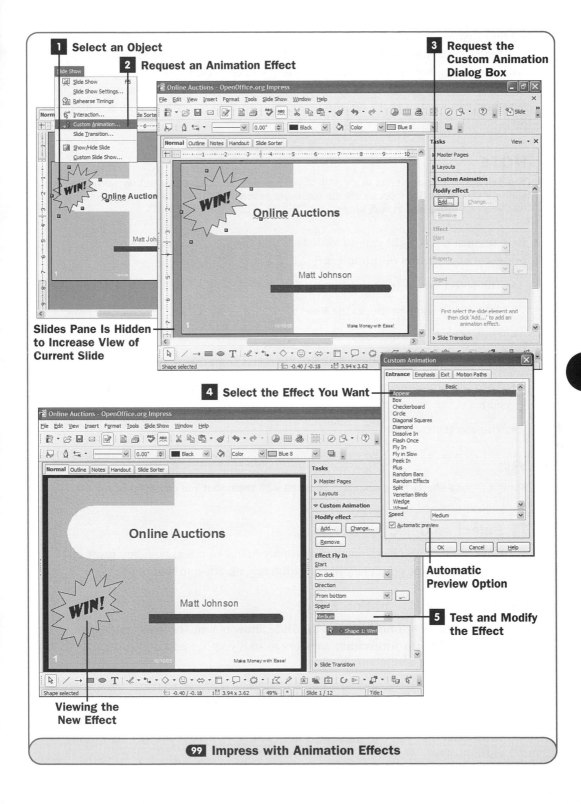

1 Select an Object

2 Request an Animation Effect

3 Request the Custom Animation Dialog Box

Slides Pane Is Hidden to Increase View of Current Slide

4 Select the Effect You Want

Automatic Preview Option

5 Test and Modify the Effect

Viewing the New Effect

Adding custom animation effects to graphics and other presentation elements can really make your presentation come alive. You can make graphic images fly onto the screen, not unlike the animated text you can cause to roll into place (see **91 Animate Text**). As with any special effects, don't overdo them. Reserve them for when you want to make an impression at a particularly critical part of your presentation.

▶ **NOTE**

You can apply special effects to graphic objects as well as other presentation elements such as text boxes. The special effects are more pronounced than the simpler animated text you can also place in text boxes.

Here are just a few of the animation effects you can apply to graphics and other presentation elements with Impress:

- The object flies in from outside the slide.
- A laser-like show produces the object.
- The object fades into place.
- The slide sparkles, slowly producing the object from the moving glitter.
- The object (graphic text works well here) snakes into the slide from one of the edges.
- The object spirals into place.

▶ **TIP**

Some of these effects have sounds associated with them that you can keep or remove.

1 Select an Object

Click to select an object, such as a graphic image or a text box. You must first click to select the object before you can apply an effect to that object.

2 Request an Animation Effect

Select **Custom Animation** from the **Slide Show** menu. The **Tasks** pane displays the **Custom Animation** category so that you can add and customize an effect.

3 Request the Custom Animation Dialog Box

Click the **Add** button in the **Custom Animation** category in the **Tasks** pane. Remember that you can hide the **Slides** pane if you want a larger view of the current slide.

▶ **NOTE**

Many of the special effects that appear in the **Animation Effects** dialog box are also available as slide transitions. See **100** **Add a Slide Transition**.

4 **Select the Effect You Want**

The **Custom Animation** dialog box contains four tabbed pages of effects you can add to the selected object. Click each tab to view the choices available. You can choose an **Entrance** effect to control how the selected object first appears (such as flying in from the left), an **Emphasis** effect to control how the object behaves on the slide (such as spinning in place), an **Exit** effect (such as having the object dissolve into the background), or a **Motion Paths** effect to add motion to the object (such as having the object move along an oval-shaped path). Choose an option from the **Speed** list at the bottom of the **Custom Animation** dialog box to adjust the speed of the selected effect.

On each tabbed page, the effects are organized into categories such as **Moderate** and **Special** to help you find the right look for your presentation. If you leave the **Automatic Preview** check box enabled, you can click any effect and see how it looks in your presentation. When you've found the right animation, click the **OK** button.

100

▶ **TIP**

Press **F9** to review your presentation and make sure that the special effect adds the flavor you want to your presentation. To change the effect, select the object again and right-click the object to reach the **Effects** context menu option.

5 **Test and Modify the Effect**

After you've assigned the desired effect, the **Custom Animation** category in the **Tasks** pane displays the current settings for the effect for as long as that object is still selected on your slide. The options in the **Tasks** pane change depending on what type of effect you have assigned. You can change the settings for the effect, for example, if you want the object to fly in more slowly or want to change the type of effect altogether. Whenever you make a change in the **Tasks** pane, the new effect plays in the work area.

100 **Add a Slide Transition**

✔ **BEFORE YOU BEGIN**	➔ **SEE ALSO**
98 Add Sound to a Presentation	**101** Make an Automatic Presentation
99 Impress with Animation Effects	

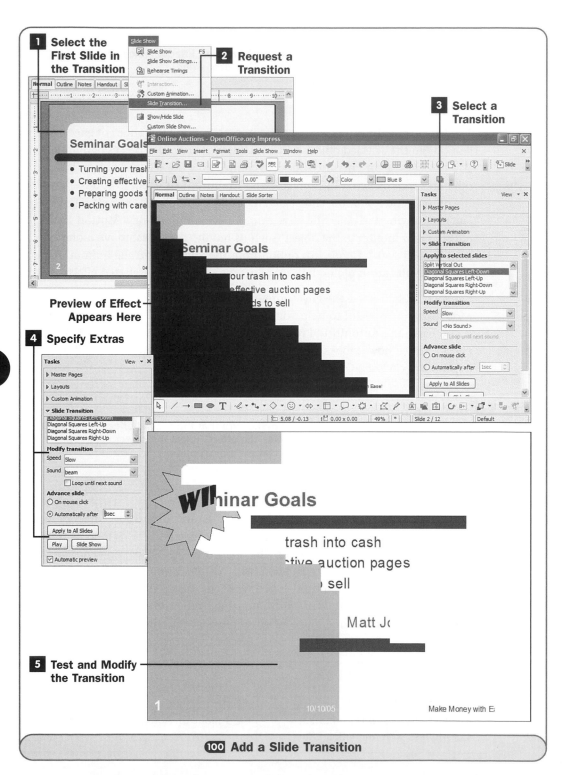

1 Select the First Slide in the Transition

2 Request a Transition

3 Select a Transition

Preview of Effect Appears Here

4 Specify Extras

5 Test and Modify the Transition

100 Add a Slide Transition

Adding a transition between slides is very much like adding custom animation to graphics and other objects on your slides (see **99** **Impress with Special Effects**). Instead of applying a special effect to a graphic image, you apply the special effect to the next transition. For example, a rolling transition would bring the next slide into view, during an automatic slide show or when you request the slide during a presentation, by rolling it in from one of the edges as it slowly overrides the previous slide.

You can apply a different transition to each slide throughout your presentation. In addition, you can apply the same transition to multiple slides. As with any special effect, don't overdo it because it's your presentation's message that is more important than the look of the physical presentation itself.

1 Select the First Slide in the Transition

Move to the slide that is to take on the transition. In other words, if you want the second slide in your presentation to appear on the screen through a special animated transition, display the second slide. Be sure the **Slide View** button is active so you can work with the slide and its transition.

2 Request a Transition

Select **Slide Show**, **Slide Transition** from the menu. The **Slide Transition Tasks** pane appears.

3 Select a Transition

Under **Apply to selected slides**, click any transition and watch a preview of it in the work area. Click to select the transition you want to apply to your slide. To apply this transition to all slides, click the **Apply to All Slides** button at the bottom of the **Tasks** pane.

▶ TIPS

To see what the transition will look like, click **Assign** once again. You can keep selecting different transitions and clicking **Assign** to see their effect until you find the one you like best.

Leave the **Automatic Preview** check box enabled at the bottom of the **Slide Transition** category in the **Tasks** pane (you might have to scroll to the bottom of the pane to see this option).

4 Specify Extras

In the **Modify Transition** section, you can adjust the speed of the transitional effect and add a sound if you want. Click the **Speed** list arrow or the **Sound**

100

list arrow to choose a different speed or sound. Remember that you can pre-view as many options as you want. The one you leave selected is the option that is used in the presentation.

▶ **TIP**

If you are controlling your own presentation (as opposed to creating an automatic pres-entation), click the **On mouse click** button so that the transition doesn't occur until you click the mouse button or press the **Spacebar** during your presentation.

You can also control whether the transition occurs manually or automatically in the **Advance slide** section. If you want the transition to occur automatical-ly after a certain time, select the **Automatically after** option and designate the amount of time the slide should stay onscreen in the text box.

5 Test and Modify the Transition

Press **F9** to review your presentation in Slide Show view and make sure that the transition works the way you want it to. To change the transition to a dif-ferent one, display the starting slide again and choose **Slide Show, Slide Transition** from the menu bar to display the **Slide Transition** category in the **Tasks** pane.

101

---

101   Make an Automatic Presentation

✔ BEFORE YOU BEGIN	→ SEE ALSO
81 Create a New Presentation	**104** Turn a Presentation into Online Web Pages
83 Open an Existing Presentation	

An automated slide show is useful for creating self-running demonstrations, prod-uct presentations, and conference information distribution. You can control each and every detail of a self-running slide show, add special and transition effects, and ensure that the show automatically runs within a given time frame.

▶ **NOTE**

Microsoft PowerPoint uses the term *kiosk* to refer to an automatic presentation.

1 Select Automation

Build your slide show. Once you've designed the slides and added the transi-tions, select **Slide Show, Slide Show Settings** to display the **Slide Show** dia-log box.

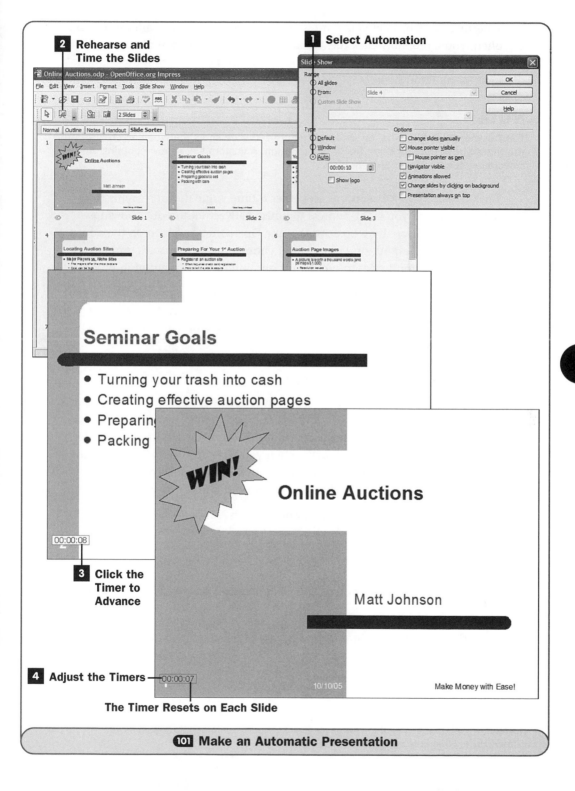

2 Rehearse and Time the Slides

1 Select Automation

3 Click the Timer to Advance

4 Adjust the Timers

The Timer Resets on Each Slide

Determine which slides you want to use in the automatic presentation. Most often, you'll probably click the **All slides** option, but you can also start the automatic slide show after a specific slide that you choose from the list box next to the **From** option.

▶ **NOTE**

The **Custom Slide Show** option shows a customized slide show that you can create from the **Slide Show**, **Custom Slide Show** menu option. A custom slide show contains only selected slides from your presentation.

Click to select the **Auto** option and enter a time value that represents the amount of time you want Impress to pause between automatic showings. Checking the **Show logo** box displays the OpenOffice.org logo on the screen between presentations, and you cannot change the logo to something else. (The logo is a small price to pay for an absolutely free presentation program!)

The remaining **Options** section of the **Slide Show** dialog box enables you to select various options for your automated presentations, such as whether you want animations to show throughout the automatic presentation. Click **OK** to close the **Slide Show** dialog box.

101

2 Rehearse and Time the Slides

In many cases, your automatic slide show is ready to go without you doing anything further. Nevertheless, Impress offers one more service that improves upon your automatic presentation's timings. You can walk through a slide show in real time, selecting exactly when you want the next slide to appear. As you rehearse the presentation in this manner, Impress records the time frame that you use for each slide and prepares automatic transitions for you.

To rehearse the automatic presentation, click the **Slide Sorter** to display your presentation from a bird's-eye view perspective.

▶ **TIP**

You can easily rearrange slides by dragging them from one location to another while in the Slide view.

Click the **Rehearse Timings** button on the **Slide View** toolbar. Your presentation begins, and the first slide appears with a timer in the lower-left corner of your screen.

▶ **TIP**

To hide any slide that you don't want to display during the presentation, click the **Show/Hide Slide** button on the **Slide View** toolbar.

3 Click the Timer to Advance

When the first slide has been on the screen as long as you wish, click the timer. Impress advances to the next slide, using a transition and sound if you've set them up, and that slide's timer begins. Continue clicking each slide's timer after each slide has appeared until the presentation ends. Impress records the display times and uses them the next time you run the presentation with automatic slide changes.

4 Adjust the Timers

When you return to the **Slide Sorter** view, the **Slide View** toolbar displays the slide's transition, the transition time, and the amount of time you've given for the slide to appear during the automatic presentation. You can click to adjust any of these settings. If, for example, you want to decrease the time a slide appears, click the down arrow to reduce the amount of time the slide shows from the time applied during rehearsal.

102   Add Notes to a Presentation

✔ **BEFORE YOU BEGIN**	→ **SEE ALSO**
85 Print a Presentation	**103** Create Presentation Handouts

102

Impress's Notes view enables you to create and edit notes for you or your presentation's speaker. When you display the notes, Impress shows the notes at the bottom of your slide while you work on your presentation. The Notes view shows the slide contents and, below it, a dialog box for your notes.

Therefore, the speaker's notes contain the slides that the audience sees as well as notes the speaker wrote to go along with each slide. Your audience does not see the speaker's notes during the presentation.

▶ TIP

Generally, the **Notes** view is best used for short reminders that you want to remember for each slide. Don't plan to write your entire presentation's text in the note area because you'll get bogged down in the details (see **105** About Giving Presentations).

The Notes view is designed to allow printing of the notes for the speaker. However, the speaker can also display the Notes Page view during a presentation to eliminate paper shuffling. If the speaker's computer has two video cards and two monitors, as most laptop setups used for presentations will be able to provide (the laptop's monitor and the overhead projector plugged into the laptop's output port), Impress can send the slides to one monitor and the speaker's slides and notes are available on the speaker's computer to follow the presentation.

102

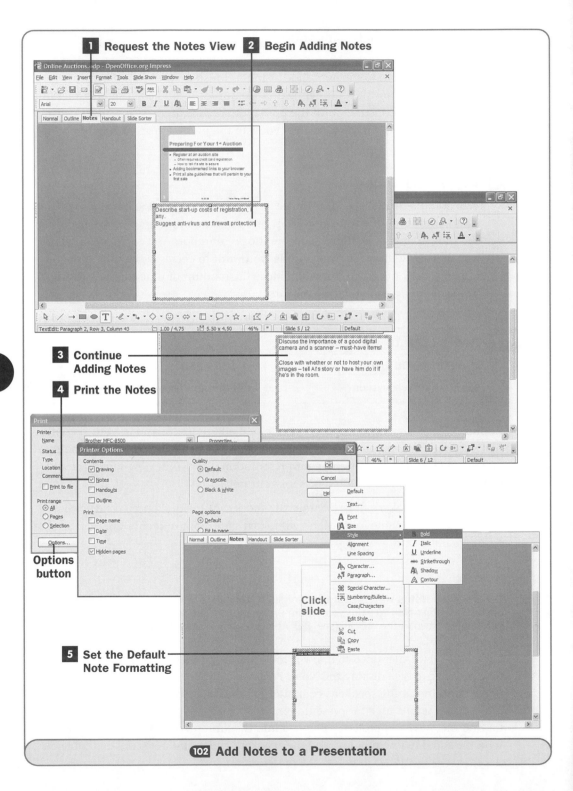

1 Request the Notes View   **2** Begin Adding Notes

3 Continue
Adding Notes

4 Print the Notes

Options
button

5 Set the Default
Note Formatting

102 Add Notes to a Presentation

▶ **TIP**

If your notes text is not large enough to read easily, expand the viewing area by using the **Zoom** command from the **View** menu.

1 Request the Notes View

Click the **Notes** tab at the top of the work area to display your slides' **Notes** view. Alternatively, choose **View, Notes Page** from the menu bar.

2 Begin Adding Notes

Double-click the text box with the placeholder text *Click to add notes*. Type any notes that go with the current slide. You can apply all the usual text-formatting commands to your notes, including increasing the font size (see **90 Format Presentation Text**).

3 Continue Adding Notes

Press **PageDown** to move to the next slide and add notes where needed throughout the rest of your presentation.

▶ **NOTE**

You don't have to add notes once you've completed all the slides. If you display the Notes view after creating each slide, you can add notes along the way.

102

4 Print the Notes

If you prefer to print your notes instead of following along on your laptop as you give your presentation, you can print each slide and the notes that go with them. Select **File, Print**, click the **Options** button in the Print dialog box, and click to enable the **Notes** check box.

5 Set the Default Note Formatting

If you want to set up a master format for your notes, you can select **View, Master, Notes Master** to show the master slide. Select the placeholder text that reads **Click here to edit the notes format** and then right-click the text to display the formatting menu. You don't have to select the text before right-clicking, but sometimes it's wise; if the note's text box and not the note text itself is still selected, the right-click menu won't display the needed formatting commands.

103	**Create Presentation Handouts**

✔ **BEFORE YOU BEGIN**	→ **SEE ALSO**
85 Print a Presentation	**104** Turn a Presentation into Online Web Pages

Handouts can benefit your audience because they can take home ideas and tips from your presentation. You control what goes into your handouts. You don't have to print every slide in the presentation. Doing so would only cost you paper and would not necessarily benefit your audience. Instead, select the slides that mean the most to your presentation. Consider the following handouts as important, depending on your presentation:

- Your presentation's title, goal, and your name

- Your contact information (website, phone number, email address, and so on)

- Critical ideas within your presentation

- Numerical examples the audience can study at their leisure

- Goals for the audience

- Take-home action items that the audience might want to do as a result of your presentation

- Products you or others sell that relate to your presentation and that will benefit your audience

▶ **TIP**

You'll use the Handout view to select specific handouts from your presentation.

1 **Request the Handout View**

Select **View**, **Handout Page** (or click the **Handout** tab atop your work area) to enter the Handout view. The *handouts master slide* appears.

▶ **KEY TERM**

Handouts master slide—A slide that shows the formatting and number of slides per handout.

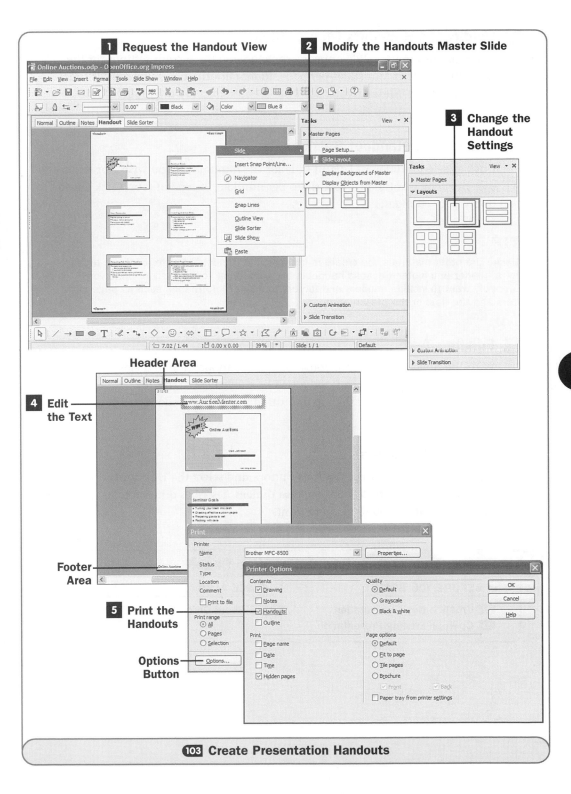

1 Request the Handout View

2 Modify the Handouts Master Slide

3 Change the Handout Settings

4 Edit the Text

Header Area

Footer Area

5 Print the Handouts

Options Button

103 Create Presentation Handouts

2 Modify the Handouts Master Slide

The handouts master slide appears, showing you the default settings for the handouts, such as four slides per page. Right-click the handouts master slide and select **Slide**, **Slide Layout** from the menu to display the **Modify Slide** dialog box.

3 Change the Handout Settings

Click to select a different Layout style for the handouts if you wish. For example, you may want to print six slides per handout instead of four. Click **OK** to apply your changes.

▶ **TIP**

Unlike the other materials you create in Impress, the Handouts Master contains areas for a header and footer. Because handouts are something you're likely to print, you'll probably want to include headers and footers to display information such as page numbers and the date of the presentation.

4 Edit the Text

With the handouts showing, you can edit, rearrange, and add elements to them. For example, you can add a text box (by clicking the **Text** button on the **Drawing** toolbar) at the top and throughout the handouts for your audience.

5 Print the Handouts

Select **File**, **Print**, click the **Options** button, and select the **Handouts** option to print the handouts. **80** **Set Impress Options** describes other options available to you when you're ready to print.

---

104 Turn a Presentation into Online Web Pages

✔ BEFORE YOU BEGIN	→ SEE ALSO
81 Create a New Presentation	**105** About Giving Presentations
83 Open an Existing Presentation	

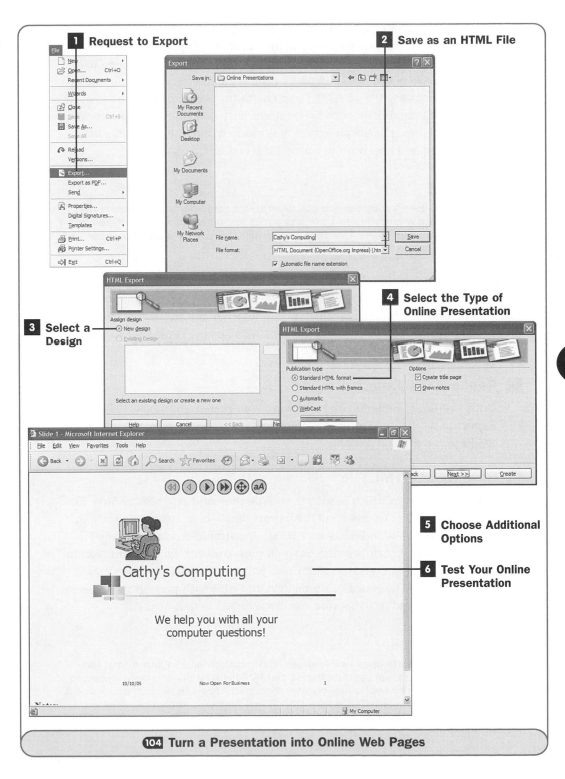

1 Request to Export

2 Save as an HTML File

3 Select a Design

4 Select the Type of Online Presentation

5 Choose Additional Options

6 Test Your Online Presentation

104

Cathy's Computing

We help you with all your computer questions!

104 Turn a Presentation into Online Web Pages

Instead of a roomful of people, why not give your presentation to the world? You can by turning your Impress presentation into a set of web pages. After converting your presentation to web content, you must upload your pages to a *web hosting service* (which will probably be the same service, either in-house or out, that hosts your website currently) and link to the presentation. When your site's visitors click the link for your presentation, they can enjoy your presentation from their web browser. If the presentation is manual and not automatic, they can click forward and backward to watch the presentation.

▶ KEY TERM

Web hosting service—A company you hire or an inside computer support center that provides disk space where you can store web pages and other online content. You might even host your own web pages from your own computer if you have the knowledge and system software to do so.

Impress makes it surprisingly easy to convert your presentation to an online presentation. The most difficult part of the process is uploading the online presentation and linking to it (neither of which is Impress's role but rather tasks you must do outside Impress—or you can find someone who has the knowledge to upload and link to your presentation for you).

104

1 Request the Export

Once you finish designing and reviewing your presentation, select **File**, **Export** to display the **Export** dialog box, where you can export your presentation as a web page.

2 Save as an HTML File

Select a location in which to save the online presentation from the **Save in** drop-down list box at the top of the **Export** dialog box. Type a filename in the **File name** field and make sure **HTML Document** is selected in the **File format** list box. When you click **Save**, Impress converts your presentation to *HTML* code and stores the resulting Web pages, with a starting Web page named the same as your **File name** field and with each page in your presentation being saved as a separate Web page linked to that one.

▶ TIP

Impress actually supports three web formats: HTML, Macromedia's *Flash* format (perhaps best if you use a lot of special effects), and PDF files (for documents you want to look the same on any computer that displays them). All three can be displayed inside a Web browser, although only HTML works with all web browsers without requiring extra add-in products. Most browsers these days, though, are equipped to display PDF or Flash files without trouble.

▶ **KEY TERMS**

HTML—Abbreviation for *Hypertext Markup Language* and refers to the code needed to make Web pages display properly inside a Web browser.

Flash—The name for an animated file format developed by Macromedia, Incorporated to give Web sites the ability to display animation using very little bandwidth.

Once you start the export, Impress opens the **HTML Export** dialog box.

3 **Select a Design**

The first page of the **HTML Export** dialog box requests that you select a design or create a new one. When you export your first presentation, you won't see any designs to choose from. As you save presentations in an online format, following through with the rest of the HTML export process, you will be able to save various Web site designs from the selections you make, keeping you from having to reselect them when you want to create similar Web presentations. For example, when you finish the process of exporting your first presentation to HTML, you then can save the HTML exporting options you chose so you later only need to select that name when another online presentation is to take on the same characteristics. Click **Next** to continue specifying the characteristics for this online presentation or **Create** if you decide to choose from an existing design.

104

4 **Select the Type of Online Presentation**

You now must select the type of Web page to create—either a standard HTML format or one with frames. If you select the framed Web site, Impress creates Web pages in a main frame with a table of contents to the left of the frame that contains a list of hyperlinks to the rest of your presentation. As you select from the **Publication type** options, the preview and related options change depending on your choice. For example, if you choose to create an automatic online presentation, Impress displays options that determine how long each slide is to be viewed before moving to the next slide (your own slide duration times will be in effect unless you specify a different duration setting here).

▶ **NOTE**

In spite of the advantages that a framed Web page seems to bring, such as the automatic table of contents, framed Web sites are generally frowned upon today due to the difficulties users often have bookmarking them. Table-based Web pages are simpler to maintain and maneuver.

The **Automatic** option creates an automatic presentation where the slides advance online, just as they do in automatic presentations that you generate on your PC (see **⬛101 Make an Automatic Presentation**). Reserve the **WebCast** option for when you have advanced server capabilities or can work with someone who does. You can use a WebCast presentation to control the presentation from your desk while teleconferencing with others who view your presentation, as you might do on a teleconferencing training call. For example, you could develop a presentation about reading stock charts and teach a phone class to a conferenced group of students around the world who would log in to your server's Web pages and view your presentation as you change slides and speak on the phone.

Finally, make sure that the **Create title page** and **Show notes** options are selected if you want a title page and your speaker notes generated for your online presentation. Click **Next** to continue exporting the online presentation.

5 Choose Additional Options

You must now specify the type of graphics (such as **GIF** or **JPG**) that you want your presentation graphics saved as. If you choose the **JPG** option, you must specify a quality value. The closer your selected value is to **100%**, the more accurate your graphics will look, but the longer they will take to display in your users' Web browsers. Unless you know the kind of hardware most of your users will have, as you might if you were developing an in-house, online training presentation, select the **Low resolution (640 × 480 pixels)** option so your presentation loads as quickly as possible for everyone who views it online. Click **Next** to continue.

In the next dialog box that opens, specify additional information to appear on the title page of your Web publication, such as the presenter's name, Web page, and other contact information. Complete these fields or leave them blank if you don't want to include this type of information. Click **Next** to continue the process.

▶ TIPS

If you don't want to include buttons in your presentation, enable the **Text Only** check box.

You don't have to complete every step in the **HTML Export** dialog box. You can click the **Create** button at any time, and OpenOffice.org creates an online presentation based on your choices so far and the default settings.

You can also choose a button style for your online presentation. Click any set of buttons in this dialog box to add it to this design and then click **Next**. In

104

the final dialog box, you can choose a different color scheme for your presentation or define specific colors for objects such as hyperlinks and visited links. When you are finished, click **Create** to generate your online presentation.

Impress asks you for a name to give to your Web page design. This name is little more than a collection of **HTML Export** dialog box settings you've given so far that you can choose from in the future instead of having to specify them again for this kind of presentation. If you did click to select **Save**, you can opt out of naming the design by clicking **Do Not Save** instead of entering a name and clicking **Save**.

Impress now generates your Web pages, creating JPG or GIF images and HTML files as needed. The name of the starting page, or the *home page* of your presentation, is the name you gave the HTML file when you first began exporting the presentation. This is the name you'll link to from other sites, once you transfer the generated online presentation files to your Web hosting service.

6 Test Your Online Presentation

Once you or someone you have help you transfers the generated files to the appropriate Web hosting service, and once you link to the files from within your Web browser (or type the address of the online presentation directly into your browser's **Address** box), your presentation is ready for you to review. Anyone viewing your presentation, even if it's an automatic presentation, can click the traversal links across the top of your presentation to move forward or backward throughout the presentation.

105

▶ TIP

You can review your online presentation from within a Web browser without uploading the files to a Web hosting service. Start your Web browser, select **File, Open**, and browse to the folder with your online presentation. Select the starting page, and your presentation begins inside your browser.

---

105 About Giving Presentations

✔ BEFORE YOU BEGIN

81 Create a New Presentation
84 Run a Presentation
101 Make an Automatic Presentation

Giving presentations seems to be as much of an art as a skill. Some extremely enjoyable, attention-getting speakers use absolutely no presentation handouts, notes, or overhead materials such as those Impress can produce. On the other hand, many professional speakers wouldn't enter a room without these tools.

You must decide what is best for you, given your comfort level, your ability to capture an audience, your material, and the environment in which you plan to present your material. One thing is for sure—tools such as Impress are so powerful, it's easy to get caught up in special effects, color, and sound so much that your presentation's details take away from your message. You must keep in the forefront that your message should take priority over the presentation in every detail.

▶ **NOTE**

Not every speech requires Impress's tools. A simple speech that you plan to give may be better presented without any overhead slides shown to your audience. But even for "low-tech" talks, you can still use Impress to develop your content and thoughts and to arrange the topics you wish to speak on.

Don't add a special effect unless that effect accents the message you're trying to convey on that slide. Don't add sound to your presentation without ensuring that you won't be speaking when the sound starts. If you create automatic presentations, you might rely a little more on sound and special effects to keep the audience's attention because you won't be there to direct things, but the message you want to convey is still paramount to the technical aspects of your presentation.

Unlike tradition, seriously consider *not* passing out handouts of your presentation, or even letting your audience know you have them, until after your presentation ends. If you do, you may lose the interest of some audience members because they will assume all the information is in the handouts. Or they may think they can study the handouts later, and in doing so, they may miss connecting important points together that you make in your speech but that may not be explicit in the handouts. Do what you can to keep your audience attentive to your message—this may mean that you buck the trend and not pass out handouts before you speak.

Don't print, word for word, your speaker notes, either on slides or on a printed piece of paper you keep with you at the podium. You need to know your presentation well enough to give it cold, without any notes other than (perhaps) a card with key words that remind you of your presentation's order.

▶ **TIP**

Know your presentation but do not memorize it. Instead of coming across knowing your material inside and out, if you recite a memorized speech, you will come off sounding stiff and boring no matter how well you know your topic and no matter how interesting your topic is.

Unless you're teaching technical material, I'd suggest that you save questions for the end of your presentation. If you do not, you may be sidetracked from your presentation, you may go over time (upsetting both your audience and possibly the host conference personnel if you're speaking at a conference), and your entire presentation runs the risk of being derailed.

Finally, even though it should go without saying, how many times have you seen a speaker get up before the audience and not know how to work the equipment? You need to arrive before your audience and prepare your hardware, get your handouts ready to pass out after the talk, and test your entire presentation system before the presentation starts. If you cannot get the ball rolling when you're supposed to start the presentation, you lose control of the situation in your audience's eyes and you must fight to regain your audience.

▶ **NOTE**

As you can see, giving a presentation requires far more important tasks than using Impress to create slides. Make Impress an important part of your presentation but don't make Impress the center of your presentation. Impress should only serve your presentation and not the other way around.

105

PART IV

Drawing on Your Inner Artist with Draw

IN THIS PART:

14

Getting Ready to Draw

IN THIS CHAPTER:

With Draw, you can generate drawings and graphics. Draw supports all popular graphics formats such as TIFF and JPEG, both for importing images as well as for the drawings you want to export. Here are just a few features Draw supports:

- *Vector graphics*—Use predefined geometric shapes to generate your drawings.

▶ KEY TERM

Vector graphics—Graphics defined by geometric shapes such as lines, curves, rectangles, and polygons. Internally, vector graphics are stored as mathematical values, helping to decrease file size.

- **3D objects**—Create three-dimensional shapes to add depth to your images.

- **Light application**—Adjust the perceived light source on the objects you draw to add realism.

- **Object groups**—Logically group objects so that when you move or resize one, other objects adjust accordingly.

- **HTML/PDF Format**—Besides exporting a drawing in any of several popular graphics formats, you can also export your drawing in HTML or PDF format to make them easy to view on the Internet. See **36 Save a Document as a PDF File** for help with PDF.

- **Multiple Slides**—Each Draw file can contain multiple slides; each slide contains a single drawing. In this way, you can keep related drawings together in a single file (such as artwork for a brochure, a print ad, and a newsletter). See **109 About Drawing with Draw**.

Draw supports a gallery that contains numerous graphic images, animations, sounds, and web graphics such as buttons, bullets, and backgrounds that you can use to spruce up your drawings. You can make your drawings more consistent by taking advantage of Draw's grids and *snap lines*.

▶ KEY TERM

Snap lines—Also called *snap-to lines* and refers to logical lines that align the objects on your drawing to one another. When requested, an object shifts to the closest snap line as soon as you drag that object close to the snap line. Items aligned along the same snap lines will stay in alignment unless you move them relatively far from their snap lines.

If you're a graphic design artist, you'll be surprised at the tools you can get in Draw considering its free price. If you're not much of an artist, like this author, you'll be thankful that Draw's tools can help make your drawings more presentable when you need to create them.

106 **Set Draw Options**

→ **SEE ALSO**

107 Create a New Drawing
108 Open an Existing Drawing

Not everybody works the same way, so not every Draw user wants to use Draw the same way. By setting some of Draw's many options, you will make Draw conform to the way you like to do things. For example, you may want to hide Draw's image placeholders because they distract you from your drawing. (**111** **Draw from Scratch** describes the use of placeholders.) The options you set control this and many other aspects of Draw.

▶ **TIP**

Even if you're familiar with Calc or another OpenOffice.org set of options, initially learning about Draw's options now gives you a preview of what Draw is able to do.

As a matter of fact, Draw has an option for just about anything! Table 14.1 describes Draw's option categories. You'll learn a lot about what Draw can do just by looking through the options available to you.

106

▶ **NOTE**

All options are available for all OpenOffice.org programs at all times. For example, you can control the display of a grid in Calc from Impress, and you can request that Impress print the date and time on all pages of output from within Draw.

TABLE 14.1   Draw's Drawing Options

Draw Option Category	Explanation
General	Describes general Draw settings, such as the initial default unit of measurements for elements within a drawing and the *scale* you want your drawings to appear in.
View	Describes how Draw appears on the screen and which Draw special elements are shown, such as rulers and graphic placeholders. You can elect to display image and text placeholders in place of actual images/text in your drawings, and to display objects as contours (no fills).
Grid	Determines whether Draw displays a grid for you on your drawing area background to help you place elements more accurately and consistently.
Print	Describes how Draw handles the printing of drawings, such as adjusting the drawing size to fit the paper.

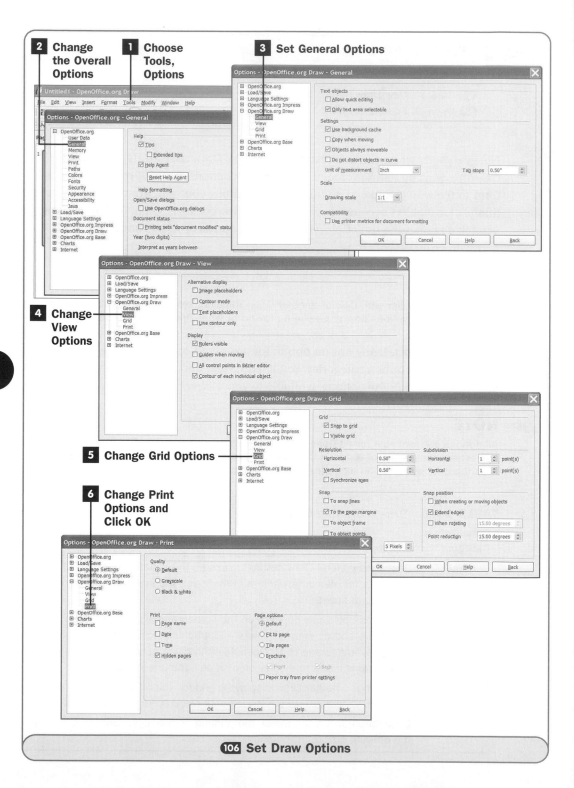

2 Change the Overall Options

1 Choose Tools, Options

3 Set General Options

4 Change View Options

5 Change Grid Options

6 Change Print Options and Click OK

106 Set Draw Options

▶ **KEY TERM**

Scale—A ratio that describes the size of objects on your screen and how that size relates to their actual printed size.

1 Choose Tools, Options

Select **Options** from Draw's **Tools** menu. The **Options** dialog box appears. From this dialog box, you can change any of Draw's options as well as the options for the other OpenOffice.org programs.

▶ **TIP**

Often you'll work in one OpenOffice.org program and realize that you need to change an overall option. For example, if you want to print several kinds of OpenOffice.org documents to a file (instead of to your printer) to send to others via email, you can change the **OpenOffice.org** option labeled **Print**, from within Draw, to apply that setting to all OpenOffice.org programs.

2 Change the Overall Options

Select any option in the **OpenOffice.org** category to modify OpenOffice.org-wide settings such as pathnames. For example, if you don't like the path-name you see when you open or save a drawing to disk, click the **Paths** option and change it to a different default file path.

If you're new to OpenOffice.org, consider leaving all the OpenOffice.org options "as is" until you familiarize yourself with how the OpenOffice.org programs work.

3 Set General Options

Click the plus sign next to the **OpenOffice.org Draw** option to display the four Draw-specific categories listed in Table 14.1 at the beginning of this task.

Click the **General** options category; the dialog box changes to show options you can select to make changes to the general Draw options. The **Text objects** section enables you to edit text objects with a single click rather than a double click, and enables you to choose whether to select a text object's outer area when clicked. The **Settings** section describes how you want Draw to use its background cache when displaying objects in a drawing (without the cache, Draw runs more slowly, although on recent computers you'll hardly notice the difference). In addition, you can specify how you wish to handle copying and moving your drawings' objects, and you may also specify how you want to handle measurements and tab stops, such as in inches or metrically. The **Scale** section shows the ratio of drawing size on your screen's rulers and how they relate to the actual printed drawing. The **Compatibility** section enables you to determine if you want Draw to use a different layout for the screen and printed drawings (typically you'll leave this option unchecked).

4 Change View Options

Click the **View** options category under the **Drawing** category; the dialog box changes to show options that handle Draw's onscreen display. The **Alternative display** section determines how and when Draw shows elements such as text and images. If you choose to show placeholders only, Draw will not display actual text and graphics but rather will show placeholders for them to speed your screen's display. During the editing of a large drawing, you can often speed up the editing process by electing to show placeholders instead of actual text and graphics. When printing your drawings, of course, Draw will show the actual text and graphics on the drawings because the placeholders would be meaningless as artwork. If you choose not to show contours, the filled objects display without their fill. The **Display** section enables you to determine how special elements such as the rulers are to show while you work within Draw.

106

▶ **TIP**

If you are new to Draw, perhaps it's best to accept Draw's default option settings. Read through them now to familiarize yourself with the terminology, however. Once you've created some drawings, you'll better understand how these options impact your work.

5 Change Grid Options

Click to select the **Grid** category under the **Drawing** option category. The **Grid** section enables you to determine whether to use the snap-to grid and whether to make the grid visible. The **Resolution** section specifies the width between each grid point measurement (decrease the width for detailed drawings). If you click to check the **Synchronize axes** option, when you change the X-axis, the Y-axis adjusts symmetrically at the same time, instead of changes to one axis not affecting the other. The **Snap** section determines how you want to use the snap-to grid to align objects. If you create many freeform drawings, such as an artist might do with a drawing tablet attached to the computer, you'll want to turn off all snap-to items. If you create commercial drawings and some educational drawings showing relationships and textual backgrounds and layouts, you may wish to require that some objects move toward the closest snap-to grid for consistency and alignment of objects.

6 Change Print Options and Click OK

Click to select the **Print** category under the **Drawing** option category. The **Quality** section controls whether your drawings are printed by default in color or in a more efficient grayscale or black and white (saving color printer ink). The **Print** section specifies what you want printed, such as the page name (if you've assigned one), date, time, or pages you've hidden within the drawing but may want to print. The **Page options** section determines how you want your drawings to fit the final page—whether they should take up the actual size specified by the ruler or whether you want Draw to shrink the drawings enough to fit on the current page. You can also specify whether you want to print on the front and back of the page as well as use the printer's own paper tray settings instead of the default settings. Click **OK**.

107 Create a New Drawing

✔ BEFORE YOU BEGIN	→ SEE ALSO
106 Set Draw Options	**108** Open an Existing Drawing
	111 Draw from Scratch

Unlike most other OpenOffice.org programs, Draw comes with no templates. Unlike common documents (such as memos) and presentations (such as those that might introduce a new product), drawings can differ from one another in such a major way that there isn't any way OpenOffice.org could provide templates that attempt to help you with what you might want to draw next.

▶ **NOTE**

Draw does support templates, and you can create your own by saving your drawing with the **File**, **Save As** menu option and selecting the **OpenOffice.org Drawing Template** option for the file type.

Most often, you'll create a brand-new drawing from scratch (or change one you've already created). Draw supplies drawing tools such as shapes and lines, and you can place graphic images and charts in your drawings also. Of course, you can put text throughout a drawing and add some effects to the text to make it look more artistic than plain text would look.

▶ **NOTE**

Unlike in Writer and Impress, AutoPilot provides no help when creating drawings.

107

107 Create a New Drawing

1 Choose New, Drawing

Select **Drawing** from the **Windows** menu to create a new drawing. Draw displays a blank drawing area on which you can work. Of course, once inside Draw, you can select **File**, **New**, **Drawing** to display a fresh drawing area where you can create your drawing. Alternatively, you can click the **New** toolbar button to open a new, blank drawing area quickly.

2 Compose Your Drawing

Create your drawing in the blank drawing area that Draw provides. You'll draw lines, add shapes, type and format text, and edit your composition depending on your drawing's goals. You can print your drawing (see **110** **Print a Drawing**) at any time.

3 Save the Drawing

After creating your drawing, select **File**, **Save** and type the name of your drawing. Draw uses the filename extension .odg for your drawing. Click **Save** to save your drawing.

If you want to use your drawing on the Web, export it (choose **File**, **Export**) in a Web-compatible format such as GIF or JPEG. You can also export a drawing as a series of web pages (choose **File**, **Export** and choose the HTML format) or as a PDF file (choose **File**, **Export as PDF**). (See **36** **Save a Document as a PDF File** for help with PDF.) If you export to HTML format, a main page is created, with links to each slide in the drawing file (each slide is saved to its own web page). If you export to PDF format, each slide in the drawing file is placed on its own page in the PDF document.

▶ **TIP**

If you want to protect your drawing from prying eyes, click to check the **Save with password** option before clicking **Save**. Draw requests a password that anyone will have to enter before editing or viewing your drawing.

108

---

108 Open an Existing Drawing

✔ **BEFORE YOU BEGIN**	→ **SEE ALSO**
107 Create a New Drawing	**109** About Drawing with Draw

Opening an existing drawing to edit within Draw is simple. You tell Draw that you want to open a drawing file and then locate the file. Draw then loads the drawing into memory, where you can edit the drawing on the drawing area.

One important Draw feature is its capability to open drawings that you create in other graphics programs. In addition to opening Draw files, Draw opens the files in many popular graphic formats such as BMP, JPEG, GIF, TIFF, WMF, and EPS, as well as exports Draw drawings to those file formats.

1 Choose File, Open

Select **Open** from Draw's **File** menu or click the **Open** button to display the **Open** dialog box.

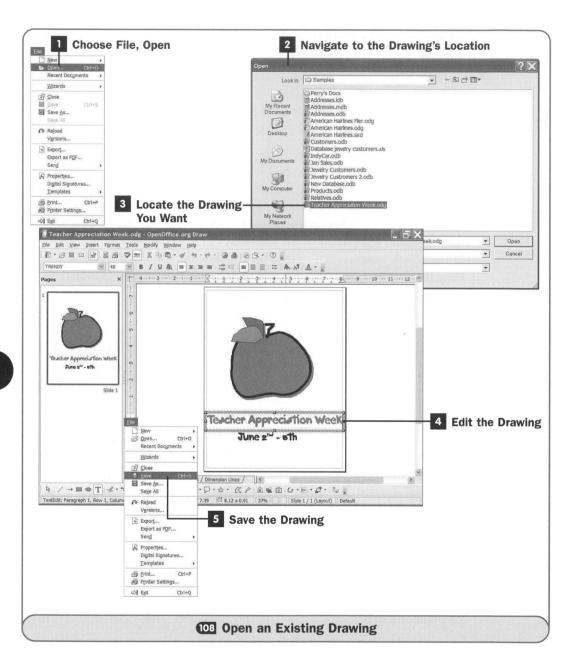

1 Choose File, Open

2 Navigate to the Drawing's Location

3 Locate the Drawing You Want

4 Edit the Drawing

5 Save the Drawing

108 Open an Existing Drawing

108

2 Navigate to the Drawing's Location

The drawing that you want to open might not appear at the default location shown in the **Open** dialog box, so navigate to the folder in which the drawing you're looking for resides using the **Look in** drop-down list.

► **TIPS**

You can open drawings from your computer's disk or from elsewhere in the file system. If you want to open a drawing located on the Web, preface the filename with the **http://** web address or the **ftp://** File Transfer Protocol address to open drawing files from those sources.

Feel free to open more than one drawing by holding down the **Ctrl** key while clicking multiple filenames. Draw opens each drawing that you select in its own window. Use the **Window** menu to select a currently opened drawing that you want to edit.

3 Locate the Drawing You Want

When you locate the folder that holds the presentation file, select the file you want to open. Then click the **Open** button to open the selected Draw file.

Draw opens the drawing and places it for you to view, edit, and print on Draw's drawing area. If the entire drawing is large, you may need to select the **View**, **Zoom** menu option and increase the zoom factor to see a close-up of your drawing's details before editing them.

4 Edit the Drawing

After the file opens on the Draw workspace, you can edit the drawing (see **109** **About Drawing with Draw**).

109

5 Save the Drawing

When you've made all the changes you want to make, choose **File**, **Save** or click the **Save** button to save your drawing. Your recent changes will be saved in the drawing file for your next editing or printing session.

---

109 **About Drawing with Draw**

✔ BEFORE YOU BEGIN	→ SEE ALSO
107 Create a New Drawing	**111** Draw from Scratch
108 Open an Existing Drawing	

Without question, Draw is the most enjoyable of all the OpenOffice.org programs. Draw is fun to use, and it's the only one of the OpenOffice.org programs that both adults and children have fun using. Draw supports all kinds of shapes. Here is only a sample of the shapes available to you as a Draw artist:

- Lines of all thicknesses, patterns, and lengths, including arrows and connectors

- Curves, circles, and ovals (ellipses of all kinds)

- Rectangles, squares, and polygons

- 3D blocks, 3D cones, 3D cylinders, 3D conclave holders, and 3D convex holders

- Artistic text

▶ TIP

Not only does Draw support multiple shapes, but you can control how those shapes over-lap. You can combine or un-combine shapes to produce different effects when you place multiple objects on the same plane.

As you use draw, you place various shapes on the drawing area. You control all aspects of the shapes you place there, including their lighting effects, their rotation angles, their size, their interaction with other objects, their color, their line thickness, and more. You can always return to shapes you place on your drawing and delete, resize, and edit them.

One of the most powerful features of Draw is its ability to combine multiple shapes so that you can treat those shapes as a single object. You can temporarily combine multiple shapes to work with them currently or you can combine them into a single shape semi-permanently (you can, through menu commands, uncombined them).

109

As you place items on the screen, you are placing them on slides, not unlike Impress slides. (See the introduction in Chapter 11, "Learning About Impress," for a quick background about Impress slides.) Each slide is basically its own graphic image; if you export your drawing to a graphic format such as JPEG, only the selected slide is saved to the file. If you export the drawing to an HTML file, how-ever, multiple web pages are created—one page for each slide, with an additional master page that contains links to the slide pages. In this manner, you can create an easy-to-navigate image gallery. If you export a drawing to a PDF file, each slide is saved to a new page in the file. (See **36** **Save a Document as a PDF File** for help with PDF.)

▶ TIPS

Another advantage to creating multiple images in a Draw file (each on its own slide) is that you can add components on a *master slide* that each image shares. Choose **View, Master** to display the master slide, and then add the common components, such as a similar background or text.

Whenever you want to place the same objects (such as a title and a background image) on all your drawing's slides, place those objects on the master slide so that they appear on all slides you create in that drawing.

Pages Pane   **Apple Is on Master Slide**

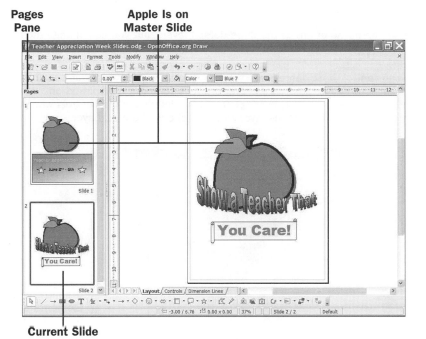

Current Slide

The Pages pane allows you to change from one slide to another in your drawing.

To insert a slide, choose **Insert, New Slide** from the menu. To change from slide to slide, click the slide you want to work on in the **Pages** pane (display this pane by choosing **View, Pages Pane** from the menu bar). The current slide is highlighted in blue.

On each slide, you can combine multiple objects, even stacking them one on top of the other to partially obscure the object underneath. If it helps you to keep these multiple objects on different *layers*, you can create extra layers as needed. Choose **Insert, Layer**, type a layer name, select layer properties (such as **Visible**), and click **OK**. You change from one layer to another on a slide by clicking the layer's tab. Each slide has three layers by default: **Layout**, **Control**, and **Dimension Lines**. You can use these layers for whatever you want, but the intention is that you keep your drawing objects on the **Layout** layer, buttons that activate sounds, movie files, and other fun stuff on the **Controls** layer, and *dimension lines* on the **Dimension Lines** layer.

▶ KEY TERMS

Layers—Groups of items, such as your drawing's graphics and text, controls you place on a drawing, or *dimension lines* for three-dimensional space control.

Dimension line—A special line you can draw that measures the length of the nearest object and displays that measurement onscreen.

▶ TIPS

You can't change the name of any of the three default layers, but you can change their properties to hide them, stop them from printing, or lock their contents.

Likewise, you can control these same three properties for any layer you create: **Visible**, **Printable**, and **Locked**. **Visible** controls whether a layer's contents is displayed on screen; **Printable** controls whether a layer's contents is printed; **Locked** controls whether or not edits are allowed. Just select the layer and then choose **Format, Layer**.

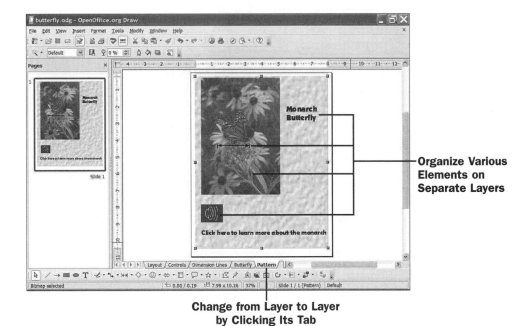

Organize Various Elements on Separate Layers

Change from Layer to Layer by Clicking Its Tab

Each slide comes with three layers you can use to organize the drawing's various elements.

Objects you draw (such as a rectangle or a line) can be stacked in any order you choose, with the object at the top of the stack obscuring objects beneath. See **118 About Grouping Objects**. If you create multiple layers, the way in which objects are stacked has nothing to do with which layer they are on; layers are only used to organize objects and to prevent certain objects from printing, displaying, or being changed.

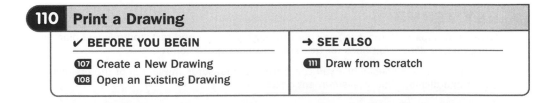

110 | Print a Drawing

✔ BEFORE YOU BEGIN	→ SEE ALSO
107 Create a New Drawing	111 Draw from Scratch
108 Open an Existing Drawing	

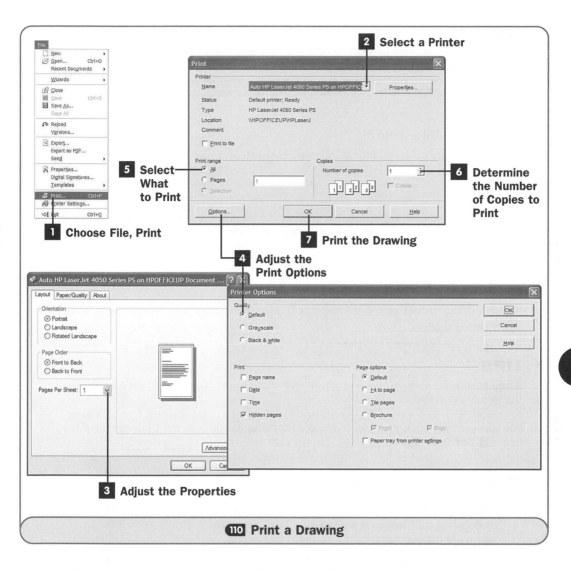

2 Select a Printer

5 Select What to Print

6 Determine the Number of Copies to Print

1 Choose File, Print

7 Print the Drawing

4 Adjust the Print Options

3 Adjust the Properties

110

110 Print a Drawing

Once you're done creating your drawing, you'll want to print it to paper. Draw supports the standard printing options that most Windows programs support. If your drawing uses color and you have a color printer, the colors print just fine. Otherwise, the colored areas will print in shades of black and gray (and still look fine!).

Be sure to save your drawing before you print it. Actually, it's a good idea to select **File, Save** or click the **Save** button to save your drawing throughout the creation and editing of that drawing. If your printer jams or the Windows print queue messes up during the printing process (rare, but it can happen), you could lose changes you made to the drawing before you printed it.

▶ **TIP**

If you select **File**, **Export as PDF**, Draw saves your document in the common PDF format, which you can send to any computer with Adobe Acrobat Reader, allowing the users to view or print your drawing even if they don't have Draw (see **36** **Save a Document as a PDF File** for information on PDF terminology and usage).

1 Choose File, Print

Select **Print** from the **File** menu. The **Print** dialog box opens.

▶ **NOTE**

Unlike Writer and Calc, Draw does not support a print preview feature—and it doesn't need one. What you see in the drawing area (in **Normal** view) is what your drawing will look like when you print it.

2 Select a Printer

Select the printer you want to print to from the **Name** drop-down list in the **Printer** section.

110

▶ **TIPS**

If you have a fax modem, you can select your fax from the **Name** list to send your drawing to a fax recipient.

You can set the print options for the majority of your drawings in the **Options** dialog box. See **106** **Set Draw Options**.

3 Adjust the Properties

If you want to adjust any printer settings, click the **Properties** button. The dialog box that appears when you click **Properties** varies from printer to printer. Click **OK** to close the printer's **Properties** dialog box once you've made any needed changes. If, for example, your printer's properties support multiple pages per sheet, you can select the number of slides you want on each printed page (as opposed to the one slide per page that Draw normally prints). You can also use the **Properties** dialog box to select the paper type and print quality you want.

4 Adjust the Print Options

Click the **Options** button to display the **Printer Options** dialog box. From the **Printer Options** dialog box, you can adjust several print settings, such as whether you want to print in grayscale or black and white (to save color ink or toner), whether you want the date and time printed, and whether you want Draw to scale down your drawing to fit a single printed page if needed.

▶ **NOTES**

Although it's called the **Printer Options** dialog box, this dialog box is not printer specific; rather, it controls the way your drawing appears when printed. If, for instance, you want to produce a brochure, you could click to select the **Brochure** option and specify whether you want Draw to print on both the front and back of the paper. For automatic double-sided printing, you need a printer that supports double-sided printing.

If you select **Tile pages**, and if the drawing's page size is smaller than the paper size you're printing on, this option prints multiple copies of each slide in a tiled pattern, on a single piece of paper. To change the page size used in a drawing, choose **Format, Page**, click the **Page** tab, select **User** from the **Format** list, and enter the dimensions you want to use for the **Width** and **Height**.

Click the **OK** button to close the **Printer Options** dialog box.

5 Select What to Print

Click to select either **All** or **Pages** to designate whether you want to print the entire drawing (assuming that the drawing contains multiple slides) or only a portion of it. If you clicked **Pages**, type the slide number you want to print, or a range of slide numbers (such as **2–5** or **1–10, 15–25**).

6 Determine the Number of Copies to Print

Click the arrow next to the **Number of Copies** option to determine how many copies you want to print.

7 Print the Drawing

Once you've determined how many pages and copies to print, click the **OK** button to print your drawing and close the **Print** dialog box.

15

Improving Your Drawings

IN THIS CHAPTER:

In this chapter, you'll learn how to put the details into your drawings. Starting with a blank drawing area, there is very little you cannot generate with Draw. With the millions of colors available, today's video cards, and high-resolution screens, you have the tools to create fine drawings that can represent any picture you want to produce.

But Draw isn't just for drawings! You can create charts and diagrams too. Commercial users who create art for logos, slogans, fliers, and other areas will feel at home with Draw's tools. The shapes and alignment tools ensure that your commercial artwork conveys the very message you need it to convey.

▶ **NOTE**

If you need to add some freehand artwork to your drawings, consider getting a drawing tablet such as the ones Watcom sells. Neither a mouse nor trackball offers the same precision control you get drawing by hand.

---

111 | **Draw from Scratch**

✔ BEFORE YOU BEGIN	→ SEE ALSO
106 Set Draw Options	**112** Place Shapes on the Drawing Area
107 Create a New Drawing	

Freehand drawing is perhaps the first thing most people want to try when they learn a new drawing program. Draw enables you to freeform draw, but on your freeform drawing you can also place all kinds of shapes and graphic images; you can mix it all up on a Draw drawing.

If you're new to Draw, the drawing tools may seem a little awkward at first. When you select a tool and draw with it, as soon as you finish the line or shape, the mouse cursor changes back to its regular pointing cursor, and to use the tool once again, you must reselect the tool. Therefore, if you need to draw several freeform objects, such as birds flying, it might seem as though you must keep selecting the freeform drawing tool each time you add to your drawing. Fortunately, although it may not be fully intuitive, there is a way to keep tools selected that you want to use multiple times, and you learn how to do that here.

1 Select Freeform Line Tool

Start Draw and go to work! It doesn't matter at this point what you draw if you're new to Draw; you need to get a feel of the basic steps necessary for drawing and placing objects on the drawing area. To start a new drawing, choose **File, New, Drawing** from the menu or click the **New** button.

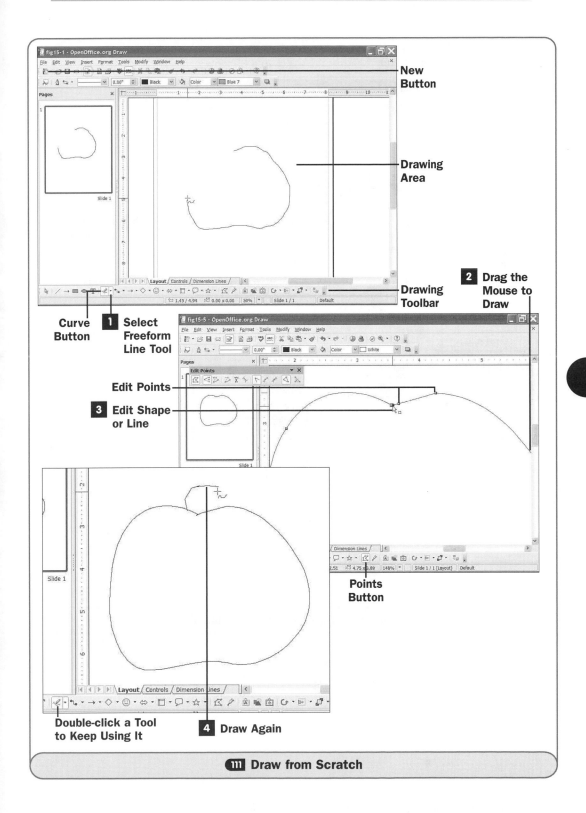

New Button

Drawing Area

Drawing Toolbar

Curve Button

1 Select Freeform Line Tool

2 Drag the Mouse to Draw

Edit Points

3 Edit Shape or Line

Points Button

Double-click a Tool to Keep Using It

4 Draw Again

111 Draw from Scratch

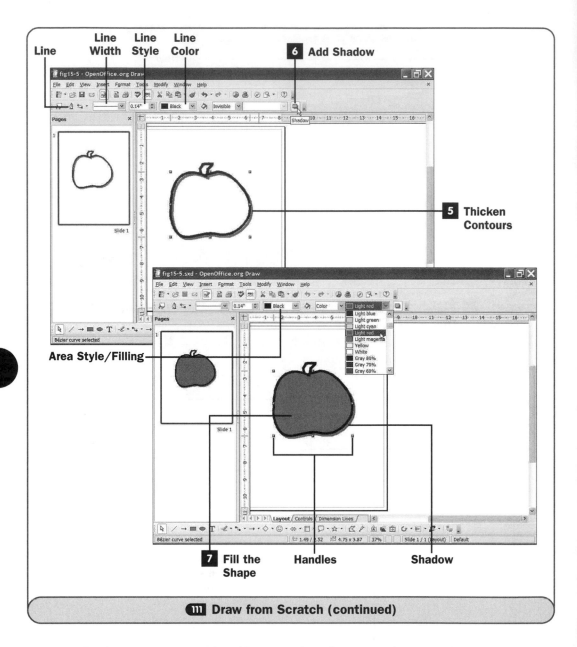

111 Draw from Scratch (continued)

The drawing area is enclosed by an outline the size you've set in the **Format, Page** dialog box (typically, this is set to 8.5" × 11"). You do not have to place objects directly on the drawing area. You can move graphics out of the way by dragging them off the drawing area temporarily until you're ready to use them.

When you're ready to draw a freeform line or shape, just long-click the **Drawing** toolbar's **Curve** tool to display the **Curve** toolbar. Click the **Freeform Curve** tool. Your mouse cursor changes from the pointer to a crosshair shape with the **Freeform Curve** icon showing next to it.

▶ **NOTES**

Objects you drag off the drawing area are not printed.

The **Curve** button changed to the **Freeform Curve** button's icon on your **Drawing** toolbar. You can click this button to reuse the **Freeform Curve** tool without having to long-click the **Curve** button first. You only have to long-click the **Curve** button again if you want to select a tool other than the **Freeform** tool on the **Curve** toolbar.

2 Drag the Mouse to Draw

Click the starting point of the line you're about to draw and hold down the mouse button as you draw a line. The line is freeform because you're using the **Freeform Curve** tool, so you can draw any line, curve, or shape you wish. When you finish, release your mouse button.

▶ **TIP**

If you want to draw a closed shape, such as the outline of a face, release your mouse button near the point at which you began drawing, and Draw will close the shape.

3 Edit Shape or Line

After you release the mouse button to indicate that you are finished drawing an open or closed shape, small *handles* appear around the new object. You can resize an object by dragging one of these handles inward or outward. See **117** **About Manipulating Objects**.

▶ **KEY TERMS**

Handles—Green boxes that surround an object when that object is selected. Resize an object by dragging one of these handles.

Edit points—Also called *data points*. Small blue squares that surround an object when it's being edited; drag an edit point inward or outward to modify a shape or freeform line's contour.

If you want to change the outline of the object, you must display its *edit points*. Click the object to select it, and then click the **Points** button on the **Drawing** toolbar. Edit points surround the object so that you can manipulate its contour. Drag an edit point in or out to reshape the contour of the line or shape at that location. See **117** **About Manipulating Objects**.

▶ **NOTE**

To delete an object, click it and press the **Delete** key. Choose **Edit**, **Undo** (or press **Ctrl+Z**) to replace what you deleted if you delete the wrong piece of the drawing.

4 Draw Again

To draw another freeform shape or line, you must click the **Freeform** button once again to use it again. In other words, each tool that you select by clicking the **Drawing** toolbar stays active only for one use of that tool. If you're doing a lot of drawing with one of the tools, such as the **Freeform** tool, you won't want to keep selecting the tool after each line you draw. Therefore, Draw lets you double-click any tool to keep that tool active (until you select another).

5 Thicken Contours

You can add thickness to the contour of an object or line using the options on the **Line and Filling** toolbar. To select every shape and line in your drawing, press **Ctrl+A**. This **Select All** command selects everything in the drawing and displays handles around the area.

With all objects selected, you can easily change the thickness of the lines used. The **Line and Filling** toolbar includes several tools you can use to modify lines and the contours of shapes, including a line type and thickness tool. With the object(s) you want to change selected, click the up arrow on the **Line and Filling** toolbar's **Line Width** control. As you click, your drawing's selected lines will thicken. You can change the line color for selected objects and lines by choosing a color from the **Line and Filling** toolbar's **Line Color** control, and you can change the line itself (from solid to dashed, for example) by selecting from the **Line Style** list box. To remove the line from around a shape, set the **Line Style** to **Invisible** (you might do this after you fill the shape with color, for example).

6 Add Shadow

The remaining **Line and Filling** toolbar's tools include a **Line** button that displays a dialog box so that you can make precise selections to a line's style and color (see **113 Draw Lines**), fill buttons you can use to fill the center of enclosed drawing areas with patterns and colors, and a **Shadow** button that adds a shadow effect to your object. Click the **Shadow** button now to add a shadow to your line so that you can see the effect. See **116 Fill an Object** for more help with shadows.

7 **Fill the Shape**

If you've drawn an enclosed shape, click the shape to select it. Select the type of fill pattern you want to add from the **Area Style/Filling** list box, such as a solid **Color**, a **Gradient**, a cross pattern of lines known as **Hatching**, or a **Bitmap** image. Then select a matching style (such as a particular color) from the second list box. **116** **Fill an Object** describes more about filling objects on your drawing area.

▶ **TIP**

You can import graphic images from files onto your drawing area, as you might do for a corporate logo that you want to label a drawing with. Remember that if you've elected to display image placeholders instead of the images themselves, an image anchor will appear as a placeholder for the image. You'll need to select the appropriate **View** option from the **Tools, Options** dialog box to see the graphic image as it will finally look in your drawing.

---

112 **Place Shapes on the Drawing Area**

✔ BEFORE YOU BEGIN	→ SEE ALSO
107 Create a New Drawing	**114** About Perfecting Shapes
	115 Create a New Shape
	117 About Manipulating Objects

112

Although you don't create anything fancy in this task, you do get a tour of Draw's shapes. You must be able to select from and place the various shapes available to you. Draw provides ovals, rectangles, *polygons*, and other shapes, including three-dimensional versions of most of these.

▶ **KEY TERM**

Polygons—Multisided shapes. A square and rectangle are four-sided polygons, and a stop sign is an eight-sided polygon. Polygons don't have to be symmetrical.

Before getting complicated, you need to master the selection and placement of these shapes on your drawing area. Once you see how to place one shape on the drawing area, the rest are just as simple to do.

▶ **TIP**

Use the ToolTips feature if you forget what a shape or tool does. For example, let your mouse pointer hover over any button on the **Drawing** toolbar and Draw pops up a ToolTip box that names the button (for example, the **Lines and Arrows** button).

112

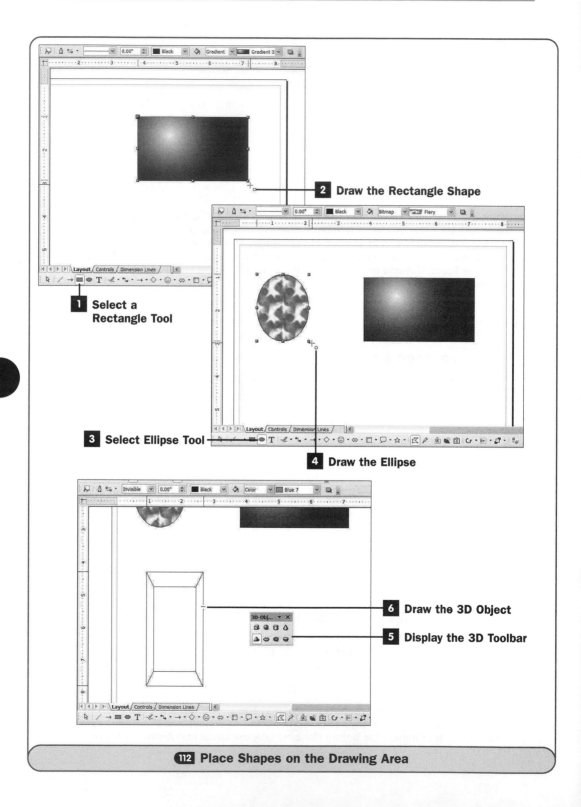

2 Draw the Rectangle Shape

1 Select a Rectangle Tool

3 Select Ellipse Tool

4 Draw the Ellipse

6 Draw the 3D Object

5 Display the 3D Toolbar

112 Place Shapes on the Drawing Area

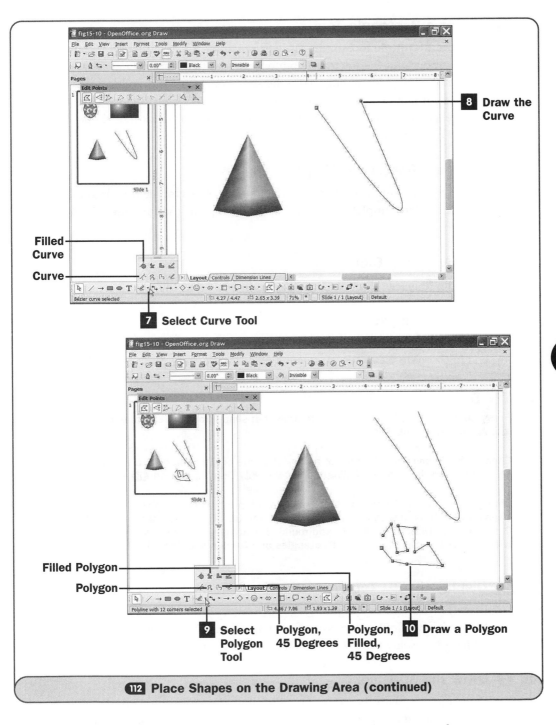

112 Place Shapes on the Drawing Area (continued)

The steps in this task walk you through the list of shapes you can place on your drawings.

1 | Select a Rectangle Tool

Click the **Rectangle** tool on the **Drawing** toolbar. Your mouse cursor changes to that shape and the **Rectangle** button changes to the shape you selected. Remember that you can only place the shape once on your drawing area before your mouse cursor will return to its normal pointer. To place several occurrences of the same shape on your drawing, double-click that shape's button before drawing.

2 | Draw the Rectangle Shape

To draw the rectangle, click to place one end of the rectangle and drag to the opposite end to complete the shape. To create a perfect square, press **Shift** as you drag.

3 | Select Ellipse Tool

Click the **Ellipse** tool on the **Drawing** toolbar to select the tool.

4 | Draw the Ellipse

To draw the ellipse, click to place one end of the ellipse and drag to the opposite end to complete the shape. To create a perfect circle, press **Shift** as you drag.

112

▶ **TIPS**

Press **Alt** and drag with a shape tool to draw that shape from the center out. See **114** **About Perfecting Shapes**.

Change the fill and line attributes of an object before or after you draw it by making selections from the **Line and Filling** toolbar. See **113** **Draw Lines** and **116** **Fill an Object**.

Change aspects of a 3D object other than line color and fill (such as the angle and intensity of light on the object) by right-clicking the 3D object and choosing **3D Effects**. Customize the **Drawing** toolbar to add rounded rectangles and various circle shapes with the buttons copied from the **Rectangles** and **Circles and Ovals** toolbars.

5 | Display the 3D Toolbar

Draw provides cubes, spheres, cylinders, cones, pyramids, and other shapes that come right out of the drawing at you. Choose **View, Toolbar, 3D-Objects** to display the **3D-Objects** toolbar. Select a 3D tool such as **Cone**.

6 | Draw the 3D Object

Click and drag with the 3D tool to place that 3D shape onto your drawing area. A wireframe appears, marking the size of the foreground area of the future object. When the object is the right size, release the mouse button.

Depending on the speed of your computer, the 3D shape will take slightly longer to draw than the other shapes because of the more complex computations taking place to render it.

▶ **NOTE**

If the **Contour mode** option is checked in your View options (see **106** **Set Draw Options**), the 3D shape will appear in the drawing area as a faint outline. You will see the object fully on the slide if the **Pages** pane is displayed, however. You must disable the **Contour mode** check box to see your 3D shape in the drawing area. (The shape will print either way.) This option is for users who work on slower computers whose screens take far too long to update every time they change a drawing that includes 3D shapes.

7 Select Curve Tool

The **Curves** toolbar, when you click the **Drawing** toolbar's **Curve** button to open it, include more tools than just curves. (For example, this the same **Drawing** toolbar button you clicked in a previous task to choose the **Freeform** tool.) From this toolbar, you can choose to draw a curve, a polygon, a 45-degree polygon, and filled versions of each.

▶ **NOTE**

In 45-degree polygons, each edge is always a multiple of a 45-degree angle from the previous edge, as is always the case with squares and rectangles.

8 Draw the Curve

To draw a curve, click the **Curve** or **Filled Curve** tool to select it. Click on your drawing area where you want to start the curve. Drag your mouse over the span of the curve and release your mouse button after you've spanned the entire curve length. Your curve initially looks like a straight line, but now the fun begins.

Unlike with most other tools, when you release the mouse button after drawing a curve, you have only designated part of the shape. You must now move your mouse to another location to begin developing the curve; as you move your mouse, the end of the line moves with your mouse, forming a curve to meet your mouse pointer. When the curve is positioned where you want it, double-click your mouse to anchor that end of the curve.

▶ **NOTE**

After you've dragged your mouse to start the curve, don't drag the mouse again. Just move your mouse to adjust the curve as needed; the curve adjusts as you move the mouse.

112

9 **Select Polygon Tool**

Once again, open the **Curves** toolbar by clicking the **Drawing** toolbar's **Curves** button. You can now draw a polygon.

10 **Draw a Polygon**

To draw a polygon, click either the **Polygon** or **45-Degree Polygon** tool to select it. Click your drawing area where you want to start the multisided polygon. Drag your mouse in the direction of the polygon's first side. Release your mouse button to anchor that side; then drag your mouse once again to draw the next side. Keep drawing the polygon's sides. To end the polygon, double-click your mouse button. If you want to draw an enclosed polygon, finish as close as you can to the starting point of your polygon before you double-click to anchor the polygon into position.

▶ **TIP**

If you're using the **Polygon** or **Filled Polygon** tool (and not the 45-Degree Polygon or 45-Degree Filled Polygon tool) you can still create 45-degree polygons; just hold the **Shift** key when dragging to create a new line that's angled at a multiple of 45-degrees from your current point.

113

113	**Draw Lines**

✔ **BEFORE YOU BEGIN**	→ **SEE ALSO**
111 Draw from Scratch	**115** Create a New Shape
112 Place Shapes on the Drawing Area	**117** About Manipulating Objects

You can easily add lines and arrows to your drawings. In addition to arrows and lines, Draw also supports the use of many kinds of connectors. With lines, arrows, and connectors, you can draw flow diagrams such as organization charts and flowcharts.

Draw gives you the choice of four kinds of connectors (with or without arrows at one or both ends):

- Standard connectors with 90-degree angle bends that form a kind of blocked Z pattern

- Line connectors with two halves whose midpoint you can adjust

- Straight connectors that draw one connecting line to another

- Curved connectors that draw curved lines from one object to the next

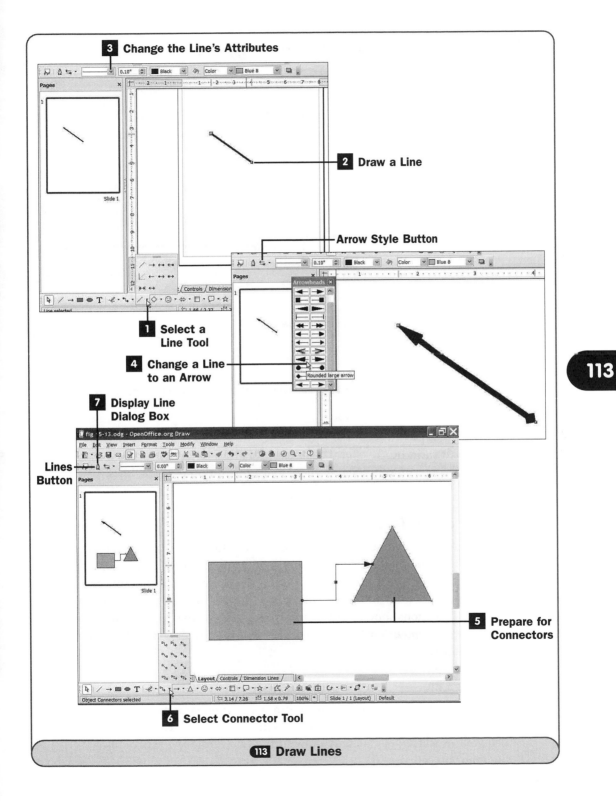

3 Change the Line's Attributes

2 Draw a Line

Arrow Style Button

1 Select a Line Tool

4 Change a Line to an Arrow

Rounded large arrow

113

7 Display Line Dialog Box

Lines Button

5 Prepare for Connectors

6 Select Connector Tool

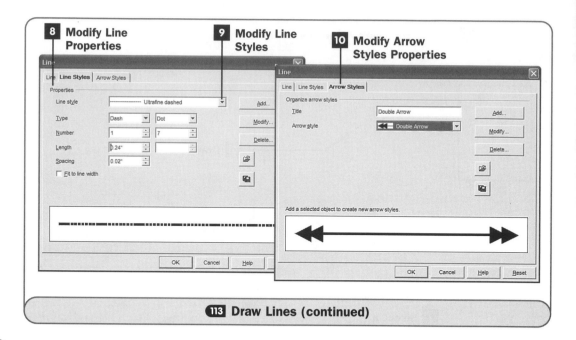

113 Draw Lines (continued)

113

▶ **NOTE**

You choose what appears on the ends of connectors, such as an arrow, a small box, or a circle.

You'll want to experiment with the various lines, arrows, and connectors until you see all that Draw has to offer. The **Line and Filling** toolbar contains the thickness and color controls you'll need to adjust the attributes of the lines, arrows, and connectors.

1 Select a Line Tool

Long-click to open the **Lines and Arrows** toolbar from your **Drawing** toolbar, and select a **Line** tool. As with any shape, you can double-click the tool to keep it active when you want to draw multiple occurrences of that line or arrow. You'll see the various lines and arrows on the toolbar; the icon on each of the buttons shows what your selected line or arrow will look like. For example, the *dimension line* is a line with arrows on each end that intersect straight lines.

2 Draw a Line

Click the starting point for the line or arrow and drag your mouse to the ending point. You can draw lines and arrows in any direction, except for the 45-degree line, which you can only draw straight up, straight down, or at a diagonal angle.

▶ **NOTE**

The direction you drag when you draw a line with an arrow determines the direction your drawn arrow will point.

▶ **TIP**

Press **Shift** as you drag to draw a line or arrow in 45-degree increments from the starting point.

3 Change the Line's Attributes

You can select a color and line thickness from the **Line and Filling** toolbar either before or after you draw the line or arrow. If you want to change an attribute after you draw the line or arrow, you can click to select the line or arrow and then change its thickness and color.

4 Change a Line to an Arrow

You can convert a line to an arrow by first clicking to select the line and then clicking the **Arrow Style** button on the **Line and Filling** toolbar. The **Arrow Style** list box appears, containing more forms of arrows, including double-headed arrows, than is available from the **Lines** toolbar. Click a style on the left side of the list box to apply it to the left end of your line; click a style on the right side to apply it to the right end of the line.

5 Prepare for Connectors

Draw two shapes on your drawing area that you will later connect with connectors.

6 Select Connector Tool

Long-click to open the **Connector** toolbar from your **Drawing** toolbar. Select a connector and click the first object you drew to connect. Drag your mouse to the next object. As you drag your mouse, Draw updates the connecting line according to the style of the connector. You can connect the same two shapes with multiple connectors, so feel free to add another kind of connecting line to familiarize yourself with the connectors.

7 Display Line Dialog Box

Draw enables you to adjust lines and connectors with precision from the **Line** dialog box. Select one of the lines or connectors you've drawn and click the **Line** button on the **Line and Filling** toolbar. The **Line** dialog box appears.

113

8 Modify Line Properties

The **Line** page lets you control the line style, color, width, and whether or not the line allows graphics beneath it to show through by the amount of the **Transparency** option. In addition, the **Line** page enables you to change or select from arrow styles, widths, and measurements. A preview at the bottom of the dialog box shows you the result of any change you make to the selected line.

9 Modify Line Styles

Click to select the **Line Styles** page. Here, you not only select a style but you can help create a new style by specifying the number of dashes or dots that follow one another across the length of your selected line. If you change the line's styles, you will be able to save that style for use later in another drawing by clicking **Save Line Styles**.

10 Modify Arrow Styles Properties

The **Arrow Styles** page enables you to adjust the look of any arrow you select in your drawing. If you change an arrow's style, you will be able to save that style for use later in another drawing by clicking **Save Arrow Styles**. Click **OK** when you want to apply your **Line** dialog box settings to your selected line, connector, or arrow.

114

---

114 | About Perfecting Shapes

✔ BEFORE YOU BEGIN	→ SEE ALSO
112 Place Shapes on the Drawing Area 113 Draw Lines	115 Create a New Shape

---

Once you learn how to apply one shape, all the other shapes are simple to add to your drawings. Draw gives you the tools you need to add shapes in a format that suits you best. Surprisingly, a judicious use of your **Shift** and **Alt** keys can dramatically improve your ability to add shapes to your drawings.

When you first learn how to add shapes to your drawings, you'll usually also learn how to adjust their thickness and color. 112 **Place Shapes on the Drawing Area** and 113 **Draw Lines** show examples of how to change these kinds of attributes. Generally, you'll be able to change all the formatting attributes you wish to change from the **Line and Filling** toolbar.

In addition to the **Line and Filling** toolbar, you have several other ways to change the way your shapes look. **117 About Manipulating Objects** describes how to use your mouse to adjust a shape's length, size, and skew. As you place shapes on your drawing, however, you can take advantage of some less obvious ways to make the shapes look the way you want them to look.

For example, if you hold the **Shift** key while drawing certain shapes, some interesting things happen:

* Hold **Shift** while drawing a straight line or arrow, and Draw limits you to 45-degree angles, meaning you can draw the line or arrow straight up and down, left or right, or at 45-degree diagonal intersections, but nowhere else. When you need to draw perfectly horizontal, vertical, or diagonal lines and arrows, remember this trick.

▶ NOTE

Using the **45-degree Line** tool is identical to using the regular **Line** tool and holding **Shift**. By using **Shift**, you can also apply 45-degree angles to many more lines and arrows.

* Hold **Shift** when drawing rectangles, even when not using the **Square** tool (which is found on the **Rectangles** toolbar), and your rectangles are drawn as perfect squares. If you've selected a **Rectangle** tool instead of one of the **Square** tools by double-clicking it, using **Shift** keeps you from having to select the **Square** tool when you need a square on your drawing.

* Hold **Shift** while drawing polygons, and each line you add with the **Shift** key is limited to 45-degree increments from the previous polygon edge.

* Hold **Shift** when drawing ellipses, even when not using a **Circle** tool (which is found on the **Circles and Ovals** toolbar), and your ellipses are drawn as perfect circles.

The **Shift** key has yet another purpose when you move selected items from one place on your drawing to another. Holding **Shift** while you drag an object keeps the movement on a 45-degree plane, making sure you move the object perfectly horizontally, vertically, or at a perfect 45-degree diagonal angle. **117 About Manipulating Objects** discusses more about selecting, moving, and copying shapes.

Depending on your drawing, it may be easier to draw your shape from its center instead of from one of its corners or edges. For example, suppose you wish to center an oval around some text. Almost always, you'll draw the oval as usual, clicking where its edge is to begin and then dragging the oval down to its other side, enclosing the text as you go. Once you place the oval on the drawing, you'll then have to drag the resizing handles to align the oval better around the text. Some of the oval, at first, might be overlapping some of the text, whereas other parts of the oval extend too far outside the text area.

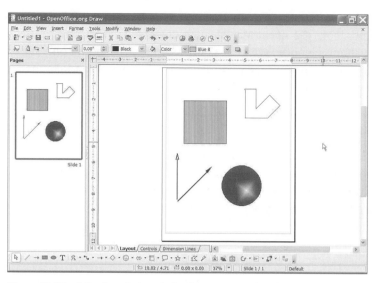

*Press **Shift** while drawing certain shapes to maintain perfect circles, squares, and 45-degree angles.*

114

Before drawing the oval (or any shape), you can press and hold the **Alt** key to draw that shape from its center. As you drag your mouse, the shape increases in size, moving away from the center where you began drawing. When you release your mouse button, the shape anchors into position. Often, by using the **Alt** key, you keep from having to adjust the shape later because you can better orient the shape around other text and objects on your drawing.

Started Drawing at Center

*Hold **Alt** to draw a shape from its center point outward, enabling you to position the shape better around objects and text.*

115 Create a New Shape

✔ BEFORE YOU BEGIN	→ SEE ALSO
112 Place Shapes on the Drawing Area **114** About Perfecting Shapes	**118** About Grouping Objects

You can create your own shapes in Draw. Although you cannot add those shapes to the **Drawing** toolbar's shape toolbars, you can reuse a shape that you create and resize and modify the shape just as you would resize and format any of Draw's built-in shapes.

▶ **NOTE**

You can only use two or more two-dimensional shapes such as the rectangles and ellipses to create new shapes. Draw does not support the construction of new shapes based on three-dimensional shapes.

To create new shapes from two or more existing shapes, you first place different shapes on the drawing area, overlapping in some way. The first object you place becomes the shape that determines the combined shape's properties. In other words, if the first shape you place on the drawing area is red, your newly created shape (after you place several more objects on that one and merge them) will also be red. You can apply any fill and hatching patterns to your new shape, just as you can apply them to any built-in shape.

115

1 Place Two Shapes to Merge

Select and place two shapes on your drawing. They don't have to be the same shape, but make sure they overlap in some way. (You can use more than two shapes to create a new shape if you ever need to do so.)

2 Select Both

Hold your **Shift** key and click both objects to select both of them.

▶ **NOTE**

117 About Manipulating Objects describes the selection and grouping of multiple shapes.

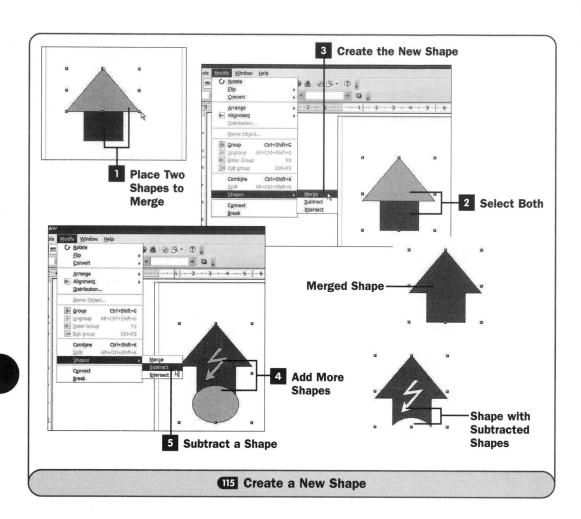

115 Create a New Shape

3 Create the New Shape

Select **Modify, Shapes, Merge** from the menu to create a new shape from the selected shapes. All the selected shapes take on the properties (such as color, line thickness, and so on) of the first shape you placed on the drawing area. If somewhere inside the shape the drawing area shows through, that hole will be left unfilled.

▶ TIP

After you've created the new shape, you can copy, move, and duplicate that shape elsewhere on your drawing without having to re-create it.

4 Add More Shapes

Draw also supports the subtraction of certain shapes. To see this in action, add two more shapes to your newly created shape. Keep in mind that your created shape is the earliest of the three shapes you applied to the drawing area, so it takes precedence when you subtract out the other objects.

5 Subtract a Shape

Press **Ctrl+A** to select all the shapes on your drawing area, including the newly created shape. Select **Modify**, **Shapes**, **Subtract** to remove all shapes that intersect your first shape (in this case, the shape you created). The two new shapes and any overlapping portions of your created shape disappear. You can use the **Subtract** menu command to pick away pieces of a shape or a drawing that you don't wish to show. (If you'd selected the **Modify**, **Shapes**, **Intersect** command instead of the **Modify**, **Shapes**, **Subtract** command, Draw would have kept only those parts of the shapes that overlap each other—that is, the intersecting pieces—and removed the rest.)

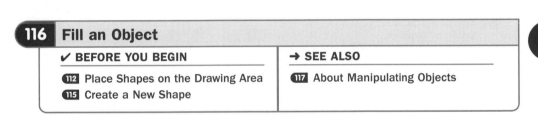

116 Fill an Object

116

✔ BEFORE YOU BEGIN

112 Place Shapes on the Drawing Area
115 Create a New Shape

→ SEE ALSO

117 About Manipulating Objects

If you've placed shapes on the drawing area already, you're probably already familiar with the **Line and Filling** toolbar's style, width, color, and fill options. (**111 Draw from Scratch** describes the use of the **Line and Filling** toolbar in detail.) Instead of relying solely on the **Line and Filling** toolbar, you can use a more complete dialog box, called the **Area** dialog box, that enables you to control every aspect of a shape's fill.

You can choose the colors, gradients, and hatching patterns, and you can even select graphic images to fill up the space inside your shapes. One timesaving feature of the **Area** dialog box is its capability to save new fill combinations that you define so that you don't have to select the same options again when you want to reuse a fill pattern on some other object.

1 Draw an Object to Fill

Draw a shape in your drawing area that you can fill.

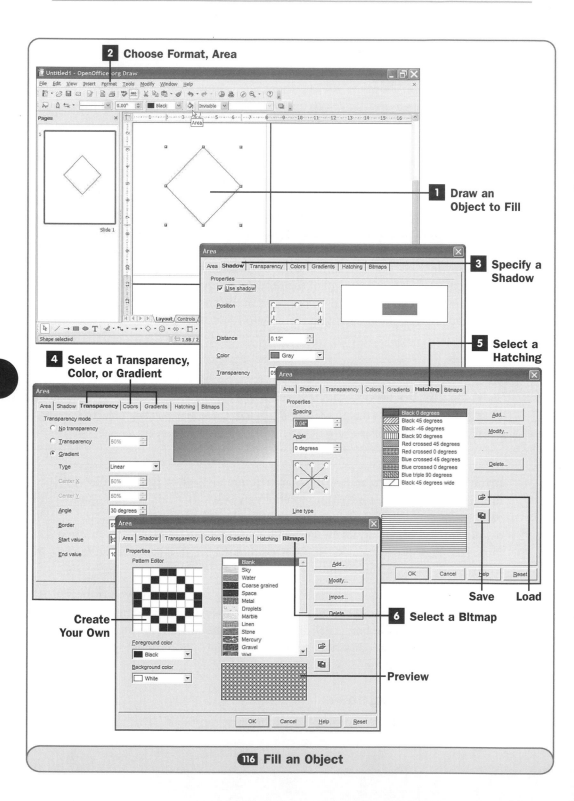

2 Choose Format, Area

1 Draw an Object to Fill

3 Specify a Shadow

4 Select a Transparency, Color, or Gradient

5 Select a Hatching

Save   Load

6 Select a Bitmap

Create Your Own

Preview

116

116 Fill an Object

2 Select Format, Area

With the shape selected, select **Format**, **Area** to display the **Area** dialog box, or click the **Area** button on the **Line and Filling** toolbar. The first page of the dialog box, **Area**, basically provides the same fill tools as the **Line and Filling** toolbar does. You can elect to use no fill, a color fill, a gradient fill, a hatching pattern fill, or a bitmap fill (from a graphic image stored on your disk). As you select the respective **Fill** section options, the **Area** page changes to reflect the options you've selected. For example, if you click the **Gradient** option, the **Area** page offers a long list of gradient patterns you can choose from and enables you to determine how dramatically the gradient moves, in incremental pixels, from one color to another.

▶ **NOTE**

Until you familiarize yourself with all the gradient patterns, save any changes you make to a new pattern by clicking **Add**.

3 Specify a Shadow

Click to select the **Shadow** page of the **Area** dialog box. Here, you can apply a shadowing effect to your selected object (including 3D text you've placed on the drawing). The **Position** option enables you to determine where the shadow will fall; for example, if you click the lower-right corner, the shadow will drop from the lower-right corner of your selected shape when you click **OK** to apply the shadow.

4 Select a Transparency, Color, or Gradient

If you have elected to add a color fill to a shape, you can determine how much of the underlying objects show through the filled area. The **No transparency** option makes the selected object's fill overwrite anything below it. If you choose the **Transparency** option, you can determine, in percentage terms, how much any objects underneath the fill area show through. If you choose the **Gradient** option, you determine how the color or other fill transitions to full transparency.

▶ **NOTE**

The **Transparency** page applies only to colors you've already filled a shape with; if you choose the **Gradient** option on this page you'll affect how the chosen fill transitions gradually complete the transparency. Use the **Gradients** page instead if you want to fill an object with a gradient pattern that transitions from one color to another.

Click the **Colors** tab to display the **Colors** page of the **Area** dialog box. Here, you can choose a color or even generate your own color by combining *RGB* *values*. Click the **Save** button if you generate a color that you might want to reuse in the future. To reuse a saved color, click the **Load** button and select the color you wish to use.

▶ KEY TERM

RGB values—The *red*, *green*, and *blue* elements of a color. All colors are composed of different combinations of the primary colors, red, green, and blue. The numbers you enter in the three RGB values determine how much of each primary color you want to include in your colored fill.

If you click the **Gradients** tab, you are able to specify exact attributes of the gradient you want to fill with. As mentioned earlier in this task, saving any changes you make to a gradient to a new pattern is recommended until you familiarize yourself with gradient effects. On the **Gradients** page, you can determine the gradient's central location, the angle of the gradient as it moves from one color to another, how much of a border the gradient will have, and the extent of the gradient's "from" and "to" colors. As with the **Colors** page, you can save a specialized gradient that you generate for later use by clicking the **Save** button.

116

5   Select a Hatching

Click to select the **Hatching** page. Here, you can select from the available hatching patterns to fill your shape. In addition, you can determine the spacing between hatch marks with the **Spacing** option. You can specify the angle used for the hatching grid lines, the direction of the hatch rotation, and the type and color of lines to use inside the hatching pattern. You can save a specialized gradient that you generate for later use by clicking **Save Hatches List**. To reuse a saved hatching pattern, click the **Load** button and select the hatching pattern you wish to use.

6   Select a Bitmap

Click the **Bitmaps** tab to display the **Bitmaps** page of the **Area** dialog box. Here, you can select from several bitmapped images to fill your shape. The **Bitmaps** page even enables you to create your own bitmap pattern and save it for reuse by clicking **Save Bitmaps List**. If you select **Blank** instead of another bitmap pattern, the **Pattern Editor** activates. Click the boxes in the **Pattern Editor** to fill them in. As you do, the preview area updates to show you what your pattern will look like as a fill. The **Foreground color** option determines the color of the selected boxes (as you click to select them), and the **Background color** option determines the pattern's background. Be sure to save your pattern by clicking the **Save** button if you want to reuse the same bitmap pattern in the future.

117 About Manipulating Objects

✔ BEFORE YOU BEGIN	→ SEE ALSO
112 Place Shapes on the Drawing Area	**119** Align Objects
114 About Perfecting Shapes	

Producing accurate drawings often requires more than just an artistic ability; you must be able to keep control of the objects on your screen. Much of the artwork you create will require that you reuse objects you've already drawn, especially in commercial artwork for logos and advertisements.

Copying and pasting of the shapes, text, and all objects you place on your drawing area works differently from copying and pasting in other OpenOffice.org programs. Draw's graphical nature requires special handling when you want to copy and paste objects.

For example, when you want to move an object, you don't really need to cut and paste it. Just click to select the object and drag it to another location. If you want to move multiple objects, select them all before dragging them to another location. If your drawing has multiple objects, you can click to select one of them. Draw moves the selection to each succeeding object (in the order you drew them) each time you press **Tab**.

▶ **TIP**

To select multiple shapes, hold the **Shift** key and click each object you want to select. Select all your drawing's objects by pressing **Ctrl+A**.

To make a copy of an object, you can do so without using the **Edit** menu to copy and paste, as you must do in most other Windows programs. Be warned, though, that it takes a little practice to make copies of Draw objects. To copy an object from one drawing location to another, follow these steps:

1. Click to select the object you want to copy. Make sure you click toward the edge of the object so you see the resizing handles and the rectangular outline of the shape instead of the edit points.

2. Before moving your mouse, but after you've clicked the shape's outline, press the **Ctrl** key.

3. While holding **Ctrl**, drag your mouse to the area where you want the copy to appear. Release both the mouse and the **Ctrl** key to place the copy into position. For best results, wait a few seconds after selecting an object and pressing **Ctrl**, and then drag to copy. The pause gives Draw the time it needs to copy the object into memory.

Resizing Handle

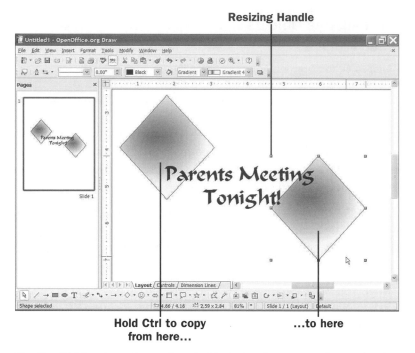

Hold Ctrl to copy
from here...   **...to here**

*Use the **Ctrl** key to make copies of objects in other areas of your drawing.*

117

If you want to copy or paste an object in one drawing to another drawing, from one slide to another, or from one layer to another, you will need to use the Windows Clipboard to do so. Click to select the object, select either **Copy** or **Cut** from the **Edit** menu, and then switch to the other drawing and select **Paste** from the **Edit** menu. The shortcut keys **Ctrl+C**, **Ctrl+X**, and **Ctrl+V** all work for the **Copy**, **Cut**, and **Paste** commands, respectively.

After you click a shape to display the shape's resizing handles, you can drag any resizing handle to resize the shape. The shape resizes, increasing or decreasing, as you drag any resizing handle outward or inward, respectively. Draw maintains the shape's scale as you resize the shape if you drag one of the four corner resizing handles. If you drag one of the resizing handles that appear in the middle of any edge, the object skews wider or taller as you drag your mouse.

▶ **TIP**

If you have a difficult time showing resizing handles when you want to display edit points, or vice versa, click the object to display either the edit points or the resizing handles. If you want to work with the other, click once on the **Line and Filling** toolbar's **Points** button.

Move Points   Insert Points
  Button   Button

Edit
Points

Points
Button

*To show the resizing handles when you see only edit points, click the **Points** button.*

The edit points enable you to edit and fine-tune the contour of objects. Different shapes utilize edit points differently. For example, when you draw a curve, the curve has only two edit points: one at the curve's starting point and one at the end. By dragging these edit points (as opposed to dragging resizing handles), you change the completeness of the curve.

▶ **NOTE**

Technically, the edit points and resizing handles of curves use different terminology. The two edit points on each end of the curve are called *data points*, and the resizing handles are called *control points*.

Polygons and other multisided shapes and lines display far more edit points. You can always click an edit point to drag that piece of the shape in or out while all the other edit points keep their locations.

Although many-sided shapes and freeform curved lines often contain many edit points, the edit points don't always fall where you need to adjust a segment of the shape. Once you click the **Line and Filling** toolbar's **Points** button to display the edit points, you can move any edit point to a more convenient location by first clicking the **Line and Filling** bar's **Move Points** button and then moving one of the edit points to a more appropriate spot on the line. Instead of moving an existing edit point, you can insert a new edit point by clicking the **Insert Points** button and then clicking where you want the new edit point to appear.

117

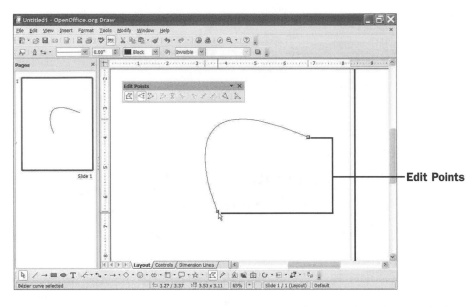

Curves support two edit points that enable you to complete or reduce the curve's shape.

117

The other **Points** buttons behave differently depending on the object. For example, clicking the **Close Bézier** button applies a straight line from any line's starting point to the end point, no matter how crooked and curved the line is. The Bézier line initially adds one control point to your line, that join the ends at a single spot.

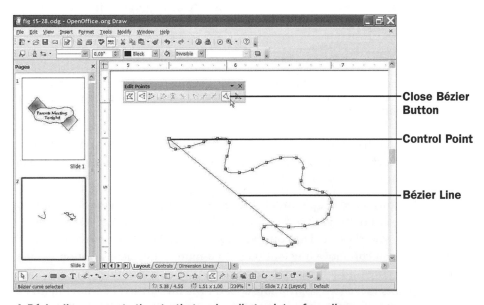

A Bézier line connects the starting and ending points of any line or curve.

118 About Grouping Objects

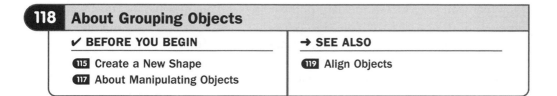

✔ BEFORE YOU BEGIN	→ SEE ALSO
115 Create a New Shape	**119** Align Objects
117 About Manipulating Objects	

As you draw objects on your drawing area, Draw keeps track of the order in which you draw them. Draw maintains a logical overlap as you lay one item on top of another. It's obvious, for example, that the rounded square in the middle was the last item placed on the following figure's drawing area and that the rightmost square was the first item placed on the figure because it falls beneath all three of the other objects. Can you tell from the placement which shapes were placed second and third?

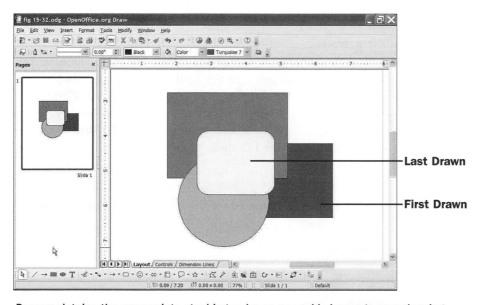

Draw maintains the appropriate stacking order as you add shapes to your drawing.

If you want to move an object down the stack or up the stack, just click to select the item, choose **Modify**, **Arrange** from the menu, and then choose the appropriate command from the submenu that appears to send the item back into the stack one level at a time, send the item to the very back of the stack, or bring the item forward as much as you want. You can also arrange objects in a stack by clicking the **Arrange** button on the **Drawing** toolbar and selecting the appropriate button from the toolbar that appears.

When you press **Ctrl+A** to select all the objects in your drawing, or when you press **Shift** and click multiple objects to select them, you then have a *group* of items. You can move, copy, resize, format, and perform other functions on the objects in a group as if they were one object. A selected group such as this is not permanent, however. As soon as you select another object, the selected group is disbanded. To create a fixed group, select the objects to group and then choose **Modify, Group**. To later ungroup the objects so that you can perform a task on a single object in the group, choose **Modify, Ungroup**. To edit the objects in a group without ungrouping them, click the group and choose **Modify, Enter Group**. Perform your edits on the individual objects as desired, and then choose **Modify, Exit Group** to return to normal editing, with the objects still grouped.

▶ KEY TERM

Group—A set of two or more selected objects in Draw.

When you work with a group as a whole, such as resizing or moving the group, Draw maintains the separate identities of the objects in that group. If you want to combine the items, you can merge the shapes into a single shape that takes on the attributes of the bottom-most object in the stack. The combined shape occupies the combined area of the original shapes, minus areas where the original shapes overlapped. To combine a selected group of objects, select **Modify, Combine** from the menu. Unlike new shapes you create (see **115** **Create a New Shape**), you can split apart combined shapes.

▶ NOTE

Blank areas will always appear where the combined objects originally overlapped.

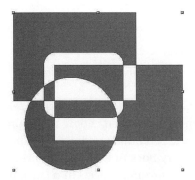

Combined objects take on the appearance of the lowerrmost object in the stack.

After the objects are combined, you can resize, copy, and move them as a single object. Instead of keeping these objects combined, however, you can uncombine them. By selecting the overall combined object and then selecting **Modify**, **Split** from the menu, you can separate the objects out once again, although they stay in their combined locations until you click and drag one of the pieces out. In addition, the separate shapes have all the color, line thickness, and other properties of the bottommost shape before you combined them. Any differentiation in color or other attributes they originally had will be gone when you split the shapes.

119 Align Objects

✔ BEFORE YOU BEGIN

112 Place Shapes on the Drawing Area
114 About Perfecting Shapes

→ SEE ALSO

81 Set Impress Options
96 Insert Graphics into a Presentation
120 Add Text to a Drawing

When arranging objects, you can use Draw's magnetic grid, with its evenly spaced vertical and horizontal lines, to align objects perfectly. To turn on the magnetic grid, choose **Tools**, **Options**, and on the **Grid** page for **OpenOffice.org Draw**, enable the **Snap to grid** option. If you want to see the grid, enable the **Visible grid** option as well. Adjust the spacing between the vertical and horizontal lines that make up the magnetic grid with the **Resolution** options. See **106** **Set Draw Options** for more information on setting grid options.

Sometimes, the magnetic grid's lines just won't fall where you want them in your drawing. Draw's *snap lines*, which you manually insert, help you ensure that your Draw shapes align properly with one another exactly as you want them to. Whether you want to display objects across or down a page, when you use snap lines, you can make your objects follow those snap lines (also called *snap to* lines) without getting... well, out of line.

You can control every aspect of your snap lines, from their width, to their direction, to their distance from one another. To turn on the snap lines option, choose **Tools**, **Options**, and enable the **To snap lines** option on **OpenOffice.org Draw's Grid** page.

▶ NOTES

You can use the grid and snaplines to align objects in Impress.

Snap lines are useful for aligning objects, but they do not print when you print your drawing and (if you use snap lines in Impress) they don't show during the presentation.

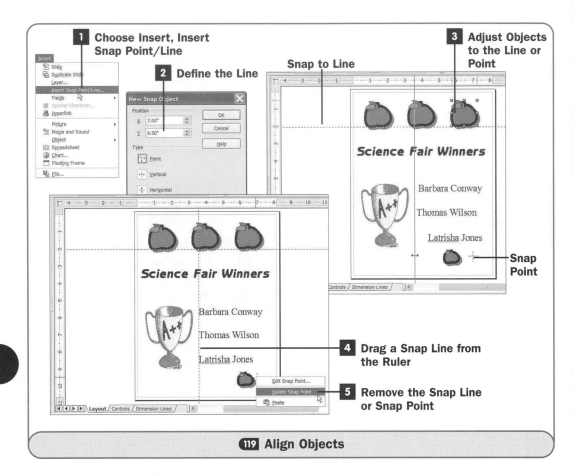

119 Align Objects

In addition to snap to lines, you can set snap to points. To use snap points, be sure to enable the **To object points** option on the **Grid** page in the **Options** dialog box. These points define locations in your drawing that you want all objects close to those points to move to. For example, you could place objects in a semi-circle by temporarily drawing a curve, and then adding snap to points along the curve. When you delete the curve, the snap to points will remain, and you can add objects to those points as desired.

1 Choose Insert, Insert Snap Point/Line

Choose **Insert, Insert Snap Point/Line** from the menu. The **New Snap Object** dialog box appears.

2 Define the Line

Define the snap line using the **New Snap Object** dialog box that appears. If you're defining a vertical snap to line, you must set the **X** position (use the ruler as a guide). If you're defining a horizontal snap to line, you must set the Y position. Therefore, if you want to align a set of images across the top of your drawing, 3 inches down from the top, you'll create a horizontal snap line with a Y setting of **3.00"**.

When creating a snap to point, you must enter both an x-axis and a y-axis value.

Click to select either **Point**, **Vertical**, or **Horizontal** to specify the kind of snap you want. Click **OK** to draw the snap line or snap point.

▶ **TIP**

If you don't like the position of any snap line or point, just click it with your mouse and drag the line or point to a new position.

▶ **NOTE**

Snap lines appear as dashed lines vertically or horizontally across your drawing. A snap point appears as a dashed crosshair showing the point of the snap.

3 Adjust the Objects to the Line or Point

The purpose of the snap line or snap point is to act as a magnet for whatever you drag close to it. If you add a snap line to an existing drawing, for example, you can drag the objects you want to snap to that line close to it. When an object's edge gets close to the snap line or snap point, Draw immediately pulls that object to the line/point.

4 Drag a Snap Line from the Ruler

Instead of using the **New Snap Object** dialog box to add your snap line, you can more quickly drag from inside either ruler out to your drawing to apply a snap line.

To draw a vertical snap line, click anywhere on the vertical ruler and drag your mouse to the left into your drawing. As you drag your mouse, the snap line appears, and when you release your mouse, the snap line will be anchored into place. To draw a horizontal snap line, click anywhere on the horizontal ruler and drag down into your drawing.

5 Remove the Snap Line or Snap Point

Right-click the snap line/snap point to produce a menu. From the menu you can edit or delete the line/point. When you select **Edit Snap Line**, for example, the **Edit Snap Line** dialog box appears, where you can type a new x-axis or y-axis value. If you select **Delete**, you'll erase the snap line/snap point.

119

<table>
<tr><td colspan="2">**120** **Add Text to a Drawing**</td></tr>
<tr><td>✔ **BEFORE YOU BEGIN**</td><td>→ **SEE ALSO**</td></tr>
<tr><td>**111** Draw from Scratch</td><td>**124** Add 3D Text</td></tr>
</table>

Drawings certainly don't rely only on lines and shapes to make their point. You can easily add text to your drawings. The **Drawing** toolbar's **Text** button is the launching point for most of the text you'll place on your drawing area.

The **Text** button enables you to place three kinds of text onto your drawing:

- Text inside text boxes.

- Text that fits itself to a frame. This kind of text behaves like a graphic image in that the text resizes when you resize the frame.

- Callouts or legends that describe parts of your drawing, with a line moving from the item being described to the text, not unlike a cartoon's caption above the characters' heads.

120

▶ **TIP**

All text is assumed to be horizontal. If you want vertical text, enable the Asian language tools by selecting **Tools**, **Options**, **Language Settings**, **Languages**. This causes the **Vertical Text** tool to appear on the **Drawing** toolbar. Use it just like the regular **Text** tool.

1 Select Text Tool

Click the **Text** button on the **Drawing** toolbar. (If you plan to add more text, double-click the **Text** button to keep it active.)

2 Drag to Create a Text Box

Click where you want the starting point of your text's text box to appear. Drag your mouse down and to the right, releasing the mouse after the text box is in place. A text cursor will appear inside the text box, waiting for you to type the text.

3 Type and Format the Text

Rarely will you draw the text box to the exact dimensions you need. That is fine. Go ahead and type your text anyway. If you need to resize the text box, click to display its resizing handles and then drag to resize the text box. You can drag any edge of the resizing outline to move the text box if you need to adjust its position.

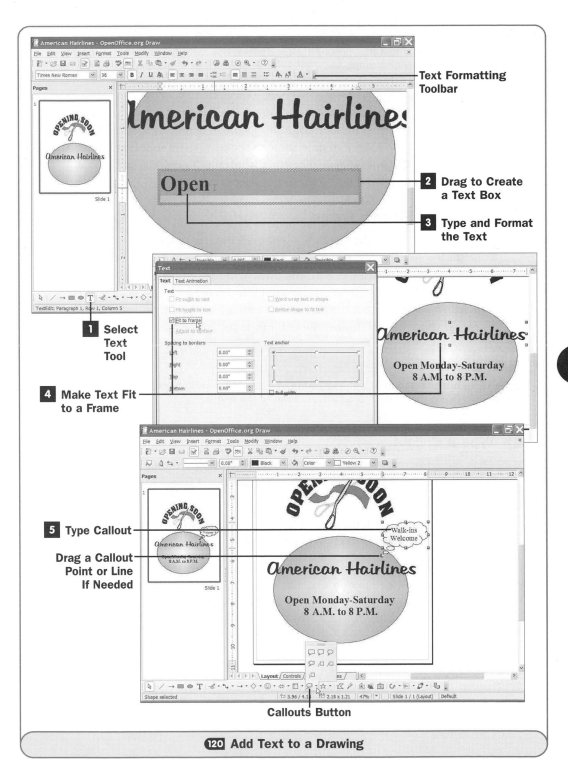

Text Formatting Toolbar

2 Drag to Create a Text Box

3 Type and Format the Text

1 Select Text Tool

4 Make Text Fit to a Frame

5 Type Callout

Drag a Callout Point or Line If Needed

120

Callouts Button

▶ **TIP**

Once you've created a text box, press **F2**, click the text box with the **Text** tool, or double-click the text box to return to the text-editing mode so you can make changes to the text just like you might in Writer.

Before or after you type the text, you can set the text formatting options you want the **Text Formatting** toolbar that appears as soon as you click the **Text** tool. To change the format of only some of the text, select that text and then select **Format**, **Character** to display the **Character** dialog box, where you can adjust the font, size, and color of the selected text.

4 Make Text Fit to a Frame

You can easily adjust the size of the text to fit the size of the frame that encloses it. Click the text box to select it. Choose **Format**, **Text**, and the **Text** dialog box appears. On the **Text** tab, disable the **Fit width to text** and **Fit height to text** options. Then enable the **Fit to frame** option. Click **OK.** When you do, you'll notice that the text formats itself to fit perfectly inside the frame. If you resize the frame, the text inside the frame resizes.

120

▶ **NOTE**

Even though the text resizes with the frame, you can still apply character-formatting commands, such as italics and a different font, to the text.

5 Type a Callout

Click the **Drawing** toolbar's **Callouts** button to display the **Callouts** toolbar. Select the callout style you want. Now drag a callout frame to the area where you want the callout.

Press **F2** or double-click the callout bubble; a text cursor appears within the callout bubble. Type the text for your callout.

After you've resized and positioned your callout properly, you might want to drag the callout line or point to a place that differs slightly from its current location. Drag the callout's edit point on its callout tail to where you want the callout's line to begin.

16

Putting on Finishing Touches with Draw

IN THIS CHAPTER:

Draw provides many useful tools that you can use for drawings. You might use Draw for months before discovering how each tool can benefit you, but you'll always feel well-rewarded when you come upon one. For example, Draw's Gallery is a comprehensive collection of graphics, sounds, and other objects that you can use in your drawings and throughout OpenOffice.org, arranged in named *themes*.

▶ **KEY TERM**

Themes—A collection of graphic files you save as a group under a theme name. The Gallery comes with several predesigned themes, such as Backgrounds and Bullets.

This chapter explains how to use the Gallery to improve your images. In addition, you'll learn to take your drawings to the next step by adding three-dimensional text. Finally, you'll learn how to import graphics and scanned images in your drawings. After these scanned images are in your drawings, you'll be able to manipulate them just as you can any other graphic images.

121   **About the Gallery**

✔ **BEFORE YOU BEGIN**	→ **SEE ALSO**
117 About Manipulating Objects	**122** Insert Gallery Objects
	123 Add New Items to Gallery

When you display the Gallery by clicking the **Gallery** button on the **Drawing** toolbar or by choosing **Tools**, **Gallery**, you'll see the following collection of predesigned themes:

- **Backgrounds**—A collection of textured patterns such as marble, gravel, cloth, and many more textures with various colors that you can use as your drawings' backgrounds.

- **Bullets**—A collection of various items you can use as bullets in your drawings when creating bulleted lists.

- **Homepage**—Web-related graphics that you can use to create web page graphics, including special buttons and navigational tools that are common on Web pages.

- **My Theme**—Collections of graphics that you've put together and saved.

- **Rulers**—Not the measuring kinds of rulers, but straight colorful edges in multiple designs that you can add to drawings to create borders.

- **Sounds**—Sounds you can add to your files.

► **NOTES**

Why sounds in drawings? Actually, all the OpenOffice.org programs support the use of the Gallery. The sounds are especially useful for Impress presentations. But you might add a sound to a drawing you intend to save in HTML format for use on the Web.

Click the **New Theme** button to add your own theme (category) to the Gallery.

To display the items in a particular theme, select the theme from those listed on the left. The items in the theme appear on the right, as icons (in **Icon** view) or as a detailed list of files with a small thumbnail (in **Detail** view). To view a particular item in a larger view, double-click it. To return to **Icon** or **Detail** view, double-click the larger thumbnail again.

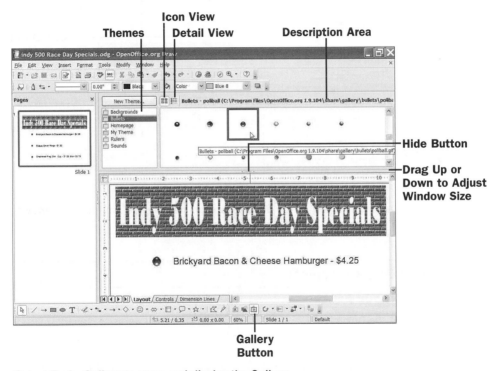

*Select **Tools, Gallery** to open and display the Gallery.*

You can display (and then remove) the Gallery from the screen by clicking the **Gallery** button on the **Drawing** toolbar. The Gallery appears above the drawing area. Resize the Gallery to make the drawing area bigger by dragging the Gallery's bottom edge up or down. You can turn the Gallery into a free-floating toolbar by clicking and dragging its top edge into the drawing area. Dock the Gallery again at the top, bottom, left or right edge of the drawing area by dragging the **Gallery** toolbar by its title bar, hovering over one edge of the drawing area until you see a dark rectangle, and then releasing the mouse button.

▶ **TIPS**

Click the **Hide** button on the Gallery pane to hide it temporarily.

Press **Ctrl** and double-click the description area at the top of the Gallery to return it to its former state—either a toolbar or a pane.

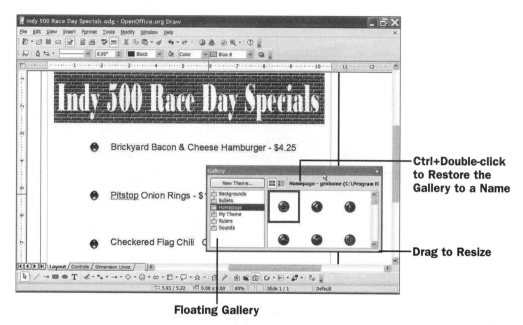

Floating Gallery

When you convert the Gallery into a floating toolbar, you can see more of your drawing area.

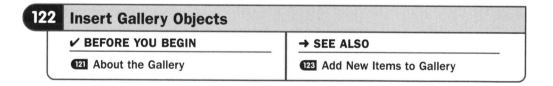

122   Insert Gallery Objects

✔ BEFORE YOU BEGIN	→ SEE ALSO
121 About the Gallery	**123** Add New Items to Gallery

Inserting Gallery objects into your drawings requires little more than displaying the Gallery, selecting a theme, selecting the item you want to insert, and then adjusting the inserted item's size and location once you place it onto your drawing.

When you insert Gallery objects, you have several choices to make:

- **Insert a copy**—Creates a copy of the Gallery item and inserts it into your drawing.

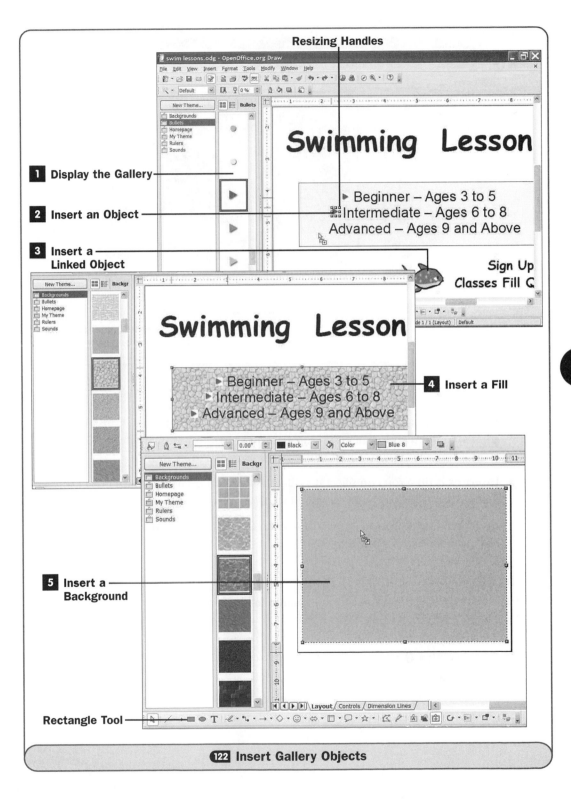

Resizing Handles

1 Display the Gallery

2 Insert an Object

3 Insert a Linked Object

4 Insert a Fill

5 Insert a Background

Rectangle Tool

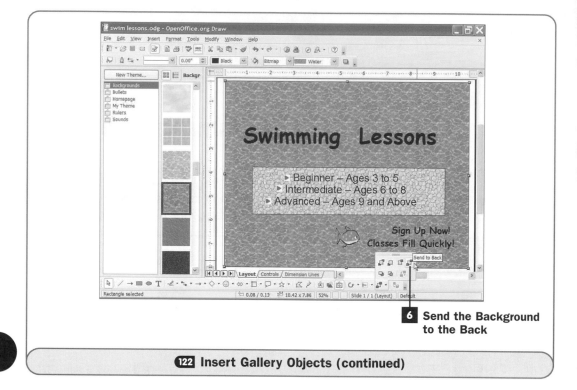

6 **Send the Background to the Back**

122 Insert Gallery Objects (continued)

- **Insert as a link**—If you change a Gallery object that's been linked (instead of copied) to a drawing, when you subsequently open that drawing for editing or printing, the Gallery object will take on its newest appearance.

- **Insert as a fill**—You can select a Gallery object and insert it into an object so that the Gallery object acts as the fill for that object.

- **Insert as a background**—You can select a Gallery object and use it as a background for your drawing.

▶ NOTE

Unless you expect that you'll be making changes to a Gallery object, you should insert Gallery objects as copies and not as links.

1 Display the Gallery

Select **Tools**, **Gallery** or click the **Drawing** toolbar's **Gallery** button to display the Gallery. Click to select the appropriate theme you want from those listed on the left. Items in the selected theme appear on the right. If you need to, scroll down to see more items.

▶ **TIP**

Click the **Detail View** button to view Gallery items by filename. Click the **Icon View** button to display Gallery items as large thumbnails.

2 Insert an Object

To simply insert an item from the Gallery into the current drawing, click and drag the object you want, and then drop it into your drawing area. When the image is in your drawing, you can move and resize it as desired. If changes are made to the Gallery object, those changes are not passed to the inserted object, so the object is as you left it in the drawing.

3 Insert a Linked Object

To insert a linked object instead of copying an object into your drawing, hold the **Shift** and **Ctrl** keys while you drag the object to your drawing.

▶ **NOTE**

As you can see, linked objects behave just as copied objects when you insert them—in other words, you can move and resize the linked objects as you like. Linked objects will change, however, if their original Gallery objects change.

4 Insert a Fill

If you want to use a Gallery object to fill a drawing object, press **Ctrl+Shift** and drag the object into the drawing, and then drop it on an object. This time, pressing **Ctrl+Shift** does not create a linked object—instead the Gallery object is tiled until it fills the drawing object's background. And in case you were wondering, changes to the Gallery object *do not* affect the fill.

▶ **TIP**

You can use the same technique described in step 4 to fill the background of a text object if you like. If you fill a text object with a background and it's too dark for you to read the text clearly, lighten the color of the text or make the fill more transparent. Click the **Area** button on the **Line and Filling** toolbar, click the **Transparency** tab, and adjust the transparency as desired. Typically, a light transparency such as 15% allows you to see the background texture clearly while making the text more readable.

5 Insert a Background

To use one of the Gallery's background objects as the background for your drawing, you basically create a rectangle shape to act as the background, then fill it with something from the Gallery.

122

Click the **Rectangle** tool on the **Drawing** toolbar and drag to create a rectangle that's as large as your drawing. Don't worry that you'll cover up all the objects in your drawing; we'll take care of that in the next step.

Click to select the **Backgrounds** theme. Background objects appear on the right. Select a suitable background object from this list. (Actually, any Gallery object can serve as a drawing background, but the ones listed in the **Backgrounds** theme are designed to be background patterns and are not really suitable as standalone objects in drawings.)

Press **Ctrl+Shift** and drag the background object onto the large rectangle and drop it. The background is tiled to fill the rectangle.

▆ Send the Background to the Back

Click the background rectangle and select **Modify**, **Arrange**, **Send to Back** or click the **Arrange** button on the **Drawing** toolbar and select **Send to Back** to move the background image to the very back of your drawing so that all the other objects and text can be seen. Adjust the background if needed to completely fill your drawing area. Be careful that your background is not so busy that it detracts from your drawing's primary elements.

123   Add New Items to Gallery

✔ BEFORE YOU BEGIN	→ SEE ALSO
121 About the Gallery	**124** Add 3D Text
122 Insert Gallery Objects	

You can add new items to the Gallery's theme categories. In addition, you can create entirely new themes. For example, if you design graphics for a sports-related organization, you'll surely create a theme called **Sports** and use it to hold all your designs.

The themes exist only so that you can group similar graphics together. Once separated into themes, all your related images appear together for you to find quicker than if they were spread across multiple themes or if all your images were included in only one theme.

▶ TIP

Resist the temptation to store new images in the theme labeled **My Theme**, unless they truly are unique. Instead, create new themes to store related groups of drawings you design.

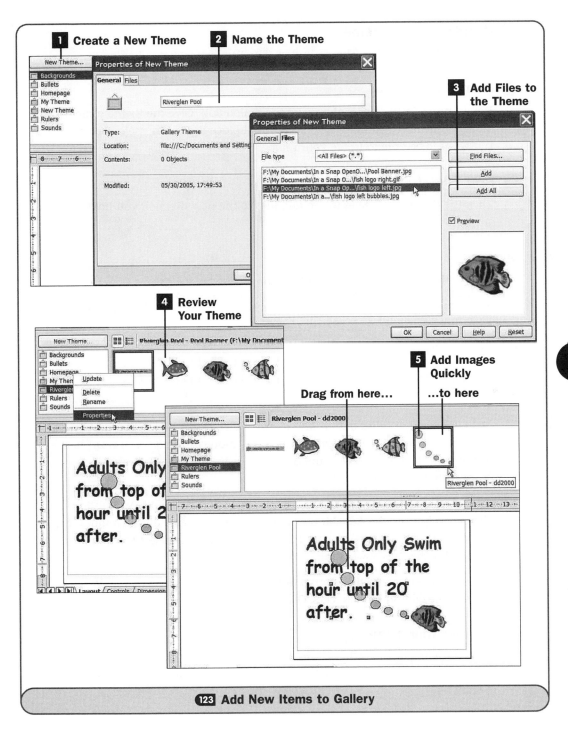

1 **Create a New Theme**

2 **Name the Theme**

3 **Add Files to the Theme**

4 **Review Your Theme**

5 **Add Images Quickly**

Drag from here...

...to here

Adults Only Swim from top of the hour until 20 after.

123

123 Add New Items to Gallery

1 Create a New Theme

Click the Gallery's **New Theme** button. The **Properties** dialog box opens.

2 Name the Theme

Type a name in the **General** page of the dialog box. Give the theme a meaningful name that relates to the objects you'll place in that theme category. You want to be able to locate your images quickly.

3 Add Files to the Theme

Click the dialog box's **Files** tab to add files to the new theme if you have any graphics to add.

► NOTES

Only graphic files such as JPEG, GIF, and TIFF, can be saved in the gallery; Draw files (files with an .odg extension) cannot be added (although you can select objects in a drawing and add them to the theme, as shown in step 5). To export a drawing to a graphic format such as JPEG, choose **File, Export**.

You can also add sound files to a theme.

Drawings you add to the Gallery can be inserted but not linked to a drawing. See **122** **Insert Gallery Objects**.

First click the **Find Files** button and use the **Select Path** dialog box that appears to select the folder that contains the image or images you want to add to your theme. Click **OK**, and a list of files in that folder appears in the **Properties** dialog box.

Select the files you want to add to the new theme and click the **Add** button. Alternatively, click the **Add All** button to add to the theme all the images in the selected folder. To preview an image before adding it, select the image and enable the **Preview** option.

Repeat this step to add files from a different folder to the new theme. When you're done adding images, click **OK**.

4 Review Your Theme

Draw displays your new theme and its contents. Review the contents and add more images if needed by right-clicking the theme name and selecting **Properties**.

123

▶ **TIP**

You can delete an image from any theme by clicking the image and pressing **Delete**. Draw confirms that you want to delete the image before removing it from the Gallery; click **Yes** to delete.

5 **Add Objects Quickly**

If you want to add objects from a drawing to an existing theme, you can do so quickly. For instance, perhaps you've created a group of small circles that form the perfect bubble path—one you don't want to duplicate again.

First, group multiple objects together so that they are easier to move as one. (See **118** **About Grouping Objects**.) Click the object, and then click it again to copy the object into Draw's temporary memory. Drag the object(s) to an empty spot in a Gallery's theme. When you release your mouse button, the Gallery creates a copy of the object(s) so that you can insert them into subsequent drawings.

---

124 **Add 3D Text**

✔ BEFORE YOU BEGIN	→ SEE ALSO
119 Align Objects	**125** Apply 3D Effects
120 Add Text to a Drawing	

124

When you want fancier text, convert that plain two-dimensional text to three-dimensional text. You can control several aspects of the 3D conversion, and you'll quickly spruce up your headlines, signs, and banners. Once you convert text to 3D, you can modify some of the three-dimensional effects, such as the rotation of the text. Text can be rotated along three axes: the y-axis, x-axis, and z-axis. If you could hold your right arm straight in front of you and the left one straight behind, they would form the z-axis. If you held your arms straight out to the sides, they would form the x-axis. Meanwhile, a pole running straight through your head and down to your toes would form the y-axis. These imaginary axes do not have to run through the center of an object at all; Draw provides a mark that denotes the center of rotation that you can move to rotate a 3D object off-center.

▶ **NOTE**

You cannot edit the characters inside text itself once you convert that text to three-dimensional text. You can edit the text's image properties, however, just as you can edit any graphic image.

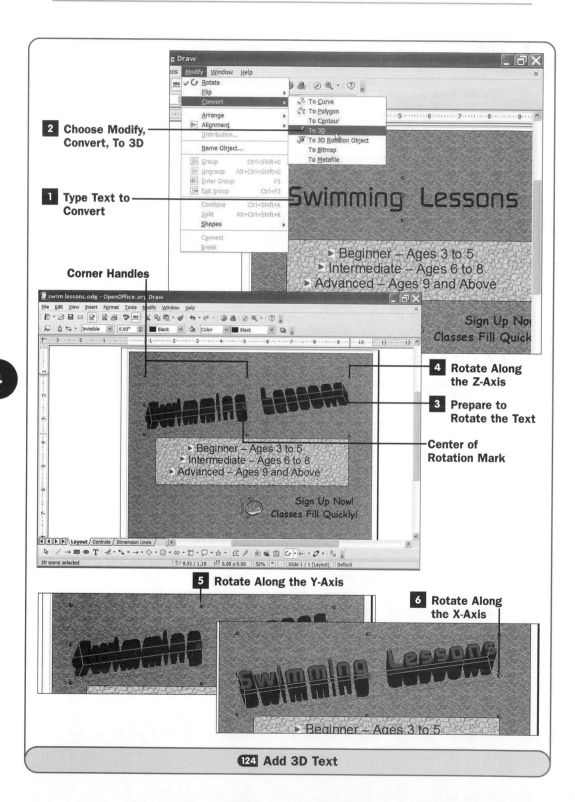

124

2 Choose Modify, Convert, To 3D

1 Type Text to Convert

Corner Handles

4 Rotate Along the Z-Axis

3 Prepare to Rotate the Text

Center of Rotation Mark

5 Rotate Along the Y-Axis

6 Rotate Along the X-Axis

124 Add 3D Text

▶ **NOTE**

You can convert a 2D object (such as a rectangle) to a 3D object (such as a cube) by following these same steps. To create simple 3D objects by just drawing them, see **112** **Place Shapes on the Drawing Area.**

1 Type Text to Convert

Click the **Drawing** toolbar's **Text** tool and type the text you want to convert to 3D. Change the size and font of the text so it's close to the size you wish to make the 3D text. Check the spelling of the text and make any necessary edits before converting the text in the next step.

2 Choose Modify, Convert, To 3D

Click to select the text object. Choose **Modify**, **Convert**, **To 3D** from the menu. Draw converts the text.

3 Prepare to Rotate the Text

You can rotate the text to change the 3D appearance. To rotate the text, you must click to select the 3D text (green resizing handles appear) and then click the 3D text once again. The resizing handles turn from green squares to red circles. These are the 3D text's *corner handles*. Your mouse pointer changes to a rotate symbol to indicate that the 3D text is ready for rotation.

If desired, click and drag the **center-of-rotation mark** to move it off-center.

▶ **KEY TERM**

Corner handles—Red circles that act as 3D resizing handles that you can drag to rotate 3D text.

4 Rotate Along the Z-Axis

To rotate the text around its z-axis (arms straight out and behind), drag one of the four corner handles up or down. The 3D text seems to tilt side to side.

5 Rotate Along the Y-Axis

To rotate the text around its y-axis (the pole from your head to your toes), click and drag one of the top or bottom center handles. The text seems to spin around that center "pole."

124

6 Rotate Along the X-Axis

To rotate the text around its x-axis (arms out to both sides), click and drag one of the left or right center handles. As you do, you'll see the 3D text tilt up or down.

▶ **TIP**

Once you convert 2D text to 3D, you can apply Draw's 3D effects to the 3D text. See **125** Apply 3D Effects for more information. These same effects can also be applied to a 3D *object*.

---

125 | Apply 3D Effects

✔ BEFORE YOU BEGIN	→ SEE ALSO
117 About Manipulating Objects	**126** Insert a Graphic Image into a Drawing
124 Add 3D Text	

125

As you learned in **124** **Add 3D Text**, Draw can actually convert a two-dimensional, flat object to a three-dimensional object. In addition, Draw provides special tools for drawing simple 3D objects (such as a cube) on its **3D Objects** toolbar. (See **112** **Place Shapes on the Drawing Area**.) After you create a 3D object, you can control many of the resulting 3D attributes, such as surface texture, lighting, and shading.

1 Choose 3D Effects

After drawing a 3D object (with the **3D Objects** toolbar) or converting a 2D shape to 3D (as described in **124** **Add 3D Text**), right-click the 3D object and choose **3D Effects** from the context menu. The **3D Effects** dialog box appears.

2 Adjust Geometry

Click the **Geometry** button at the top of the **3D Effects** dialog box if needed, to display the **Geometry** settings. Here you can adjust the amount of roundness in the **Rounded edges** of your object, and the ratio of the front face of the object to its back face (the **Scaled depth**). The **Rotation angle** applies only to a *3D rotation object* and controls whether the profile is rotated a complete 360 degrees to create the object. You can adjust the amount of extrusion by changing the **Depth**.

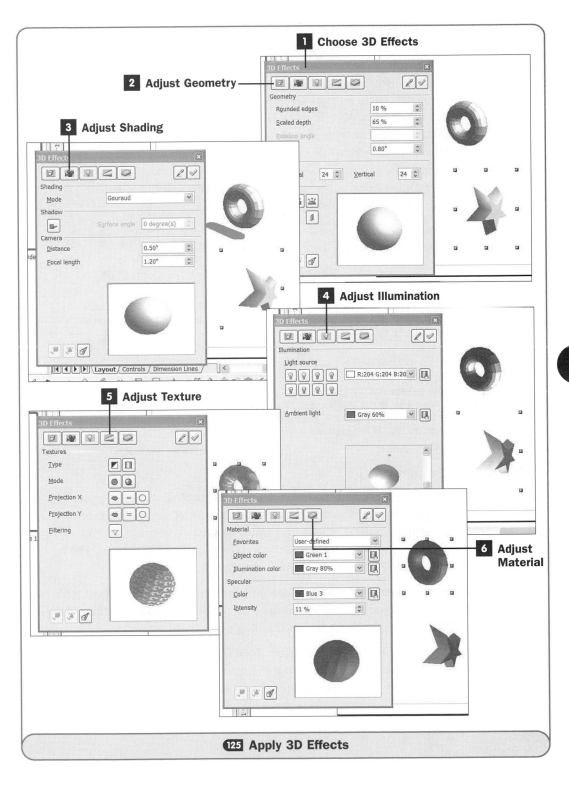

1 Choose 3D Effects

2 Adjust Geometry

3 Adjust Shading

4 Adjust Illumination

5 Adjust Texture

6 Adjust Material

125

125 Apply 3D Effects

The **Horizontal** and **Vertical Segment** amounts apply to rounded shapes; by increasing these values, you can make a rounded shape more smooth. The higher these values, however, the longer your shape will take to draw. The **Normals** affect how your object's surface is rendered when lit and when a texture is applied. These settings are best left at **Object Specific**, which selects the best formula for each object. With **Flat**, you can let each of the vertical and horizontal segments become more apparent, or smooth them with **Spherical**. You can invert the **Normals**, which makes an object appear as if lit from within. You can choose **Double-Sided Illumination**, which simulates both interior and exterior lighting. You can also create **Double-Sided**, or open ended, 3D objects, like an open ended box.

On each page of this dialog box, after setting the effects you want, click the **Checkmark** button to apply them to the selected 3D object.

▶ KEY TERM

3D rotation object—Created with the **Modify, Convert, To 3D Rotation Object** command, this type of object starts as a profile which is then rotated 360 degrees through its y-axis (a pole running up and down through its center).

125

▶ NOTE

Understanding all the mathematics that produce appropriate 3D effects is fairly advanced. This task just skims the surface of the 3D effects you can apply. Fortunately, you can always try one of the options, adjust the 3D effect, and then select the **Undo** command to back up and try something else.

3 Adjust Shading

Click the **Shading** button at the top of the **3D Effects** dialog box to display the **Shading** settings. Here you can adjust the amount of shadow and the shading type (the **Shading Mode**). The **Shading Mode** is best left to **Gouraud**, unless you want quicker rendering (and less smoothness), in which case you might try **Flat**. **Phong** produces medium-rough shadows.

By clicking the **Shadow** button, you can add a shadow to your 3D object. The **Surface angle** lets you adjust the length of the shadow by adjusting the angle of the surface on which the 3D object appears to sit.

By adjusting the **Camera's Distance** and **Focal length**, you can change the perspective. The distance directly affects the object's apparent size (further away, an object appears smaller), while the focal length affects its apparent depth (shorter focal lengths provide greater depths).

4 Adjust Illumination

Click the **Illumination** button at the top of the **3D Effects** dialog box to display the **Illumination** settings. Here you can set up to eight different light sources, specifying the position of the light and its color. Click the first lit lightbulb button to select the settings for that light source. You can select the color of the light and that of the ambient light, as well as the source's position (by dragging the glowing star on the illustration in the lower-right corner). Double-click an inactive lightbulb button to activate it, and then adjust its settings.

5 Adjust Texture

Click the **Texture** button at the top of the **3D Effects** dialog box to display the **Texture** settings. This page applies only to 3D objects filled with a bitmap, as explained in **116** **Fill an Object** and **122** **Insert Gallery Objects**.

You can display the bitmap texture in black and white or color by clicking the appropriate **Type** button. You probably won't want to choose the **Mode** button, **Only Texture**, which displays only the texture across the surface of the object, without the shading that makes an object appear 3-dimensional. Instead, leave **Mode** set to **Texture and Shading**.

You can control how the bitmap is rendered over the surface of the object horizontally (**Projection X**) and vertically (**Projection Y**) by choosing between **Object-specific**, **Parallel**, or **Circular**.

6 Adjust Material

Click the **Material** button at the top of the **3D Effects** dialog box to display the **Material** settings. You can adjust these settings whether or not you've filled your 3D object with a bitmap.

Here you can apply one of several common textures (such as wood) or design your own texture by selecting the color of the object, the color of the lighting, the color of the reflection (the hot spot), and its intensity.

After you've chosen and applied the settings from each page as desired, click the **X** to close the **3D Effects** dialog box.

125

126 Insert a Graphic Image into a Drawing

✔ BEFORE YOU BEGIN	→ SEE ALSO
111 Draw from Scratch	**127** Scan a Picture into Draw
117 About Manipulating Objects	

Draw supports virtually every kind of graphics file in use today, and you can easily insert these graphic images into your drawings. For example, you might insert a piece of royalty-free clipart to spice up a sign you're making. After an images is inserted into a drawing, you can resize, move, copy, duplicate, and perform similar tasks.

▶ NOTE

You can insert an image into your drawing or link to an image. Either way, the image appears in your drawing. However, if you link instead of insert the image, your drawing will update if the original image ever changes.

126

1 Click from File

Choose **Insert, Picture, From File** from the menu or click the **From File** button on the **Drawing** toolbar to display the **Insert Picture** dialog box, where you can locate the image you want to insert into your drawing.

2 Insert the Image

Browse to the location where your image is located, select it, and click **Open**. The image is inserted into the drawing. You can resize the image by clicking it and dragging one of its *handles* inward or outward. Move the image by clicking and dragging it to a new location.

▶ NOTE

Click the **Link** option if you want Draw to link to the image instead of inserting it into your drawing. You can convert a linked image to a copy by selecting **Edit, Links** from the menu and selecting **Break Link** from the dialog box that appears.

3 Edit the Image

Select the image, and the **Picture** toolbar automatically appears at the top of the screen, providing you with the following options:

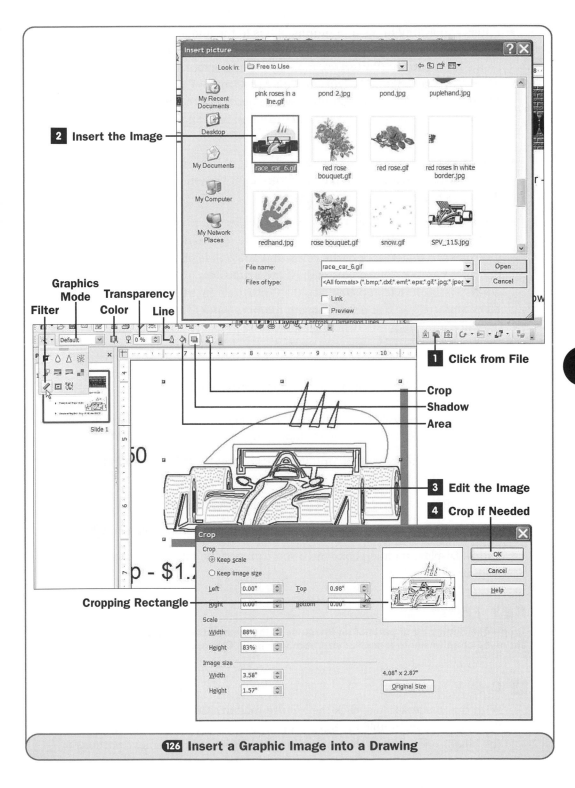

2 Insert the Image

Graphics Mode

Filter   Transparency   Color   Line

1 Click from File

126

Crop
Shadow
Area

3 Edit the Image

4 Crop if Needed

Cropping Rectangle

126 Insert a Graphic Image into a Drawing

- **Filter**—Apply any number of graphic filters to the image to create marvelous effects, such as inverting the colors (**Invert**), reducing the number of colors to create large patches (**Posterize**), making the image look old (**Aging**) and simulating artistic looks (**Solarization**, **Pop Art**, **Charcoal Sketch**, **Relief**, and **Mosaic**). In addition, you can improve the quality of the image by lowering (**Smooth**) or increasing the contrast (**Sharpen**), reducing noise and imperfections (**Remove Noise**).

- **Graphics mode**—Select a graphics mode such as black and white or **Watermark**, which places a pale and very light version of your image on the drawing's background.

- **Color**—Displays the **Color** toolbar, which allows you to change the amount of the three primary colors in your image—red, green, and blue. Here, –100% indicates a complete lack of the color, and 100% indicates the heaviest use of the color possible. You can also adjust the **Brightness** from –100% (complete darkness) to 100% (completely lit), the **Contrast** from –100% (no contrast) to 100% (full contrast), and the **Gamma** (*gamma value)* from 0 (lowest gamma) to 10 (highest possible gamma value).

126

▶ **KEY TERM**

Gamma value—The brightness of an image's midtones (middle values).

- **Transparency**—Specifies how much transparency, from 0% to 100%, that the image has, which affects whether underlying objects show through it.

- **Line**—Adjust the style, color, and thickness of the line (border) around the perimeter of a graphic.

- **Area**—Fill transparent parts of a graphic with your selection.

- **Shadow**—Add a shadow beneath the graphic. See **111 Draw from Scratch**.

- **Crop**—Displays a dialog box where you can *crop* the image. See the next step for details.

▶ **KEY TERM**

Crop—The cutting off of parts of an image or, in the case of Draw images, the scaled shrinking of an image to a smaller size from within the **Crop** dialog box.

4 Crop if Needed

With the image selected, click the **Picture** toolbar's **Crop** button to open the **Crop** dialog box. Enable the **Keep scale** option to retain the ratio between the height and width of the original image. If you want to remove portions of the image but maintain its size in the drawing, enable the **Keep image size** option instead.

If you choose **Keep scale**, enter values in the **Left**, **Right**, **Top**, and **Bottom** boxes to tell Draw how much to trim off that side of the image. If you chose **Keep image size,** the values you enter tell Draw how much to increase or decrease the vertical or horizontal scale of the image. The preview shows you how your entries will affect the final image—the cropping rectangle displays the portion of the image that will be kept if you crop.

Using the **Width** and **Height** boxes in the **Scale** area, you can adjust the scale of the image by the percentage you enter. For example, you can stretch the image horizontally and make it twice as wide as it was by entering 150% in the **Width** box only. With the **Width** and **Height** boxes in the **Image size** area, you can keep the image proportions, but change its relative size. To restore the image to its original size and proportions if you overcrop, you can click the **Original Size** button. Click **OK** to apply your cropping instructions.

▶ **NOTE**

Playing with the scale of an image using the **Crop** dialog box distorts the image but can create some interesting effects.

127

---

127 | **Scan a Picture into Draw**

✔ **BEFORE YOU BEGIN**

[117] About Manipulating Objects
[119] Align Objects

If you want to insert a graphic into your drawing but the graphic resides on paper, or perhaps in a magazine or book, you can scan the image directly into your drawing. As long as you use a TWAIN-compliant scanner, as most are, Draw can accept your scanned image directly. (See [27] **Insert Graphics in a Document** for information on TWAIN devices.)

▶ **NOTE**

You can scan a picture and save it as a graphic image and then insert that image into your drawing if needed. By scanning directly into your drawing, however, you save the extra step of saving the graphic as a separate file.

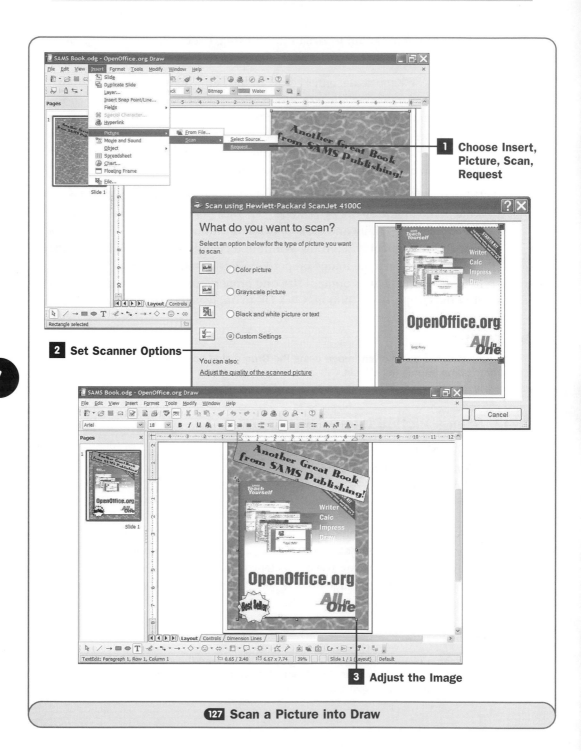

127

127 Scan a Picture into Draw

When your scanner is TWAIN compliant, your scanner will often scan using its own scanning routines. So the exact steps for scanning images into Draw varies depending on the scanner and its supplied driver software. Nevertheless, the general step-by-step procedure for inserting scanned images remains the same no matter what kind of scanner you use.

1 Choose Insert, Picture, Scan, Request

Choose **Insert**, **Picture**, **Scan**, **Request** from the menu. (If you have more than one scanning device or program, choose **Insert**, **Picture**, **Scan**, **Select Source** to choose the source you want to use.) A dialog box with options for your particular scanner appears.

2 Set Scanner Options

Depending on your scanner's software, you will be given the chance to scan a preview first, adjust resolution and color mode (such as grayscale), and modify other aspects of the scan. After making your selections, click **Scan** to scan the image into your drawing.

▶ TIP

Scanned images can be huge. Decrease your scanned image resolution if possible from within your scanner's software if you want to send your drawing to others over email.

127

3 Adjust the Image

Your scanned image will rarely come into your drawing at the exact placement and size you want to see. When your scanned image appears inside your drawing, you'll need to adjust the image's placement by clicking and dragging to move the image into position; adjust the image's size by dragging the green resizing *handles* that appear around the outside of the image when the image is selected. Use the **Modify**, **Arrange**, **Send Backward** command, if needed, to send the scanned image back in the stack and reveal other objects in your drawing.

PART V

Enhancing Your Work with OpenOffice.org's Other Features

IN THIS PART:

17

Enhancing Your Work with More OpenOffice.org Features

IN THIS CHAPTER:

As we begin Part V, you'll get a taste of some of OpenOffice.org's more advanced features, such as the automation of certain OpenOffice.org tasks. If you find yourself repeating the same series of keystrokes or menu selections over and over in Writer or Calc, you can automate those steps to speed the work in the future. In addition, you'll learn how to manage more extensive Writer documents, such as you'll use when writing complete books with Writer. Maintaining chapters and all the elements that go into such a large, multi-part document is no longer a chore when you learn how to use the concept of *master documents*.

▶ KEY TERM

Master document—A repository of document files managed as a single group, within a single window. Its components are called *subdocuments*, each of which might be a chapter or other composite element, but all of which together form a collective volume.

The integration of OpenOffice.org's programs is crucial to using OpenOffice.org successfully. Any document, produced from within any OpenOffice.org application, can contain functional components of any other OpenOffice.org application—such as a Calc spreadsheet in a Writer document, or a Draw composition in an Impress presentation. You can integrate all these components together within OpenOffice.org's consistent interface, using far fewer steps than if each OpenOffice.org had replicated the functionality of every other one just to get the job done.

To be honest, OpenOffice.org's integrated power shines in its support for loading and saving Microsoft Office documents, spreadsheets, and presentations. You can load, edit, and save virtually all Microsoft Office files within OpenOffice.org—for instance, Writer can open any document you select that has Microsoft Word's .doc filename extension. There's a good chance you're an OpenOffice.org user yourself because you did not want to continue paying high upgrade costs to keep up with Microsoft Office. So for you, it's critical that OpenOffice.org opens, edits, and saves all the work you've previously created with Microsoft Office.

128	**About OpenOffice.org Macros**

✔ **BEFORE YOU BEGIN**	→ **SEE ALSO**
Just jump right in!	**129** Create and Use a Macro

The purpose of a *macro* is to automate any repetitious task that would normally require you to enter a big sequence of commands. OpenOffice.org perceives menu commands, keystrokes, and (in the case of Writer) movements of the mouse pointer, as *instructions*. When you have OpenOffice.org "record" a macro, what you're asking it to do is watch you perform a series of instructions and then remember that series so that it can repeat it later at your discretion.

▶ KEY TERM

Macro—A sequence of recorded actions that can be played back at any time, for any number of times, to perform an oft-used, repetitive, or tedious task.

Why would you want the same series of instructions repeated? In most computer applications, you'll often find yourself making the same additions or alterations to *different* items or to *different* areas of the document. In Writer, the location of those changes is indicated with the cursor; in Calc, it's the cell pointer. So with each application, you can choose a different thing to change and then have a macro make the same change to it. That's what's so useful about a macro—not that it does the same thing in the same way, but that it makes the same series of additions or alterations to whatever you designate.

The type of task you'd record with a macro is most likely something that maybe only you would ever need—which is why it wasn't built into the OpenOffice.org suite to begin with. For example, suppose that you quite frequently copy selected passages of text from within a Writer document to the end of the document for a summary. You want the copied passage formatted as a bulleted list. You can set up a macro that performs all the commands that make this possible—after you've already pointed to the copied paragraph in Writer. Such a macro might represent the kind of functionality that you and only a few other users might ever require.

128

▶ NOTES

You can record macros only in Writer and Calc.

The macro-recording process is sensitive to three things: the keys you press, the items you click with the mouse (menu commands, toolbar buttons, elements in the document), and the entries you make in dialog boxes. The process does *not* record your mouse *movements*, such as "up and to the right." Specifically, the macro recorder isn't concerned with where your mouse pointer is located, as much as with what it's pointing to when you click.

Creating macros is simple. OpenOffice.org learns by example! As **129** **Create and Use a Macro** shows, when you're ready to create a macro, you only need to tell Writer or Calc to begin recording your next interactions with the program, either from the keyboard or mouse. When you tell the application to stop recording the keystrokes, you name the macro and store it as a file. To run the macro without calling it up as a file (for instance, from some kind of "Open" menu), you can assign some kind of trigger, such as a dedicated keystroke or menu command.

▶ **TIPS**

One of the under-appreciated qualities of a macro is not just how it saves time, but how it reduces the chance of user error. When you find yourself performing the same sequence of commands repeatedly, it's possible that you lose track (or lose interest) in what you're doing, slip up, and then find yourself selecting **Undo**—maybe several times—until you reset the application to the point before the error occurred. With a properly recorded and debugged macro, you eliminate most chances for errors to crop up because of improper entries.

In Writer, to record the act of selecting a passage of text, such as a word or a paragraph, use keystrokes as described in ❹ **Type Text Into a Document**. The recorder does not pay attention to selecting elements with the mouse, but it does record movements of the cursor using the arrow keys and the **Shift** and **Ctrl** keys. At such a time, the recorder only takes note of the *type* of element you're selecting (word, line, paragraph), not the *content* of the selection ("When in the course of human events...").

As a macro is recorded, the commands you enter are reinterpreted as textual instructions, written in OpenOffice.org's version of the BASIC programming language. You do not have to know anything about BASIC to record macros, nor do you ever have to edit a macro with BASIC to use the macro. However, you do need to know that once they're converted to BASIC, macros are stored in OpenOffice.org using a compartmentalized structure that's meant to help those who actually do use BASIC. This knowledge of something related to a discipline you may never want to know comes into play when you save a recorded macro, and when you assign a recorded macro to a keystroke or toolbar button for playback on demand. So here's the minimum you need to know:

128

- You can save a macro within an OpenOffice.org **document file**. Doing so means that the macro will pertain only to that file, and can only be used when that file is open. If a Calc macro would only ever apply to a particular spreadsheet, you might want to save your macro this way.

- OpenOffice.org recognizes two *volumes*, separate from open documents, that contain macros that can apply to any open document in any application. **My Macros** is the volume where all your recorded macros are stored. **OpenOffice.org Macros** is the volume where example macros, from OpenOffice's own authors, are stored.

- A **module** is a text file where several recorded macros can be stored. This text file can be edited in OpenOffice.org's own macro editor.

- A **library** is a grouping of one or more modules, which is often used for storing macros with similar functions. Separating macros into individual libraries is done for the convenience of users who know how to edit in the BASIC language; you might never find yourself needing to create separate libraries for your recorded macros. However, you'll have to pay attention to the fact that recorded macros are located by default in **Module1** of the **Standard** library of **My Macros**, unless you explicitly state otherwise.

129 | Create and Use a Macro

✔ BEFORE YOU BEGIN	→ SEE ALSO
128 About OpenOffice.org Macros	**133** Associate OpenOffice.org and Microsoft Office Files

The process of recording a macro (a recorded sequence of commands) is mainly comprised of performing the commands as you normally would, only with the recorder turned on. The trick to making a proper recording, however, is setting up your document beforehand so that the commands you're recording can apply to *any* document you may be editing in the future, not just the one you're looking at now.

After recording is completed, it's actually a bit trickier to assign that macro to a *shortcut key*. When that's finally done, you can type a single keystroke to have your OpenOffice.org application replay that macro very, very quickly.

▶ KEY TERM

Shortcut key—A keystroke, such as **Ctrl+Shift+B**, that represents a command otherwise located within an onscreen menu or toolbar.

① Prepare Your Document

In either Writer of Calc, set up your document or spreadsheet to appear exactly as it should before you would normally execute the first action you intend to record as a macro. For example, if your macro is to change the formatting of a selected paragraph in Writer, select a paragraph now, and let that be the "guinea pig" selection for your macro recording.

② Start Recording

To begin recording, choose **Tools**, **Macros**, **Record Macro**. The **Record Macro** toolbar appears, containing a single button, **Stop Recording**.

③ Perform Actions to Be Recorded

Carefully reproduce all the actions you want the macro to repeat for you. The recorder takes note of every command you execute through the menu bar, a toolbar, or a keystroke shortcut. It will *not* record actions made with the mouse directly to an open document, such as selecting a graphic on a page, clicking a different cell, or selecting a passage of text, so whenever possible, use the keyboard to perform such actions (for more, see **128** **About OpenOffice.org Macros**).

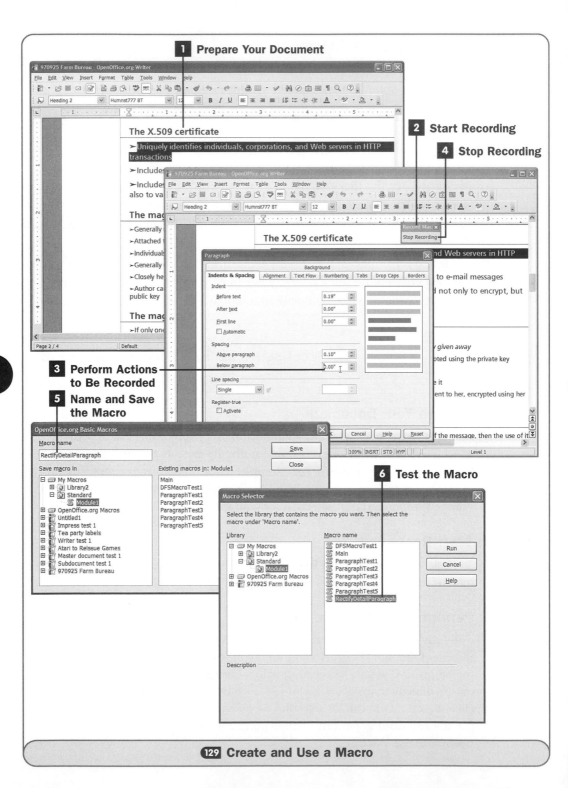

1 Prepare Your Document

2 Start Recording

4 Stop Recording

3 Perform Actions to Be Recorded

5 Name and Save the Macro

6 Test the Macro

129 Create and Use a Macro

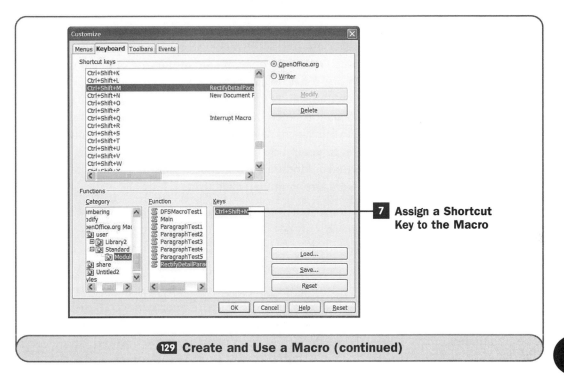

7 Assign a Shortcut
Key to the Macro

129 Create and Use a Macro (continued)

129

4 Stop Recording

When you're satisfied that your sequence of commands has been completely demonstrated for the recorder, click **Stop Recording**. If the recorder has taken note of any commands that can be saved to a macro, the **OpenOffice.org Basic Macros** dialog box appears; otherwise, recording stops with no response from the application.

5 Name and Save the Macro

In the **Macro name** text box, enter a name for your macro. In place of spaces, use an underscore, such as **Format_Heading**. It is perfectly safe to leave recorded macros in the **Module1** module of the **Standard** library in the **My Macros** volume. If you'd rather store the macro along with an open document—thus ensuring that the macro is used only with that document—choose that document from the **Save macro in** list. To store the macro, click **Save**.

▶ TIP

When the **OpenOffice.org Basic Macros** dialog box first appears, the default choice in the **Save macro in** list is the name of the module from which you last executed a macro—even if you cannot or should not store your newly recorded macro in that location. Make sure that you choose a safe location, such as **Module1** of the **Standard** library in **My Macros**. For more on macro locations, see **128** About OpenOffice.org Macros.

6 Test the Macro

This is a good time to make certain that the macro works the way you intend. Prepare a document—either the open one or, in the case of macros saved to the **Standard** library, a new document—whose conditions approximate those from which you'll normally use your macro. Select **Tools**, **Macros**, **Run Macro**. The **Macro Selector** dialog box appears. From the **Library** list, choose the location where your macro was stored. Unfortunately, this choice is not made automatically, so you must recall the location manually (by default, **My Macros**, **Standard**, **Module1**). In the **Macro name** list, choose the name of your recorded macro, and then click **Run**.

The commands recorded in the macro are executed. You will not notice each step of the execution; you will only see the *results* of the macro, instantaneously. This is because OpenOffice.org stops updating its own windows when executing a macro, which speeds things up tremendously.

Examine the results closely. If something appears amiss, repeat the test. If you don't get the results you intend after a second test, you can record the macro over again. Repeat this procedure from step 1, but in step 5, instead of entering a new name, choose the bad macro's name from the **Existing macros in** list, and click **Save**. A dialog box asks you to confirm overwriting the existing macro; click **Yes**.

7 Assign a Shortcut Key to the Macro

When the recorded macro works perfectly in simulated work conditions, you can assign it to a command or shortcut key so that you don't have to plow through libraries to get to it. Select **Tools**, **Macros**, **Organize Macros**, **OpenOffice.org Basic**. The **OpenOffice.org Basic Macros** dialog box appears. You do *not* have to choose your macro's name at this point; instead, just click **Assign**. The **Customize** dialog box appears. Here, you can determine how the macro is to be triggered in the future.

For example, to assign the macro to a shortcut key, click the **Keyboard** tab. To make this key execute the macro in all OpenOffice.org applications, click **OpenOffice.org** in the upper-right corner; otherwise, click the name of the application from which you recorded the macro.

The **Shortcut keys** list shows all possible keystrokes; those to which commands are presently assigned have the associated commands listed in the rightmost column. Unavailable keystrokes are shown in gray. Preferably, you should choose an unassigned keystroke from this list.

In the **Category** list, choose **OpenOffice.org Macros**, **user**, followed by the location of your recorded macro (for instance, **Standard**, **Module1**). In the

129

Function list, choose the macro to which you want to assign the keystroke. Then click **Modify**. The name of your macro should appear in the right column of the **Shortcut keys** list, and the chosen keystroke should appear in the **Keys** list. Click **OK** to finalize this assignment, and then click **Close**.

▶ **TIPS**

Elsewhere in the **Customize** dialog box, the **Menus** tab enables you to assign macros to menu commands. The **Toolbars** tab lets you create new perennially visible buttons for your macro. Finally, the **Events** tab is where you can assign a macro to be triggered by a specific event, such as every time a document is saved. This way, for instance, you can create a "diagnostic" macro that makes certain your document contains a feature you might specifically require before the document is saved to disk.

If you need to make certain that *nothing* is selected before the main body of your macro proceeds—for instance, so that anything your macro might add to a document doesn't overwrite existing text—for the first keystroke in your recording, press the **Esc** key.

---

130 **About Master Documents**

✔ **BEFORE YOU BEGIN**	→ **SEE ALSO**
21 Create a Table of Contents	**131** Create a Master Document
22 Create an Index	
35 Add a Footnote or Endnote	

In Writer, a master document is a repository of separate Writer document files, gathered together in a collective volume, not unlike the way books such as this one are comprised of chapters. The master document system enables you to manipulate large texts as a single unit, within a single window, without having to save the contents of that window as a huge, single file.

Within its single window, a master document is comprised of *subdocuments*. Here, their pages are numbered collectively, their document and page formats are maintained collectively, and (most importantly) an index at the end can refer to any contents that appear throughout the master document and can link to any page within it. In reality, the master document file does not actually contain the subdocuments, but instead acts as an enclosure for them. When you print a master document, all its subdocuments are printed in their proper consecutive order.

▶ **KEY TERM**

Subdocument—One of multiple files collected together within a master document. It can be edited individually if necessary, within its own window; when the master document is re-opened, the contents of the subdocument reflect those changes.

The most important benefit of using master documents is that page numbering, footnotes, figure captions, indexes, and table of contents are all numbered in the collective context, rather than in the context of each individual file. Suppose that a master document collected together the components for a complete book. If its Introduction's subdocument contained only one footnote numbered **1**, then Chapter 1's first footnote would be numbered **2**. Furthermore, if you were to remove a footnote from the middle of the book, all subsequent chapters' footnotes would automatically be renumbered accordingly. Without the master document to provide a collective context, every chapter file's first footnote would be numbered **1**.

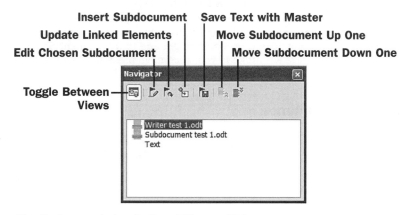

The Navigator window in OpenOffice.org Writer.

Writer's **Navigator** window is the optimum tool for maneuvering through subdocuments. When you have a master document open, the **Navigator** window lists all the master document's components, and provides the tools for managing those components. In the **Navigator** window, you can do any of the following:

- Add existing subdocuments to your master document

- Create new subdocuments

- Rearrange the order of the subdocuments

- Remove subdocuments from the master document

- Quickly edit a subdocument

- Update the master document when a subdocument changes

130

---

131 **Create a Master Document**

✔ **BEFORE YOU BEGIN**

130 About Master Documents

When you're using a master document, the **Navigator** window shows its true colors. It becomes a "table of contents" for the entire document, giving you functions for reorganizing those contents and creating and updating indexes. It also serves as a launch pad for subdocument windows because you cannot edit a subdocument's contents from within the master document's window.

1 Create a New Master Document

From Writer's menu bar, select **File**, **New**, **Master Document**. Writer creates a new, blank master document that looks just like a normal document. In addition, Writer opens the **Navigator** window. For safety, you should save this master document now: Choose **File**, **Save**, and then in the **Save As** dialog box, choose a location, enter a new name, and click **Save**.

2 Add Files to the Master Document

131

The **Navigator** window's first entry is always **Text**, which refers to the text content of the new master document you just created. For example, you might enter a title and an introductory paragraph into the master document. However, although the **Text** element always exists, it can be blank.

To add an existing Writer document, from the **Navigator** window, click and hold the **Insert** button, and choose **File** from the popup menu. The **Insert** dialog box opens. Choose the documents to be added to your master document, and then click **Insert**.

To create a new document for immediate enrollment in the master document, click and hold **Insert**, and from the popup menu, select **New Document**. A fresh window is created, and the **Save As** dialog box appears. Choose a location for the document and click **Save**. With the new document window open, the **Navigator** window switches to content view for that document; to return to the table of contents, activate the master document window.

3 Rearrange Subdocument Order as Necessary

To change the order in which a subdocument appears in the master document, from the **Navigator** window, click and drag its entry in the list to its new location. A horizontal line indicates where the document will be moved in the list when you release the mouse button.

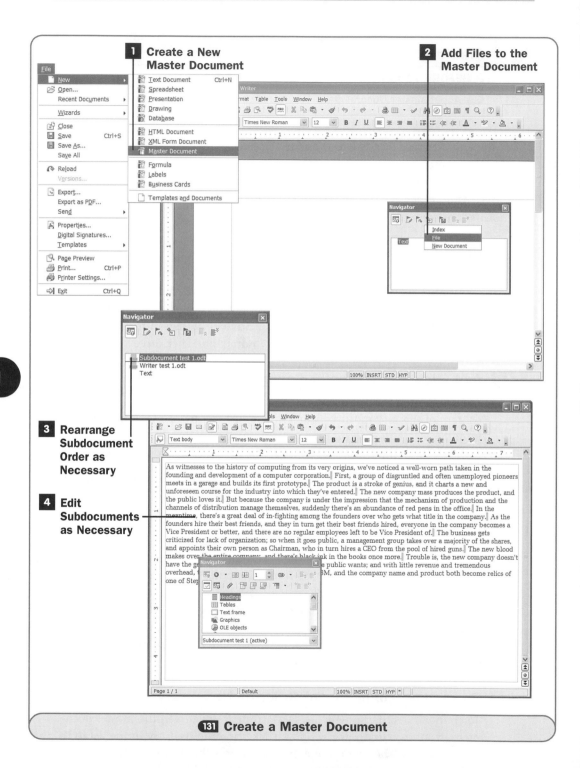

131 Create a Master Document

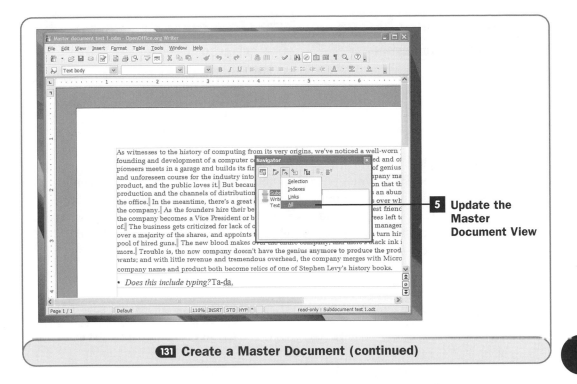

5 Update the
Master
Document View

131 Create a Master Document (continued)

131

4 Edit Subdocuments as Necessary

Although the master document window shows the contents of the entire volume as they will appear collectively, you cannot make changes to the contents of subdocuments appearing within this window. (Here, you can edit the **Text** element of the master document only.) Instead, you edit a subdocument by launching it within its own separate window.

Think of the **Navigator** window for the master document as the launch pad for any subdocument. For example, to edit Chapter 2, from **Navigator**, simply double-click that subdocument's name. A document window appears with the contents of Chapter 2. Make your changes. To finalize the edits, save the subdocument with the usual **File**, **Save** command.

5 Update the Master Document View

Changes made and saved to subdocument files are *not* automatically reflected in the master document window. To force an update here, activate the master document, and then from **Navigator**, click and hold **Update**, and from the popup menu, select **All**. A dialog box will confirm; click **Yes**. Writer reloads every subdocument in the master document, and updates any links— such as footnote and index entries. Click **Save** to finalize these updates.

132 About Sharing OpenOffice.org Files with Other Applications

✔ BEFORE YOU BEGIN	→ SEE ALSO
Just jump right in!	133 Associate OpenOffice.org and Microsoft Office Files
	134 Upgrade OpenOffice.org to a New Version

OpenOffice.org plays well with others! Specifically, and most importantly, OpenOffice.org reads and writes Microsoft Office files with ease, but it can open files created in just about any similar program you can name. When saving your work in Writer, Calc, or Impress, the **Save As** dialog box always provides you with both OpenOffice.org-based file types as well as Microsoft Office file types. In addition, OpenOffice.org saves files in the StarOffice format.

▶ **NOTE**

To use a Base database throughout OpenOffice.org, or to use a Calc database in Base, you must *register* it first. You must also register databases created in other applications such as Microsoft Access or Excel before they can be used. See 140 **Access an Existing Database**.

OpenOffice.org saves in several formats, as indicated by this long list.

In reality, it is Microsoft Office that is not compatible with OpenOffice.org! Microsoft Office offers no way to save files in OpenOffice.org's native file format. To convert an Office file to OpenOffice.org format, you must first open the Microsoft Office file in OpenOffice.org, and then save the file in OpenOffice.org's native format.

Another powerful OpenOffice.org feature is its capability to export documents directly into Adobe's PDF format, which can then be viewed with Adobe Reader on all computer platforms. See **36** **Save a Document as a PDF File** for information on the PDF format.

▶ NOTE

Microsoft Word master document files are saved with the `.doc` **extension as used for standard Word documents; they become master documents when subdocuments are inserted into them, in Word's Outline view. OpenOffice.org Writer's master document files are saved as** `.odm` **files rather than** `.odt` **files. So when importing a Microsoft Word master document file, don't look for an unusual filename extension.**

When loading Microsoft Office documents, spreadsheets, and presentations into OpenOffice.org's programs, you may run into conversion problems. For Microsoft Office documents, these features will not always convert in OpenOffice.org:

- Revision marks

- Non-standard embedded OLE objects, especially those not provided by either application suite

- Embedded ActiveX controls, such as PivotTables in Excel spreadsheets

- Some textual form fields, which OpenOffice.org might convert into dialog box input fields

- Hyperlinks and bookmarks

- WordArt graphics

OpenOffice.org does not support Visual Basic for Applications (VBA), which is Microsoft Office's native macro language. As a result, although OpenOffice.org can import any Microsoft Office document's native *content*, it cannot import its embedded functionality. However, OpenOffice.org does copy the *text* of Microsoft's VBA macros into the **Standard** library of the imported copy of the Microsoft file. Because the VBA text cannot be executed by OpenOffice.org's BASIC interpreter, though, the importer "remarks out" (adds Rem statements to) the instructions it cannot interpret, which constitute about 98% of all instructions. If you are familiar with OpenOffice.org BASIC, you can edit the syntax and native contexts of many of the imported instructions, changing them into their Sun-compatible equivalents. All that having been said, there are no Sun-compatible equivalents

132

for VBA instructions that use Microsoft Office-specific functionality. So you'll probably have to re-record any Office macros after you import a corresponding document into OpenOffice.org.

OpenOffice.org does include import and export support for some Object Linking and Embedding (OLE) objects that one would expect to find within a Microsoft Office document, especially those which Office generates automatically. For example, for typesetting explicit and exact mathematical formulas within any document, Microsoft Office provides a tool called MathType; OpenOffice.org provides its own Math component (see **30 Use Mathematical Formulas in Documents** for details on how to use it). In both cases, these objects are created using embedded components generated by separate programs. From the **Options** dialog box, you can set whether the contents of certain Microsoft-embedded objects are imported when an Office file is loaded, or whether the contents of their OpenOffice.org counterparts are saved when its documents are exported to Microsoft format. To bring up this dialog box, from any OpenOffice.org application, choose **Tools**, **Options**, then from the list at the left, expand **Load/Save**, and choose **Microsoft Office**.

133

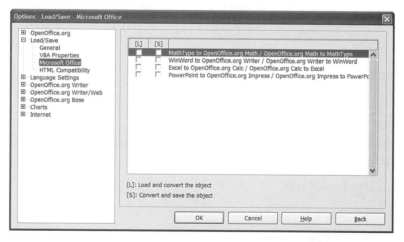

Options for converting OLE object data to and from Microsoft Office format.

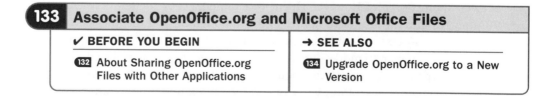

133	**Associate OpenOffice.org and Microsoft Office Files**
✔ **BEFORE YOU BEGIN**	→ **SEE ALSO**
132 About Sharing OpenOffice.org Files with Other Applications	**134** Upgrade OpenOffice.org to a New Version

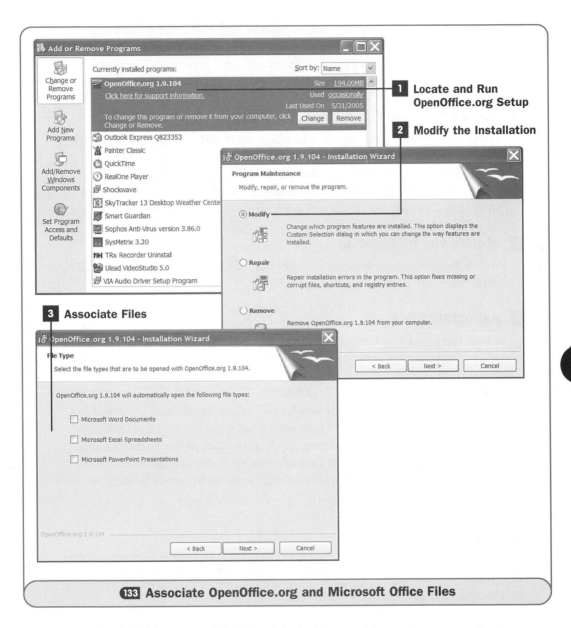

1 **Locate and Run OpenOffice.org Setup**

2 **Modify the Installation**

3 **Associate Files**

133 **Associate OpenOffice.org and Microsoft Office Files**

If you have both Microsoft Office and OpenOffice.org installed on the same computer, you should keep their respective native file types separate from one another, especially so that a Microsoft Office document launched from a Microsoft Office application doesn't launch an OpenOffice.org application instead. But, if you prefer OpenOffice.org but you must regularly edit Microsoft Word documents, you might want to be able to click a Word document, which ends with the .doc filename extension, and have Writer start and load the document automatically—instead of having your computer load the document in Word. If you have both Office and

OpenOffice.org installed, your current file associations might make Word open the file instead. Similarly, you'll have to determine whether Impress or PowerPoint should be the default application for opening PowerPoint .ppt presentation files, and whether you prefer Calc or Excel for working with Excel (.xls) spreadsheet files.

1 Locate and Run OpenOffice.org Setup

From the Windows **Start** menu, select **Control Panel**, and then double-click **Add or Remove Programs**. The **Add or Remove Programs** dialog box appears. In the **Currently installed programs** list, choose the entry for **OpenOffice** (the current version number is shown next to the name), and then click **Change**. The **Installation Wizard** appears; click **Next** to continue.

2 Modify the Installation

In the **Program Maintenance** panel of the Installation Wizard, click **Modify**, click **Next**, and then click **Next** again.

3 Associate Files

Check the boxes for all Microsoft Office files that you want OpenOffice.org to open automatically, instead of letting Office open them: Word, Excel, and/or PowerPoint. Remember, you're telling Windows which program will automatically open files that end in Microsoft's .doc, .xls, and .ppt filename extensions when you double-click those files in a Windows Explorer window. Click **Next** to continue, and then click **Install** to have Setup alter OpenOffice.org's Registry settings to accommodate your changes. Despite the button's name, and despite the progress report that appears next, this action does *not* reinstall the entire application suite. It only updates the Windows Registry. When the process concludes, click **Finish**.

▶ NOTES

You can always open Office files in Office if you like. After starting the appropriate Office program, just click **Open** and select the file you want to edit. In addition, you can always open Office files after starting OpenOffice.org, without completing this task first. Just start an OpenOffice.org component, click **Open**, and open any Office file.

To install the latest version of OpenOffice.org on your computer, see **134** Upgrade OpenOffice.org to a New Version.

134 Upgrade OpenOffice.org to a New Version

✔ **BEFORE YOU BEGIN**

132 About Sharing OpenOffice.org with Other Applications

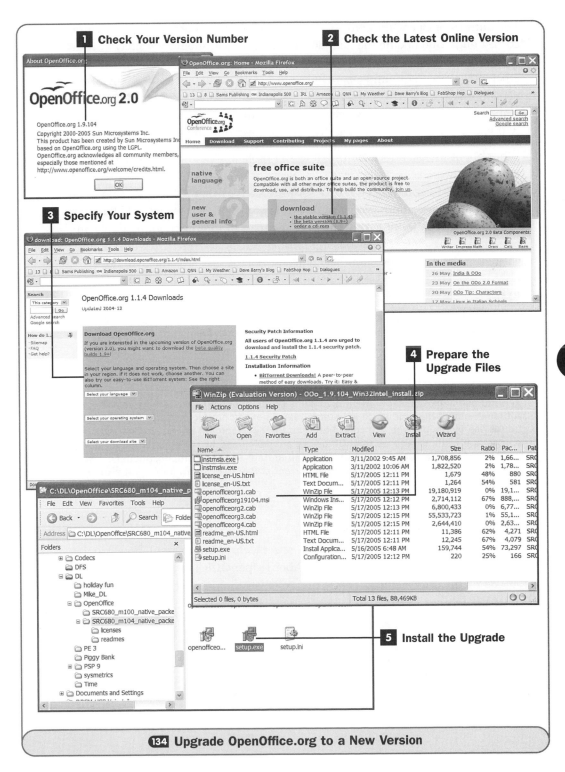

134 Upgrade OpenOffice.org to a New Version

The authors of OpenOffice.org continually update the programs to add features, correct bugs, and update the help documentation. You should routinely visit the OpenOffice.org website to check for updates and add-on programs for OpenOffice.org. Upgrading OpenOffice.org requires that you check your current version and see if a newer one is available on the product's Web site. If so, you can easily download the new version (this download might not be quick, especially if you don't have a broadband Internet connection) and install it.

What about the old adage stating, if it isn't broken, don't fix it? Whereas commercial software is upgraded every few years or so—though it may seem longer to some—the evolution of open-source software such as OpenOffice.org is an ongoing and continual affair. Rather than waiting for new features and old bug fixes to collect and ruminate so that the publisher can spring them on the public in one massive premiere, open-source publishers such as Sun produce new builds with even the most minor improvements as soon as they become available.

▶ **NOTE**

All data files you've created in previous versions of OpenOffice.org remain on your disk unchanged when you upgrade. None of your personal documents are deleted.

134

▶ **TIP**

Unlike with commercial software, the makers of OpenOffice.org make available to the general public certain experimental versions of their software, called *beta releases*. Although newer than the so-called *stable release* of the product, a beta release is intended for use by people who are contributing to the development of this product. Open-source applications such as OpenOffice.org are developed by contributions from both professional and amateur programmers who are not seeking compensation. For everyday use, you should download the most current *stable* release available, not a beta release.

1 **Check Your Version Number**

From any OpenOffice.org program, select **Help**, **About OpenOffice.org** to see the current version number in the **About OpenOffice.org** dialog box. Don't go by the graphic logo; look at the exact version number on first line of text. Click **OK** to close the dialog box.

▶ **TIP**

With the **About** dialog box still open, you can press **Ctrl+S+D+T** to view a scrolling list of the names of the developers who created OpenOffice.org.

2 Check the Latest Online Version

Start your web browser and go to **http://www.openoffice.org/**. Sun will list the latest version number on its link to the stable version, generally in the **Download** frame on the home page. If this number is greater than the one shown in your **About** dialog box, you should upgrade. To proceed, click the link to the most recent stable edition.

3 Specify Your System

From the downloads page, choose your spoken language, operating system (**Windows**), and your closest geographical download site location. You might see a request for funds donation; click **Donate Funds** to give the amount of your choice to this open-source project, or click **Continue to Download** to proceed. Your Web browser will show a file downloading dialog box. Specify a download destination and click **Save** (if you're using Internet Explorer) or **OK** (if you're using Firefox) to begin the transfer.

4 Prepare the Upgrade Files

OpenOffice.org installation packages for Windows are distributed as ZIP files, which are compressed files that are now natively supported by Windows XP. Use Windows or the compression utility of your choice (see `http://www.filzip.com` for a superb freeware alternative) to extract the compressed contents of this ZIP file into a secure location. Among the uncompressed files, check to see whether the **readmes** directory exists; if it does, open it and read either of the files contained there for special instructions. These instructions might include tasks you might have to perform manually before installing the new version—especially whether you must install an old version first.

5 Install the Upgrade

After you have thoroughly read the **readme** files and followed their precautions, from Windows Explorer, in the root directory of the extracted setup files, double-click **setup.exe** to begin the installation process. Instructions are given to you onscreen as setup proceeds.

18

Organizing Your Data with Base

IN THIS CHAPTER:

A **database** (or **data source** as it is sometimes called) is an organized collection of information. You can use a database to organize any set of related data, such as relatives' names and addresses, customer contact data, travel expenses, rental listings, or product inventory.

Data in a database is organized within **tables**. For example, if you were a big Indy 500 fan and you wanted to keep track of your favorite drivers and teams within a database, you might create several tables: a driver table, a team table (because an IRL team often has several drivers), and a car table (because an IRL driver often has a main car and a backup car). After you set up at least one table in your database, you enter data into it one **record** at a time. A record is a collection of data related to the same item. For example, in your Indy driver table, you'll find one record for each race driver. Each record is divided into different **fields**—each field represents a different type of data such as a person's first name, last name, best start, best finish, championship points, YTD earnings, and so on.

▶ KEY TERMS

Database—Organized collection of data, such as employees, customers, and so on.

Data Source—Registered database that can be used in any OpenOffice.org component.

Table—A collection of related data. A database can have multiple tables.

Record—Data related to one item in a database, such as a single person.

Field—One part of a record; each field represents a different type of data such as a person's city, state, and zip code.

▶ NOTE

To create and work with databases in OpenOffice.org, you must have Java JRE (Java Runtime Environment) installed. Download it from Java's Web site at **www.java.com**. Register its use by choosing **Tools, Options, OpenOffice.org, Java** from the Base menu bar.

---

135 Create a Database

✔ BEFORE YOU BEGIN	→ SEE ALSO
Just jump right in!	**136** Enter Data Using a Form
	137 Create a Form
	138 Access an Existing Database

If you want to keep track of related data—such as relative's names and addresses—create a **database**. You can then use the information in this database with any of your OpenOffic.org components. For example, you could use your new **Relatives** database to address reunion party invitations for your parents, brothers, sisters, aunts, uncles, and cousins using the **MailMerge Wizard** as described in **37** **Use the MailMerge Wizard**.

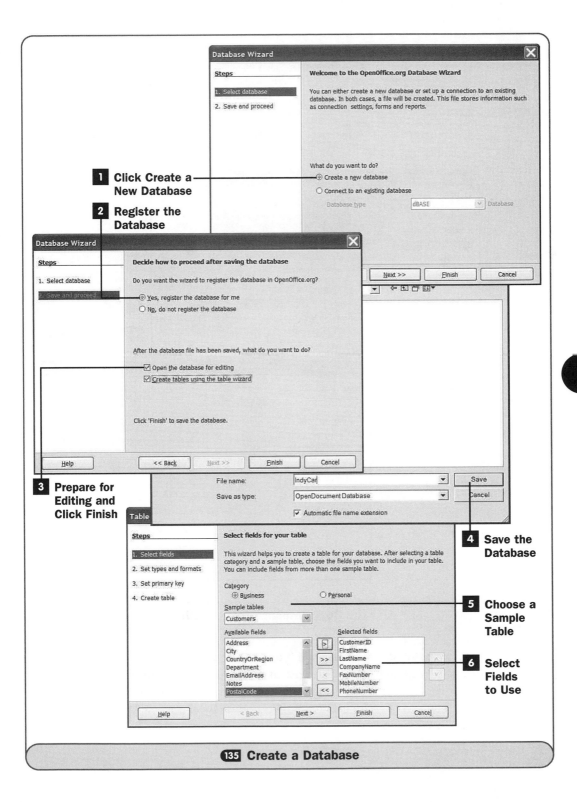

1 Click Create a New Database

2 Register the Database

3 Prepare for Editing and Click Finish

4 Save the Database

5 Choose a Sample Table

6 Select Fields to Use

135

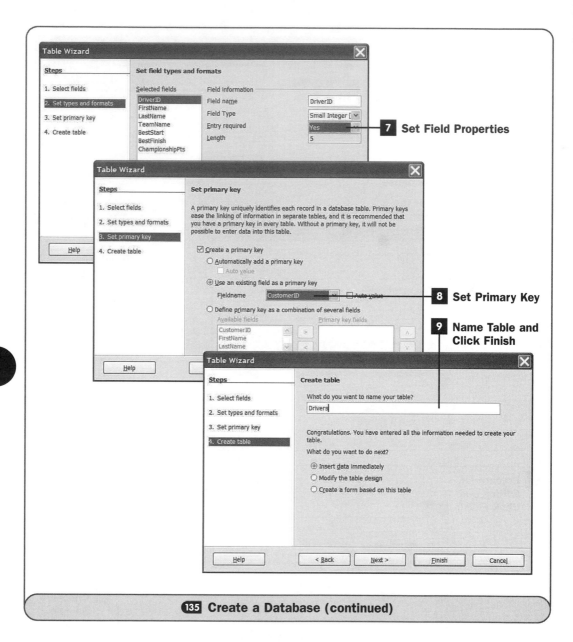

7 Set Field Properties

8 Set Primary Key

9 Name Table and Click Finish

135

135 Create a Database (continued)

After creating a database, you can open it again for editing from any OpenOffice.org component (and start Base at the same time) by simply choosing **File, Open** or clicking the **Open** button. If you're not running OpenOffice.org at the moment, you can open an existing Base database by double-clicking the database file in Windows Explorer.

▶ **NOTE**

If you start Base from the **Start** menu, you'll have only two options, as you'll learn in this task: to create a new database, or to register and edit a database created in some other application such as dBASE or Microsoft Access. You cannot open an existing Base database this way.

1 **Click Create a New Database**

Start Base, and in **Step 1** of the **Database Wizard** which automatically launches, select the **Create a new database** option and click **Next**.

▶ **NOTE**

If you're already working in Base and you want to create a new database, click the **New** button on the **Standard** toolbar, and then choose **Database** from the menu that appears. The **Database Wizard** starts, and you can continue to step 2.

2 **Register the Database**

In **Step 2** of the **Database Wizard**, select Yes, **register the database for me.** This option allows you to use the database in other OpenOffice.org components. If you intend to use the new database only in Base, you can select **No, do not register the database.**

135

3 **Prepare for Editing and Click Finish**

In **Step 2** of the **Database Wizard**, enable the **Open the database for editing** check box so that you can work on the database after the initial file is created and saved.

Also enable the **Create tables using table wizard** check box. Because you must create at least one table in a database before you can start entering data, enabling this second option allows you to get started on that right after the database is created and saved. Click **Finish**. The **Save As** dialog box appears.

4 **Save the Database**

In the **Save As** dialog box, type a name for your new database in the **File name** text box. Change to the folder in which you want to save your database and then click **Save** to save the file. Because you enabled the **Create tables using table wizard** check box in step 3, the **Table Wizard** appears to help you create the first table in your database.

5 **Choose a Sample Table**

In **Step 1** of the **Table Wizard**, select a sample table to build your first table from. First, choose a **Category**, either the **Business** or **Personal**. Then choose a table from the **Sample tables** list. A list of fields in that table category appears in the **Available fields** list.

6 Select Fields to Use

Select the first field you want to use from those listed in the **Available fields** list and click > to add that field to the list of **Selected fields** for your table. Typically, the first field you select is the *primary key*, which is a field with "ID" in its name. Here I choose **CustomerID**, with the intent of using it to enter each driver's unique driver number. If you don't have some field in mind that's unique to each record, you can have Base add a primary key field for you in step 8. If you choose a field to act as the primary key, you will designate it as the primary key in step 8.

Repeat this step (selecting a field and clicking >) to add each additional field you want the table to have to the **Selected fields** list. You can change to a different sample table by repeating step 5 if you want to use a field located in some other sample table. When you're done adding fields to your table, click **Next**.

▶ TIPS

135

If you can't find the exact field you want to use, select one that's similar and then modify the field to suit your exact needs in step 7.

You can rearrange the fields in the **Selected fields** list by clicking a field and then pressing the ↑ or ↓ key on your keyboard to move that field up or down within the listing.

▶ KEY TERM

Primary key—A field that is never duplicated in any record in a database.

7 Set Field Properties

In **Step 2** of the **Table Wizard**, change the properties of each field as needed. Start by selecting a field from the **Selected fields** list. Then change the **Field name**, **Field Type**, and so on as needed. Repeat this step for each field in the table, and then click **Next**.

I selected my primary key (**CustomerID**) and changed its **Field name** to **DriverID** which made more sense to me. I also changed the **FieldType** to a small integer because the driver ID number is small, from 1 to 99. I then selected each field in my table and made adjustments as needed. For example, I selected **FirstName** and changed the **Entry required** field to **Yes** to ensure that a first name is always entered for each driver. I did the same thing with the **LastName** field. I changed the **CompanyName** field to

TeamName, and made that field required as well. I made similar changes to other fields until everything was set up as I wanted.

8 Set Primary Key

In **Step 3** of the **Table Wizard**, set up your primary key. First, enable the **Create a primary key** check box.

If you didn't select a field to act as your primary key in step 6, then choose **Automatically add a primary key** and enable the **Auto value** option, which will cause Base to add a primary key field and create a unique number for each record.

If you have a field in the table that can serve as the primary key, choose **Use an existing field as primary key**, and then choose that field from the **Fieldname** list. Here I choose **DriverID** (which shows up in the list under its original name, which was **CustomerID**). I didn't want to enable the **Auto value** option because I intend to enter the **DriverID** myself, but if you want to have Base automatically fill the field you select as the primary key with a unique number, enable the **Auto value** check box.

If you have several fields that *together* form a unique ID that won't be duplicated by any other record, choose the **Define primary key as a combination of several fields** option, and then select the first field you want to use in forming the primary key and click > to add it to the **Primary key fields** list. Repeat this step to add other fields to the list to create a primary key from that combination of selected fields.

When you have established the primary key for your table, click **Next**.

9 Name the Table and Click Finish

In **Step 4** of the **Table Wizard**, type a name for the table in the **What do you want to name your table?** text box. I named my table **Drivers** because it will hold the data for each Indy Car driver.

Choose the **Insert data immediately** option (to enter data using **List** view) or **Create a form based on this table** (to enter data using a form) and then click **Finish** to add the table to the database. If you chose **Insert data immediately**, the table appears in **List** view. See **136** **Enter Data in List View** for help in entering data into the table in this view. If you chose **Create a form based on this table**, see **137** **Create a Form** for help in creating an entry form you can use to enter data more easily into a complex table with lots of fields. Because you don't really need to make any modifications to the table you created in steps 5–8, there's no need to choose **Modify the table design**, which takes you to **Design** view so you can modify the table.

135

▶ **TIP**

You can add more tables to your database if desired. After entering data for my **Drivers** table using **List** view, I added a **Team** table for team data and a **Car** table for data about each car by clicking the **Tables** icon in the **Database** pane, clicking the **Use Wizard to Create Table** option, and following steps 5 to 9 in this task to create another table in my database.

---

136 | **Enter Data in List View**

✔ **BEFORE YOU BEGIN**	→ **SEE ALSO**
135 Create a Database	**139** Enter Data Using a Form

After creating a *table* in Base, you can enter data into it in one of two ways. For a table that contains simple data, you can enter information in **List** view. **List** view looks remarkably like a Calc sheet, as described in **38** **About Sheets and Spreadsheets**. In List view, the *fields* in your table are displayed in individual columns; as you add *records* to the table, each record is displayed in its own row. The other method you can use to enter data into a table is to use a form, as described in **139** **Enter Data Using a Form**.

136

▶ **NOTE**

You might want to enter data into a table using a form. Some tables contain a lot of fields that will be easier to view or arrange in a logical order when they appear on a form. A form also lets you select repetitious data from a list that's linked to a simple table of values you create beforehand.

1 **Click Tables**

To add data to a table, you must first open the table. Click the **Tables** icon in the **Database** pane. A list of tables in the current database appears on the right side of the Base window.

2 **Double-Click Table**

In the **Tables** list, double-click the table you want to add data to. The table is opened in **List** view, ready for you to add data. On the **Navigation** toolbar at the bottom of the screen, the current record number is displayed, along with a total of the records in the table.

3 **Enter Data in Record**

The first empty row in the table is marked with a yellow asterisk on the left. The current row is marked with a green pencil icon on the left. If needed, click in the first field (column) of the first empty row (record).

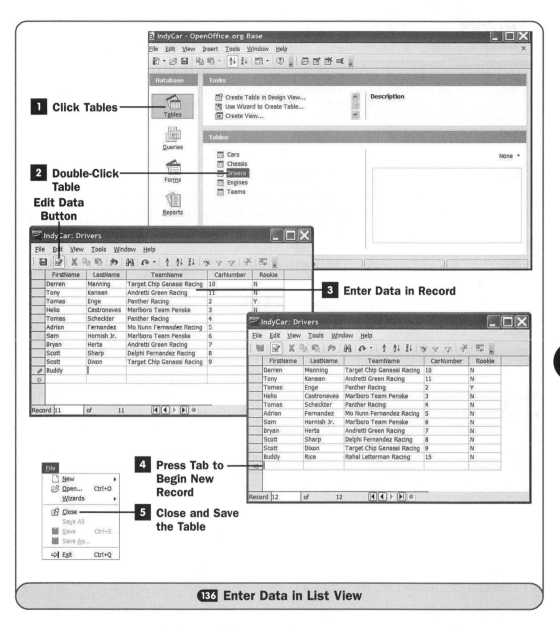

1 Click Tables

2 Double-Click Table

Edit Data Button

3 Enter Data in Record

4 Press Tab to Begin New Record

5 Close and Save the Table

If the first field in this empty row is an *auto value*, skip it by pressing **Tab**. Type data for the field, and then press **Tab** to move to the next field. Continue to press **Tab** and enter data into each field in the record (row).

▶ **KEY TERM**

Auto Value—A field in a table that's automatically filled in a value that increases with each new record. Typically, the *primary key* is set up as an auto value.

▶ NOTES

You can skip any fields that do not apply to the current record by pressing **Tab** to bypass them.

If you need to make changes to an existing record, click in the appropriate field (the **Edit Data** button on the **Table Data View** toolbar is now enabled, indicating that you can now make changes), and then make your changes directly to the field. To remove a record from the table, right-click at the beginning of that row and choose **Delete Rows** from the context menu that appears.

4 Press Tab to Begin New Record

To begin a new record, press **Tab**. The cursor moves down one row to the first field in the next row. Repeat step 3 to enter data into each field in the record and to add all the records you want into the table.

5 Close and Save the Table

When you're done entering and editing table data, choose **File, Close** from the menu. A table is saved each time a record is completed (each time you press **Tab** to move to a new record/row), so most likely when you close your table, you won't have to save it. If you're prompted to save, click **Yes.** The table is saved and you're returned to the Base main window.

137

137 Create a Form

✔ BEFORE YOU BEGIN	→ SEE ALSO
Just jump right in!	**138** Modify a Form
	139 Enter Data Using a Form

To help you enter data into a complex table that contains a lot of *fields*, you can create a form to help you arrange those fields in a more compact and perhaps more logical order. Unlike entering data in **List** view, with a form, you can add instructions and informational text or graphics that make the form easier for someone else to enter the right data into the table.

If you think you might be entering the same information in multiple records, you can enter that data in a simple table with only one field, and then link to the resulting one-column list from the form. For example, to make entering the data for each CD in a music collection table easier, you might create a simple one column/field music categories table, with entries such as **jazz**, **rock**, **country**, and so on. You could then make this music category list available to the CD form, so when you use the form later on to enter your CD collection, you can select the music category for each CD from a list instead of having to type the various categories over and over again as you enter information about each CD.

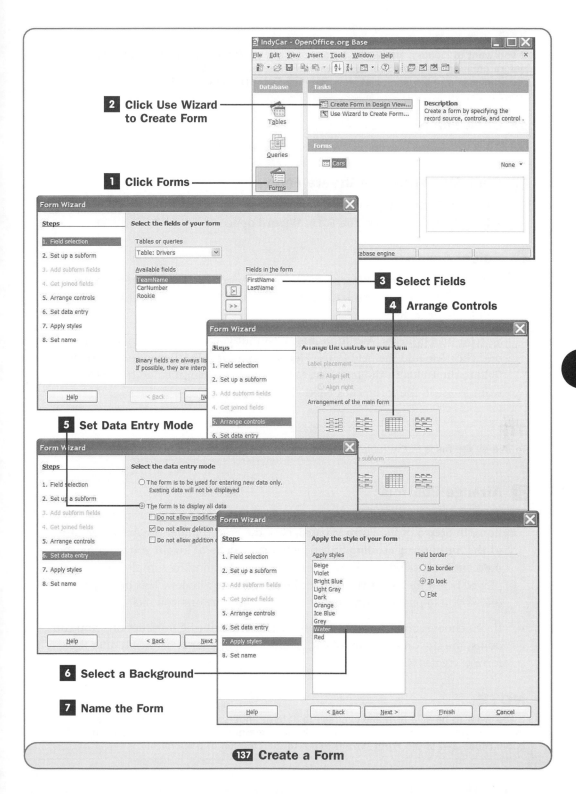

2 Click Use Wizard to Create Form

1 Click Forms

3 Select Fields

4 Arrange Controls

5 Set Data Entry Mode

6 Select a Background

7 Name the Form

137

137 Create a Form

▶ **TIP**

If you want to create a simple list for use in the form, create the one-field table *first*, before creating the form. See 🔢 **Create a Database**, steps 5–9. Then enter the data for the single-column list using **List** view. See 🔢 **Enter Data in List View**.

1 Click Forms

Click the **Forms** button on the **Database** pane of the Base window.

2 Click Use Wizard to Create Form

Click the **Use Wizard to Create Form** link, shown in the **Tasks** list on the right side of the Base window. The **Form Wizard** appears.

3 Select Fields

In **Step 1** of the **Form Wizard**, select the table for which you're creating this form from the **Tables or queries** list. The fields in that table appear in the **Available fields** list.

Select a field from the **Available fields** list that you want to use on the form and click > to add the field to the **Fields in the form** list. Repeat to add each field to the **Fields in the form** list. When you have identified all the fields you want to use in the form, click **Next**.

▶ **TIP**

To use all the fields in the table on the form, click **>>** instead.

4 Arrange Controls

Click **Next** again to skip **Step 2**, **Step 3**, and **Step 4** (see Note for more information). In **Step 5** of the **Form Wizard**, click the button under the **Arrangement of the main form** heading that represents the general layout you want for the data entry boxes on the form. After you click a button, the sample layout is displayed below the **Form Wizard**, in the actual form window. This arrangement allows you to preview each layout until you find the one you like.

If you choose something other than the sheet layout (the third option), you can adjust the size and position of each control to suit your exact needs after the form is created. Click **Next**.

▶ **NOTE**

If you want to be able to make changes to data in another table while entering data in this table, you can add a subform. This advanced feature is beyond the scope of this book. Steps 2–4 of the **Form Wizard** relate to the creation of a subform.

5 Set Data Entry Mode

In **Step 6** of the **Form Wizard**, select the type of data entry mode you want and click **Next**. For example, if you intend to use the form to enter data but not to review it, choose **The form is to be used for entering new data only. Existing data will not be displayed.**

If you want the user to be able to scroll through previously entered records using the form, choose **The form is to display all data.** Then choose any restrictions you want by enabling the appropriate check box. For example, to prevent a user from deleting previous records, enable the **Do not allow deletion of existing data** option. Click **Next.**

6 Select a Background

In **Step 7** of the **Form Wizard**, select the background color you want to use from the **Apply styles** list. Again, as you select a color, you can see a preview of how your color selection will look on the actual form under the **Form Wizard**.

Select how you want the border around each field to appear (such as 3D) from the **Field border** options on the right side of the wizard window. Click **Next.**

138

7 Name the Form

In **Step 8** of the **Form Wizard**, type a name for the form in the **Name of the form** text box, or simply leave the suggested name as is.

To start entering data into your table using the form, choose **Work with the form.** (See **139 Enter Data Using a Form.**) To make changes to the form before you use it, choose **Modify the form.** (See **138 Modify a Form.**) Click **Finish.** The form is created and displayed in a window.

---

138 Modify a Form

✔ BEFORE YOU BEGIN	→ SEE ALSO
137 Create a Form	**117** About Manipulating Objects
	139 Enter Data Using a Form

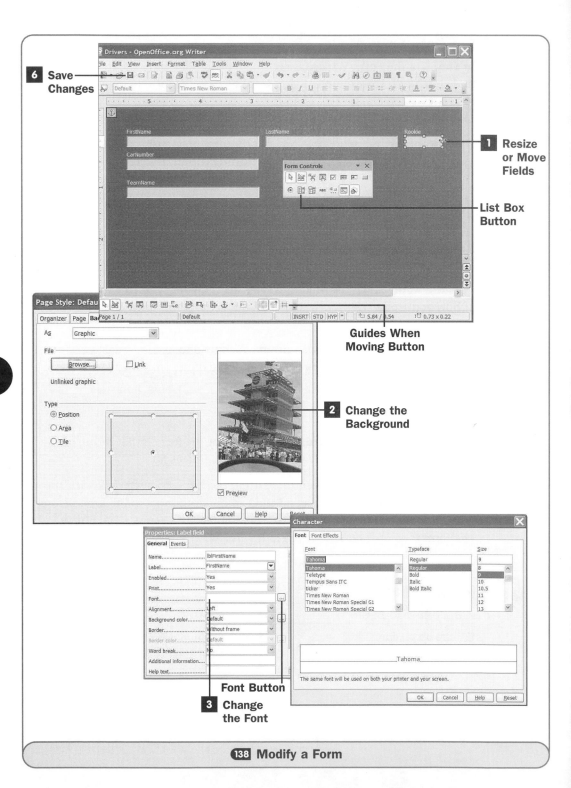

138 Modify a Form

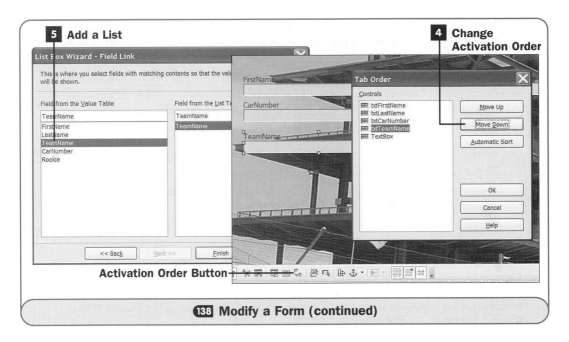

5 Add a List

4 Change Activation Order

Activation Order Button

138 Modify a Form (continued)

After creating a form, you can modify it before using it to enter data into its associated table. For example, you might want to reposition a few *controls* so that the table data will be in a more logical order, or be visible onscreen at the same time. Or you might want to simply add a few personal touches, such as selecting the font used for data entry or for the labels.

Normally, data is entered in a form in the order in which the controls appear onscreen—in other words, when a user presses **Tab**, the cursor automatically advances to the nearest control onscreen. However, you might prefer to change this activation order to make it easier for a user to enter data. For example, if the user has to pull data from several sources, you might want to have the cursor automatically move between just the fields being pulled from the source one, skipping any fields whose data comes from a secondary source. After the first fields are filled in, you can then have the cursor jump back to any fields you skipped the first time.

▶ **KEY TERM**

Controls—An object on a form similar to those you find in a typical dialog box, such as a text box, list box, check box, or option button.

Handles—Small green boxes that appear around a selected object.

1 **Resize or Move Fields**

As you learned in **117** **About Manipulating Objects**, you must first select an object before you can resize or move it. When you click an object such as a form control, small *handles* appear around its perimeter. To resize an object, drag one of these handles inward (to make the object smaller) or outward (to make it bigger). The pointer looks like a two-headed arrow when it's positioned correctly over a handle for resizing. One caution however: When you click on an object in **Design** mode, typically both the object (such as a text box) and its label are selected. You probably don't want to resize the label too, so to select just the text box, press and hold the **Ctrl** key and then click.

To move a selected object, click within its borders and drag. The pointer looks like a four-headed arrow when it's positioned correctly over the object for moving. Typically, you want to move both the text box and its label, so just click the object to select both, then drag to move them.

▶ TIPS

If the form is not currently displayed in **Design** mode, just right-click the form in the Base main window and select **Edit** from the context menu.

Display helpful guidelines whenever you move an object by enabling the **Guides When Moving** button on the **Form Design** toolbar.

138

2 Change the Background

You can change the color used for the form's background, or replace it with a texture or graphic image. Choose **Format**, **Page** from the menu. The **Page Style** dialog box appears. Click the **Background** tab if needed.

To apply a color to the form's background, choose **Color** from the **As** list, and then click the color you want from the palette on the left.

To use a texture or other graphic as the form's background, choose **Graphic** from the **As** list. Then click **Browse**, select the graphic you want to use, and click **Open**. You're returned to the **Page Style** dialog box.

Select where you want the graphic positioned from the options in the **Type** area. The **Position** option allows you to click the position in which you want the graphic placed, using the map on the right. The **Area** option stretches the graphic to fill the form. The **Tile** option repeats the graphic from left to right and top to bottom, to fill the form.

▶ TIP

You'll find textures and other graphics you can use in the **OpenOffice.org****share**\ **gallery** folder.

3 | Change Font

You can change the font used in labels or data entry boxes. Press **Ctrl** and click the label or text box you want to change. Right-click the selected object and choose **Control** from the context menu that appears. The **Properties** dialog box appears.

Click the **Font** button, and the **Character** dialog box appears. On the **Font** tab, select the **Font**, **Typeface**, and **Size** you want. On the **Font Effects** tab, add special effects and select the **Font color**. The preview at the bottom of the dialog box displays your changes. Click **OK**. You're returned to the **Properties** dialog box. If you want to select another object to change, leave it open, otherwise, click the **X** to close the **Properties** dialog box.

▶ TIP

To change the background color used in a data entry box, select it, display the **Properties** dialog box, and then on the **General** tab, select a different color from the **Background color** list.

4 | Change Activation Order

If you want to change the order in which data is entered into the various fields on a form, adjust the activation order of the form. Click any field to select it. Then click the **Activation Order** button on the **Form Design** toolbar. The **Tab Order** dialog box appears.

The fields appear in the list in the order in which they will be activated when a user presses **Tab** to move from field to field during data entry. To adjust a field's position in this list, select the field and click the **Move Up** or **Move Down** button as needed. When you're done rearranging the order of the fields, click **OK**.

5 | Add a List

If you've created a single-entry table to provide a list of choices for a field in your form, you can add a list box to replace the field's normal text box on the form. First, click the field you want to replace, and then press **Delete** to remove it from the form.

On the **Form Controls** toolbar, click the **List Box** button. Click on the form and drag downwards and to the right to draw the list box. When you release the mouse button, the **List Box Wizard** appears. On the **Table Selection** page of the Wizard, select the table into which you typed your list from the tables shown on the right. I'm creating a form for my **Drivers** table. To make

138

it easier, I decided I wanted to make a list for all the team names. So I created a single column table called **Teams**, and entered the various team names into the one column. Because my list source is the **Teams** table, I selected that in this step. Click **Next**.

On the **Field Selection** page of the Wizard, from the **Existing fields** list, select the field whose contents you want to use in the list. My **Teams** table only has one field, so the selection process was pretty easy; I choose the only field there was, which is called **TeamName**.

I also replaced my **Rookie** field with an option button that would put **Yes** in the field if the option was enabled by the user when entering a new record. If the option was not enabled, **No** would be put in the **Rookie** field. I used the **Option Button** tool on the **Forms Control** toolbar to draw the button, and then displayed the **Control** dialog box and entered **Yes** and **No** values on the **Data** tab. If you want this field to appear on the form with some other name, change the name shown in the **Display field** box. Click **Next**.

The **Field Link** page of the Wizard appears. The fields in the table that's associated with the form appear on the left. From the **Field from the Value Table** list, select the field in the form for which you want to substitute the list. The table for which I'm creating this form is called **Drivers**, so the fields in the **Drivers** table appear on the left. The field I want to substitute a list for is called **TeamName**, so I select that from the **Value Table**.

From the **Field from the List Table** list, select the field from the list table that contains the data you want to use in the list. My list table is called **Teams**. It has only one field, called **TeamName**, and that field contains the data I want the list box to show when I open it on the form. So I selected **TeamName** from the **List Table**. Click **Finish**. The list box is complete; when you enter data in the form, the contents of the field you selected in the source table will appear in a list, and you can choose one of its items for the current record rather than typing in the data. In my case, my **Drivers** form now has a list box in place of the text box for the **TeamName** field, and when I open that list box, the data in the **TeamName** field of the **Teams** table appears. (If you want to see my final form, it appears in the next task, **139 Enter Data Using a Form**.)

6 Save Changes

Click the **Save** button on the **Standard** toolbar to save your changes to the form. Then close the form window to return to the main Base window where you can enter data into the table using your new form. See **139 Enter Data Using a Form**.

139 Enter Data Using a Form

✔ BEFORE YOU BEGIN	→ SEE ALSO
137 Create a Form	**136** Enter Data in List View
138 Modify a Form	

After creating a form, you can use it to add data to the table that's associated with the form. You might have added controls to make data entry easier, such as a list box with entries from which a user can choose. Or you might simply have reorganized the fields on the form so that they follow a more natural flow. In any case, in this task, you'll learn how to use your form to enter data into its table.

▶ **NOTE**

Even after creating a form for a table, you can still enter some of the data using List view if you want. See **136** **Enter Data in List View**.

1 **Click Forms**

To add data to a table using a form, you must open the form first. Click the **Forms** icon in the **Database** pane of the Base window. A list of forms associated with the current database appears on the lower-right side of the window.

139

2 **Double-Click Form**

In the **Forms** list, double-click the form you want to use to enter data. The form opens, ready for you to add data. On the **Form Navigation** toolbar at the bottom of the screen, the current record number is displayed, along with a total of the records in the table.

3 **Enter Data in Record**

If the table already has data in it, the data for the first record might be currently displayed in the form fields. If so, you need to clear the fields and start a new record so that you can enter new data. To do that, click the **New Record** button on the **Form Navigation** toolbar.

Enter data in the first field. If the first field is an *auto value*, its value will be automatically updated for each record you create, so skip that field. Press **Tab** to move to the next field, and enter its data. Continue this process to enter data for the entire record.

1 Click Forms

2 Double-Click Form

3 Enter Data in Record

4 Press Tab to Begin New Record

New Record Button

5 Close Form

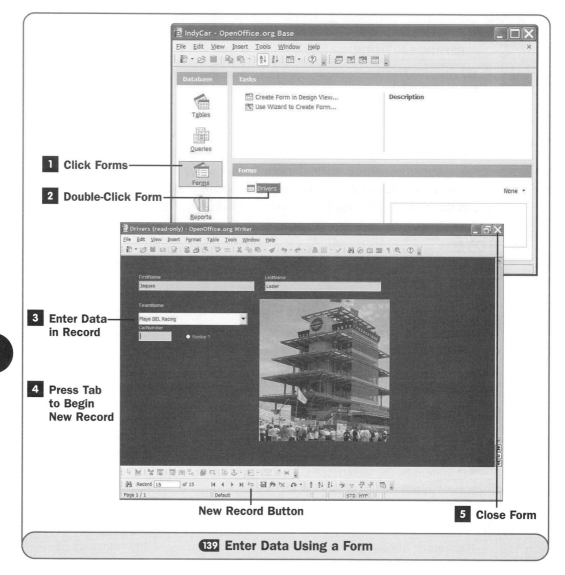

139 Enter Data Using a Form

▶ **NOTES**

You can skip any fields that do not apply to the current record by pressing **Tab** to bypass them.

If you have to make changes to an existing record, display that record by clicking the < or > buttons on the **Form Navigation** toolbar. Then make your changes and press **Tab** to advance to the next record. To remove the record from the table, click the **Remove Record** button (the red X) on the **Form Navigation** toolbar.

4 Press Tab to Begin New Record

Press **Tab** after entering data in the last field of the record; the record is saved and a new blank record appears. *Do this even if you don't want to add a new record, because pressing **Tab** after the last field in a record also saves the last record.* If you want to enter data for another record, repeat steps 3 and 4.

5 Close Form

When you're through entering data, close the form by clicking the **X** in the upper right corner of the window. If you pressed **Tab** after entering data in the final record, you won't be prompted to save the table because each record you added has already been saved to the database. If prompted, however, click **Yes** to save the table.

---

140 Access an Existing Database

✔ BEFORE YOU BEGIN	→ SEE ALSO
Just jump right in!	**135** Create a Database

140

You can use any database within Base or any other OpenOffice.org component if that database is registered as a **data source**. Typically, when you create a database in Base, you register it so that it can be used as a data source by any OpenOffice.org component (see **135 Create a Database**). But what about databases that were created using some other program such as Calc, Microsoft Excel, Microsoft Access, or Thunderbird (an email program with an address database)? In this task, you'll learn how to register such a database so that you can use it whenever you want, throughout OpenOffice.org. For example, you can use a registered database in Base or in a Writer Mail Merge operation, or you can copy its data into a Calc spreadsheet.

After creating a database in Base, *do not follow these steps to open it again for editing.* Instead, open an existing Base database from any OpenOffice.org component (and start Base at the same time) by choosing **File, Open** or by clicking the **Open** button. If you're not running OpenOffice.org right now, you can open an existing Base database by double-clicking the database file in Windows Explorer.

1 Click New, Database

2 Select Database Type

3 Select Database

4 Register Database and Click Finish

5 Save the Database

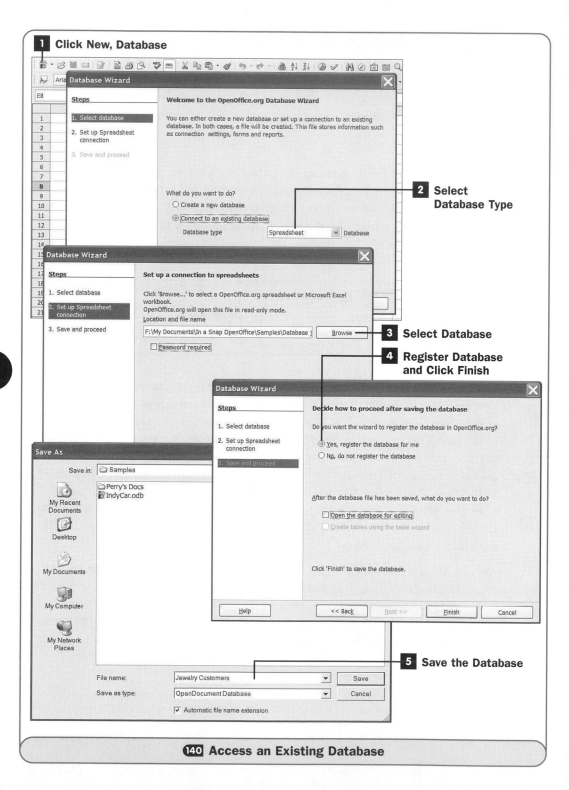

140 Access an Existing Database

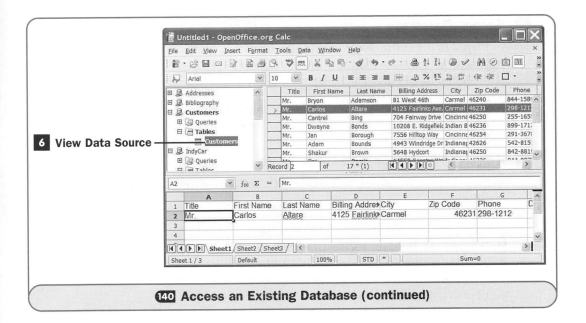

6 View Data Source

140 **Access an Existing Database (continued)**

▶ **NOTES**

140

If you start Base from the **Start** menu, you'll have only two options, as you'll learn in this task: to create a new database, or to register and edit a database created in some other application such as dBASE or Microsoft Access.

To use a database created in Calc (as explained in **76 Create a Calc Database**) within another OpenOffice.org component such as Base or Writer, you'll need to register it by following the steps given in this task.

After registering a foreign database (such as a Microsoft Access database) and converting it to Openoffice.org format, you can remove the original version from your system if you decide you don't need it. Choose **Tools, Options, OpenOffice.org, Databases.** Select the database to remove and click **Delete.**

1 Click New, Database

In any OpenOffice.org component, click the **New** button on the **Standard** toolbar and choose **Database** from the menu. Base starts and displays the **Database Wizard.**

2 Select Database Type

In **Step 1** of the **Database Wizard**, select **Connect to an existing database.** Select the type of database you want to register from the **Database type** list. In this example, I wanted to convert an Excel database for use in Base, so I chose **Spreadsheet.** You'd make this same choice to register a Calc database. Click **Next.**

3 Select Database

In **Step 2** of the **Database Wizard**, click **Browse.** Change to the folder that contains the database file you want to open, select it, and click **Open.** You're returned to the **Database Wizard**.

If a password is required to access the database (if you or someone else password-protected the file), enable the **Password required** option. Click **Next.**

4 Register Database and Click Finish

In **Step 3** of the **Database Wizard,** select the **Yes, register the database for me** option.

Disable the **Open the database for editing** option, unless you need to make changes to the database before you use it. If you do select this option, you might also be able to build the tables yourself, rather than letting OpenOffice.org create them by selecting **Create tables using the table wizard** option (if present). Click **Finish.**

5 Save the Database

The **Save As** dialog box appears. OpenOffice.org will convert the database to Base format, register it for use, and save it in a new file. Select the folder in which you want to store the new database, and enter a name in the **File name** box. Base automatically adds the extension .odb to the filename. Click **Save.** The converted database is saved, and it can now be used within any OpenOffice.org program.

If you opted to edit the data source, the converted file is opened in Base so that you can make changes.

6 View Data Source

To view any registered data source from within Calc, Writer, or Impress (if you're creating a spreadsheet slide), choose **View, Data Sources** or press **F4.**

The **Data Source** pane appears above the document window. Click the plus sign in front of the data source you want to use. Click the plus sign in front of **Tables,** and the tables in the database are listed. Click one of these tables to view its data.

▶ **NOTES**

If you must enter a password to access a data source, you'll be prompted for it when you click the plus sign in front of that data source to view its contents.

After a table is displayed, you can drag and drop a single row, column, or all the data into the OpenOffice.org component you are currently using (Calc, Writer, or Impress). You can also drag information from a component file (such as a Calc spreadsheet) into a Base database file.

To edit a data source in Base, right-click the source and choose **Edit Database File** from the context menu.

---

141 | **Find Data in a Database**

✔ **BEFORE YOU BEGIN**

135 Create a Database

One of the best things about a database is that it keeps your information organized. Whenever you need to, you can quickly locate the exact data you need. One way to find information in a database is to create a *query*. A query is like a question that is posed to the database—what you get for an answer is a simple list of records that match your query criteria.

Because a query is a question and not an actual report, you can run the query again and again as your data changes, and get results based on current information. A query can search the data in as many tables as you like, and combine that information in various ways for presentation, as you'll see in this task.

▶ **KEY TERM**

Query—A "question" asked of the current data in a database. The result is a report of matching records.

▮ **Click Queries**

Click the **Queries** button in the **Database** pane of the Base window.

▮ **Click Use Wizard to Create Query**

Click the **Use Wizard to Create Query** link in the **Tasks** list, shown on the right side of the Base window. The **Query Wizard** appears.

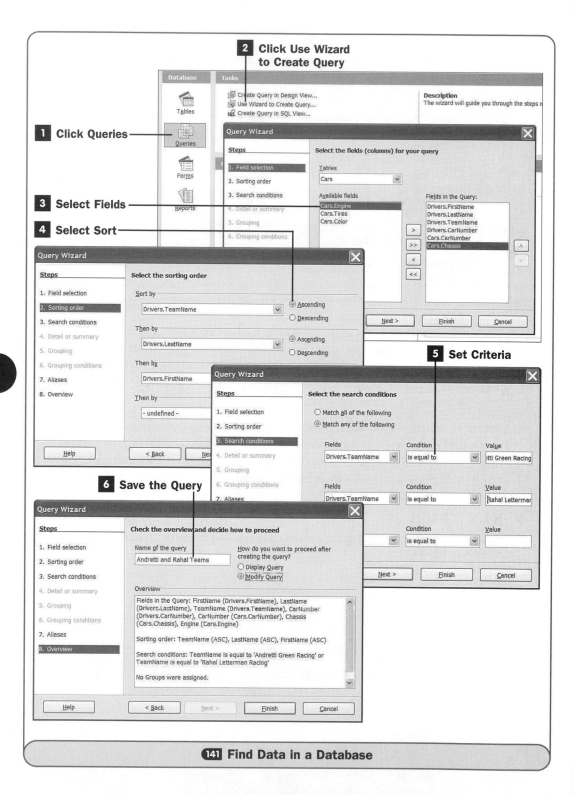

141

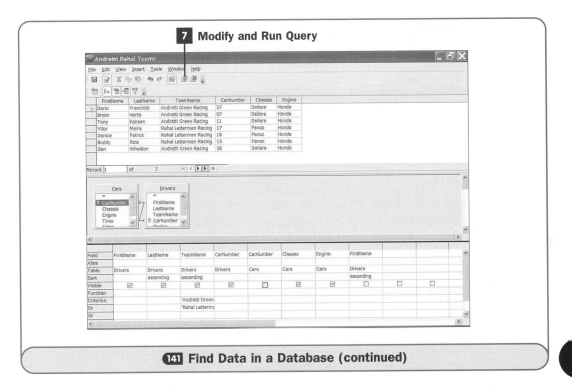

7 Modify and Run Query

141 Find Data in a Database (continued)

141

3 Select Fields

In **Step 1** of the **Query Wizard**, select the first table whose fields you want to search (or view in the resulting report) from the **Tables** list. The fields in that table appear in the **Available fields** list. For the query I'm creating, I want to list all the drivers on the Andretti Green and Rahal Letterman teams, so I'll pull information from the **Drivers** table.

Select a field from the **Available fields** list that you want to search through or display on the resulting report and click > to add the field to the **Fields in the Query** list. Repeat to add more fields from the selected table to the query list. Change to another table if desired and add more fields if you like. I wanted to show information on each driver's car, so I pulled additional data from the **Cars** table. Click **Next**.

▶ **TIP**

To use all the fields from the selected table on the query report, click **>>** instead.

4 Select Sort

On **Step 2** of the **Query Wizard**, choose a field by which to sort the resulting report from the **Sort by** list, and then choose **Ascending** or **Descending** to specify the sort order.

Add additional sorting levels by selecting a field from the **Then by** list, and choosing the sort order—**Ascending** or **Descending**. You can add as many as four sort levels. Click **Next**.

5 Set Criteria

In **Step 3** of the **Query Wizard**, set limits on which records you want in the resulting report. Select a field to search from the **Fields** list, select a **Condition**, and then enter a **Value**. For example, I want to show only drivers on the Andretti Green and Rahal Letterman teams, so I started by selecting **TeamName** (from the **Drivers** table), and then set the other options to search for records where **TeamName** is equal to Andretti Green Racing.

To find a field that's empty, look for one that's **NULL**. If you choose the "like" condition, you can match part of the text using wildcards. For example, I could have used this condition: **TeamName like Rahal***, which searches for "Rahal" at the beginning of the **TeamName** field, followed by any number of characters. Likewise, I could have searched for **Ra?al**, where *Rahal*, *Rajal*, and *Rabal* are all matches.

Because I also want to list the members of the Rahal Letterman team, I selected the **Match any of the following** option, and then set the second condition to search for records with Rahal Letterman in the **TeamName** field. You can set a third search criteria if you like. Click **Next**.

▶ **NOTES**

Unless you have a value field (a field in a table with a number value), you'll automatically skip **Step 4**, where you can choose to display all records, or just a summary (such as a total of all the sales from the North region). **Step 5 Grouping** and **Step 6 Grouping conditions,** when available, allow you to group similar records in the report.

You can change the labels for each field in the query report in **Step 7** by creating "aliases," but this step is optional and often not needed, especially if you use understandable field names when you create your tables.

6 Save the Query

Because a query is a question you can ask over and over, using the current data in a database, you'll want to save your query. For example, because new drivers can be added to a team just for the Indy 500, I can run my query

141

against the database and get an updated report on the current drivers for the Andretti Green and Rahal Letterman teams. In **Step 8** of the **Query Wizard**, type a name for the query in the **Name of the query** box.

You can display the resulting report immediately by selecting the **Display Query** option, but typically you'll want to modify the query first, especially if you're combining data from multiple tables like I am. Choose **Modify Query** and click **Finish.** The query is saved and opened for editing.

7 Modify and Run Query

The tables you selected for the query appear in the middle of the window. (The result of a final query, shown here, appears above the tables.) Below the tables is a pane in which you can control the **Sort**, the searching **Criterion**, and the fields that appear on the report (they have a check mark in the **Visible** box.

If you're pulling data from multiple tables, you'll want to link the fields from each table that match (contain the same data). Being able to link related tables is what makes Base a *relational database* program. Linking shared data from different tables allows you to display related data on a single line in the resulting report. In other words, by linking my two tables, my report will show not only the driver data, but data on the car that particular driver is using, all on one line in the report.

To link two fields, drag a matching field from one table, and drop it on the matching field in the second table. Lines connect the two fields, showing that they are linked. In the example, the **CarNumber** field in the **Cars** table is linked to the **CarNumber** field in the **Drivers** table.

Make any other changes you want and then click the **Run Query** button on the **Query Design** toolbar to run the query and display a report. The report appears at the top of the window. If it's not right, make other changes to the criteria and run the query again.

141

19

Browsing the Internet with Firefox

IN THIS CHAPTER:

The World Wide Web is a collection of pages on the *Internet*; these pages are filled with text, graphics, movies, sound, and animations. Web pages are "linked together" like the strings of a spider web so that you can easily move from one related page to the next. The Web is just one part of the Internet, but it's certainly the most popular part. On the Web, you can find information on just about anything—some of it true, some of not, some of it just opinion. To view a web page, you need an Internet connection and a program called a *web browser* such as Mozilla Firefox.

▶ KEY TERMS

Web browser—A program that allows you to view pages on the World Wide Web.

Internet—A world-wide network of computers, originally linked together by the government for the purpose of sharing information and research.

---

142 Navigate the Web

✔ BEFORE YOU BEGIN	→ SEE ALSO
Just jump right in!	**143** Search the Web
	146 Browse with Tabbed Windows
	148 Bookmark a Favorite Page

When you start Firefox, it displays your Home page—a web page you've arbitrarily selected to view first whenever you launch the browser. (See **147** **Set Your Home Page**.) You move from page to page on the World Wide Web by either clicking a *link* on a web page, or by typing the address of the page you want to view into your web browser (Firefox). After you've viewed a few web pages during a session, you can easily move back to view some previous page if needed.

If you find a web page that's especially interesting, you can *bookmark* it so that you can easily revisit it whenever its information is updated. See **148** **Bookmark a Favorite Page**. You can also save a favorite page and its contents on your hard disk permanently. See **150** **Save a Web Page**.

▶ KEY TERM

Link—A bit of text or a graphic image that, when clicked, causes a particular web page to be displayed. When the mouse pointer is moved over a link, the pointer changes to a hand.

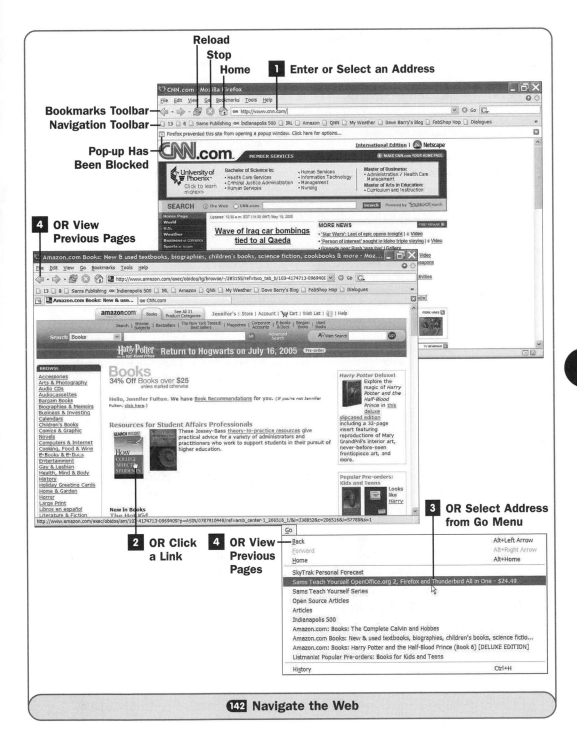

Reload

Stop

Home

1 Enter or Select an Address

Bookmarks Toolbar

Navigation Toolbar

Pop-up Has Been Blocked

4 OR View Previous Pages

3 OR Select Address from Go Menu

2 OR Click a Link

4 OR View Previous Pages

142 Navigate the Web

❶ Enter or Select an Address

To view a particular web page, type its address in the **Location** bar on the **Navigation** toolbar and press **Enter** or click the **Go** button. For example, type **www.samspublishing.com** and press **Enter**. You can also open the **Location** drop-down list and select an address that you've previously typed.

Typically, the new page and its contents replaces the currently viewed page in the browser. But you can set up Firefox to create a tabbed window for each new page if you like, so that you can jump back and forth quickly, between a series of pages you're interested in. See **146 Browse with Tabbed Windows**.

▶ TIPS

To view a page full screen (hiding the menu bar and all the toolbars except the **Navigation** toolbar), choose **View, Full Screen** or press **F11**.

Some web pages automatically display pop-up ads and similar small windows that pop up over a page's content; Firefox will typically block these for you and display a message telling you it is doing so. If you want to display the popup anyway, click the message bar, which appears under the toolbars.

142

If a page has trouble displaying correctly, you can try reloading it. Click the **Reload** button on the **Navigation** toolbar. Stop a page from displaying by clicking the **Stop** button.

❷ OR Click a Link

After a web page is displayed, you can move to a related web page by clicking a *link*. A link typically appears as blue, underlined text, although it can be formatted differently. A link might also appear as a graphic or a button. You can identify a link by moving the mouse pointer over it and watching the pointer change to a hand.

If you've set up Firefox for tabbed browsing, click the link with the middle mouse button or press **Ctrl** as you click to automatically open that page in a new tabbed window. See **146 Browse with Tabbed Windows**.

❸ OR Select Address from Go Menu

To revisit a page you've viewed previously in this browser session, open the **Go** menu and select the web page you want to revisit from the list. To view a page you've visited during some previous viewing session, use the browser's History. See **145 Use History**.

When you return to a previous page, any links you visited typically appear as purple, underlined text, rather than in blue. This color change helps you identify which pages you've looked at already.

4 OR View Previous Pages

To revisit the page you just left, click the **Back** button on the **Navigation** toolbar. To return to the page you were on when you jumped backward, click the **Forward** button. To jump back or forward several pages in your viewing history, click the arrow on the **Back** or **Forward** button and select a page from the list that appears.

To revisit the **Home** page at any time, click the **Home** button on the **Navigation** toolbar.

---

143   Search the Web

✔ BEFORE YOU BEGIN	→ SEE ALSO
142 Navigate the Web	**145** Search a Page
	146 Browse with Tabbed Windows

143

The Web is a wonderful place to learn about lots of different new and interesting things, but to do that, you must find the appropriate pages. Firefox makes it easy for you to search the Web for pages related to whatever topic you choose. Firefox doesn't actually do the searching; instead, it sends your search request to the *search engine* you choose, such as Google or Yahoo!, which then displays a list of matching web pages.

When you're searching the Internet for information on some topic, chances are you'll visit quite a few web pages. Tabbed browsing can help you keep the useful pages open (even displaying the initial results page in its own tabbed window) as you continue to search. See **146** **Browse with Tabbed Windows**.

▶ KEY TERM

Search engine—A website whose primary function is to maintain a searchable database of web pages.

1 Type Search Text

Click in the **Search** bar and type the topic you're interested in, such as **"father's day" crafts**. Typically, I place short phrases in quotation marks, in order to eliminate pages that might contain the word *father's* and the word *day*, but not next to each other.

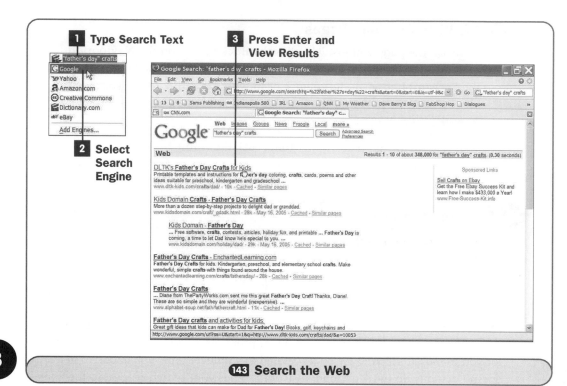

143

143 Search the Web

2 Select Search Engine

The logo for the current search engine appears in front of your search text. For example, you might see a G for Google. If needed, click the logo and select a different *search engine* to use from those listed. For example, you might want to search Amazon.com, eBay, or Dictionary.com.

3 Press Enter and View Results

Press **Enter** to begin your search. A listing of web pages that match your search request appears. Browse this listing and click a *link* to view that page.

▶ TIPS

To search for information related to some text on a web page, select the text, right-click, and choose **Search Web for XXXX** from the context menu.

To add more search engines to the listing, select **Add Engines** from the search engine list shown in Step 2. The Mozilla Web site appears, listing various search engines you can add. Click a link to add that engine to the listing.

You can add the Google toolbar to Firefox, making it even easier to search the Web. See **152 Customize the Browser**.

✔ **BEFORE YOU BEGIN**	→ **SEE ALSO**
142 Navigate the Web	**143** Search the Web

Web pages can be quite lengthy, and sometimes scanning a page to find what you're looking for can be tedious. Luckily, Firefox can help you find specific text on a web page. It can even highlight the search text as it appears throughout a page, making it easy for you to quickly scroll through a web page and find the exact instance of the search text that you're looking for.

1 Choose Edit, Find in This Page

To begin a search on a web page, choose **Edit, Find in This Page** from the menu bar or press **Ctrl+F**. The **Find** bar appears at the *bottom* of the browser window.

▶ **TIP**

To search the text within a framed area of the page, click within the frame, and then begin your search.

144

2 Type Search Text

In the **Find** box, type the word or phrase you want to search for. As you type, the first occurrence of that bit of text is highlighted on the page.

▶ **NOTE**

If you want to find an exact match (in uppercase and lowercase letters) to the search text as you typed it, enable the **Match case** option.

3 Click Find Next or Highlight

To find the next occurrence of the search text, click the **Find Next** button in the **Find** bar at the bottom of the browser window. To find a previous occurrence of the search text, click **Find Previous**. To highlight all occurrences of the search text, click **Highlight**, as I've done here. Click **Highlight** again to turn the highlighting off.

When you're through searching, click the **X** at the left end of the **Find** bar to hide it again.

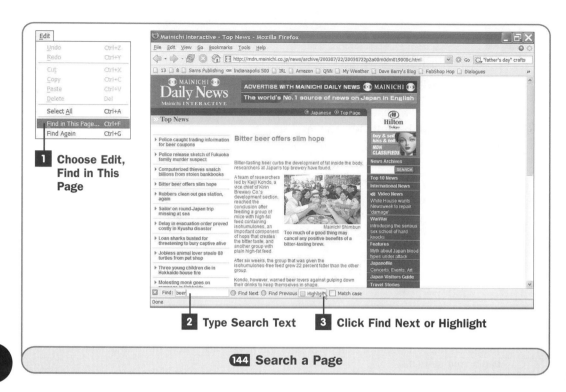

1 Choose Edit, Find in This Page

2 Type Search Text   **3** Click Find Next or Highlight

145   **(144)** Search a Page

145 Use History

✔ **BEFORE YOU BEGIN**

(142) Navigate the Web

After browsing the Web and viewing many different pages, you might find yourself wishing you could return to some previously viewed page and look at it again. The trouble is, you don't exactly remember the Web site on which you saw the page. Luckily, Firefox maintains a history of the web pages you've viewed, and you can use that history to revisit a previously viewed page.

Firefox normally maintains a nine-day history, including today. You can maintain a larger or smaller history file as desired (a smaller history file takes up less room on the hard disk). To change the history file size, choose **Tools, Options** and on the **Privacy** page, under **History**, set the **Remember visited pages for the last XX days** to the value you want to use and click **OK**.

Choose View, Sidebar, History

Choose **View, Sidebar, History** from the menu bar, or press **Ctrl+H**. The **History** sidebar appears on the left side of the browser window.

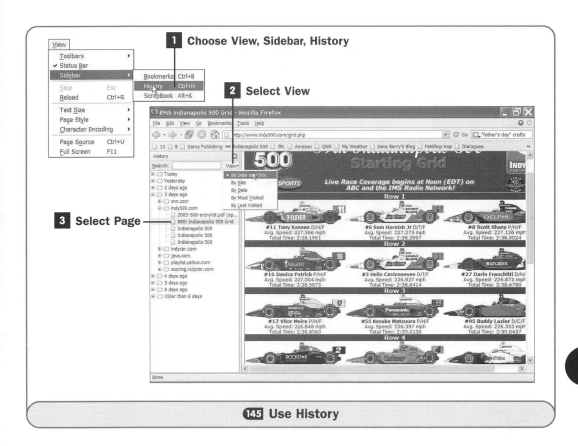

1 Choose View, Sidebar, History

2 Select View

3 Select Page

145 Use History

2 Select View

Open the **View** menu at the top of the **History** sidebar and select how you want the history displayed, such as **By Date and Site**.

3 Select Page

If needed, open a folder in the **History** sidebar to display its contents by clicking its plus sign. For example, open the folder of pages visited three days ago by clicking the plus sign in front of **3 days ago**. Continue this process of opening folders until the page you want to visit is listed.

Click the name of the page you want to revisit. The web page is displayed in the browser window.

▶ NOTE

Although Firefox maintains a history of pages you've visited, it's only a listing of the web pages' addresses and not their content. When a page is redisplayed, its current content is shown. If you want to save the content of a page for viewing later (and not have it change), see **150 Save a Web Page**.

You can search the **History** listing for a particular page if you like; just click in the **Search** box on the **History** sidebar, type the search text, and press **Enter**. Firefox searches its list of web page titles for a match.

---

146 | **Browse with Tabbed Windows**

✔ BEFORE YOU BEGIN	→ SEE ALSO
142 Navigate the Web	**143** Search the Web
	152 Customize the Browser

As you browse the Internet, you might encounter some pages you'd like to keep open so that you can refer to them again, even as you continue to look around. Firefox allows you to display a linked web page in a tabbed window, and to switch from window to window by clicking the window's tab.

In this task, you'll learn several different ways in which you can open a web page in a tabbed window. You can customize whether a tabbed window is opened automatically in certain instances by choosing **Tools**, **Options** and displaying the **Tabbed Browsing** pane. For example, you can have Firefox display a page in a new tab if you type its address in the **Location** bar, or if you initiate a search from the **Search** bar. See **152** **Customize the Browser**.

1 Right-Click and Choose Open Link in New Tab

One way you can open a link in a tabbed window is to right-click the link and then choose **Open Link in New Tab** from the context menu.

A tab for the current window *and* for the new window appear on the **Tab** bar at the top of the browser window. Click the tab of the window you want to view.

▶ TIPS

Scroll between tabbed windows with the keyboard by pressing **Ctrl+Page Up** (or **Ctrl+Tab**), **Ctrl+Page Down** (or **Ctrl+Shift+Tab**).

You can open a set of tabbed windows and save the collection in a bookmark folder so that you can easily open those same windows (with current data) at a later time. See **148** **Bookmark a Favorite Page**.

You can also set a series of tabbed windows to your Home "page," and have them open all automatically when you start Firefox. See **147** **Set Your Home Page**.

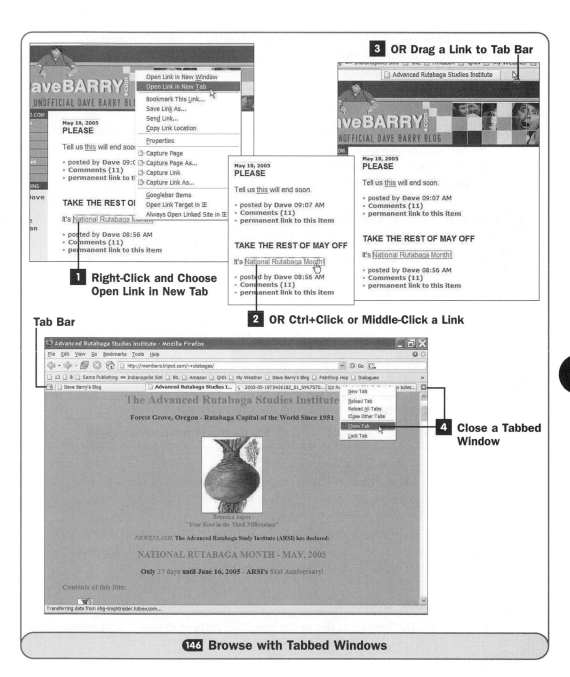

3 OR Drag a Link to Tab Bar

1 Right-Click and Choose Open Link in New Tab

Tab Bar

2 OR Ctrl+Click or Middle-Click a Link

4 Close a Tabbed Window

146

146 Browse with Tabbed Windows

2 OR Ctrl+Click or Middle-Click a Link

Another way to open a link in a tabbed window is to press **Ctrl** and click the link.

Assuming that you've enabled the **Load middle-clicked URLs in new tabs** option on the **Tabbed Browsing** pane (choose **Tools**, **Options** and display the

Tabbed Browsing pane to see the options available for tabbed browsing), you can also click a link with the middle button of your mouse (even if the "middle button" is a scroll button) to open that link in a tabbed window.

3 OR Drag a Link to Tab Bar

If the **Tab** bar is visible (in other words, you have at least two tabbed windows open), you can drag a link and drop it on an open area of the bar to open that link in a new tabbed window. If you drop the link on an existing tab, the contents of that tabbed window is replaced by the linked page.

4 Close a Tabbed Window

To close a tabbed window, click its **Close** button (the **X**), or right-click the tab you want to close and choose **Close Tab** from the context menu. To close all tabs but one, right-click the tab you want to keep open and choose **Close Other Tabs** from the context menu.

When you close multiple tabbed windows, you might see a warning reminding you of what you are doing. Click **Close Tabs** to continue.

---

147 Set Your Home Page

✔ **BEFORE YOU BEGIN**	→ **SEE ALSO**
142 Navigate the Web	**146** Browse with Tabbed Windows

As you learned in **142 Navigate the Web**, when you start Firefox, it displays your Home page automatically. You don't have to set your home page to a single page; instead, you can set it to a series of tabbed windows and have them all open for you whenever you start Firefox. You can also set Firefox to open with a blank page, which might be useful if you have a slow Internet connection and you'd like to fully load the program before you begin browsing.

1 Choose Tools, Options

Choose **Tools, Options** from the menu bar. The **Options** dialog box appears.

▶ TIPS

If you want to set the home page to a series of tabbed windows, you might want to open those windows first, before beginning this task. (If the tabbed windows you want to use as a home "page" are already saved in a single bookmark folder, you can skip this part.)

Likewise, if you want to set a single home page, you might want to display it first in the browser window.

1 Choose Tools, Options   **2** Click General

3 Set Options and Click OK

Choose a Bookmarked Page or Set of Pages

147 Set Your Home Page

---

2 Click General

Click the **General** button in the left pane to display the options on the **General** tab of the **Options** dialog box.

3 Set Options and Click OK

Select the home page option you want, and click **OK**.

- You can set the home page to the current page in your browser (or *pages*, if you've already displayed them in tabbed windows) by clicking **Use Current Page.**

- Set the home page to a page (or pages) you've already bookmarked by clicking **Use Bookmark**. (See **148** **Bookmark a Favorite Page** for more about bookmarks.) The **Set Home Page** dialog box appears; click a single page or a folder (to set the home page to a series of tabbed windows). Click **OK** to return to the **Options** dialog box.

- Set the home page to a blank page by clicking **Use Blank Page**.

---

148 **Bookmark a Favorite Page**

✔ BEFORE YOU BEGIN	→ SEE ALSO
142 Navigate the Web	**146** Browse with Tabbed Windows
	147 Set Your Home Page
	149 Manage Your Bookmarks
	150 Save a Web Page

148

When you find an especially interesting or helpful web page, you can bookmark it to make it easier for you to revisit that page at a later time. For example, you might bookmark a favorite news site so that you can check what's happening each morning. If you happen to have multiple tabbed windows open, you can quickly bookmark each of them.

You can save your favorite bookmarks to the **Bookmarks** toolbar. Each bookmark added to this toolbar appears as a button; click a button to display the associated web page. Thus, the **Bookmarks** toolbar allows you to visit your favorite places on the Web quickly and easily. The **Bookmarks** toolbar normally appears just under the **Navigation** bar; to display it, choose **View**, **Toolbars**, **Bookmarks** from the menu.

This task shows you how to bookmark a web page. You can also bookmark a live feed, such as updated RSS news headlines. Just navigate to the web page containing the live feed and click the **Live Bookmark** icon (an orange sound horn), located at the right end of the **Status** bar on pages that contain a live feed. Select the live feed you want to bookmark from the list that appears. You might be prompted to select the program you want to process the feed, such as NewzCrawler or Sage.

▶ **NOTE**

Bookmarks created in another web browser (such as Internet Explorer) are automatically imported into Firefox when you install Firefox. If your existing bookmarks were not imported, choose **File, Import** to import them now.

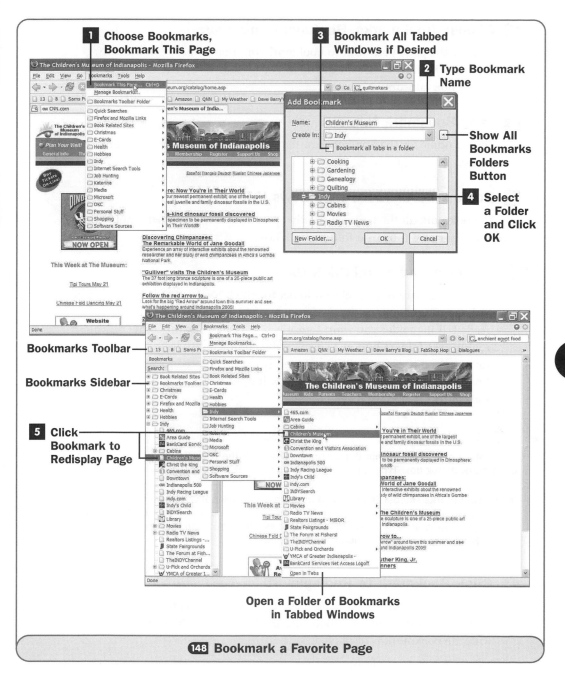

1 Choose Bookmarks, Bookmark This Page

3 Bookmark All Tabbed Windows if Desired

2 Type Bookmark Name

Show All Bookmarks Folders Button

4 Select a Folder and Click OK

Bookmarks Toolbar

Bookmarks Sidebar

5 Click Bookmark to Redisplay Page

Open a Folder of Bookmarks in Tabbed Windows

1 Choose Bookmarks, Bookmark This Page

Display the page you want to bookmark and then choose **Bookmarks, Bookmark This Page** from the menu, or press **Ctrl+D**. The **Add Bookmark** dialog box appears.

2 Type Bookmark Name

Type a name for the bookmark in the **Name** box, or accept the default page name.

3 Bookmark All Tabbed Windows if Desired

To bookmark all the pages currently open in tabbed windows, enable the **Bookmark all tabs in a folder** check box.

4 Select a Folder and Click OK

Open the **Create in** list, select a folder in which to save the bookmark and click **OK**. Click the plus sign in front of a folder to display its subfolders if needed. If the folder you want to use is not listed, click the **Show all the bookmarks folders** button to display the complete list of bookmark folders at the bottom of the dialog box and then select the desired folder. If you choose the **Bookmarks** folder, the bookmark will appear as a button on the **Bookmarks** toolbar.

148

▶ TIPS

To create a new folder within the current folder, click the **New Folder** button in the **Add Bookmark** dialog box. Type a name for the new folder and click **OK** to create it.

If the **Bookmarks** sidebar is displayed in the browser window, you can drag an address from the **Locations** bar and drop it on the appropriate folder in the **Bookmarks** listing of web pages you've already saved to create a bookmark. You can also drop the bookmark on the **Bookmarks** toolbar to add it as a button.

5 Click Bookmark to Redisplay It

To use a bookmark you've saved, open the **Bookmarks** menu, open the folder the bookmark is in, and then click the bookmark. The web page associated with the bookmark is displayed.

To open all the bookmarks in a folder within tabbed windows, select **Open in Tabs** at the bottom of that folder's submenu on the **Bookmarks** menu.

▶ **TIPS**

If a bookmark appears on the **Bookmarks** toolbar, click its button to visit that page.

Display your bookmarks in the **Bookmarks** sidebar by choosing **View, Sidebar, Bookmarks** or pressing **Ctrl+B**. Then click a bookmark to display the page associated with it.

To locate a bookmark, type all or part of its name in the **Search** box located at the top of the **Bookmarks** sidebar.

---

149 **Manage Your Bookmarks**

✔ **BEFORE YOU BEGIN**

142 Navigate the Web
148 Bookmark a Favorite Page

It's not soon after you start creating bookmarks that you realize you should probably start organizing them better. You might rename a bookmark, for example, to make it easier to identify. You might also move the bookmark into a different folder to make it easier to find. You can perform other maintenance tasks as well, such as refining the address the bookmark points to, deleting unwanted bookmarks, and sorting the bookmarks list.

149

▶ **TIP**

You can perform most of these maintenance tasks using the **Bookmarks** sidebar, rather than displaying the **Bookmarks Manager**. To display the sidebar, choose **View, Sidebar, Bookmarks**. Just right-click the bookmark you want to change, and select the appropriate command from the menu, such as **Delete**.

1 **Choose Bookmarks, Manage Bookmarks**

Choose **Bookmarks, Manage Bookmarks** from the menu. The **Bookmarks Manager** window appears.

2 **Select Bookmark**

If needed, click the plus sign in front of a folder in the left pane to display its bookmarks in the right pane. Click the bookmark you want to change.

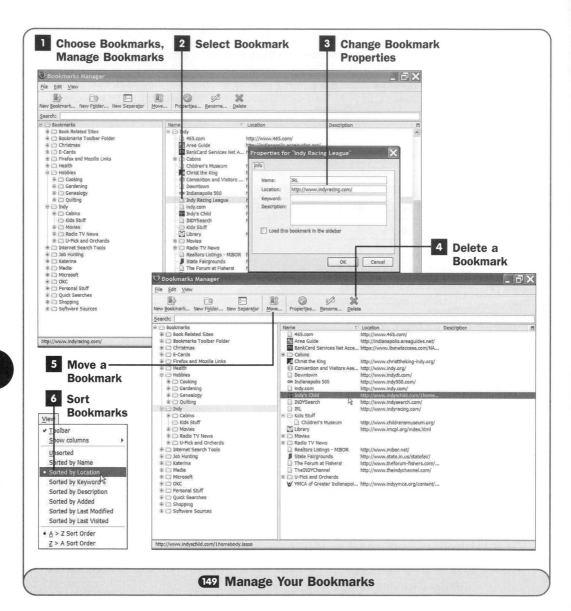

1 Choose Bookmarks, Manage Bookmarks

2 Select Bookmark

3 Change Bookmark Properties

4 Delete a Bookmark

5 Move a Bookmark

6 Sort Bookmarks

149

149 Manage Your Bookmarks

3 Change Bookmark Properties

Click the **Properties** button in the toolbar at the top of the **Bookmarks Manager** window. The **Properties** dialog box appears. Change the bookmark's name by typing a new name in the **Name** box. Edit the **Location** (the URL, or address, of the web page) if desired. You can type a **Keyword** and/or a **Description**, and use this information when you sort the bookmarks list. Click **OK** to accept the changes to the bookmark.

▶ **NOTE**

Enable the **Load this bookmark in the sidebar** check box in the **Properties** dialog box to display the associated web page in the sidebar. You might do this with a search engine bookmark, for example, to keep its results page handy in the sidebar as you display the links you click on the right, in the main window (this assumes the web page recognizes that it's in a sidebar—some pages do not, and simply display the result of a clicked link in the sidebar).

4 Delete a Bookmark

To remove the selected bookmark, click the **Delete** button in the toolbar at the top of the **Bookmarks Manager** window. The bookmark is removed from the list.

5 Move a Bookmark

To move the selected bookmark, drag it up or down in the listing. If you place a bookmark in the **Bookmarks Toolbar** folder, the bookmark appears as a button on the **Bookmarks** toolbar in the main browser window. You can also move a bookmark by selecting it, clicking the **Move** button in the toolbar at the top of the **Bookmarks Manager** window, selecting a folder for the bookmark from the **Move to** list that appears, and clicking **OK**.

6 Sort Bookmarks

Normally, bookmarks and folders are sorted alphabetically. To sort them in a different order, open the **View** menu in the **Bookmarks Manager** window, and select the sort order you want from those listed. For example, you can sort the listing by Web address by choosing **Sorted by Location**. If you choose **Sorted by Name**, you can select **A > Z Sort Order** or **Z > A Sort Order.** You can also click the column headings at the right side of the window to sort the listing by that column. The entire bookmarks listing is resorted, using the sort order you chose. When you're done organizing your bookmarks, close the **Bookmarks Manager** window.

150

---

150 | **Save a Web Page**

✔ **BEFORE YOU BEGIN**

142 Navigate the Web

If you're browsing the Internet for information and you find an especially useful web page, you might want to save its contents to you computer's hard disk for further review. If you simply bookmark the page, you can return at any time, but that does not guarantee that the page's information will still be the same or that the page will still be available.

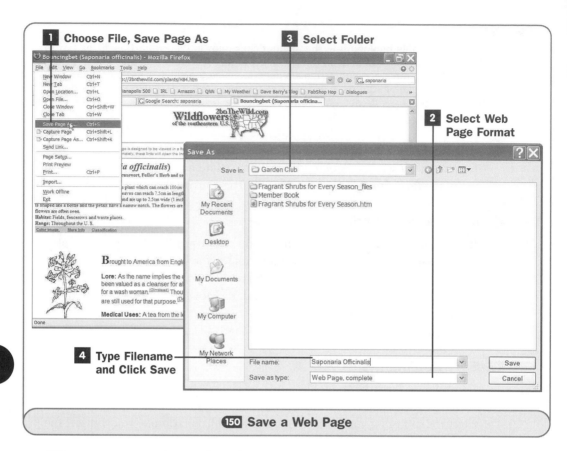

150

150 Save a Web Page

When you save a web page by following the steps in this task, sometimes all the graphics are not saved, even when you choose to save them with the page. This is not an error, but rather a reflection of the web page's design. If you want to ensure that all graphics are saved, you might want to install and use Scrapbook, a Firefox extension. See **152 Customize the Browser**. Scrapbook also lets you capture a portion of a web page, a linked web page without displaying it, or just an image if you like.

1 Choose File, Save Page As

Display the web page you want to save to your hard disk. If you want to save the contents of a web page currently displayed in a frame, click within that frame first. Then choose **File, Save Page As** from the menu bar. The **Save As** dialog box appears.

2 Select Web Page Format

Open the **Save as type** list and select the web page format you want to use. If you choose the **web page, HTML only** option, embedded graphics are not saved. If you choose the **Web Page, complete** option, the graphics and text are saved in a separate file. If you choose the **Text Files** option, just the text is saved.

▶ TIPS

If you've installed the Scrapbook extension, you can use the **File, Capture Page** command to save a web page and all its graphics. To capture files linked to the page such as sound or movie files, choose **File, Capture Page As**.

To save just a web page graphic with Scrapbook, right-click the image and choose **Save Image As** from the context menu. You can also send the image in an email, use it as Windows wallpaper, and copy the image to the Windows Clipboard—choose the desired option from the context menu.

3 Select Folder

Open the **Save in** list and select the folder in which you want to save the web page.

4 Type Filename and Click Save

Type a name for the web page in the **File name** text box and click **Save**. The web page is saved to the hard disk. To view it again, choose **File, Open File** from the menu, select the web page you saved, and click **Open**.

151

---

151 Manage Your Downloads

✔ BEFORE YOU BEGIN

142 Navigate the Web

Some web pages provide links to files you can copy (download) to your computer. Rather than wait for a download to finish, you might want to continue working in Firefox, browsing the Internet. The **Download Manager** allows you to do just that, because it keeps track of the file(s) you download and their statistics as you work. For example, at any time during a download session, you can display the **Download Manager** and see just how much of a large file has been copied to your system and how much longer it might take to complete the job. If there's a problem during the download, you can retry the process with a simple click of a button. You can even pause and resume the process if downloading is slowing down your computer too much.

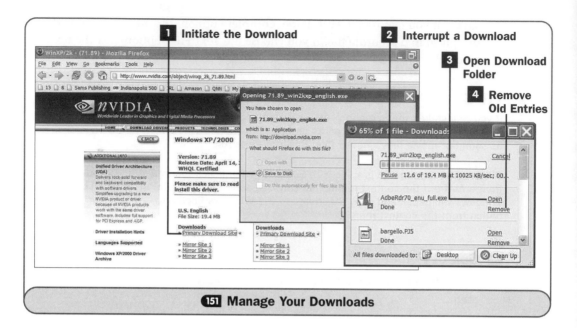

1 Initiate the Download   **2** Interrupt a Download

3 Open Download Folder

4 Remove Old Entries

151 Manage Your Downloads

151

▶ **TIP**

Files are downloaded to the Desktop by default, but you can place them in a different folder if you like. Choose **Tools, Options**, click the **Downloads** button, and select the download options you want, such as which folder you want to use for downloading and whether you want **Download Manager** to appear automatically every time you select a file to download.

1 Initiate the Download

A download is typically initiated by clicking a link to a file. You might also initiate a download by right-clicking an object or link and choosing **Save Image As** or **Save Link As**. With some files, you'll be asked if you want to open them or save them on your system. If so, click **Save to Disk** and click **OK** to start the download.

After a download begins, the **Download Manager** automatically appears. You can use it to pause the download, for example, or you can simply switch back to the main Firefox window and keep working. **Download Manager** keeps track of what's going on and if there are any problems, so you can check back later whenever you want.

▶ **NOTE**

After a download is finished, you can redisplay the **Download Manager** to review download statistics by choosing **Tools, Download**.

2 Interrupt a Download

If a download is still in progress, you can pause it temporarily by selecting the download from those listed and clicking **Pause**. Click **Resume** to pick up the download where you left off.

To cancel a download completely, select the listing and click **Cancel**. To retry a failed download, select the listing and click **Retry**.

3 Open Download Folder

After a download is complete, you can open the file in its associated program (for example, open a zipped file in WinZip) by clicking **Open**.

4 Remove Old Entries

The **Download Manager** keeps track of all of your downloads until you remove them from its listing. To remove a single download listing, select it and click **Remove**.

To remove all entries in the **Download Manager**, click **Clean Up**.

152

152 Customize the Browser

✔ BEFORE YOU BEGIN	→ SEE ALSO
Just jump right in!	**145** Use History
	146 Browse with Tabbed Windows
	147 Set Your Home Page
	151 Manage Your Downloads

You don't have to use Firefox to browse the Web just like everyone else; instead, you can customize it to fit the way you work. In addition to changing options, you can install *extensions*, *plug-ins*, and *themes* that complement the web browser. For example, you might install the Googlebar extension, which helps you refine your Google searches, or the Acrobat Reader plug-in, which displays PDF documents within the browser window.

▶ KEY TERMS

Extensions—Small add-on programs that add specific functionality to Firefox.

Plug-in—A program that can be called by Firefox to open, play, or display a file of a particular type, such as a sound or movie file.

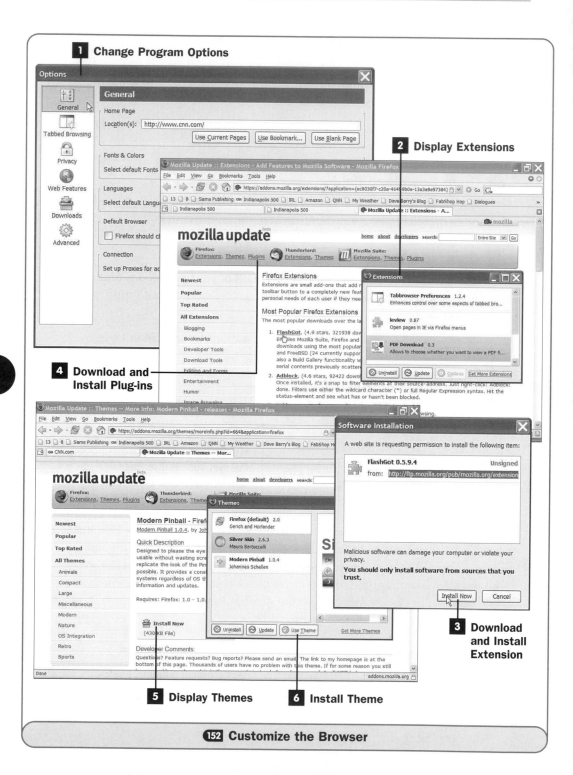

1 Change Program Options

2 Display Extensions

4 Download and Install Plug-ins

3 Download and Install Extension

5 Display Themes

6 Install Theme

152 Customize the Browser

1 Change Program Options

Choose **Tools, Options** from the menu bar. The **Options** dialog box appears. Click the button in the left pane for the type of option you want to change:

- **General**   Here you can set your Home page, select default fonts and colors for web pages that don't specify them, set the default language for the browser to use, allow Firefox to check whether it is the default web browser, and set up *proxies* (intermediaries that try to complete a task before passing it on to the browser).

- **Tabbed Browsing**   Here you can tell Firefox when to automatically create tabbed windows and other options. See **146 Browse with Tabbed Windows**.

- **Privacy**   Here you can set the number of days of history to track, have Firefox save data normally entered into Web forms and log-in screens, limit the size of the **Download Manager** history, control how *cookies* are handled, and set the size of the browser *cache*.

▶ KEY TERMS

Cookies—Information stored on your computer by a Web site, such as your preferences when viewing data on that site.

Cache—A temporary storage area on your computer for web pages you visit so that they can be displayed more quickly should you visit them again.

- **Web Features**   Here you can tell Firefox to block popup windows, stop Web sites from installing programs on your system, block images from displaying, and stop Java and JavaScript programs from running.

- **Downloads**   Here you can pick the folder into which you want to save downloads, prevent **Download Manager** from appearing automatically, and associate various file types with the programs you want to handle them, such as selecting the movie viewer you want to use to view movie files.

- **Advanced**   Here you can set options that make Firefox easier to use if you're disabled, control how images and text are displayed in the browser, control how tabbed browsing works by default, allow Firefox to check for new updates automatically, and establish how you want the browser to send and receive secure data.

Options associated with the button you select appear on the right side of the **Options** dialog box. Set options as desired and click **OK**.

2 Display Extensions

Choose **Tools, Extensions** from the menu. The **Extensions** dialog box appears, displaying a list of currently installed extensions. You can select an installed extension and click **Uninstall** to remove it, or select the extension and click **Update** to check the Web for a possible update to that extension.

Click **Get More Extensions**. The **Mozilla Update** web page appears, displaying a list of the most popular Firefox extensions. To display all extensions of a particular type, click that type in the list on the left. For example, perhaps you want to see all the **Blogging** extensions. When you find an extension you're interested in, click its link. A full description of the extension appears on another page, with some images of the extension in action.

3 Download and Install Extension

Click **Install Now.** The **Software Installation** dialog box appears. Click **Install Now** to download and install the extension.

The **Download Manager** appears so that you can review the download if you like. After the extension has been downloaded to your system, close and restart Firefox to complete the installation.

4 Download and Install Plug-ins

At the top of the **Mozilla Update** page, click the **Firefox Plugins** link. A list of plug-ins for Firefox appears. In the **Download** section for the plug-in you want, click the appropriate link for your operating system.

If prompted, click **Save to Disk** to download the plug-in, and click **OK**. After the plug-in is downloaded, follow the program's instructions to install it.

5 Display Themes

At the top of the **Mozilla Update** page, click the **Firefox Themes** link. A list of the most popular Firefox themes appears. To display all themes of a particular type, click that type from the list on the left.

When you find a theme you like, click its image to read reviews of your selected theme and to view more sample images. Click **Install Now.** The theme is downloaded to your system.

6 Install Theme

The **Themes** dialog box appears. Select the theme and click **Use Theme** to install it. To complete the installation, close and restart Firefox.

152

20

Emailing with Thunderbird

IN THIS CHAPTER:

In today's hustle and bustle world, instant communication is almost a given. Gone are the days when a person would write a letter, mail it, and then wait days and even weeks for an answer. Now, when you need to share some important information and get an answer right away, you can exchange *emails*. To send and receive emails, you need an Internet connection and an email program such as Mozilla's Thunderbird.

▶ KEY TERM

Email—An electronic message sent over the Internet using an email program.

An email message can contain more than text. You can attach images and other files to the message to send them along to a co-worker or friend. To send an email to someone, you'll need their email address, such as **best.friend@faraway.net**.

---

153   Create an Email Account

✔ BEFORE YOU BEGIN	→ SEE ALSO
Just jump right in!	154 Get Your Email
	156 Send a Message

153

Before using Thunderbird, you need to provide it with information regarding the Internet service you use for email. Specifically, you must tell Thunderbird your email address (such as **jennifer.fulton@fake.net**), the name of your incoming and outgoing mail server (**pop.fake.net** and **smtp.fake.net**), the server type (such as POP or IMAP), and the login and password you use to access your mail service. If you don't know this information, obtain it from your email service, Web service, or your Internet Service Provider before setting up the email account.

▶ TIPS

If you use multiple email services, you must repeat these steps to set up each email account. In step 1, the **Account Settings** dialog box appears instead of the **Account Wizard**. Click the **Add Account** button to display the wizard so that you can create a new email account.

When you set up different accounts, Thunderbird assumes you'll use the same outgoing server for all of them. If your secondary service has problems passing along messages sent from a non-compatible email address, select **Outgoing Server (SMTP)** in the **Account Settings** dialog box and click **Advanced** to enter the outgoing server information for that second account. After setting up the additional outgoing server, display the **Server Settings** page for that account in the **Account Settings** dialog box, click **Advanced**, and select the secondary outgoing server.

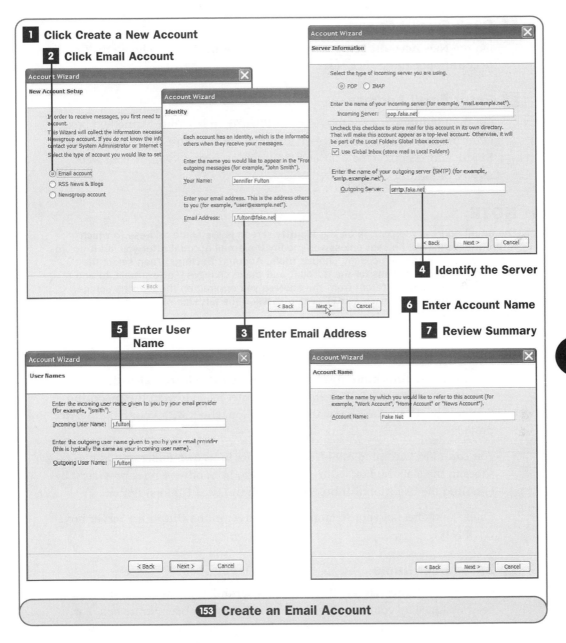

1 Click Create a New Account

2 Click Email Account

4 Identify the Server

6 Enter Account Name

7 Review Summary

5 Enter User Name

3 Enter Email Address

153

153 Create an Email Account

1 Click Create a New Account

When Thunderbird first starts, it displays the **Local Folders** page with links to common tasks. Click **Create a new account** in the list on the right. If you don't see the **Create a new account** link, click **Local Folders** in the **Folders** list on the left to display the link, or choose **Tools, Account Settings** from the menu bar and click **New Account**. The **Account Wizard** appears.

2 Click Email Account

On the **New Account Setup** screen of the **Account Wizard**, choose the **Email account** option and click **Next**.

3 Enter Email Address

On the **Identity** screen of the **Account Wizard**, in the **Your Name** text box, enter the name you want to use to identify your messages to others. In the **Email Address** box, type your email address as given to you by your web service or ISP. Click **Next**.

▶ NOTE

The email address you provide on the **Identity** screen is the same address to which return messages will be sent unless you modify the email account after you set it up. To modify an existing email account, choose **Tools, Account Settings**. Then select the appropriate page of options for the account and make changes. For example, to add a reply-to address that's different from the address you entered on the **Identity** screen, click the account name (such as ATT or Comcast) on the left side of the **Account Settings** dialog box.

153

4 Identify the Server

On the **Server Information** screen of the **Account Wizard**, select the incoming email server type (POP or IMAP), and enter its address in the **Incoming Server** box. If you don't know this information, check with your email service provider.

You can place incoming mail from this server in its own folder or add messages to the global inbox (with email coming from other service providers) by enabling the **Use Global Inbox (store mail in Local Folders)** option.

Enter the address of your outgoing email server in the **Outgoing Server** box. Click **Next**.

5 Enter User Name

On the **User Names** screen of the Account Wizard, type the user name you've been assigned by your email service in the **Incoming User Name** box. For example, type `jennifer.fulton@fake.net` or j.fulton. In most cases, this same name should be entered in the **Outgoing User Name** box as well. If you don't know this information, check with your email service provider. Click **Next**.

6 Enter Account Name

On the **Account Name** screen in the **Account Wizard**, type a name for this email account in the **Account Name** box and click **Next.** This name helps you identify this email account from others you might set up so that you can use any name you like (I typically use the name of the email service provider such as ATT, Comcast, Company Email, Google, and so on).

7 Review Summary

Review the summary of your settings. If needed, click **Back** to return to a previous screen to change a setting. Enable the **Download messages now** option if you want Thunderbird to check this account for email now (this will happen anyway if this is your first email account). When you're ready, click **Finish** to save the email account.

---

154 Get Your Email

✔ BEFORE YOU BEGIN	→ SEE ALSO
153 Create an Email Account	**156** Send a Message

154

After setting up an email account, as explained in **153 Create an Email Account**, you're ready to begin using Thunderbird to manage your email. The first thing you'll probably want to do is to check and see if you have any new messages. After you receive an email message, you can read through it, reply to it, forward it to someone else, and add the person who sent you the message to your address book.

You can import mail from your old email program if you like, or you can start fresh in Thunderbird and import only new messages as described in this task. To import mail from another program, choose **Tools, Import** from the menu. In the **Import** dialog box, select **Mail** and click **Next.** Select your old email program from the next screen and click **Next** again. You'll see a message telling you how many messages were imported into Thunderbird; click **Finish**.

1 Click Get Mail

By default, Thunderbird checks for new messages every 10 minutes and notifies you if there are any new ones. In most cases, Thunderbird also retrieves those messages for you. However, to retrieve new email messages *now* instead of waiting for 10 minutes, click the **Get Mail** button on the **Mail** toolbar.

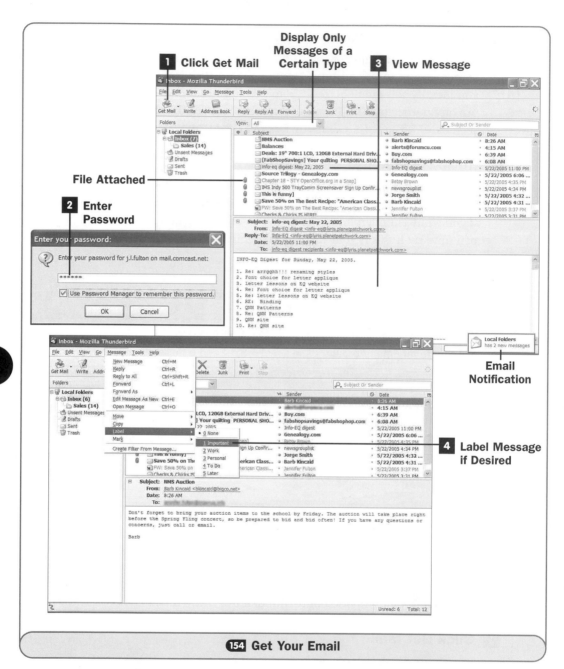

1 Click Get Mail

Display Only Messages of a Certain Type

3 View Message

File Attached

2 Enter Password

Email Notification

4 Label Message if Desired

154 Get Your Email

▶ **NOTES**

To change how often email is checked, choose **Tools, Account Settings**, and display the **Server Settings** page for an account. Then change the value in the **Check for new messages every XX minutes** box. To automatically retrieve new mail, enable the **Automatically download new messages** option as well.

If you have multiple email accounts set up, all email is typically retrieved when you click **Get Mail**. However, if you've set up email accounts that are not linked to the main account, click the arrow on the **Get Mail** button and select the account whose mail you want to retrieve.

You can link an email account to the main account by clicking the **Advanced** button on the account's **Server Settings** page in the **Account Settings** dialog box and enabling the **Include this server when getting new mail** option.

2 Enter Password

The first time you get mail from an account during a session, you'll be prompted for your password. This is the password your email service provider gave you so that you could access your email. Type your password in the text box and click **OK**.

New messages are retrieved, and a notification appears on the status bar. The number of messages in the current folder, along with the number that have not yet been read, also appears on the status bar.

▶ **TIPS**

If you don't want to have to type in your password each time you retrieve email, enable the **Use Password Manager to remember the password** option.

The email notification appears even if you're working in some other program and not Thunderbird, so you'll always know when you get a new message. Click the link within the notification to change over to Thunderbird to view (and download, if needed) your messages.

3 View Message

Typically, incoming messages are placed in the **Inbox** folder, although you can create subfolders for special messages and have messages directed to those folders. (See **161 Organize Incoming Mail**.) So, if needed, click the folder that contains the message you want to read. Messages in that folder appear in a list on the right side of the Thunderbird window.

Unread messages appear in bold; the number of unread messages in the current folder appears in the status bar. To view a message, click its header. The message content appears in a viewing pane below the message header listing. You can change the location and size of this viewing pane by selecting the view you want to use from the **View**, **Layout** menu.

Some messages contain images that are not displayed; if you want to view such images, click the **Show Images** button that appears just above the view pane.

Some messages have files attached to them. These messages are identified with a small paper clip icon in front of their subject line in the message header listing. When you view a message with file(s) attached, the attachments are listed below the message text in the view pane. See **158** **Attach a File to a Message** for help in viewing and saving such attachments.

4 Label Message if Desired

If you want, you can label a message as important, work related, personal, and so on. Each label type is a different color, and when you assign a label to a message, the message's header appears in that color, making the message easy to identify.

With the message still selected, choose **Message**, **Label**, and then select the label type from the submenu that appears. For example, if you label a message as important, then its header appears in red. Sort messages by their label by choosing **View**, **Sort By**, **Label** from the menu.

To display only messages of a particular label, open the **View** list box just above the message headers and select that label type such as **Personal**. You can also use the **View** list to limit the display of messages in other ways—for example, you can display messages only from "people you know" (people listed in the address book). See **155** **Find a Message**.

---

155 Find a Message

✔ **BEFORE YOU BEGIN**

154 Get Your Email

It won't take too long before you receive so many email messages that you'll find it difficult to just scroll through and locate the one message you want to read right now. Luckily, Thunderbird makes it easy for you to locate a specific message by searching through the message headers, the sender information, the subject line, and even the message text itself.

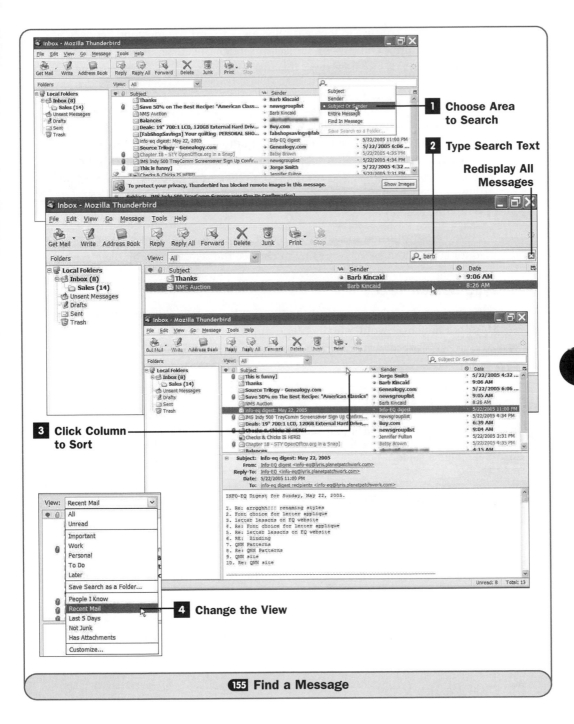

1 Choose Area to Search

2 Type Search Text

Redisplay All Messages

3 Click Column to Sort

4 Change the View

155 Find a Message

Another method you can use to locate a message is to sort the message headers. You can sort them alphabetically by subject or sender, of course, as well as in a variety of other ways as you'll learn in this task.

1 Choose Area to Search

The portion of each message that will be searched appears in faint text within the **Search** box on the **Search** bar. For example, it might be set to **Subject or Sender**, which searches the subject line and the sender field of each message in the current folder. You can search a different message area instead by clicking the **Magnifying Glass** button in front of the **Search** box and selecting the area to search.

After you select an area to search such as **Entire Message**, that area will be used for subsequent searches until you change the selection again.

2 Type Search Text

Click in the **Search** box and type the text or phrase you want to search for. Messages matching your search criteria appear in the listing.

155 ▶ TIPS

To redisplay all message headers after performing a search, click the **X** that appears at the right end of the **Search** box.

To place the headers that match your search in an email folder of their own, click the **Magnifying Glass** button while the results of your search are still displayed, and choose **Save Search as a Folder**.

3 Click Column to Sort

To sort your messages so that you can find a particular one, click the column heading by which you want to sort. For example, to sort the messages by **Sender**, click that column. If you click the column again, messages are sorted in reverse alphabetical order. Here, I'm sorting by **Subject** line.

▶ TIP

To sort messages by a field that's not displayed, choose **View, Sort by** from the menu and then select a sort option from the submenu that appears.

4 Change the View

Another way to quickly locate an email image is to change the view. For example, you learned in 154 **Get Your Email**, how to label messages and then display only messages with a particular label. Open the **View** list on the **Search** bar and select the view you want.

In addition to displaying only messages with a particular label such as *Important*, you can use the **View** list to display only mail you haven't read yet, recent mail (from the last two days), mail from the last five days, mail from people in your **Contacts** list, email with attached files, and email that's not identified as junk. If you choose **Customize** from the **View** list, you can set up your own criteria and create a custom view—for example, a view that shows only messages from your family or messages that are replies to messages you've sent.

---

156 | **Send a Message**

→ **SEE ALSO**

157 Reply or Forward a Message
159 Add New Contacts

When you have a quick message or important news to share, you can send out an *email*. To send an email message, you'll need to know the recipient's email address. Typically, you're sending email to people who've already sent you a message, so this is usually no problem.

After you send an email to someone, their address is automatically copied to the **Contacts** list (address book), making it easier to address and send messages to friends and colleagues. You can also add addresses to the **Contacts** list manually, before sending an email message. Also, you can import existing addresses and contact data from your old email program. See **159** **Add New Contacts** for help.

1 Click Write Button

To reply to or forward a message you've just been sent, see **157** **Reply or Forward a Message** for help. To begin composing a new message, click the **Write** button on the **Mail** toolbar. The **Compose** window appears.

2 Type To Address

Your default email address appears at the top of the window. If you have more than one address, you can open the **From** list and select a different address if desired.

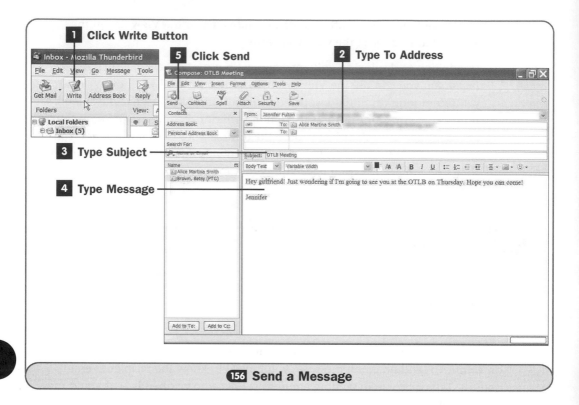

156 Send a Message

Click in the **To** box and type the address to which you want to send this message. If this person's address is in the **Contacts** list (because you've sent them an email before, or because you added the address to the **Contacts** list yourself), you'll probably only need to type a few letters before the **Address Autocompletion** feature completes the address for you. In such a case, press **Enter** to accept the suggested address. If **Address Autocompletion** displays multiple addresses that match what you've typed, use the arrow keys to select the address you want, or just click it.

Enter additional email addresses by repeating this step. Each email address is entered on its own **To** line, which appears as soon as you press **Enter** to complete an address.

▶ TIPS

If for some reason **Address Autocompletion** suggests the wrong address or none at all, you can display the **Contacts** list (by clicking the **Contacts** button at the top of the **Compose** window) and insert the correct address yourself (by selecting the address from those listed and clicking the **Add to To** button at the bottom of the **Contacts** sidebar. You can also drag and drop the address in the **To** box within the **Compose** window.

To send a copy of this message to someone else, click the arrow on the **To** button and select **Cc**. To send a blind carbon copy of this message, select **Bcc** instead.

3 Type Subject

Click in the **Subject** box and type a short description of the message topic.

4 Type Message

Type your message in the message area. Assuming that your recipient uses an HTML compatible email program (most are), you can add formatting to your text as desired using the tools on the **Formatting** toolbar.

You can create a signature file (a text file that typically contains your name, address, and phone number) and have its contents added to all your messages automatically. A signature file saves you the trouble of adding common information at the bottom of your email messages. After creating the text file in Writer (be sure to save the file in text format with the .txt file extension), choose **Tools, Account Settings**, and click the name of the email account for which you created the signature. Enable the **Attach this signature** option, click **Choose**, select your text file, and click **Open**.

5 Click Send

If you want to attach a file to the message, do so now. See **158** **Attach a File to a Message** for help. Click the **Send** button to send the message. If prompted, select the message format to use: text, HTML, or both. Copies of messages you send are placed in the **Sent** folder unless you've configured Thunderbird to do something else with your sent messages. To configure Thunderbird to behave differently, choose **Tools, Account Settings**, display the **Copies & Folders** page for the account you want to change, and in the **When sending messages, automatically** section, choose the option you want to apply to messages you send.

Optionally, instead of clicking **Send**, you can click **Save**, which saves the message in the **Drafts** folder. Later you can change to the **Drafts** folder by selecting it from the **Folders** list in the main Thunderbird window, double-click the message to open it, make additional edits, and click **Send** to send it.

You can also choose **File, Send Later** instead of clicking **Send**. This command places the message in the **Unsent Messages** folder. To send such messages, choose **File, Send Unsent Messages** from the main Thunderbird menu.

156

▶ **TIP**

Click the **Spell** button to check your spelling before sending the message. Better yet, set up Thunderbird to check the spelling of all messages automatically. Choose **Tools, Options**, display the **Composition** page, and enable the **Check spelling before sending** option.

157   Reply or Forward a Message

✔ BEFORE YOU BEGIN	→ SEE ALSO
154 Get Your Email	**156** Send a Message

Instead of composing an original message, you might want to reply to a message you've been sent. When replying, you can choose to send your reply only to the originator of the message, or to the originator and all other recipients of the original message. When you reply to a message, the original text is typically copied into the new message (depending on your email settings) so that your recipients will know what you're referring to.

If a message is interesting and you want to share it with someone who did not receive it originally, you can forward the message. When you forward a message, the text of the original message is copied into the new message, or simply attached (depending on your email settings). You can easily add your own comments as desired and then send the resulting message.

157

▶ TIPS

To change how the original text is treated when you forward a message, choose **Tools, Options**, and on the **Composition** page, open the **Forward messages** list and choose **As Attachment** or **Inline**.

To change how original text is handled in replies, choose **Tools, Account Settings** and display the **Composition & Addressing** page for the email account you want to change. Enable the **Automatically quote the original message when replying** option to copy the text, and then select where you want the text placed (at the bottom of the new message, for instance) from the **Then** list.

1   Click Reply, Reply All, or Forward

Select the message you want to forward or reply to, and then click the appropriate button on the **Mail** toolbar: **Reply** (to send a reply to the originator of the message), **Reply All** (to send a reply to the originator plus all recipients), or **Forward** (to send the message along to a new recipient).

2   Type To Address if Needed

If you're sending a Reply or a Reply All message, the new message is automatically addressed for you.

If you're forwarding a message, click in the **To** box and type an email address, or display the **Contacts** list (by clicking the **Contacts** button) and insert an address by selecting the address from those listed and clicking the **Add to To** button at the bottom of the **Contacts** sidebar.

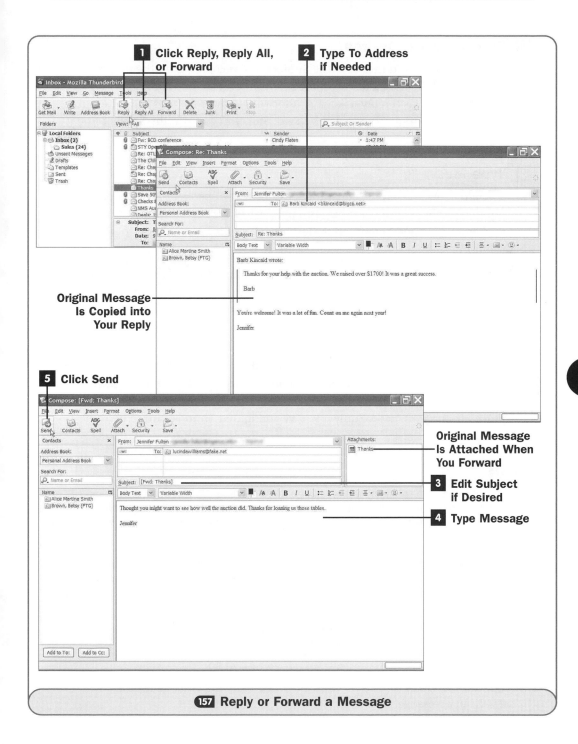

1 Click Reply, Reply All, or Forward

2 Type To Address if Needed

Original Message Is Copied into Your Reply

5 Click Send

Original Message Is Attached When You Forward

3 Edit Subject if Desired

4 Type Message

157

3 Edit Subject if Desired

When you reply to a message, the **Subject** line is copied from the original message and the letters **Re:** are added in front of it so that the message is easy to identify as a reply. Likewise, a forwarded message uses the same subject line as the original preceded by **Fwd**. Still, you can edit the **Subject** line if you like.

4 Type Message

If you're replying to a message, the message text appears in the message pane, typically with the cursor positioned below the copied text. If you're forwarding a message, the original message is attached and the message pane is empty.

Type your message in the message area. Assuming that your recipient uses an HTML compatible email program (most are), you can add formatting to your text as desired using the tools on the **Formatting** toolbar.

5 Click Send

If you want to attach a file to the message, do so now. See **158 Attach a File to a Message**. Click the **Send** button to send the message. If prompted, select the message format to use: text, HTML, or both. Copies of message you send are placed in the **Sent** folder (unless you've configured Thunderbird to do something else).

▶ TIPS

Click the **Spell** button to check your spelling before sending the message. Better yet, set up Thunderbird to check the spelling of all messages automatically. Choose **Tools, Options**, display the **Composition** page, and enable the **Check spelling before sending** option.

Messages you've replied to appear with a special icon in the Inbox: an envelope with a green arrow that sweeps to the left. Forwarded messages are marked with an icon with an envelope and a purple arrow that sweeps to the right.

---

158 **Attach a File to a Message**

✔ BEFORE YOU BEGIN	→ SEE ALSO
154 Get Your Email	**157** Reply or Forward a Message
156 Send a Message	

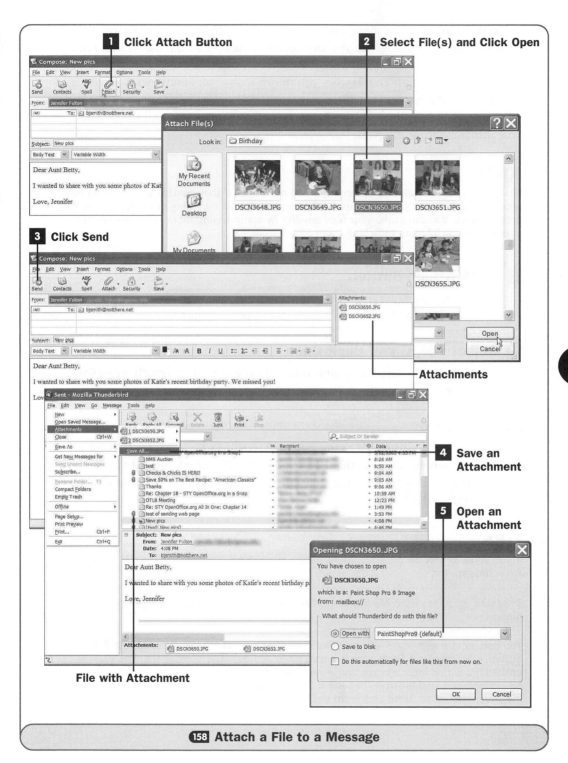

1 **Click Attach Button**

2 **Select File(s) and Click Open**

3 **Click Send**

Attachments

4 **Save an Attachment**

5 **Open an Attachment**

File with Attachment

158

158 Attach a File to a Message

Through email, you can share more than just text. When you want to say more than you can with just words, you can attach a file and send it along with your message. You might attach an image, for example, to share a recent family photo with friends and relatives. Likewise, you might receive an email message with a file attached. But how do you open an attached file, or save it to your system? In this task, you'll learn how to attach files to outgoing messages and to open or save attachments sent to you.

▶ NOTE

Most email servers will stop incoming email messages if they contain attachments over a certain size—usually 5 MB or so. Some servers stop all incoming email messages with attachments. You can make your files smaller by compressing them (with WinZip or a similar program) before attaching them to a message.

1 Click Attach Button

After composing and addressing your message, click the **Attach** button on the **Mail** toolbar. The **Attach File(s)** dialog box appears.

2 Select File(s) and Click Open

Change to the folder that contains the file(s) you want to attach. Press **Ctrl** and select as many files as you like, and then click **Open**.

3 Click Send

The files you've attached to the message appear in the **Attachments** list in the upper-right corner of the mail window. Double-check this list to make sure that you've attached the right file(s), and then click **Send** to send the email message.

▶ TIPS

If you want to preview an attachment before you send it, double-click the file in the **Attachments** list.

Drag and drop files from **My Explorer** into a Compose window to quickly attach the file(s).

You can send a web page with an email message by clicking the arrow on the **Attach** button, selecting **Web Page**, typing a web page address, and clicking **OK**. The page is embedded within the message and a web page link is attached to the message that can be opened in a web browser. To send a link to a web page from within Firefox, right-click the page and select **Send Link** from the context menu.

158

4 Save an Attachment

If you receive a message with files attached, a small paper-clip icon appears in front of the message header. When you view the message, the file(s) attached to it are listed below the message text. To save all of the attached file(s) in the same folder, choose **File, Attachments, Save All**. To save a particular attachment from a group of files attached to a single message, choose **File, Attachments**, select the file from those listed, and then choose **Save As**. A dialog box appears; select the folder in which you want to save the file, and then click **OK** or **Save**.

5 Open an Attachment

To open an attachment you've received in an email message rather than save it, choose **File, Attachments**, select the file from those listed, and then choose **Open**. You can also simply double-click the attachment's name which appears below the message text. The **Opening** dialog box appears; select the program you want to use to open the file from the **Open with** list, and click **OK**.

159 Add New Contacts

✔ **BEFORE YOU BEGIN**	→ **SEE ALSO**
Just jump right in!	**156** Send a Message
	157 Reply or Forward a Message

159

To send an email message, you need the recipient's email address. You can store frequently used addresses in the **Contacts** list (also known as the address book). By default, Thunderbird automatically saves the addresses of the people you send email to so that they are available should you need them again. When needed, you can easily grab addresses from incoming email and add them to the **Contacts** list as well. In addition, you can manually add addresses to the **Contacts** list for people you've neither received nor sent emails to.

The address book actually has two sections: **Personal Address Book** and **Collected Addresses**. Typically, addresses you enter yourself are stored in the **Personal Address Book** section, while addresses Thunderbird gathers for you from incoming or outgoing messages are placed in the **Collected Addresses** section.

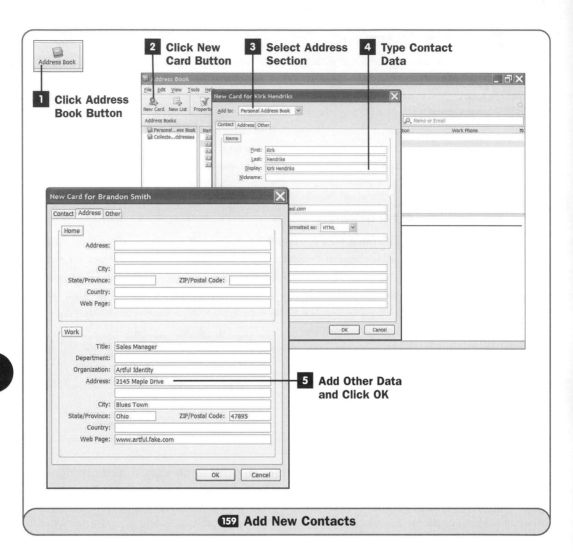

159 Add New Contacts

▶ TIPS

To import addresses from an old email program, choose **Tools, Import,** choose **Address Books** and click **Next,** select your email program from those listed and click **Next,** and click **Finish.**

To make changes to the way Thunderbird collects outgoing email addresses (or to turn the option off), choose **Tools, Options,** and on the **Advanced** page, in the **General Settings** section, enable the **Automatically add outgoing e-mail addresses to my** option, and choose the section you want the addresses stored in (such as **Collected Addresses**).

To add an email address from an incoming message to your **Contacts** list, display the message and, in the message header that appears above the message pane, click the sender's address and choose **Add to Address Book** from the context menu that appears.

1 Click Address Book Button

Click the **Address Book** button on the **Mail** toolbar in the main Thunderbird window. The **Address Book** appears.

2 Click New Card Button

Click the **New Card** button on the **Address Book** toolbar. The **New Card** dialog box appears.

3 Select Address Section

Open the **Add to** drop-down list and select the section of the address book into which you want to save the new contact—either **Personal** or **Collected**.

4 Type Contact Data

Enter the contact data on the **Contact** tab. At a minimum, you should enter the contact's first and last name and email address. You might also want to select the format (HTML or text) that you want to use when sending messages to this address.

5 Add Other Data and Click OK

If desired, click the **Address** tab and add the contact's home and/or business addresses and web page addresses. If you enter an address and then later display that contact by opening the **Address Book**, you can click the **Get Map** button that appears to open Firefox and display a map to the address.

If you have data that you want to enter and you can't find an appropriate field, click the **Other** tab and enter that data in one of the custom fields. Click **OK.** The contact appears in the **Address Book** listing.

▶ **NOTE**

To make changes to an existing contact, open the **Address Book**, select the contact, and click the **Properties** button. For example, you might want to add the email format your contact prefers (such as HTML) to prevent Thunderbird from asking you what format to use each time you send that person an email. To remove the contact, click the **Delete** button instead.

160 Handle Junk Mail

✔ BEFORE YOU BEGIN	→ SEE ALSO
154 Get Your Email	**161** Organize Incoming Mail

160

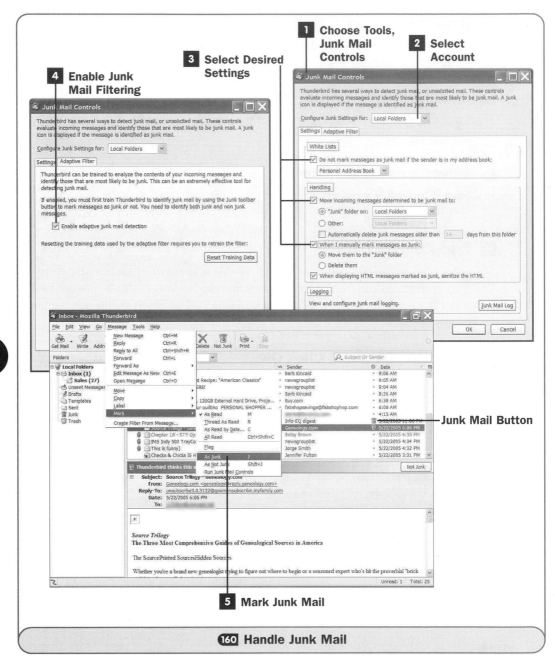

1 Choose Tools, Junk Mail Controls

2 Select Account

3 Select Desired Settings

4 Enable Junk Mail Filtering

Junk Mail Button

5 Mark Junk Mail

160 Handle Junk Mail

Unfortunately, even with the convenience of almost instant communication through *email*, there's a downside—anyone who has your address can send you email. This means that, just like your mail box at home, you can't prevent junk mail (spam) from arriving. Although your email service provider might provide some spam controls (and you should enable them, when they're available), the truth is that because large email providers are typically targeted by spammers, spam gets through anyway. What you can do with junk mail that gets through, however, is to teach Thunderbird what to do with it—from moving it into a special folder so that you can review it when you have time, to simply deleting it as soon as it arrives.

1 Choose Tools, Junk Mail Controls

Choose **Tools**, **Junk Mail Controls** from the menu. The **Junk Mail Controls** dialog box appears.

2 Select Account

Open the **Configure Junk Settings for** list, and select the email account for which you want to set junk mail controls. Here, I selected **Local Folders**, which covers both of my email accounts (both accounts are under the **Local Folders** heading in the **Folders** list of the main Thunderbird window).

3 Select Desired Settings

On the **Settings** tab, select the junk mail options you want. Under **White Lists**, you can make sure that emails from people in your address book are not marked as junk.

Under **Handling**, you can tell Thunderbird what to do with junk mail. You can move the junk mail to a special folder or delete the messages.

Under **Logging**, click the **Junk Mail Log** button to create a file that tracks junk mail activity. You might use such a file to track what happened to a particular message, for example.

4 Enable Junk Mail Filtering

Unless you want to manually mark all junk mail messages, you should turn on junk mail filtering. Click the **Adaptive Filter** tab and turn on the **Enable adaptive junk mail detection** option. Click **OK**.

5 Mark Junk Mail

To get the most out of Thunderbird's junk mail adaptive filter, you should mark specific messages as junk when they come in. That way, Thunderbird learns to identify the type of junk mail you get and takes care of similar messages in the future.

To mark a message as junk, select it and choose **Message**, **Mark**, **As Junk** or click the **Junk Mail** button to the right of the **Sender** column in the message header.

▶ **TIP**

If you've accidentally marked a message as junk, select the message again, and you'll see a note from Thunderbird (just above the message header detail) telling you that it thinks this message is junk mail. Click the **Not Junk** button to remove the message's junk mail status.

---

161 **Organize Incoming Mail**

✔ **BEFORE YOU BEGIN**

154 Get Your Email

You won't have Thunderbird up and running for very long before you start pondering the universal problem of managing all that mail. In **155** **Find a Message**, you learned to sort your mail and to search for a particular message. In **160** **Handle Junk Mail**, you learned how to enable Thunderbird's automatic junk mail handler to manage most if not all of your incoming junk mail. Still, what should you do with messages from your department head, email from your kid's teachers, personal email from friends and family, and so on? One way to tackle the problem is to delete email after you've read it, unless you're sure you'll need to refer to it again. Messages you keep can then be organized into special folders. You can even set up *filters* that handle some of this organizing for you automatically. For example, you can have emails from Uncle Bill and Aunt Judith automatically routed into the **Family** folder.

▶ **KEY TERM**

Filter—A set of instructions that tells Thunderbird what to do with particular pieces of incoming mail.

1 **Click Delete**

If a piece of incoming mail was interesting but not important enough to keep, delete it by selecting the message and clicking the **Delete** button on the **Mail** toolbar.

▶ **NOTE**

Deleted messages are moved to the **Trash** folder for that particular email account, where they are kept until the trash is "emptied." To do that, select the email account from the **Folders** list, choose **File, Empty Trash**. To have Thunderbird empty the **Trash** folder for an account every time you close the program, choose **Tools, Account Settings**, select the **Server Settings** page for that email account, and enable the **Empty Trash on Exit** option.

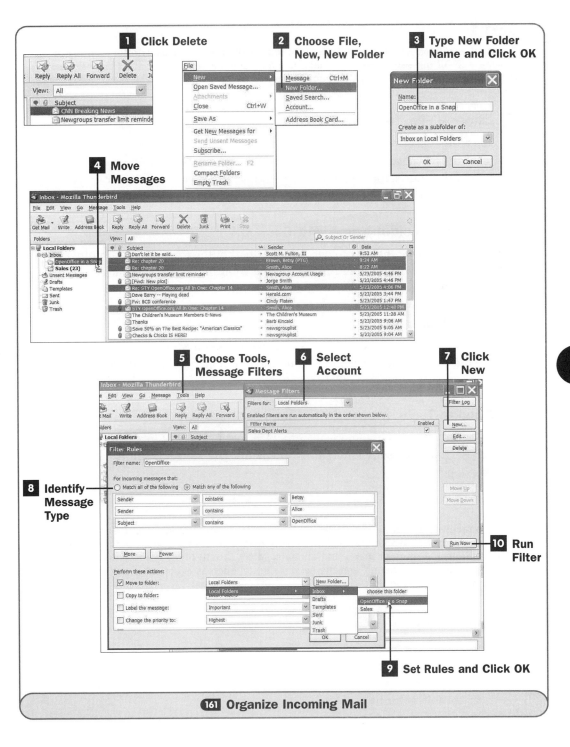

1 Click Delete

2 Choose File,
New, New Folder

3 Type New Folder
Name and Click OK

4 Move
Messages

5 Choose Tools,
Message Filters

6 Select
Account

7 Click
New

8 Identify
Message
Type

9 Set Rules and Click OK

10 Run
Filter

161 Organize Incoming Mail

▶ **NOTE**

Compact email folders from time to time to reduce their size, expecially after deleting or moving a lot of messages. Select a folder (such as **Local Folders**) from the **Folder** list on the left, and then choose **File, Compact Folders**.

2 Choose File, New, New Folder

To create a new folder in which to place specific messages, select the folder into which you want this new folder placed from the **Folders** list on the right side of the Thunderbird window. Then choose **File, New, New Folder** (or **New Subfolder**). The **Create New Folder** (or **Subfolder**) dialog box appears.

3 Type New Folder Name and Click OK

Type a **Name** for the new folder. Then verify that the **Create as a subfolder of** list box shows the folder into which you want this new folder placed and click **OK**. The folder appears in the **Folders** list.

4 Move Messages

Now that you have a folder for specific messages you want to organize, select the message(s) you want to move into the new folder and then drag and drop them on that folder in the **Folders** list.

5 Choose Tools, Message Filters

To create a filter to automatically organize specific types of incoming mail, choose **Tools, Message Filters** from the menu. The **Message Filters** dialog box appears.

▶ **TIP**

If you've received a message you'd like to use as a basis for a filter, select that message and, in the message header that appears just above the message text, click the **From** address. From the shortcut menu that appears, select **Create Filter from Message**. The **Filter Rules** dialog box opens, and the sender's email address is copied to the criteria section described in step 8.

6 Select Account

From the **Filters for** list, select the email account for which you want to set up this filter. I wanted the filter to apply to both my email accounts; because both accounts are included under **Local Folders**, I selected **Local Folders** from the **Filters for** list.

161

7 Click New

Click **New** to create a new filter. The **Filter Rules** dialog box appears.

8 Identify Message Type

Type a name for the new filter in the **Filter name** box. Then set criteria that identify the type of message you want filtered. First, choose either **Match all of the following** or **Match any of the following** criteria. In the list boxes, make selections that identify the message type. For example, if you want to filter messages that come from a specific individual, select **From** in the first list, **Contains** in the second list, and type all or part of the person's name from the third list.

Click **More** to add more criteria as desired. For example, you might want to filter messages from your boss that contain the word *meeting* in the subject heading.

9 Set Rules and Click OK

In the bottom part of the **Filter Rules** dialog box, you tell Thunderbird what to do with messages that meet your criteria. You can have the messages moved to a specific folder, copied to a folder, labeled, deleted, prioritized, or marked as junk. You can make multiple selections here; for example, you can have a message moved to a folder *and* labeled **Important**. Click **OK** to create the filter. You're returned to the **Message Filters** dialog box.

10 Run Filter

To run the filter now on existing messages, click **Run Now**. Messages that match your criteria are identified, and the action you selected is taken. The filter you just created is automatically run against any incoming messages from this point forward.

▶ **TIP**

In the **Filter Rules** dialog box, you can create a folder into which Thunderbird will copy or move the matching messages by clicking the **New Folder** button, entering a folder **Name**, and selecting a folder into which you want it placed from the **Create as a sub-folder of** list.

161

Index

D

E

F

G - H - I

O

P

Q - R

S

T

X - Y - Z

License Agreement

By opening this package, you are also agreeing to be bound by the following agreement:

You may not copy or redistribute the entire CD-ROM as a whole. Copying and redistribution of individual software programs on the CD-ROM is governed by terms set by individual copyright holders.

The installer and code from the author(s) are copyrighted by the publisher and the author(s). Individual programs and other items on the CD-ROM are copyrighted or are under an Open Source license by their various authors or other copyright holders.

This software is sold as-is without warranty of any kind, either expressed or implied, including but not limited to the implied warranties of merchantability and fitness for a particular purpose. Neither the publisher nor its dealers or distributors assumes any liability for any alleged or actual damages arising from the use of this program. (Some states do not allow for the exclusion of implied warranties, so the exclusion may not apply to you.)

What's on the CD-ROM

The companion CD-ROM contains OpenOffice.org 2.0 pre-release, Firefox 1.0.4, and Thunderbird 1.0.2 for Linux and Windows.

Windows Installation Instructions

1. Insert the disc into your CD-ROM drive and double-click on the My Computer icon.

2. Double-click on the icon representing your CD-ROM drive.

3. Double-click on start.exe. Follow the onscreen prompts to finish the installation.

Linux and Unix Installation Instructions

These installation instructions assume that you have a passing familiarity with UNIX commands and the basic setup of your machine. As UNIX has many flavors, only generic commands are used. If you have any problems with the commands, please consult the appropriate man page or your system administrator.

Insert CD-ROM in CD drive. If you have a volume manager, mounting of the CD-ROM will be automatic. If you don't have a volume manager, you can mount the CD-ROM by typing:

```
mount -tiso9660 /dev/cdrom /mnt/cdrom
```

/mnt/cdrom is just a mount point, but it must exist when you issue the mount command. You may also use any empty directory for a mount point if you don't want to use /mnt/cdrom.

Open the readme.htm file for descriptions and installation instructions.

Key Terms

Don't let unfamiliar terms discourage you from learning all you can about OpenOffice.org. If you don't completely understand what one of these words means, flip to the indicated page, read the full definition there, and find techniques related to that term.